hugo

Danish
in Three Months

Knud Ravnkilde

A DK Publishing Book
www.dk.com

A DK PUBLISHING BOOK

www.dk.com

First American Edition, 1999
10 9 8 7 6 5 4 3 2 1

Published in the United States by
DK Publishing, Inc.
95 Madison Avenue
New York, New York 10016

Library of Congress Cataloging-in-Publication Data
Ravnkilde, Knud.
Danish in three months / by Knud Ravnkilde. -- 1st American ed.
p. cm. -- (Hugo)
Includes index.
ISBN 0–7894–4425–9 (alk. paper). -- ISBN 0–7894–4434–8 (w/cassette)
1. Danish language--Grammar. 2. Danish language--Textbooks for foreign speakers--English. I. Title.
II. Series: Hugo (Series)
PD 3105.R38 1999
439.8'182421 -- dc21 98–48011
CIP

Set in 10/12pt Palatino by
Traverso Design Consultants, London, Great Britain
Printed and bound by LegoPrint, Italy

Preface

This new and expanded edition of Hugo's 'Danish in Three Months' is designed for those people who want to acquire a good working knowledge of the language in a short time, and who will probably be working at home without a teacher. The 'Three Months' series as a whole is renowned for its success in self-tuition, but the books are equally useful as sources of reference if you happen to be attending language classes.

The author, Knud Ravnkilde, is a Danish journalist, translator and writer resident in Britain; he has taken the layman's approach to his native language, teaching only what is necessary, without too much dry and dusty grammar. Where more formal explanation was required we called on the expertise of Robin Allan, Senior Lecturer in Danish at University College London.

'Danish in Three Months' begins with an explanation of the sounds of the language, as far as this is possible in print. If you are working without a teacher, you will find that our system of 'imitated pronunciation' simplifies matters considerably. Using this book together with the related audio cassettes which we have produced as optional extras will add another dimension to your studies. Ask the bookshop for Hugo's Danish 'Three Months' Cassette Course.

In each chapter, elements of grammar are examined, explained and illustrated; there is an exercise or two, with vocabulary lists of useful new words, and the all-important need to build up your conversational skill is one of the foremost considerations in this course. Answers to exercises are at the back of the book.

Ideally you should spend about an hour a day on the course (maybe a little less if you've not got the cassettes), although there is no hard and fast rule on this. Do as much as you feel capable of doing; it is much better to learn a little at a time, and to learn that thoroughly. At the beginning of each day's session, spend ten minutes recalling what you learned the day before. When you read a conversation, say it out loud if possible (listen to the tape and see how closely you can imitate the native speakers). Study each rule or numbered section carefully and re-read it to ensure that you have fully understood the grammar and examples given. Try to understand rather than memorize; if you have understood, the exercise will ensure that you remember the rules through applying them.

When the course is completed, you should have a good knowledge of Danish – more than sufficient for general holiday or business use, and enough to act as a basis for further studies. We hope you'll enjoy 'Danish in Three Months', and wish you success in learning.

ACKNOWLEDGEMENTS

Grateful thanks to Katie Lewis for her painstaking editing and constructive help in putting this course together; and to the Storm P. Foundation for permission to reproduce some of Storm P.'s 'Flies'.

Picture Credits

Jacket: CORBIS UK: Paul Almasy bottom right; Dave Bartuff top left centre, top centre, centre above right, centre below right; Gillian Darley/Edifice top right; Bob Krist bottom left, back, spine top; Carmen Rendondo centre below right centre; Adam Woolfitt centre below left centre, centre below right, bottom above; ROBERT HARDING PICTURE LIBRARY: Paolo Koch top left; MICHAEL JENNER: spine bottom; NEIL SETCHFIELD: centre above left.

Contents

Welcome to Danish!

En bedrøvet lektor, tynget af personlige erfaringer: – Oprindeligt var sproget et middel til forståelse – men efterhånden er det blevet et middel til misforståelse.

Soon, you will be able to read for yourself that this says: 'A sad lecturer, weighed down by personal experience: "Originally, language was an aid to understanding – but in the course of time, it has become an aid to misunderstanding."

So wrote the Danish cartoonist and humorist Robert Storm Petersen, known as Storm P., whose drawings and writing during the first half of this century came to represent the quintessence of Danishness. His 'Flies', philosophical asides, speckle this books as an aid to understanding what tickles Danes and make them tick.

As he also made a thoughtful character say: *'Selvom man ikke kan stave ordet 'desinficere', kan man godt leve i bedste velgående og opnå en høj alder.'* 'Even if one cannot spell the word "disinfect" it is quite possible to live in the best of health and reach a great age.'

True, true, Storm P. But there's a lot of joy in getting to know people of other nationalities better – and the brave purchaser of this book wants to start with <u>your</u> Danes . . .

Danish is <u>not</u> a difficult language to learn when compared to French, German, Italian and many others. Its grammar is considerably less complex, and in some respects even easier than English, with which it shares a good deal of vocabulary and structural rules. On paper, therefore, it should be one of the easiest languages for an English-speaker to learn. It belongs to the Germanic group of languages, as does English – in which one frequently meets words absorbed from Danish in Viking times. In modern times, the Danish glossary has had such an influx of English/American terms that it alarms language purists!

What is more, and probably very surprising, even though Danish is not written in a phonetic way, English-speaking people have few problems with its pronunciation if they approach it boldly, without the self-hypnosis of the ridiculous 'We-British-are-not-good-at-languages' attitude. In fact, all of its non-English sounds are very familiar to Scots, especially Glaswegians! Once Britons have learnt the language, most of them speak it without a strong accent. This is really quite natural, English itself being composed of more tongues than any other language.

It is a help when you meet Danes, of course, that a large proportion of Denmark's population speaks English well – or even excellently. (A help, that is, if you can make it clear to them that you want to learn Danish and not be impressed by their English!) More important is the fact that the level of primary and secondary education in Denmark is uniform and the general quality of the spoken Danish good. No social or geographical sector speaks significantly more carelessly than others. Furthermore, today only about five per cent have a strong dialect.

As an additional bonus, many who have learnt Danish confirm that they also understand a fair amount of Norwegian and even of Swedish.

The long-proven Hugo method is to teach only what is really essential. We assume that you want to learn Danish from a practical angle, so the lessons contain those rules of grammar that will be of most help in this respect. Few people remember grammatical theory and expressions from their school days. Whereas it is impossible in any course to avoid 'grammarese' completely, we have endeavoured to reduce it to a minimum. The English translations are not, of course, in polished English, but remain reasonably literal to help you master the Danish constructions.

So, without more ado, let's start work with the pronunciation of Danish – remember, it's not as hard as you might think!

Pronunciation

The Danish alphabet has three vowels – æ, ø and å – that are not found in English, and the language features a few sounds which often amuse English speakers. Pronunciation, however, can be an entertaining part of learning and if you read and practise this section carefully, you will soon get used to it.

While written Danish is certainly not phonetic, there is greater uniformity than in English in the relationship between written and spoken Danish. The same group of letters tend to carry the same sound. There is no equivalent to 'thorough, through, rough, Slough'.

In Danish as in English, many letters are pronounced in more than one way. Study the points below, and your pronunciation should come close to correct Danish. Hugo's Imitated Pronunciation system is provided in the early chapters as an approximation, and the right-hand column below shows the English letters chosen to represent the sound concerned in the Imitated Pronunciation. The best route to correct pronunciation, though, is to use our audio-cassettes of selected extracts from this book.

Accents are used only to indicate stress on the letter **e** in some words: **dér er det** '*there* it is'; **allé** [al-<u>ley</u>'] as opposed to **alle** [<u>al</u>-l*e*]. Umlauts (ä, ö and ü) are occasionally seen in names of foreign origin. They correspond in sound to the Danish æ, ø and y respectively.

The glottal stop, or **stød**, is a distinctive feature of the Danish language. It is produced by briefly interrupting the sound, as if abruptly applying a brake – something like the Cockney glottal stop in 'wha'?' Don't worry if you find these glottal stops difficult at first; some regional variants of Danish don't feature them at all. For the sake of accuracy, however, glottal stops are indicated, by an apostrophe, in the Imitated Pronunciation:

kalv [kal'] **kalve** [kal-v*e*]

In the Imitated Pronunciation, stress is shown in words of more than one syllable by underlining the stressed syllable.

Vowels

In general, Danish vowel sounds are much shorter than English vowels. In the Imitated Pronunciation we have marked long vowel sound with a colon (:). Where you see a vowel without a colon, remember to keep it short, even if it would be long in English.

Before a double consonant, vowels are always short. Before a single consonant followed by another vowel, they are almost always long.

siden [see:-th*e*n]; **sidde** [si-th*e*]

Vowel sounds are pure, never diphthongs, and where two vowels appear side by side they are sounded separately, as two separate syllables, rather than running together into a diphthong, as English vowels do. (Words of foreign origin are sometimes excepted.)

Danish vowel		*Imitated Pronunciation*
a	short, as in the English 'cat': **mad** [math]; **lappe** [lab-b*e*]	[a]
	And long, the same sound lengthened: **lave** [la:-v*e*]; **have** [ha:-v*e*]	[a:]
	Before **r** the sound is broader, as in English 'far': **var** [vah]; **far** [fah:]	[ah]

e

short, as the ‘e’ sound in French ‘les’ or the beginning of the ‘ey’ in ‘they’: [ey]
se [sey’]; **regulere** [rey-goo-ley-r*e*]

long, the same sound lengthened: [ey:]
lede [ley:-th*e*]

Before **r** it often takes on the sound of English ‘air’: [ay]
er [ayr]; **dér** [day’r]; **her** [hay’r]

But **-er** at the end of the word, where unstressed, is rather like the English ‘or’: [or]
maler [ma’-lor]

Similarly, unstressed **-e** is very like the ‘e’ of ‘the’ in English: [*e*]
hale [ha:-l*e*]

i

long, as the English ‘ee’ in ‘seen’: [ee:]
lide [lee:-th*e*]; **time** [tee:-m*e*]

short, the same sound but shorter: [ee]
ti [tee’]; **energi** [ey-nayr-gee’]

sometimes as ‘i’ in ‘ink’: [i]
blink [blink]; **ringe** [ring-*e*]

o

like the French ‘eau’, the Northern English ‘o’ of ‘coal’ or German ‘o’ of Chancellor Kohl: [oh]
tro [troh’]; **trone** [troh:-n*e*]

Sometimes **o** sounds more like a short **å** (see below): [o]
kop [kop]

And sometimes, especially before **r**, a sound approaching English ‘aw’ as in ‘law’: [aw]
derfor [dayr-faw]; **hvor** [vaw’]

u

short, as English ‘oo’ in ‘fool’, only shorter: [oo]
sult [sool’t]; **nu** [noo]

long, the same sound lengthened: [oo:]
mulig [moo:-lee]

Sometimes **u** sounds similar to the 'u' sound of English 'put': [u]
kul [ku'l]; **lunden** [lun'-*e*n]

y

This is a pure sound that doesn't exist in English. It is very like the 'ü' of German and the French 'u' in 'lune'. You can produce it by rounding your lips and saying 'ee': [ew]
ny [new']; **by** [bew']; **flyve** [flew-v*e*]

æ

very like the English 'e' in 'bed': [e]
mænd [men']
long, the same sound lengthened: [e:]
sæde [se:-th*e*]
Sometimes the sound comes closer to the first part of the English 'ay' in 'tray': [ay]
træet [tray-*e* t]

ø

Another difficult sound for English speakers. [uh]
It is like the German 'ö' and French 'eu' in 'peu', and can be produced by rounding your lips and saying 'e' (as in 'bed'):
kø [kuh']; **øst** [uhst]; **købe** [kuh:-b*e*]
Before **r** it comes close to the English 'ur' of 'fur': [ur]
mørke [mur-k*e*]; **før** [fur']

å

short, like the 'o' in 'hot': [o]
måtte [mot-t*e*]; **trådte** [trot-t*e*]
long, something like the English 'o' of 'oh': [oh]
åen [oh:-*e*n]; **på** [poh']

Diphthongs

Danish diphthongs occur when some vowels precede **g, j** or **v.** Preceded by a vowel, **g** and **j** become very soft, like 'i':

ig, ej, eg	This sounds like the English 'i' of 'fine' or 'y' as in 'my': **mig** [my]; **rejser** [ry-sor]	[y]
øj, øg	something like the English 'oy' of 'boy': **støj** [sdoy']; **røg** [roy']	[oy]

Preceded by a vowel, the **v** often becomes very soft, almost like an unstressed 'u':

av, ov	as in English 'how': **hav** [how'], **lov** [low'].	[ow]
ev	**evne** [eyu-ne]	[eyu]
øv	**søvnig** [suhu:-nee]	[uhu]
iv	**livlig** [liu-lee]	[iu]
yv	**syv** [sew'u]	[ew'u]

Consonants

b	as in English: **bål** [bo'l]	[b]
c	as 's' in 'sit': **cigar** [si-gah']	[s]
d	at the beginning of a word, as in English: **dam** [dam]	[d]
	After a vowel, very soft as 'th' in 'the' (never as 'th' in 'thistle'): **tid** [tee'th] (remember soft 'th', not 'teeth'!); **bede** [bey:-the]	[th]
	It is always silent before **t** and after **l, n** and **r**, and often silent before **s**: **godt** [got]; **ild** [eel']; **mand** [man']; **jord** [yaw'r]	

f as in English:
fuld [fool']; [f]
straf [straf]

g At the beginning of a word, the [g]
hard 'g' of 'good':
godt [got]
In words of foreign origin, it [sj]
occasionally sounds like 'sh'
in 'shell':
geni [sjey-nee']; **genert** [sjey-ney:rt]
Following a vowel, as in
diphthongs, the **g** is almost silent,
or often like an English 'i', and is
represented in a variety of ways
in the Imitated Pronunciation:
bag [ba:'i]; **dage** [da:-y*e*]; **ryge**
[rew:-y*e*]; **pigen** [pee:-y*e*n]
In the ending **-ig, g** is frequently silent:
endelig [en-n*e*-lee]
Many **-og** endings, as in **bog**, have
a long 'oh' sound followed by a
breath through almost closed
teeth [boh:'h].
ng is always pronounced as in [ng]
English 'sing', never with a separate
'g' sound as in 'finger':
englænder [eng-len-or]

h as in English: [h]
hænderne [hen'-nor-n*e*]
except before **v** and **j**, where
it is silent:
hjælp [yel'b]; **hvilken** [vil-g*e*n]

j like English 'y' in 'yet': [y]
jord [yaw'r]
In words taken from English, [dj]
occasionally 'j' as in 'jungle':
job [djob]

In a few words of foreign origin (especially French), like 'sh' as in 'shell': [sj]
journalist [sjoh-na-leesd]

k as in English: [k]
kartoffel [kah-tof-f*e*l]
except that, unlike in English, it is sounded before **n,** like English 'acne': [cn]
knive [cnee:-*ve*]; **Knud** [cnoo'th]
In the middle of a word often softer like **g:** [g]
ikke [ig-g*e*]; **malke** [mal-g*e*];
skole [sgoh-*le*]

l as in English 'light': [l]
lys [lew's]

m as in English: [m]
meter [mey'-dor]

n as in English: [n]
nej [ny']

p at the beginning or end of a word, as in English: [p]
par [pah]; **klip** [kleep]
sometimes within a word, and particularly when doubled, like a 'b': [b]
suppe [sub-b*e*]

q very rare: **qu** as 'kv': [kv]
quiz [kvees]

r Slightly guttural, like the Scottish 'r': [r]
røvere [ruh:-v*e*-r*e*]
At the end of a word or syllable, almost silent like the 'r' in 'where':
bedstefar [be-sd*e* -fah:]

s	as the English ‘s’ in ‘sit’ and never as in ‘rise’: **sid** [si’th]; **næse** [ney:-s*e*]	[s]
t	as in English : **tit** [//]	[t]
	except in the middle of a word, where it softens to a ‘d’ (particularly when doubled): **tante** [tan-d*e*]; **atten** [ad-d*e*n] and at the end of a word, where it is sometimes mute: **det** [dey] There is a growing tendency to pronounce the **-et** ending as a soft **d**, so that **huset** becomes [hoo’-s*e*th].	[d]
v	as in English: **hvordan** [vaw-dan] except in diphthongs (see above): **navn** [now’n] and after **l** at the end a syllable, when it is usually silent: **tolv** [tol’]; **halv** [hal’]	[v]
w	very rare except in names etc. of foreign origin: as ‘v’, and **wc** is [vey’-sey’]	[v]
x	rare, at the beginning of a word like ‘s’: **xylofon** [sew’-loh-foh’n]	[s]
	at the end of syllable or word as in English: **saxofon** [saks-oh-foh’n]	[‘ks’]
z	(also rare) like ‘s’: **zebra** [sey:-brah]	[s]

The Danish alphabet

A [a']	I [ee']	Q [koo']	X [egs]
B [bey']	J [yoth]	R [ayr]	Y [ew']
C [sey']	K [koh']	S [es]	Z [sed]
D [dey']	L [el]	T [tey']	Æ [e']
E [ey']	M [em]	U [oo']	Ø [uh']
F [ef]	N [en]	V [vey']	Å [oh']
G [gey']	O [oh']	W [dawb-belt vey']	
H [hoh']	P [pey']		

Hugo's Imitated Pronunciation

Any system of 'imitated pronunciation' (where the sound of the foreign word is written down as if it were in English syllables) is bound to have drawbacks. The author of this book has strong reservations about the system, since it is impossible to reproduce the subtleties of foreign sounds through English sounds. Authentic Danish pronunciation can only be achieved by listening to native speakers and copying them. However, some students will not have access to native Danes, either in person or on our cassettes, so we have included this well-known feature of Hugo language courses which has proved helpful for such students in the past.

Remember that in the Imitated Pronunciation:

[a] is as in 'cat', not as in 'fate'
[e] is as in 'bed', not as in 'me'
[i] is as in 'ink', not as in 'bite'
[u] is as in 'put', not as in 'cut'
[g] in as in 'get', not as in 'gentle'
[s] is as in 'sit', not as in 'rise'
[th] is as in 'the', not as in 'think'
[ng] is as in 'sing', not as in 'finger'

Underlining indicates stress. A colon (:) means the vowel is long, and an apostrophe (') shows the glottal stop. // indicates that the pronunciation is as in English.

Chapter 1

> *This first chapter teaches you some greetings and ways of saying goodbye. It also introduces the main building blocks of Danish:*
>
> - *the key verbs 'to be' and 'to have' and the subject pronouns*
> - *the indefinite and definite articles*
> - *nouns and their plurals.*

1 Subject pronouns ('I', 'we') and key verbs ('to be', 'to have')

As in English, the two verbs **at være** ('to be') and **at have** ('to have') are particularly important. Feast your eyes on this:

at være	[at vay-r*e*]	to be
jeg er	[yai (rhyme with 'my') ayr]	I am
du er	[doo]	you *fam sing* are
De er	[dee]	you *pol sing* are
han er	[han]	he is
hun er	[hoon]	she is
den er	[den]	it *common gender* is
det er	[dey]	it *neuter gender* is
vi er	[vee]	we are
I er	[ee]	you *fam plur* are
De er	[dee]	you *pol plur* are
de er	[dee]	they are

at have	[at <u>ha</u>:-*ve*] or [ha] or [ha:']	to have
jeg har	[hah]	I have
du har		you *fam sing* have
De har		you *pol sing* have
han har		he has
hun har		she has
den har		it *common gender* has
det har		it *neuter gender* has
vi har		we have
I har		you *fam plur* have
De har		you *pol plur* have
de har		they have

The form of Danish verbs ('doing words') is the same regardless of who or what they refer to, a feature found in few other languages!

On the other hand, Danish, in common with most European languages, has different forms of the verb for the present, past etc. Most of them change according to a regular pattern, whereas others – such as these two – are irregular. Regular or irregular, the present tense, as here, almost always end with an **r**: 'they run': **de løber** [<u>luh</u>'-bor]; 'we walk': **vi går** [gaw']. More about this in Lesson 2.

Danish, like many other languages, features an informal, familiar form of address, **du** (or **I** when talking to more than one person), and a polite or formal form, **De** (used for both singular and plural). Whichever form you use makes no difference to verbs, adjectives or adverbs. The formal **De** and the informal **I** are both spelt with capital letters (which avoids confusion with **de** and **i** 'in').

There is a strong trend in Denmark towards dropping the polite form altogether. On the other hand, particularly with people older than yourself, or customers, it is wise to *begin* with the formal address and leave it to them to use **du** if they wish. This is all reminiscent of the unwritten first name rules in English!

The two words for 'it', **den** and **det**, are used to refer to different genders (common and neuter), which are explained in the next section.

2 Articles and nouns – 'a house', 'the dog'

In English, gender is only shown by pronouns ('he', 'she' and 'it'). It has no effect on the other components of a sentence. In other European languages there are different words for 'a' and 'the' depending on gender (French 'le', 'la'; German 'der', 'die', 'das').

In Danish, nouns (things, beings, concepts, etc.) are either 'common' (**en** [in]) or 'neuter' (**et** [it]) gender, abbreviated to *c* and *n* respectively.

In the indefinite ('a') form, **en** and **et** precede the noun – as in 'a house', **et hus** [et hoo's], 'a dog', **en hund** [en hoon']. In the definite ('the') form, they are added to the *end* of the word: 'the house', **huset** [hoo'-s*e*th], 'the dog', **hunden** [hoon'-n*e*n].

These examples show the indefinite ('a') form and the definite ('the') form:

(common gender)		
en dansker	**danskeren**	Dane
[dan-sgor]	[dan-sgor-*e*n]	
en mand	**manden**	man
[man']	[man'-n*e*n]	
en by	**byen**	town
[bew']	[bew'-*e*n]	
en kø	**køen**	queue
[kuh']	[kuh'-*e*n]	
(neuter gender)		
et loft	**loftet**	loft, ceiling
[lofd]	[lof-d*e*th]	
et ben	**benet**	bone, leg

[bey:'n]	[bey:'n-eth]	
et hold	**holdet**	team
[hol']	[hol'-eth]	
et forsøg	**forsøget**	attempt
[faw-suh']	[faw-suh'-eth]	
et træ	**træet**	tree
[tray']	[tray'-eth]	

So if it is **n** fore, it's **n** aft, as **t** follows **t**. Remembering this will make it much easier to learn other aspects of Danish, though the effects of the gender on other components of a sentence are relatively limited and not too complex.

If the noun ends with an unstressed **e** the definite form only adds the **n** or the **t.**

kaffe	**kaffen**	coffee
[kaf-fe]	[kaf-fen]	
en pige	**pigen**	girl
[pee:-ye]	[pee:-yen]	
en kvinde	**kvinden**	woman
[kvin-ne]	[kvin-nen]	
et tæppe	**tæppet**	carpet
[tep-pe]	[tep-peth]	
et menneske	**mennesket**	human being
[men-ne-ske]	[men-ne-sketh]	

Nouns which end with a stressed **e** still, however, take the full ending. These are likely to have one syllable only, or to have an accent on the **e** to show stress.

te	**teen**	tea
[tey']	[tey'-en]	
en ske	**skeen**	spoon
[skey']	[skey'-en]	
en kafé	**kaféen**	café
[ka-fey']	[ka-fey'-en]	

In nouns which end with a stressed vowel followed by a single consonant (and in one or two other cases) the consonant is often doubled before the usual ending is added. This consonant doubling should be noted from the outset because it is a pattern which occurs in other Danish words as well.

en kop	**koppen**	cup
[kop]	[kop-pen]	
en stak	**stakken**	stack
[stak]	[stag-gen]	
et kys	**kysset**	kiss
[kuhs]	[kuhs-seth]	

A limited number of nouns ending with unstressed **el, en, er** drop an **e** in the definite form, though in some cases either is correct:

en cykel	**cyklen**	bicycle
[sew-kel]	[sewk-len]	
en himmel	**him(me)len**	heaven/sky
[him-mel]	[him-(mel-)len]	
et teater	**teat(e)ret**	theatre
[tey-a'-tor]	[tey-a'-t(e-)reth]	
en frøken	**frøk(e)nen**	unmarried woman
[fruh'-gen]	[fruh'-gen-en]	

This is a pattern which occurs in other areas of Danish as well.

No western language has a hard and fast rule by which you can determine the gender of a noun. Even the fact that, in Danish, the vast majority of beings and their occupations are **en** is of limited use. The gender has to be remembered. You may find this easier if when learning your vocabulary you include the definite form **pigen** 'the girl' rather than just **pige** or **en pige.** So, when you practise while walking the dog, be definite and repeat **en hund – hunden, et træ – træet, et ben – benet** in your mind, rather than **en hund** on its own.

In Danish, the article 'a/an' is often left out, particularly where profession, nationality etc. are concerned (perhaps because you can be one Dane, journalist, etc. only!) Also, nationalities are not spelt with a capital letter.

Jeg er dansker, De er skotte. [Yai ayr dan-sgor, dee ayr sgod-d*e*]

I am a Dane, you are a Scot.

Han er journalist, hun er fotograf. [Han ayr sjoh-na-leesd, hoon ayr foh-toh-grah'f]

He is a journalist, she is a photographer.

Exercise 1

Aided by the c *and* n *indications, give the definite form of the words below. An asterisk * indicates that the single consonant is doubled.*

1	**vindue** *n*	[vin-doo]	window
2	**gulv** *n*	[gul']	floor
3	**lampe** *c*	[lam-p*e*]	lamp
4	**klubhus** *n*	[kloob-hoo's]	clubhouse
5	**mursten** *c*	[moor-stey'n]	brick
6	**fabrik*** *c*	[fa-breek]	factory
7	**knæ** *n*	[cney']	knee
8	**bager** *c*	[ba:-yor]	baker
9	**bog** *c*	[boh:'h]	book
10	**æg*** *n*	[e:'g]	egg

3 Plural of nouns – 'women', 'houses'

There are some similarities between English and Danish where the plural of nouns is concerned. In both languages, the plural is sometimes formed simply by changing the vowel of the stem ('man – men'; Danish: **mand – mænd** [men']). While, in English, plurals are commonly formed by adding 's' or 'es', the most common Danish plurals end in **e** or **er** in the *indefinite*. The *definite* plural always adds a further **ne** or **ene.**

Plural endings are not affected by gender.

(a) The majority of Danish nouns add **er** for the indefinite plural, or, if they already end in unstressed **e**, just **r**. In the definite form they add a further **ne.**

flower	**en blomst**	**blomster**	**blomsterne**
	[blom'sd]	[blom'-sdor]	[blom'-sdor-n*e*]
piano	**et klaver**	**klaverer**	**klavererne**
	[kla-vey'r]	kla-vey'-ror]	[kla-vey'-ror-n*e*]
woman	**en kvinde**	**kvinder**	**kvinderne**
	[kvin-n*e*]	[kvin-nor]	[kvin-nor-n*e*]
Scot	**en skotte**	**skotter**	**skotterne**
	[sgod-d*e*]	[sgod-dor]	[sgod-dor-n*e*]
meeting	**et møde**	**møder**	**møderne**
	[muh-th*e*]	[muh-thor]	[muh-thor-n*e*]
garden	**en have**	**haver**	**haverne**
	[ha:-v*e*]	[ha:-vor]	[ha:-vor-n*e*]

And so on:

lady	**en dame**	**damer**	**damerne**
	[da:-m*e*]	[da:-mor]	[da:-mor-n*e*]
place	**et sted**	**steder**	**stederne**
	[sdeth]	[sde-thor]	[sde-thor-n*e*]
idea	**en idé**	**ideer**	**ideerne**
	[ee-dey']	[ee-dey'-or]	[ee-dey'-or-n*e*]

As with the definite ending, most nouns ending with a stressed vowel followed by a consonant double that consonant when adding the plural ending:

bus	**bus(sen)**	**busser**	**busserne**
	[boos]	[boos-sor]	[boos-sor-n*e*]
cigarette	**cigaret(ten)**	**cigaretter**	**cigaretterne**
	[see-ga-ret;	see-ga-ret-tor;	see-ga-ret-tor-n*e*]
principle	**princip(pet)**	**principper**	**principperne**
	[prin-seep;	prin-seep-por;	prin-seep-por-n*e*]
shop	**butik(ken)**	**butikker**	**butikkerne**
	[boo-teek;	boo-teek-kor;	boo-teek-kor-n*e*]

toffee	**karamel(len)** [ka-ra-mey'l;	**karameller** ka-ra-mey'l-lor;	**karamellerne** ka-ra-mey'l-lor-n*e*]

Usually, if the vowel in the last syllable is long the consonant remains single:

camel	**kamel(en)** [ka-mey:'l]	**kameler** [ka-mey:'-lor]	**kamelerne** [ka-mey:'-lor-n*e*]

Nouns ending with **er, en** or **el** in the singular often lose the **e** of their ending when the plural ending is added, and any double consonant before the **e** becomes a single consonant:

sister	**en søster** [suhs-dor]	**søsteren** [suhs-dor-*e*n]	**søstre** [suhs-dr*e*]	**søstrene** [suhs-dr*e*-n*e*]
uncle	**en onkel** [on-k*e*l]	**onklen** [on-kl*e*n]	**onkler** [on-klor]	**onklerne** [on-klor-n*e*]
fork	**en gaffel** [gaf-f*e*l]	**gaflen** [gaf-l*e*n]	**gafler** [gaf-lor]	**gaflerne** [gaf-lor-n*e*]
prison	**et fængsel** [feng'-s*e*l]	**fængslet** [feng'-sl*e*th]	**fængsler** [feng'-slor]	**fængslerne** [feng'-slor-n*e*]
bicycle	**en cykel** [sew-k*e*l]	**cyklen** [sew-kl*e*n]	**cykler** [sew-klor]	**cyklerne** [sew-klor-n*e*]

(b) Some *indefinite* plural forms add **e**, with a further **ne** in the *definite* form.

house	**hus(et)** [hoo'-s*e*th]	**huse** [hoo-s*e*]	**husene** [hoo-s*e* -n*e*]
knife	**kniv(en)** [cnee'-v*e*n]	**knive** [cnee:-v*e*]	**knivene** [cnee:-v*e* -n*e*]
sparrow	**spurv(en)** [spoo:r-ven]	**spurve** [spoo:r-v*e*]	**spurvene** [spoo:r-v*e* -n*e*]
leaf	**blad(et)** [bla:-th*e*th]	**blade** [bla:-th*e*]	**bladene** [bla:-th*e* -n*e*]
table	**bord(et)** [baw'-r*e*th]	**borde** [baw-r*e*]	**bordene** [baw-r*e* -n*e*]

In some nouns of common gender which end in **er** the final **e** of the indefinite plural disappears in the definite plural before the **ne** ending. Native Danes tend to pronounce the

ere ending as one long indistinct sound:

butcher	**slagter(en)** [slag-tor-*e*n]	**slagtere** [slag-tor-*e*]	**slagterne** [slag-tor-n*e*]
baker	**bager(en)** [ba:-yor-*e*n]	**bagere** [ba:-yor-*e*]	**bagerne** [ba:-yor-n*e*]
Dane	**dansker(en)** [dan-sgor-*e*n]	**danskere** [dan-sgor-*e*]	**danskerne** [dan-sgor-n*e*]

This group also includes a few English-speaking nationals, such as:

amerikanerne [a-me-ree-ka:'-nor-n*e*], **australierne** [ow-stra:'-lee-or-n*e*], **canadierne** [ka-na:'-dee-or-n*e*] **englænderne** [eng-len'-or-n*e*], **irerne** [ee'-ror-n*e*], **waliserne** [va-lee'-sor-n*e*].

Again, some nouns ending in **er, en** or **el** in the singular often drop the **e** of their ending and make double consonants single before the plural ending:

warehouse	**lager(et)** [la:-yor-*e*th]	**lag(e)re** [la:-ror]	**lag(e)rene** [la:-ror-n*e*]
summer	**sommer(en)** [som-mor-*e*n]	**somre** [som-ror]	**somrene** [som-ror-n*e*]
winter	**vinter(en)** [veen'-tor-*e*n]	**vintre** [veen-tror]	**vintrene** [veen-tror-n*e*]

(c) One group of nouns is the same in the singular and plural *indefinite*, and adds **ene** in the definite plural:

leg	**ben(et)** [bey'n-*e*th]	**ben** [bey'n]	**benene** [bey'n-n*e*-n*e*]
animal	**dyr(et)** [dew'-r*e*th]	**dyr** [dew'r]	**dyrene** [dew'-r*e*-n*e*]
train	**tog(et)** [toh'-*e*th]	**tog** [toh:'h]	**togene** [toh'-*e*-n*e*]
mouse	**mus(en)** [moo:'s-*e*n]	**mus** [moo:'s]	**musene** [moo:'s-*e*-n*e*]
glass	**glas(set)** [glas-*e*th]	**glas** [glas]	**glassene** [glas-*e*-n*e*]

The last example is of a noun which does not change in the *indefinite* plural but where the extra consonant still has to be added in the definite plural.

(d) Others in all three groups also change the stem vowel, just like the English 'woman – women'.

en ko a cow	**køer** cows	**køerne** the cows
[koh']	[kuh'-or]	[kuh'-or-n*e*]
en bonde a farmer	**bønder** farmers	**bønderne** the farmers
[bohn-n*e*]	[buhn'-nor]	[buhn'-nor-n*e*]
et barn a child	**børn** children	**børnene** the children
[bah'n]	[bur'n]	[bur'-n*e*-n*e*]
en mand a man	**mænd** men	**mændene** the men
[man']	[men']	[men'-*e*-n*e*]
en gås a goose	**gæs** geese	**gæssene** the geese
[goh's]	[ges]	[ges-s*e*-n*e*]

This change of vowel in the plural occurs in several nouns referring to family members. Three of these offer the slight complication that whilst their original form is the basis for the plural, a shortened, modern form is now used almost exclusively in the singular:

mother	**moder(en) (mor)**	**mødre**	**mødrene**
	[moh:-thor (maw)]	[muhth-r*e*]	[muhth-r*e*-n*e*]
father	**fader(en) (far)**	**fædre**	**fædrene**
	[fa:-thor (fah:)]	[fayth-r*e*]	[fayth-r*e*-n*e*]
brother	**broder(en) (bror)**	**brødre**	**brødrene**
	[broh:-thor (braw)]	[bruhth-r*e*]	[bruhth-r*e*-n*e*]

(e) Teasers

One complete irregularity is:

øje (**t**) eye	**øjne** eyes	**øjnene** the eyes
[oy-*e*th]	[oy-n*e*]	[oy-n*e*-n*e*]

Menneske(t) 'human being' is regular in the indefinite plural, but has an unexpected definite plural: **mennesker, menneskene** [men-ne-skor, men-ne-ske-ne].

Two examples of nouns which are singular in English but plural in Danish: **penge, pengene** [peng-e-ne] 'money, the money' and **møbler, møblerne** [muh-blor-ne] 'furniture'. (**Et møbel** is 'a piece of furniture'.)

As with gender, you will need to learn the way each noun forms its plural, so from now on we shall include this information in vocabulary lists, e.g. **kvinde (-n, -r)** means that **kvinde** is common gender (**en kvinde**) and takes **-r** in the plural (**kvinder**). If the stem changes, as with **barn**, the full word will be given: (**-et, børn**). And if it stays the same in the indefinite plural, like **glas**, that will be indicated by a dash (**-set, -**). Try it out in Exercise 2.

Exercise 2

Form the plural, indefinite and definite, of these nouns, some of which you've met before:

Example: **pæl (-en, -e)** [pey'l] pole
pæl – pæle – pælene

1	**dreng (-en, -e)** [dreng]	boy
2	**top (-pen, -pe)** [//]	top
3	**hund (-en, -e)**	
4	**by (-en, -er)**	
5	**familie (-n, -r)** [fa-mee'l-ye]	family
6	**skotte (-n, -r)**	
7	**dansker (-en, -e)**	
8	**ske (-en, -er)**	
9	**soldat (-en, -er)** [sul-da't]	soldier
10	**tag (-et, -e)** [ta:'h]	roof
11	**æg (-get, -)**	

12	**pas (-set, -)** [pas]	passport
13	**kys (-set, -)**	
14	**tæppe (-t, -r)**	
15	**hold (-et, -)**	
16	**forsøg (-et, -)**	
17	**ideal (-et, -er)** [ee-dey-a:'l]	ideal
18	**dyr (-et, -)**	

4 Greetings

These are the most usual forms of greeting and leave-taking:

goddag [goh-da']	good day
godmorgen [goh-mawn]	good morning
godaften [goh-af-d*e*n]	good evening
godnat [goh-nat]	good night
velkommen [vel-kom-*e*n]	welcome
farvel [fah-vel]	goodbye
på gensyn [poh' gen-sew'n]	see you again

Casual forms:

hi [hy']	hi
dav [dow'] **davs** [dow's]	hello

Hvordan har du det? [vo-dan] 'How are you?' is not an automatic opening and if it is said, an answer, such as **Godt, tak** [got, tak] 'well, thank you', or **Faktisk ikke så godt** [fak-tisk ig-g*e* so got] 'not too well, actually' is expected! **Går det godt?** [gaw'] or **Har du det godt?** 'Are you well?' are often used instead.

Here's a very simple conversation in Danish. Use the vocabulary list to see how much of it you can understand, or even translate into English, before looking at the translation which follows it.

Vocabulary

fru [froo']	Mrs
brev (-et, -e) [bray'u]	letter
til Dem [ti' dem]	for you
tusind tak [too:'-s*e*n tak]	thank you very much
gæst (-en, -er) [gest]	guest
hos [hohs]	with, at the house of
tror [traw]	believe
ja [ya]	yes
hvad hedder du? [va hi'th-or doo]	what is your name?
jeg hedder	my name is, I am called
studerende (en, -) [sdoo-dey'-r*e*-n*e*]	student
mange [mang-*e*]	many
ikke sandt [ig-g*e* san't]	don't you, isn't it, etc. (not true)
du må gerne [doo moh' gáyr-n*e*]	you are welcome to
sige [see: -y*e*]	say
åh [oh:']	oh
kun [koon]	only
to [toh']	two
kat (-ten, -te) [kad]	cat
pony (-en, -er) [pon-new] or [pon-nee]	pony
og [ow] or [o]	and

CONVERSATION

Malcolm	**Godmorgen, fru Poulsen, jeg har et brev til Dem.**
Fru Poulsen	**Tusind tak. Du er gæst hos familien Frandsen, tror jeg?**
Malcolm	**Ja, jeg er englænder.**
Fru Poulsen	**Hvad hedder du?**
Malcolm	**Jeg hedder Malcolm.**
Fru Poulsen	**Er du studerende?**
Malcolm	**Ja. De har mange dyr, ikke sandt?**
Fru Poulsen	**Du må gerne sige 'du'. Åh, jeg har kun to katte, en hund, en pony – og to børn.**

TRANSLATION

Malcolm	**Good morning, Mrs Poulsen, I have a letter for you.**
Mrs Poulsen	**Thank you very much (a thousand thanks). You are a guest (at the house) of the Frandsen family, I believe?**
Malcolm	**Yes, I am an Englishman.**
Mrs Poulsen	**What's your name?**
Malcolm	**My name is Malcolm.**
Mrs Poulsen	**Are you a student?**
Malcolm	**Yes. You have many animals, don't you [not true]?**
Mrs Poulsen	**You are welcome to say 'du'. Oh, I have only two cats, a dog, a pony – and two children.**

Chapter 2

In this chapter you will meet the first snippet from Storm P. You will also learn:

- *the present tense of some more verbs*
- *the object pronouns 'me', 'him', etc.*
- *the order of words in statements and questions*
- *the question words 'who' and 'what'.*

5 Verbs – basic form and present tense – 'to hear/I hear'

Verbs are the words with which we describe any form of action or happening ('doing words'), and change according to when events take or took place. In many Western languages, they change not only with the past, present and future but also with the person, singular or plural. Danish and English both have fewer variations than most, Danish having the particular advantage – remember? – that the person makes no difference at all: **jeg hører, han hører** [huh:-ror] 'I hear, he hears'.

The infinitive (to hear: **at høre** [at huh:-r*e*]) is the basic form of verbs, and the one found in dictionaries. In Danish, the vast majority end with an unstressed **e**, the others with a stressed vowel (**at stå** [sdoh'] – to stand).

At høre er at adlyde. [ath-lew-th*e*] To hear is to obey.
In both instances, the present tense is formed by the addition of an **r**: **hører, står** [sdaw'].

Børnene står i skoven og hører fuglene synge. [bur-n*e*-n*e* sdaw' ee skow-*e*n o huh:-ror foo:-l*e*-n*e* sew-ng*e*]
The children stand in the wood and hear the birds sing.

The stressed syllable is usually short in the present tense, even where it is long in the infinitive.

Infinitive		*Present tense*
at tale	to speak	**taler**
[ta:-l*e*]		[ta'-lor]
at spise	to eat	**spiser**
[spee:-s*e*]		[spee'-sor]
at løbe	to run	**løber**
[luh:-b*e*]		[luh'-bor]
at bruge	to use	**bruger**
[broo:-*e*]		[broo'-or]
at blive	to remain/become	**bliver**
[blee:-v*e*]		[blee'-vor] or [blee'r]
at komme	to come	**kommer**
[kom-m*e*]		[kom'-mor]
at ligge	to lie	**ligger**
[lig-g*e*]		[lig-gor]
at lægge	to put, lay	**lægger**
[leg-g*e*]		[leg-gor]
at sidde	to sit	**sidder**
[si-th*e*]		[sith'-or]

When the infinitive ends with a stressed vowel, it always has a glottal stop on the final vowel. These verbs retain the glottal stop in the present tense.

Infinitive		*Present tense*
at forstå	to understand	**forstår**
[faw-stoh']		[faw-staw']
at se	to see	**ser**

[sey′]		[sey′r]
at slå	to hit	**slår**
[sloh′]		[slaw′]
at le	to laugh	**ler**
[ley′]		[ley′r]
at gå	to walk, go	**går**
[goh′]		[gaw′]
at befri	to free	**befri(e)r**
[bey-free′]		[bey-free′r]
at sy	to sew	**sy(e)r**
[sew′]		[sew′r]

The last two are examples of **er** sometimes being added, though the pronunciation all but ignores the **e**.

Blive expresses some kind of change, like the English 'turn', 'go' and 'grow':

Læreren bliver rasende. [lay′-ror-*e* n blee′r rah:-s*e* -n*e*]
The teacher is getting furious.
Det bliver koldt nu. [kol′t]
It's turning/growing/getting cold now.

It also means 'remain' and 'stay':

Bliver du eller går du? [el-or]
Are you staying or leaving?

And on the subject of **gå: gå** on its own means 'walk' or 'leave'. Linked with a preposition or an adverb, it may mean 'go', but only if it is possible to go on foot.

Du skal gå, ikke løbe. [sgal] or [sga]
You must walk, not run.
Vi går nu.
We're leaving/going now.
Han går over til vinduet. [ow-or til]
He goes/walks over to the window.

A very few verbs form their present tenses differently, including two common verbs:

Infinitive		*Present tense*
at gøre	to do	**gør**
[gur-re]		[gur]
at vide	to know	**ved**
[vee:-the]		[vi'th]

Vide means 'to know' in the sense of knowing a fact. The verb for knowing a person or a place, 'to be acquainted with', is **kende** [ken-*e*].

Jeg ved, hvor han bor, men jeg kender ham ikke
[baw'; ken'-or]
I know where he lives but I don't know him.

There are a limited number of verbs which commonly end in **s** in the infinitive and present tense. We shall be looking at this group again in Section 41:

at skændes [sken-*e*s] to quarrel
vi skændes we are quarrelling
at synes [sew:-n*e*s] to think (be of the opinion)
Jeg synes, det er grimt. [grim'd] I think it is ugly.
Synes du om filmen? [om feel'-m*e*n] Do you like the film?

Using the present tense

Forget all about the English '-ing' form ('I am drinking'), which is expressed in Danish in exactly the same way as the simple present: 'I drink': **Jeg drikker** [drig-or]. Similarly with the English 'do' and 'don't': 'I do drink, but I don't smoke'. **Jeg drikker, men jeg ryger ikke** [rew:-yor].

Just as in English, the present tense is often used with a future meaning, mostly by adding an indication of time.

Ja, jeg kommer snart. [snah't]
Yes, I'm coming soon.
Toget til København går om et øjeblik. [kuh-b*e*n-how'n; oy-*e*-blik]
The train to Copenhagen is leaving in a moment.

Svigermor rejser i morgen – desværre. [svee'-or-maw ry-sor i mawn – des-vayr-*e*]

Mother-in-law is leaving (travelling) tomorrow – unfortunately.

Vocabulary

meget [my-*e*t]	much, a lot
men [men]	but
lidt [lit]	(a) little
forår (**-et, -**) [faw-aw']	spring
snart [snah't]	soon
at gø [guh']	bark
at bide [bee:-th*e*]	bite
om	about
i	in
zoologisk [soh-oh-loh'-gisg]	zoological
at sælge [sel-y*e*]	sell
wienerbrød (**-et, -**) [vee-nor-bruh'th]	Danish pastry
hans [hans]	his
når [naw] or [naw']	when
høne (**-n, -r**) [huh:-n*e*]	hen
dér	there
at falde [fal-l*e*]	to fall

Exercise 3

Translate:

1 Han taler meget, men siger kun lidt.
2 Foråret kommer snart.
3 Jeg ser toget komme.
4 Hunden gøer og bider.
5 De fortæller om kamelerne i Zoologisk Have.
6 Bageren sælger wienerbrød.
7 Vi synger om en bonde og hans dyr.
8 Jeg ler meget, når jeg ser Victor Borge.
9 Hønen lægger to æg – dér ligger de.
10 Han falder og slår knæet.

6 Personal pronouns as objects – 'me', 'him', 'them'

He gives *me* the money.
I love *you*, you love *me*. We love *them* but they hate *us*.

The emphasised words in these examples are known as object pronouns. The Danish object pronouns are:

mig [my]	me
dig [dy]	you *fam sing*
Dem [dem]	you *pol sing*
ham [ham]	him
hende [hen-n*e*]	her
den/det [den'; dey]	it
os [os]	us
jer [yayr]	you *fam plur*
Dem	you *pol plur*
dem	them

So here is the Danish for the examples given, and a couple more:

Han giver mig pengene. [gee'r]
Jeg elsker dig, du elsker mig. Vi elsker dem, men de hader os. [els-gor; ha:-thor]
Vinen er til jer, øllet til dem [vee'-n*e*n; uhl'-l*e*t]
The wine is for you, the beer for them.
Henter du mig, eller jeg dig? [hen-tor]
Are you collecting me, or I you?

Hinanden [heen-an-n*e*n] means 'each other':

De arbejder med hinanden. [ah-by-tor; me *or* meth]
They are working with each other.
Mændene giver hinanden hånden på det. [hon'-*e*n]
The men shake hands on it (give each other the hand on it).

Vocabulary

til [til]	to
mod [moh'th]	towards
ad [ath]	at
for [faw]	for

Exercise 4

Translate the English pronouns in italics into Danish:

1. Han taler meget til *me,* men siger kun lidt om *you (fam sing).*
2. Foråret kommer snart til *us.*
3. Jeg ser toget komme mod *me.*
4. Hunden gøer ad *you* (*fam plur*) og bider *me.*
5. De fortæller *each other* om kamelerne.
6. Bageren sælger wienerbrød til *her.*
7. Vi synger for *each other.*

Vocabulary

at elske [els-ge]	to love
at kalde [kal-e]	to call
kujon (-en, -er) [koo-yoh'n]	coward
at give [gee:-ve] or [gee']	to give
vin (-en, -e) [vee'n]	wine
at spørge [sbuh-re]	to ask
at svare [svah:-re]	to answer
at bringe [bring-e]	to bring
held (-et, -) [hel']	luck
gave (-n, -r) [ga:-ve]	gift
ikke [ig-ge]	not

Exercise 5

Translate:

1 Hans and Grete, we love you.
2 Hans and Grete love each other.
3. I call you a coward.
4 They give the wine to her.
5 I ask them and they answer me.
6 They are bringing us luck.
7 The are giving each other presents.
8 I understand you, not her.

7 Sentence building – questions and answers

Danish word order is very often the same as English, but there are some important differences. In simple Danish sentences, the verb always comes second, whatever the sentence begins with. Look at the following sentences:

Jeg køber en bil i dag. [bee'l; ee-da:']
I'm buying a car today.
I dag køber jeg en bil.
Today I'm buying a car.
Jens og Peter møder en ven i København. [yen's; pey'-dor; muh'-thor; ven']
Jens and Peter are meeting a friend in Copenhagen.
I København møder Jens og Peter en ven.
In Copenhagen Jens and Peter are meeting a friend.

So when the sentence begins with a word or phrase which is not the subject, the subject will always come immediately after the verb, and not before it as it does in English. This is known as 'inversion', i.e. the subject and verb are inverted so that the verb precedes the subject.

Pigen ligger dér og sover. [sow'or]
The girl lies there sleeping (and sleeps).

Dér ligger pigen.
There lies the girl.

Straightforward questions in Danish, i.e. those formed without an interrogative or 'question word', are formed by inversion (the verb comes first and is followed immediately by the subject):

Kommer du alene? [a-ley:-n*e*] Are you coming alone?
Bor du her? Do you live here?
Køber du en bil i dag? Are you buying a car today?
Forstår du tysk? [tewsg] Do you understand German?
Kører du til Danmark eller flyver du? [kur-or; dan-mahg; flew'-vor]
Are you driving to Denmark, or are you flying?
Møder de ham i København?
Are they meeting him in Copenhagen?

The affirmative reply is **ja** [ya] 'yes'.

Ja, jeg forstår tysk. Yes, I understand German.

The negative answer is **nej** [ny'] 'no' and **ikke** 'not' :

Neg, jeg forstår ikke tysk.
No, I don't understand German.
Neg, jeg kører ikke til Danmark.
No, I'm not driving to Denmark.

So **ikke** comes directly *after* subject and verb. The same thing happens with a few other words (see Section 26, Adverbs), such as **aldrig** [al-dree] 'never', **altid** [al'-tee'th] 'always', **nu** [noo] 'now', **tit** [//] 'often'.

Til Danmark kører jeg aldrig. Jeg flyver altid – til København.
I never drive to Denmark. I always fly – to Copenhagen.
Bilen køber jeg ikke i dag, men jeg rydder op i garagen. [rew-thor op ee ga-rah-sj*e*n]
I am not buying the car today but I am tidying up (in) the garage.

Knud drikker altid te. [cnoo'th]
Knud always drinks tea.
Peter kender aldrig svaret. [svah'-r*e*t]
Peter never knows the answer.

If the object of the verb is a pronoun rather than a noun, words like **ikke** are placed directly after the pronoun object, rather than following the verb:

Jeg drikker den ikke i dag.
I'm not drinking it today.
Jens og Peter møder ham altid i København.
Jens and Peter always meet him in Copenhagen.
Køber du den ikke idag?
Aren't you buying it today?

If the question is negative: **Forstår du ikke? Kører du ikke? Køber du ikke en bil i dag?** but the reply is affirmative, the word to use is not **ja** but **jo** [yoh']:

Jo, jeg forstår.
Yes, I (do) understand.

Ikke is frequently added at the end of a sentence, requesting confirmation, like the English 'isn't it?' and so on:

Det er koldt i dag, ikke?
It's cold today, isn't it?

Vel [//] is often added in the same way at the end of a negative sentence:

Franskmændene spiller aldrig godt mod os, vel? [fransg-men-*e*-ne: sbil-lor]
The French never play well against us, do they?

Vocabulary

morgenmad (-en) [maw-*e*n-math]	breakfast
at flyve [flew-v*e*]	to fly
mellem [mel-l*e*m]	between

København	Copenhagen
politibetjent (**-en, -e**) [poh-lee-tee-bey-tyeyn't]	policeman
skole (**-n, -r**) [sgoh-l*e*]	school
ferie (**-n, -r**) [fayr'-ree-*e*]	holiday

Exercise 6

Answer all these questions in the affirmative and negative, using all the words again:

1 Spiser du altid morgenmad?
2 Flyver SAS mellem København og Alaska?
3 Taler politibetjenten engelsk?
4 Har skolen ikke ferie nu?
5 Hedder du ikke Søren?

8 Question words – 'who', 'what'

Here are some questions using the most common Danish question words.

Hvem taler dansk? [vem'; dan'sg]
Who speaks Danish?
Hvem møder du i København?
Who(m) are you meeting in Copenhagen?
Hvem giver du boret til? [baw'-r*e*t]
Who are you giving the drill to?
Hvor er benzinstationen? [vaw'; ben-see'n-sta-sjoh'n-*e*n]
Where is the petrol station?
Hvornår sender Margrethe brevet? [vaw-naw' sen-nor mah-grey'-t*e*]
When is Margrethe sending the letter?
Hvordan køber du en ny bil i dag? [vo-dan]
How are you buying a new car today?
Hvor stor er byen? [vaw sdaw']
How big is the town?

Hvad spiser du? [va]
What are you eating?
Hvad siger du? [see-or] or [seer]
What do you say?
Hvis bil kører du i dag? [vis]
Whose car are you driving today?
Hvis er campingvognen? [//-vow'n-*e*n]
Whose is the caravan?
Hvorfor læser du bogen? [vaw-faw ley's-or]
Why are you reading the book?

Storm P.

– Hvad kommer først, årsag eller virkning?
– Det gør årsagen.
– Ja, men hvad så med en mand, der skubber en trillebør?
[fursd; aw-sa:'h; veerk-ning; sgub-bor; tril-*le*-bur']

– What comes first, cause or effect?
– The cause does.
– Yes, but then what about (what then with) a man who pushes a wheelbarrow?

Hvad hjælper det, at man har paraply, når man har hul i skoene?
[yel'-bor; pa-ra-plew'; hu'l; sgoh'-*e*-*ne*]

What good is it (helps it) that one has an umbrella when one has a hole in one's (the) shoes?

Vocabulary

at holde ferie [hol-*e*]	to spend a holiday
i år [aw']	this year
eller	or
at tage med [ta: -*ye* *or* ta *or* ta:'; meth *or* me]	go/come along
din [dee'n]	your
mand (-en, mænd)	husband
måske [mo-sgey']	perhaps

færdig [fayr-dee]	finished
at sejle [syl-*e*]	to sail
Nordspanien [ŋaw-sba'-nee-*e*n]	Northern Spain
selvfølgelig [sel-fuhl'-y*e*-lee]	of course
naturligvis [na-toor'-lee-vee:'s]	of course
at tage	to take
Italien [i-ta:'-lee-*e*n]	Italy
at slappe af [slab-b*e* a:']	to relax
Firenze [fee-ren-s*e*]	Florence
at	that
at bo [boh:']	to live (reside)
at skrive [sgree:-v*e*]	to write
adresse (-n, -r) [a-dres-s*e*]	address
så [so]	so that
kan [kan] or [ka]	can
at besøge [bey-suh'-y*e*]	visit
hav [ha] or [ha:']	have
god [goh'] or [goh'th]	good

CONVERSATION

Peter Bertelsen **Hvor holder I ferie i år? Eller tager din mand ikke med – måske er han ikke færdig med bogen?**

Maria Gording **Vi sejler til Nordspanien i år. Og jo, Jan tager selvfølgelig med – *naturligvis* tager han med. Men hvad gør du og Merete?**

Peter **Vi tager toget til Italien og slapper af i Firenze. Du og Jan, I kender byen, gør I ikke?**

Maria **Ih, jo. Ved du, at Walter Nissens familie bor der? Jeg skriver adressen, så I kan besøge dem. Og hav en god ferie!**

TRANSLATION

Peter Bertelsen	**Where are you spending your holiday this year? Or isn't your husband going along (with you) – perhaps he has not finished the book?**
Maria Gording	**We are sailing to Northern Spain this year. And yes, Jan is of course coming (along) – *of course* he is (coming along). But what are you and Merete doing?**
Peter	**We are taking the train to Italy and relaxing in Florence. You and Jan, you know the town, don't you?**
Maria	**Oh, yes. Do you know that Walter Nissen's family lives there? I'll write the address so that you can visit them. And have a good holiday!**

Chapter 3

In Chapter 3 you will find out:

- *how to use adjectives to describe nouns*
- *how to give an instruction or command*
- *how possession is expressed in Danish*
- *the names of the days and months, seasons and holidays.*

9 Adjectives – 'good', 'large'

Adjectives are words used to describe characteristics – looks, size, etc. In English, they change only in comparison (good – better – best). In Danish, they also change with the gender of the noun as well as with its definite ('the') or indefinite ('a') and plural forms. Don't let this daunt you, though: the changes follow relatively simple patterns.

The *basic* form of a Danish adjective (as you will find it in the dictionary) is used unchanged in connection with nouns of common gender, singular, in their *indefinite* form ('a').

en sød kage [suh'th ka:-y*e*] a sweet cake
en god kvinde a good woman
en stor waliser a large Welshman
en morsom anekdote [maw-som a-neg-doh-t*e*]
an amusing anecdote
en blå bil [bloh'] a blue car

When adjectives are used to describe a singular neuter noun they usually require the addition of a **t:**

et sødt smil [suht smee:'l] a sweet smile
et godt hjerte [got yayr-d*e*] a good heart
et stort måltid [mol-tee'th] a large meal
et morsomt eventyr [e:-v*e*n-tew'r] an amusing fairy tale/adventure
et blåt gardin [blot gah-dee'n] a blue curtain

In the indefinite plural most adjectives end with an **e:**

søde sager [suh:-th*e* sa:-yor] sweet things
gode gerninger [goh-th*e* gayr-ning-or] good deeds
store begivenheder [bey-gee'-v*e* n-hi'-thor] great events

When an adjective is placed before a noun in the *definite* ('the') form, the definite ending is not added to the noun. Instead the adjective is preceded by another word, meaning 'the', which is the same as the words for 'it' and 'they': **den** for common gender singular, **det** for neuter singular, and **de** for plural. The ending on the adjective, though, is the same for all three: **e.**

den søde smerte [smayr-t*e*] the sweet pain
det store måltid the large meal
de dejlige oplevelser [dy-lee-*e* op-ley'-v*e* l-sor]
the lovely experiences

If you want to say 'the red one, the big ones' in Danish, you do this simply by using the appropriate form of **den, det, de** followed by the adjective ending in **e: den røde** [ruh:-th*e*], **de store.**

When the adjective is not directly in front of the noun and is used with verbs such as **at være** 'to be', **at blive** 'to become', the indefinite forms are used:

Bogen er dårlig. [daw-lee]
The book is bad.

Vejret bliver dårligt. [ve'-r*e* t; daw-leet]
The weather is getting bad.
Cigarerne er dårlig. [si-gah'-r*e* -n*e* ; daw-lee-*e*]
The cigars are bad.

Exceptions

Some adjectives do not add **t** in the neuter. These include those ending in **sk**, those already ending in **t**, those ending in a vowel other than **å** (except the adjectives **ny** [new'] 'new' and **fri** [free'] 'free'), those that end with **s**, and the adjectives **glad** [glath] 'happy' and **fremmed** [frem-m*e*th] 'foreign, strange'.

et engelsk program [eng'-*e*lsg proh-gram']
an English programme
et malet ansigt [ma:-l*e*t an-sigt]
a painted face
et fremragende forslag [frem-row-*e*-n*e* faw-sla:'h]
an outstanding suggestion
et snu trick [snoo' //]
a cunning trick
et stakkels dyr [sdag-*e*ls]
a poor (pitiable) animal
et glad menneske
a happy person
et fremmed skib [skee'b]
a foreign ship

Some adjectives don't add **e**. These include those ending with **s**, and those ending with a vowel (except the adjectives **ny** and **fri**):

det fremragende forslag
de gammeldags værdier [gam-*e*l-da:'s vayr-dee'-or] the old-fashioned values
det blå værelse [vayr-*e*l-s*e*] the blue room
but
det frie liv under den nye demokratiske regering [free-*e*lee'u un'-or den new-*e* dey-moh-krah'-tee-sg*e* rey-gey'-ring] the free life under the new democratic government

An **et** ending of an adjective with two or more syllables is turned into **ede**:

snavset: de snavsede fingre [snow-s*e*th; snow-s*e*-th*e* fing-r*e*]
the dirty fingers
udmattet: den udmattede kok [ooth-mat-t*e* th; ooth-mat-t*e*-th*e* kok]
the exhausted cook

Like nouns, adjectives that end with a single consonant preceded by a stressed vowel often double the consonant when taking the **e** ending, as do adjectives ending in **som:**

dum: det dumme grin [dum'; dum-*e* gree'n] the stupid grin
smuk: øjnene er smukke [smuk; oy-n*e*-n*e* ; smug-g*e*]
the eyes are beautiful
let: lette frokoster [led; led-d*e* froh-kost-or]
light lunches
de morsomme skuespillere [sgoo:-*e*-spil-lor-*e*]
the amusing actors

Those that end in **el**, **er**, or **en** drop the **e** of their ending when the **e** is added, and if the **el**, **er** or **en** is preceded by a double consonant, that consonant is simplified.

mager: den magre abe [ma:-yor; ma:-r*e* a:-b*e*] the thin monkey
lækker: den lækre suppe [leg-gor; leg-r*e* sub-b*e*]
the delicious soup
gammel: de gamle minder [gam-m*e*l; gam-l*e* min-nor]
the old memories

Teaser: **lille** [leel-l*e*] and **små** [smoh'] both mean 'small', in singular and plural respectively. **Lidt**, which you have already met, is not an adjective but an adverb, and means 'a little/rather/somewhat . . .'.

Den lille skomager er lidt træt. [sgoh-ma:-yor; tret]
The little shoemaker is a little tired.

Exercise 7

Produce the definite/plural form of the following adjectives, as in the example. Once again an asterisk indicates where consonants need to be doubled.

Example: **let*** light, easy: **lette**

1	**kort** [kaw't]	short	10	**tapper** [tab-bor]	brave
2	**dejlig**	delightful	11	**blød** [bluh'th]	soft
3	**rar** [rah:]	kind	12	**gammel**	old
4	**høj** [hoy']	high	13	**slap*** [slab]	limp
5	**tung** [tung']	heavy	14	**violet***[vee-oh-let]	purple
6	**farvet** [fah-veth]	coloured	15	**privat** [pree-va:'t]	private
7	**grå** [groh']	grey	16	**svanger** [svang-or]	pregnant
8	**falsk** [fal'sg]	false	17	**hullet** [hul-leth]	holey
9	**tysk**	German			

Vocabulary

eventyr (-et, -)	fairy tale, adventure
gardin (-et, -er)	curtain
mønster (-et, -stre) [muhn'-stor]	pattern
redningshelikopter (-en, -e) [reth-nings-hel-lee:-kob-tor]	rescue helicopter

Exercise 8

Give the form some of the adjectives from the previous exercise would have in Danish when used in the following contexts:

He told a (1) *short* but (2) *delightful* fairy tale.
It was a (3) *heavy*, (4) *coloured* curtain with a (5) *grey* pattern. A (6) *German* rescue helicopter made a (7) *brave* attempt. We have a (8) *soft* (9) *purple* carpet.

Vocabulary

grøn [gruhn']	green
hurtig [hoor-dee]	fast
løber (-en, -e) [luh:-bor]	runner
seng (-en, -e) [seng']	bed
fin [fee'n]	fine
flydende [flew-th*e* -n*e*]	fluent
restaurant (-en, -er) [resd-o-rang]	restaurant
vidunderlig [veeth-un-nor-lee]	wonderful
værelse (-t, -r)	room
ung [ung']	young
klog [kloh:'h]	clever, wise
fodboldhold (-et, -) [fohth-bolt-hol']	soccer team

Exercise 9

Translate:

1 Skolen er stor, men god.
2 Huset har et grønt tag.
3 Søren Andersen er en hurtig løber.
4 Sengen er blød, med et fint tæppe.
5 MacPherson er skotte, men taler flydende dansk.
6 Der er en dejlig lille restaurant her.
7 Lars har et vidunderligt værelse.
8 De har høje idealer.
9 Det er et ungt, klogt dyr.
10 Vi har to fodboldhold, og dér er det nye klubhus.

10 The command form

The base, or stem, of any Danish verb, its very shortest form, is used for the command or imperative – **hør!** 'listen!' In verbs whose infinitives end with an unstressed **e**, the imperative is formed by removing that final **e.**

Here are some verbs you have met already and others you have not:

Infinitive		*Imperative*
at løbe	to run	**løb!** [luh'b]
at adlyde	to obey	**adlyd!** [ath-lew'th]
at bruge	to use	**brug!** [broo'h]
at skrive	to write	**skriv!**
[skree:-v*e*]		[skree'v]
at springe	to jump	**spring!**
[sbring-*e*]		[sbring']
at arbejde	to work	**arbejd!**
[ah-by'-th*e*]		[ah-by'th]
at smøre	lubricate, spread	**smør!**
[smuh:-r*e*]	(butter etc.)	[smuh'r]

The imperative almost invariably calls for a glottal stop.

If the **e**-ending of the infinitive follows a double consonant, one of these consonants disappears along with the **e** in the imperative form.

Infinitive		*Imperative*
at komme	to come	**kom!** [kom']
at ligge	to lie	**lig!** [li'g]
at lægge	to put, lay	**læg!** [le'g]
at berette	to report	**beret!**
[bey-ret-*e*]		[bey-re't]
at hoppe	to hop	**hop!**
[hob-b*e*]		[hop']
at snitte	to carve	**snit!**
[snee'd-d*e*]		[snee't]
at skylle	to rinse	**skyl!**
[sguhl-l*e*]		[sguh'l]

If the infinitive ends with a stressed vowel, the imperative is exactly the same: **stå!** A few examples:

Infinitive		*Imperative*
at stå	to stand	**stå!**
at forstå	to understand	**forstå!**
at sy	to sew	**sy!**
at efterse [ef-tor-sey']	to check	**efterse!**
at befri	to set free	**befri!**
at undgå [un-goh']	to avoid	**undgå!**

Simple 'command sentences' begin with the verb, followed by the other elements of the sentence in the same order as in other simple sentences:

Spis nu ikke for meget!
Don't eat too much now!
Køb en ny bil i dag!
Buy a new car today!
Drik ikke mere vin!
Don't drink any more wine!
Send ham det ikke!
Don't send him it!

In practice, however, any 'negative command' tends to use the verbs **skulle** or **måtte,** which you will be meeting in the next chapter, or the colloquial **Lad være med** [la' vayr' meth] or **Hold op med** [hol']:

Lad nu være med at spise for meget.
Don't eat too much now.
Hold op med at drikke vin nu.
Stop drinking wine now.

Lade means 'to let, to allow':

Lad mig prøve. [pruh'-v*e*]
Let me try.
Lad os gå i biografen. [bee-oh-grah'-f*e*n]
Let's go to the cinema.

'Please', basically, is **Vær (så) venlig at . . .** [ven-lee] ('be so kind as to') but is more often implied with idiomatic terms:

Ræk mig lige saltet. [rek; lee' sal'-teth]
Please pass me the salt.
Tag lige og hjælp her. [ta']
Could you help here, please?

Exercise 10

Produce the imperative of these verbs:

1	**at save** [sa:-ve]	to saw
2	**at kopiere** [koh-pee-ey'-re]	to copy
3	**at tro** [troh']	to believe
4	**at undersøge** [un-nor-suh:'-ye]	to investigate
5	**at stoppe** [sdob-be]	to stuff, mend
6	**at forny** [faw-new']	to renew
7	**at hente** [hen-de]	to fetch
8	**at glo** [gloh']	to stare
9	**at flytte** [fluhd-de]	to move
10	**at fløjte** [floy-de]	to whistle

11 The possessive – 'the child's'

Just as in English, the possessive (or genitive) form adds an **s** to the noun, or '(s) if the word already ends in an **s:**

barnets værelse [bah'-nets] the child's room
kattens skarpe kløer [skah-pe kluh:-or]
the cat's sharp claws, the sharp claws of the cat
Jens' cykel [yen's-es] Jens' bicycle
børnenes farverige billeder [fah-ve -ree:-ye bil-e -thor]
the children's colourful pictures
øjnenes charme [sjah-me] the charm of the eyes
danskernes inspirerende sprog [in-spee-rey'-re-ne sbroh:'h]
the inspiring language of the Danes

The possessive with **s** is much more common than in English and is often used where the English phrase is likely to be 'of the'. This does not mean that **af** [a] 'of' is never used.

Sangerens klare stemme er som en englelyd/lyden af en engel. [sang-e-rens klah:-re sdem-me; som; eng-le-lew'th]
The clear voice of the singer is like the sound of an angel.

Sometimes compounds are used where the English word would use a possessive form, as in:

børneværelset the children's room
katteklØer cats' claws
urmagerbutikken [oor-ma:-yor-] the watchmaker's shop

Vocabulary

træner (**-en, -e**) [tray'-nor]	trainer
glæde (**-n, -r**) [glay-the]	pleasure
kød (**-et, -**) [kuh'th]	flesh
farve (**-n, -r**) [fah-ve]	colour
side (**-n, -r**) [see-the]	page
gul [goo'l]	yellow
gård (**-en, -e**) [gaw']	farm
ejer (**-en, -e**) [y-or]	owner
forældre [fawr-el'-dre]	parents
hjem (**-met, -**) [yem']	home
resultat (**-et, -er**) [res-ool-ta:'t]	result
stærk [stayrk]	strong
angreb (**-et, -**) [an-grey'b]	attack
høj	loud
gøen (**-en**) [guh'-en]	barking
rasende [rah:-se-ne]	furious
magt (**-en, -er**) [magd]	power

Exercise 11

Translate:

1 the butcher's shop
2 the trainer of the foreign team
3 the pleasures of the flesh
4 The colour of the eyes is blue.
5 The pages of the book are yellow now.
6 Hans's father is the owner of a farm.
7 There is the parents' home.
8 the result of the strong attack
9 the loud barking of a furious dog
10 The power of money is great.

12 Days and months

The days of the week, in English, are an inheritance of the country's Viking past – Thursday, for instance, being called after the war god of Nordic mythology, Thor. Not surprisingly, their Danish counterparts are not much different:

søndag [suhn'-da]	Sunday
mandag [man'-da]	Monday
tirsdag [teer's-da]	Tuesday
onsdag [un's-da]	Wednesday
torsdag [taw's-da]	Thursday
fredag [frey'-da]	Friday
lørdag [lur-da]	Saturday

Equally alike are the months of the year and, incidentally, neither weekdays and months nor seasons and holidays are spelt with a capital letter.

januar [ya-noo-ah']
februar [fey-broo-ah']
marts [mahds]
april [a-pree'l]
maj [my']
juni [yoo'-nee]
juli [yoo'-lee]
august [ow-goosd]
september [seb-tem'-bor]
oktober [og-toh'-bor]
november [noh-vem'-bor]
december [dey-sem'-bor]

And the seasons (you know three of them already):

forår	spring
sommer	summer
efterår (-et, -) [ef-dor-aw′]	autumn
vinter	winter

Early and late summer: **forsommer** [faw-som-mor] and **sensommer** [seyn-som-mor]

In spite of religion's modest role, many more holy days are public or semi-official holidays in Denmark than in English-speaking countries – with the addition of a few others:

nytrårsdag [newd-aws-da:′]	New Year's Day
skærtorsdag [skayr-taws-da]	Maundy Thursday
langfredag [lang-frey′-da]	Good Friday
første og anden påskedag [furs-d*e* ; an-*e*n poh-sk*e*-da:′]	Easter Sunday and Monday
store bededag [bey:-th*e*-da:′]	(Great prayer day) 4th Friday after Easter
Kristi himmelfartsdag [kris-dee him-m*e*l-fahds-da:′]	Ascension Day
majdag [my-da:′]	May Day – industrial and bank holiday
(første og anden) pinsedag [pin-s*e* -da:′]	Whit Sunday and Monday
grundlovsdag [grun-lows-da:′]	Constitution Day (5 June)
juleaften [yoo-l*e* -af-d*e*n]	Christmas Eve
første og anden juledag	Christmas Day and Boxing Day
nytårsaften [newd-aws-af-d*e*n]	New Year's Eve

And the main red-letter days or events:

fødselsdag (-en, -e) [fuh-s*e*ls-da:′]	birthday
bryllupsdag (-en, -e) [bruhl-ups-da:′]	wedding day/anniversary
årsdag (-en, -e) [aws-da:′]	anniversary

sølv/guldbryllup [suhl-/goo'l-bruhl-lup]	silver/golden wedding

Vocabulary

kone (**-n, -r**) [koh:-n*e*]	wife
hukommelse (**-n**) [hoo-kom-m*e*l-s*e*]	memory
lige så. . .som [lee-so som]	just as. . . as
min [mee'n]	mine
syttende [suhd-*e*n-*e*]	seventeenth
dag (**-en, -e**) [da:']	day
fest (**-en, -er**) [//]	celebration
at vente [ven-t*e*]	to wait
indtil [in-til]	until
fireogtyvende [feer-o-twe:-v*e*-n*e*]	twenty-fourth
at fejre [fy-r*e*]	to celebrate
altsammen [alt-sam-m*e*n]	all (of it)
heldig [hel-dee]	lucky
at finde [fin-n*e*]	to find
i morgen [i-mawn]	tomorrow
at holde bryllup med	to marry
mærkelig [mayr-k*e*-lee]	remarkable, strange
vores [vaw-r*e*s]	our
kunne [koo-n*e*] or [koo]	could
at spare [sbah:-r*e*]	to save
jamen [ya-men]	well
så [so]	then
fik [fik]	received, got
selv [sel']	self (here: myself)
én [ey'n]	one
skat (**-ten, -te**) [sgat]	darling (treasure)

CONVERSATION

Manden **Hvornår er det Kirstens fødselsdag? Hun er 17 nu, ikke?**

Konen **Din hukommelse er lige så dårlig som min. Men jeg ved, at det er den syttende marts, og det er en fredag, så det er god dag for en lille fest.**

Manden **Hvorfor venter vi ikke indtil den fireogtyvende april, når vi har sølvbryllup, så kan vi fejre altsammen den dag.**

Konen **Hvis du er heldig, finder Kirsten en dejlig ung mand i morgen og holder bryllup med ham den dag. Det er mærkeligt, at det ikke er vores bryllupsdag juleaften, så du kunne spare en gave.**

Manden **Jamen, så fik jeg selv kun én gave, skat!**

TRANSLATION

The husband	**When is it Kirsten's birthday? She is 17 now, is she not?**
The wife	**Your memory is just as bad as mine. But I know that it is on the seventeenth of March and that is a Friday, so it is a good day for a little celebration.**
The husband	**Why don't we wait until the twenty-fourth of April when we have our silver wedding, then we can celebrate every-thing on that day.**
The wife	**If you are lucky, Kirsten will find (finds) a lovely young man tomorrow and marry him on that day. It is strange that it is not our wedding anniversary on Christmas Eve so that you could save a present.**
The husband	**Well, then I would get (got) only one present myself, darling.**

Chapter 4

> *This chapter covers:*
>
> - *the indispensable 'auxiliary' verbs 'can', 'shall' and 'will' and expressions using them*
> - *the words for 'somebody', 'something', 'nobody', 'nothing' and so on*
> - *the demonstratives 'this', 'that', 'which' and 'such', in their common, neuter and plural forms.*

13 Auxiliary verbs – 'can', 'shall', 'will'

'Shall', 'can' and 'will' belong to the key group of verbs which are indispensable for use in conjunction with other verbs: 'can', 'may', 'will', 'shall', 'must', 'ought', and 'dare'.

In Danish, just as in English, these verbs have no command form, but unlike their English counterparts (except 'dare') they have an infinitive.

Infinitive	*Present*	
at kunne [koon-n*e*]	**kan** [ka]	can, is able to
at skulle [sgool-l*e*]	**skal** [sgal] or [sga]	shall, is to, must
at ville [vil-l*e*]	**vil** [vil] or [vi]	will, wants to
at måtte [mot-t*e*]	**må** [moh']	may, must
at burde [boo:r-d*e*]	**bør** [bur]	ought to
at turde [too:r-d*e*]	**tør** [tur]	dare(s)

As in English, these verbs (particularly the first four) have a wide range of uses.

Kunne means 'can', 'be able to', and is sometimes used without another verb, with a meaning similar to 'to know (how to)':

Det er godt at kunne svømme. [svuhm-m*e*]
  It's good to be able to swim.
Kan du engelsk?
  Can you speak English?

Skulle is often used in suggestions and commands:

Skal vi prøve?
  Let's (Shall we) try.
Du skal gå, ikke løbe.
  You must walk, not run.
Den syge dame skal ligge ned. [sew-y*e*; ne'th]
  The sick lady must/is to lie down.
Loven siger, at vi skal tænde nu. [low'-*e*n; ten-n*e*]
  The law says that we must switch our lights on now.

Vil is sometimes used for 'going to' with a future sense:

Du vil blive meget glad for gaven.
  You are going to be very pleased with (become very happy for) the present.

It is also very often used with **gerne** [gayr-n*e*] and **godt**, which you will meet in the next section.

Må can be either 'must' or 'may':

Mor siger, vi må ride, men vi må love at være forsigtige. [ree-th*e*; loh:-v*e*; faw-sig-dee]
  Mummy says we may ride but we must promise to be careful.

As 'may' it is also often used with **gerne** and **godt** (see the next section).

Frequently, the verb following **vil** and **skal** is implied only:

Han vil/skal (gå) ud af skolen. [oo'th]
    He wants to/has to leave (go out of) the school.

As you see, these verbs occupy the usual position of the verb in the sentence, followed by the infinitive of the other verb, but if the sentence contains a word such as **ikke**, then that is placed before the infinitive:

Jeg kan ikke købe en ny bil i dag.
I dag kan jeg ikke købe den.
Vil du ikke gerne møde stjernen? [sdyayr-n*e*n]
    Wouldn't you like to meet the star?

It is possible to begin a sentence with the infinitive:

Tænke kan han. [ten-k*e*]
    He can think.
Spise kan han ikke. [sbee-s*e*]
    He cannot eat.

14 Idioms with 'would like' and 'may'

Danes use a number of 'filler words', not least in order to qualify auxiliary verbs, and these can seldom be translated by just one English word. None is more common than **gerne** [gayr-n*e*] 'willingly'.

With **vil/ville**, it usually means 'would like to':

Jeg vil gerne lære en jysk dialekt. [yewsg dee-a-legt]
    I would like to learn a Jutlandic dialect.

With **må/måtte** it can mean 'may' or 'be welcome to':

Ja, Morten, du må gerne tale nu. [maw-d*e*n]
    Yes, Morten, you may/are welcome to speak now.

Related to **gerne** are the words **hellere** and **helst** or **allerhelst** [hel-le-re; al-lor-hel'sd]. **Jeg vil hellere** means 'I would rather', and **jeg vil helst** 'I would prefer' or 'like best of all':

Jeg vil gerne have te, men endnu hellere kaffe og allerhelst et glas champagne. [en-noo; sjam-pan-ye]
I will willingly have tea, but I'd rather have coffee and best of all I'd like a glass of champagne.
Du må gerne komme, og meget gerne bo her, og helst i lang tid. [tee'th]
You're welcome to come, and very welcome to stay (live) here, preferably for a long time.
Jeg vil hellere end gerne gøre det. [en]
I'll be more than pleased to do it.

Another word like **gerne** is **godt** 'good/well', which has overtones of agreement or of 'in fact', and is often used as 'please':

Du må godt gøre det.
Yes, you may do it.
Vi vil godt gøre det.
We agree to do it.
Jeg vil godt have én til.
I would in fact like one more.
Mor, må jeg godt gå ud og lege? [ly-e]
Mummy, may I go out and play?
Må jeg godt holde din hest? [hesd]
May I hold your horse, please?
Vil I ikke godt holde op?
Won't you please stop?

Vocabulary

biograf (-en, -er)	cinema
at tie stille [tee' sdil-le]	to be quiet, stop talking
hjem	home
alt for [alt faw]	far too
virkelig [veer-ke-lee]	really
allerede [al-e-rey:-the]	already
nød (-den, -der) [nuhth]	nut

chokolade (-n, -r) [sjoh-koh-la:-the]	chocolate
at få [foh']	to get, receive
at dø [duh']	to die
end	than
at opgive [op-gee-ve] or [op-gee']	to give up
at spille [sbil-le]	to play
bordtennis [baw-ten-nis]	table tennis

Exercise 12

Translate:

1 Skal vi ikke gå i biografen, eller vil du hellere i teateret?
2 Du bør tie stille, men du vil aldrig høre, hvad jeg siger.
3 Du kan, hvis du vil, eller hvis du tør.
4 Hvor skal I sejle til i ferien?
5 Jeg vil hjem nu, skal vi sige godnat?
6 Familien Sørensen bør sælge det alt for store hus.
7 Skal I virkelig gå allerede?
8 Jeg vil gerne have nødderne, du må godt få chokoladen.
9 De vil hellere dø end opgive.
10 Jeg vil hellere spille bordtennis.

15 'Some', 'any', 'none', 'others', 'all'

'Some', 'any'

Two key Danish words, **nogen** [noh:n] and **noget** [noh:-eth], cover a range of English words referring to unspecified things, people and quantities. **Nogen** means 'somebody' and 'anybody' and **noget** means 'something' and 'anything':

Kommer nogen med til koncerten? [kon-sayr-den]
Is anyone coming along to the concert?
Nogen har taget min ordbog. [ta:-eth; aw-boh:'h]
Someone has taken my dictionary.
Er der noget, De ønsker? [uhn-sgor]
Is there anything you want?

Der er noget galt! [ga:'lt]
    There is something wrong.

Used with singular nouns, **nogen** (*c*) and **noget** (*n*) also mean 'some', 'a little' or 'any':

Gør det overhovedet nogen gavn? [ow-or-hoh-th*e* t; gow'n]
    Is it of any use (at all)?
Ja, det gør nogen gavn, men kun nogen!
    Yes, it is of some use, but only some!
Det er noget møg! [moy']
    That is (some) rubbish!

You will also find **noget** used with adjectives, meaning 'somewhat':

Den grammofonplade er noget slidt. [gram-moh-foh:'n-pla:-th*e*; sleet]
    That gramophone record is somewhat worn.

'Any' in the plural is **nogen** again, while 'some' meaning 'a certain number', 'a few' is **nogle** (pronounced like **nogen**!):

Har du nogen kirsebær? [keey-s*e*-bayr]
    Have you any cherries?
Nogle sangere glemmer altid ordene. [sang-or-*e*; glem-mor; aw'-r*e*-n*e*]
    Some singers always forget the words.
Her er nogle penge til mælk. [mel'g]
    Here is some money for milk.
Ikke mange, tak, blot nogle få. [blot; foh']
    Not many, thank you, just a few.

'None', 'nothing'
An extremely important use of **nogen/noget** is in conjunction with **ikke. Ikke nogen** means 'nobody', 'none', and so on, while **ikke noget** means 'nothing'.

Ingen [ing-*e*n] and **intet** [in-t*e*th] cover the same ground as **ikke nogen** and **ikke noget** respectively, following the same pattern, and **ingenting** [ing-en-ting'] is another word for 'nothing'.

Jeg gør ikke noget/intet/ingenting.
I'm not doing anything.
Det gør ikke noget/intet/ingenting.
It doesn't matter.
Der er ikke nogen/ingen herinde. [hayr-in-n*e*]
There is no one in here.
Der er ikke nogen/intet/ingenting i vejen. [vy'-*e*n]
There is nothing wrong.
Ingen af dem taler klart.
None/Neither of them speaks clearly.

Watch out, though: **De giver ikke hinanden noget** cannot be replaced by **De giver hinanden intet/ingenting.** 'They don't give each other anything/They give each other nothing.'

Ikke nogen/noget and **ingen/intet** also correspond to 'no', 'not a' and suchlike:

Generalen er ikke nogen/ingen god leder. [gey-ney-rah' -l*e*n; ley:thor]
The general is not a good leader.
ikke noget/intet godt menneske not a good person
Vi har ikke nogen/ingen sorger. [saw-yor]
We have no sorrows.

Ingen in the sense of 'no one' is the only one that can be made possessive:

Intelligens er ingens fødselsret. [int-el-li-gen's; fuh-s*e*ls-ret]
Intelligence in no one's birthright.

'Another', 'someone else'

'Other' in Danish is **anden** [an-*e*n] *(c)*, **andet** [an-*e*th] *(n)* in the singular, and **andre** [and-r*e*] in the plural.

Har du fundet en anden? [fun-n*e*t]
Have you found someone else?
Kør den anden vej.
Drive the other way.

Der er ingen anden løsning (or **ikke nogen anden løsning**). [luh:s-ning]
There is no other solution.
Det er et helt andet spørgsmål. [sbuhrs-moh'l]
That's quite a different/another question.
Mange andre har intet/ingenting i sammenligning med os. [sam-men-lee-ning]
Many others have nothing in comparison with us.

Andre folks børn er altid artige. [ah-tee-ye]
Other people's children are always well-behaved.
en eller anden somebody (or other)
et eller andet something (or other)
en eller anden undskyldning [un-sgewl'-ning] some excuse or other
et eller andet sted somewhere or other

'All', 'every'

To be all-embracing you use **al** *(c)*, **alt** *(n)* and **alle/allesammen**:

Al den støj! [sdoy']
All that noise!
Kan du spise alt det?
Can you eat all that?
Alle kyllingerne er væk. [kewl-ling-or-ne; vek]
All the chickens are gone.
De har allesammen influenza. [in-floo-en-sa]
All of them have 'flu.

Danish has two alternatives for 'every', 'each' – **hver(t)** and **enhver/ethvert** [vayr'(t)]:

Det er enhver embedsmands pligt. [em-beyths-man's pligt]
It it every civil servant's duty.
Ethvert barn har brug for kærlighed. [kayr-lee-hi'th]
Any/Every child needs love.
Sømanden har en pige i hver havn. [suh-man'-nen; how'n]
The sailor has a girl in every port.

Vocabulary

forskel (**-len, -le**) [faw-skel']	difference
om	(here:) in
elev (**-en, -er**) [el-lay'u]	pupil
at sige stop	to call a halt
tilbage [ti-ba:-y*e*]	(here:) left
optaget [op-ta:-y*e*th]	occupied
nogle få	a few
ledig [leyth-ee]	free, unoccupied
at tænke	to think
at vente	to expect
øjeblik (**-ket-ke**)	moment
på	on
jord (**-en**)	earth
metode (**-n, -r**) [me-toth-*e*]	method
fordel (**-en, -e**) [faw-deyl']	advantage

Exercise 13

Translate:

1 Der er kun nogen forskel mellem dem.
2 Om nogle dage er alle eleverne her.
3 De kan alle(sammen) se alle dyrene.
4 Ikke enhver forstår at sige stop, men nogle gør.
5 Har du ingen penge tilbage?
6 Ikke alle bordene er optaget, nogle få er ledige.
7 Ingen af dem ved, hvad de andre på holdet tænker.
8 Vi venter dem hvert øjeblik.
9 Intet andet på jorden er så smukt.
10 Med den anden metode har du alle fordelene.

16 Demonstratives: 'that', 'these', 'which', 'such'

'This', 'that'

You learned at the outset that 'it' is either **den** (common) or **det** (neuter), with **de** for 'they' regardless of gender, and you've seen the same words used as 'the' with adjectives. They also serve as the demonstrative 'that' and 'those' as used when pointing something out: **Se den elefant** [ey-l*e*-fan't] 'See that elephant'. **Det gulv er glat** [glat] 'That floor is slippery'. The only difference is in the pronunciation, which is more emphatic. It is also normal though not compulsory in written Danish to apply the accent: **dén – dét.**

When you single something out with 'this', however, you use **denne** [den-n*e*] *(c)* or **dette** [ded-d*e*] *(n)*, and 'these' is **disse** [dees-s*e*]. The two alternatives in schematic form:

this	*(c)*	**denne**	that	*(c)*	**den**
	(n)	**dette**		*(n)*	**det**
these		**disse**	those		**de**

Den vin er ikke så god som den, jeg selv laver. [la:-vor]
That wine is not as good as the one I make myself.
På denne måde kommer vi ingen vegne. Dette er meget bedre [moh:-th*e* ; vy-n*e*; beth-r*e*]
In this way we'll get nowhere. (Doing) This is much better.
Disse grammatikalske udtryk er en hovedpine. [gra-ma-tee-ka'l-sg*e* ooth-truhk; hoh:th-*e*-pee:-n*e*]
These grammatical terms are a headache.
***Har* du set de pragtfulde tomater!** [pragd-fool-*e* toh-ma:'t-or]
Have you seen those magnificent tomatoes!

In colloquial Danish, however, instead of **disse** and **denne/dette** you are likely to hear **den/det/de/dem** used together with **der/her** to mean 'this (one/these (ones) (here)' or 'that (one)/those (ones) (there)':

Det kyllingelår her tager jeg, den vinge dér får du. [kew-ling-*e*-law'; ving-*e*]
This leg of chicken here I take, that wing there you get.
De tæpper (her) er dyre.
The carpets here are expensive.
De drenge dér er frække. [freg-g*e*]
Those boys there are cheeky.
De skruer dér passer ind i disse huller/hullerne her. [sgroo-or; pas-sor; hul-lor]
Those screws there fit into these holes here.

Den dér må du få, jeg vælger dén (her). [vel-yor]
That one you can have, I choose this one (here).
Foretrækker du virkelig dem dér?
[faw-r*e* -treg-gor; veer-k*e*-lee]
Do you really prefer those (there)?

As in so many other connections, emphasis is important: **de stramme bukser** [sdram-m*e* bugs-or] is 'the tight trousers' but *de* **stramme . . .** is 'those tight . . .'

'Which?'

In questions concerning choice, the Danish for 'which' is **hvilken** [vil-g*e*n] *(c)* and **hvilket** [vil-g*e*th] *(n)*, with **hvilke** [vil-g*e*] in the plural. A popular alternative in spoken Danish is **hvad for en** [va faw in] *(c)*, **hvad for et** [va faw it] *(n)* or **hvad for nogle** (plural):

Hvilken bog vil du have?
Which book do you want?
Hvilket hus bor han i?
Which house does he live in?
Hvilke aviser læser du? [a-vee-sor]
Which newspapers do you read?
Hvad for en bil køber du?
Which/What car are you buying?
Hvad for nogle bøger læser du?
Which books are you reading?

'Such'

For the English 'such', Danish uses **sådan** [so-dan].

Sådan en forfærdelig støj! [faw-fayr-d*e* -lee]
Such a terrible noise!
Sådan nogle billeder kan jeg godt lide. [bil-l*e*-thor; lee']
I like (can suffer) that kind of picture (such pictures).

The exclamation 'What (a) . . .' or 'How . . .' is mostly **sikke en/et** [sig-g*e*] and **sikke nogle** in the plural, a much used derivation from **se hvilken/hvilket.** In spoken Danish you will hear **Sikken støj! Sikket billede! Sikke billeder!** without the article.

Sikken et/Sikket held, at han fandt sådan en velhavende kæreste. [fan'd; vel-ha:-ve-ne; kayr-esd-e]
What luck that he found such a well-heeled sweetheart.

Sikke store øjne du har, bedstemor. [besd-e-maw]
What big eyes you have, Grandmother.
Sikke slank den bokser er nu. [slank; bogs-or]
How slim that boxer is now.

Vocabulary

sort [sawd]	black
billig [bil-lee]	cheap
lang [lang']	long
ved [vith] or [vi]	by
uskyldig [oo-sgewl'-dee]	innocent
farlig [fah-lee]	dangerous
at opnå [op-noh']	achieve
at vælge	to choose
karriere (-n, -r) [kah-ree-ayr-e]	career
kursus (kurset, kurser) [koor-soos]	course

Exercise 14

Translate:

1 De sorte cykler her er billige.
2 De børn har sådan en god mor.
3 Der er sådan nogle lange køer ved de to teatre, men ikke ved det dér.
4 Disse blå øjne er uskyldige, men sikke farlige de er!
5 Sådan nogle resultater opnår jeg aldrig!.
6 Hvis du vælger dén karriere, skal du gå på dét kursus.

Vocabulary

fra [frah]	from
dyreforretning (-en, -er) [dew-re-faw-ret-ning]	pet shop
forskellig [faw-skel-lee]	different
hunderace (-n, -r) [ra:-se]	dog breed
ekspeditrice (-n, -r) [egs-epy-di-tree:-se]	saleswoman
flere [fley-re]	several
glimrende [glim-re-ne]	splendid
hundeelsker (-en, -e)	dog lover
mest [mey'sd]	mostly
billede (-t, -r)	picture
pris (-en, -er) [pree's]	price
normalt [naw-ma:'lt]	normally
krone (-n, -r) [kroh-ne]	krone (main unit of Danish currency)
uge (-n, -r) [oo-e]	week
udsalg (-et, -) [ooth-sal']	sale
at koste [kos-de]	to cost
at se . . . ud	to look . . .
at læse	to read
karakter(-en) [ka-rag-tey'r]	character
fodring (-en) [fohth-ring]	feeding
behandling (-en, -er) [bey-han'-ling]	handling, treatment
og så videre [o so vith-e-re]	and so on
derovre [dayr-ow-re]	over there
hylde (-n, -r) [hewl-le]	shelf
slags (-en) [slags]	kind
begge to [beg-ge toh']	both
i alt [ee al't]	in all
da [da]	then
også [os-se]	also
hundemad (-en)	dog food
fantastisk [fan-tas-disg]	fantastic
tilbud (-et) [til-boo'th]	offer
først	first
krokodille (-n, -r) [kroh-koh-dil-le]	crocodile
at købe [kuh:-be]	to buy

CONVERSATION

Fra dyreforretningen

Ung mand **Har I en bog om forskellige hunderacer?**

Ekspeditricen **Ja, vi har flere. Denne her er glimrende til hundeelskere, mest billeder, allesammen i farver. Prisen er normalt 185 kroner, men i denne uge har vi udsalg, så nu koster den kun 125.**

Ung mand **Ja, de billeder ser godt ud. Men jeg vil gerne læse om hunderacernes karakter, om fodring og behandling og så videre. Er de bøger derovre på hylden ikke med i udsalget?**

Ekspeditricen **Jo, de er. Her er to af den slags, du taler om, denne her er til 85 kroner, den anden til 75 kroner, men den har ingen farvebilleder.**

Ung mand **Må jeg få begge to for 150 kroner i alt?**

Ekspeditricen **Ja, OK da. Vi har også billig hundemad. Se der, et fantastisk tilbud.**

Ung mand **Tak, jeg skal først sælge min krokodille og købe hund . . .**

TRANSLATION

From the pet shop

Young man	**Have you a book about different dog breeds?**
Saleswoman	**Yes, we have several. This one is splendid for dog lovers, mostly pictures, all in colour. The price is normally 185 kroner but (in) this week we have a sale, so now it only costs 125.**
Young man	**Yes, those pictures look good. But I want to read about the character of the dog breeds, about feeding and handling and so on. Aren't those books over there on the shelf in the sale?**
Saleswoman	**Yes, they are. Here are two of the kind you are talking about, this one at 85 kroner, the other at 75 kroner, but it has no colour pictures.**
Young man	**May I have both (two) for 150 in all?**
Saleswoman	**Yes, OK then. We also have cheap dog food. Look (there), a fantastic offer.**
Young man	**Thank you, I must first sell my crocodile and buy (a) dog . . .**

Chapter 5

Chapter 5 teaches you the numbers from zero to two million and also introduces the past tenses. You will learn:

- *the simple past tense of regular verbs (e.g. 'stayed')*
- *the perfect tense of regular verbs (e.g. 'have stayed')*
- *the simple past and perfect tense forms of some frequently used irregular verbs.*

17 Numbers

Tha Danish figures are quite straightforward for English speakers until twenty-one, where Danes start with the 'one': one-and-twenty.

0	nul	[nul]			
1	én/ét	[ey'n, it]	1st	første	[fur-sde]
2	to	[toh']	2nd	anden	[an-nen]
3	tre	[trey']	3rd	tredie	[treth-ye]
4	fire	[fee:-e]	4th	fjerde	[fye-re]
5	fem	[fem']	5th	femte	[fem-de]
6	seks	[segs]	6th	sjette	[sje:-de]
7	syv	[sew'u]	7th	syvende	[syoo'-e-ne]
8	otte	[oh-de]	8th	ottende	[o-de-ne]
9	ni	[nee']	9th	niende	[nee'-e-ne]
10	ti	[tee']	10th	tiende	[tee'-e-ne]

11	elleve	[el-ve]	11th	elvte	[elf-de]
12	tolv	[tol']	12th	tolvte	[tol-de]
13	tretten	[tre-den]	13th	trettende	[tre-de-ne]
14	fjorten	[fyaw-den]	14th	fjortende	[fyaw-de-ne]
15	femten	[fem-den]	15th	femtende	[fem-de-ne]
16	seksten	[sys-den]	16th	sekstende	[sys-de-ne]
17	sytten	[suh-den]	17th	syttende	[suhd-de-ne]
18	atten	[ad-den]	18th	attende	[ad-de-ne]
19	nitten	[nid-den]	19th	nittende	[nid-den-ne]
20	tyve	[tew:-ve]	20th	tyvende	[tew:-ve-ne]
21	enogtyve	[ey'n-o-tew:-ve]	21st	enogtyvende	[ey'n-o-tew-ve-ne]
22	toogtyve		22nd	oogtyvende	
30	tred(i)ve	[tre:th-ve]	30th	tre(i)vte	[trethv-de]
40	fyrre	[fur-e]	40th	fyrretyvende	[fur-e-tew:-ve-ne]
50	halvtreds	[hal-tres]	50th	halvtredsindstyvende	[hal-tres-ins-tew:-ve-ne]
60	tres	[tres]	60th	tresindstyvende	
70	halvfjerds	[hal-fyers]	75th	femoghalvfjerdsindstyvende	
80	firs	[fee'rs]	80th	firsindstyvende	
90	halvfems	[hal-fem's]	99th	nioghalvfemsindstyvende	
100	(et) hundrede	[hoon-re-the]	100th	den/det hundrede (!)	
101	hundrede og én/ét		101st	hundredeførste	
113	hundrede og tretten				
231	to hundrede og enogtredive				
8,010	otte tusind og ti	[too'-sen]			
100,000	(ét) hundrede tusind				
2,000,000	to millioner	[meel-lee-oh'-nor]			

The peculiar figures 50, 60, 70, 80 and 90 may be easier to learn if you understand their origin, which comes from the time when the Danes counted in twenties: **tre(d)s** is a shortened version of **tredsindstyve** or **tre sinde tyve, sinde** being the now defunct word for **gange** [gang-e] – 'times'. Fifty, then, was half-way from forty to sixty or **halvtredsindstyve**, now shortened to **halvtreds**. The full old form, as you see, is still used for ordinal numbers.

In the same breath:
halvanden one and a half BUT
to-en-halv, tre-en-halv etc. after that for 2 ½, 3 ½, . See also Section 36.

Note that, in figures, punctuation is the opposite of English: '0.1 – nought point one' in Danish is **0,1: nul komma én.** What would be '10,000.45' in English is 10.000,45 in Danish. A full stop is **et punktum.**

Other numerical expressions:

først	first
den/det tredie	the third
for det første	firstly
for det andet	secondly
én gang	once
to gange	twice
tre gange	three times
én ad gangen	one at a time
(den) første gang	the first time
for tusinde gang	for the thousandth time (no 'the')
hver femte gang	every fifth time
hundreder af mennesker	hundreds of people

Vocabulary

år (-et, -) [aw']	year
jubilæum (-æet, -æer) [yoo-bee-ley-um]	jubilee, anniversary
hr. [hayr]	Mr
at beskrive [bey-skree-ve]	to describe
avis (-en, -er)	newspaper
brevkasse (-n, -r) [brayu'-kas-se]	letter box
at advare [ath-vah'-re]	to warn
at lytte [lew-de]	to listen

Exercise 15

Translate:

1 Vi har femogtyveårsjubilæum i april.
2 Hr. Frederiksen, beskriv dem én ad gangen.
3 Han lægger avisen fra den trettende juli i din brevkasse.
4 For dig koster det kun fem tusind ni hundrede og fireoghalvtreds kroner.
5 Det er den enogtresindstyvende gang, jeg advarer dig, men du lytter aldrig til mig.

You should by now have become used to the Danish sounds, so from here on we are no longer including the Imitated Pronunciation.

18 Past tenses of verbs: 'spoke', 'has spoken'

As in English, some Danish verbs are *regular*, which basically means that there is no change of the stem vowel, while there is a change in the majority of the *irregular* verbs. As with the gender and plural of nouns, the only way to know which group a verb belongs to is to learn it for each one, and we shall help you with this in our vocabulary lists. A brief explanation will be a help in getting the feel of the patterns.

Like English, Danish has a simple past tense ('spoke') and the perfect and pluperfect tenses ('have spoken', 'had spoken'). These are formed in a very similar way to the English tenses. The perfect and pluperfect tenses are made up of a past participle ('spoken') and the appropriate tense of **have** or **være.** So let's look at the past tenses of those two verbs first.

Infinitive	*Present*	*Past*	*Perfect*	*Pluperfect*
have	**har**	**havde**	**har haft**	**havde haft**
være	**er**	**var**	**har været**	**havde været**

Jeg har haft influenza.
I have had influenza.
Lægen havde selv været meget syg.
The doctor had himself been very ill.

In the vast majority of regular verbs, to make the simple past tense you add **ede** to the stem of the verb – **at hoste, hostede** 'to cough, coughed'. (To make the stem of the verb, refer back to Section 10 on the command form.) If the infinitive has a double consonant before the final **e**, though, the past tense will keep that double consonant (**at kysse, kyssede**, 'to kiss, kissed').

To make the past participle, you add **et** to the stem of the verb, again retaining the double consonant of the infinitive if it has one (**hostet, kysset**).

Infinitive		*Past*	*Perfect*
kysse	kiss	**kyssede**	**har kysset**
sejle	sail	**sejlede**	**har/er sejlet**
hoste	cough	**hostede**	**har hostet**
handle	act, trade	**handlede**	**har handlet**
hamre	hammer	**hamrede**	**har hamret**

A much smaller group of verbs adds **te** to the stem for the past tense, and **t** for the past participle. We shall indicate these verbs in the vocabulary lists by adding (**-te, -t**).

Infinitive		*Past*	*Perfect*
tale	speak	**talte**	**har talt**
spise	eat	**spiste**	**har spist**
høre	hear	**hørte**	**har hørt**
bruge	use	**brugte**	**har brugt**
rejse	travel, depart	**rejste**	**har/er rejst**

De hørte, da barnet hostede, og handlede straks.
They heard when the child coughed and acted immediately.

As in many languages, there are also a number of irregular verbs, some of which take the **te, t** endings, while others are altogether different. Many of them change their stem vowel. A list of these is found at the end of the book, and in the vocabulary lists they are indicated by an asterisk. Here are a few characteristic irregular verbs:

Infinitive		*Past*	*Perfect*
bede	ask, pray	**bad**	**har bedt**
blive	stay, become	**blev**	**er blevet**
bringe	bring	**bragte**	**har bragt**
følge	follow	**fulgte**	**har fulgt**
få	get	**fik**	**har fået**
give	give	**gav**	**har givet**
gøre	do	**gjorde**	**har gjort**
gå	walk, leave	**gik**	**har/er gået**
komme	come, put	**kom**	**har/er kommet**
ligge	lie	**lå**	**har ligget**
lægge	lay	**lagde**	**har lagt**
ryge	smoke	**røg**	**har røget**
se	see, look	**så**	**har set**
sidde	sit	**sad**	**har siddet**
sige	say	**sagde**	**har sagt**
smøre	grease, butter	**smurte**	**har smurt**
spørge	ask	**spurgte**	**har spurgt**
sælge	sell	**solgte**	**har solgt**
sætte	put, set	**satte**	**har sat**
tage	take	**tog**	**har taget**
tælle	count	**talte**	**har talt**

Apart from the 'did' and '-ing' forms being absent, the use of the past tense does not differ much from English.

Vi sad ved floden og så, da båden kom.
We were sitting by the river and saw when the boat came.

There is even an equivalent to the English 'used to' in the sense of 'was in the habit of': the Danish verb **at pleje** (literally 'to nurse', look after') is used in this sense in the simple past. Watch out, though – 'used to' in the sense of 'accustomed to' is **vant til:**

Jeg plejede at ryge – nu er jeg vant til tyggegummi i stedet for.
I used to smoke – now I'm used to chewing (chewing) gum instead.

Have or være?

In English 'to have' is the dominant auxiliary for forming the perfect and pluperfect tenses. More often than not, **at have** is used similarly in Danish.

Andre havde gjort det hårde arbejde.
Others had done the hard work.
Holdet har trænet godt.
The team has trained well.
Hansens har bygget et hus.
The Hansens have built a house.
Jeg har elsket og levet.
I have loved and lived.
De havde brugt alt.
They had used everything.
Har du ikke set ham?
Haven't you seen him?

However, some verbs form the perfect and pluperfect with a form of **at være.** These are verbs of motion or change of state such as **at forsvine** ('to disappear'), **at rejse, at komme, at blive.** Sometimes verbs of motion may be used with **at have** instead of **at være.**
When this happens the emphasis is not on where the movement is to, but on the type of movement.

Nu er de endelig gået.
Now they have finally gone.
Har du gået langs stranden?
Have you walked along the beach?

Det var blevet koldt.
It had become/turned cold.
Ulykken er sket.
The accident has happened.
Det er begyndt at sne.
It has begun to snow.
Det var begyndt at regne.
It had begun to rain.
Kassereren er ikke gået, for assistenten er ikke kommet.
The cashier has not left, for the assistant has not arrived.
Henning har rejst hele året og nu er han rejst til Alaska.
Henning has travelled all year and now has gone to Alaska.

It may be of help to know that **at blive** 'to become' is only ever used with **er** and **var.**

Vocabulary

kilometer (**-en, -**)	kilometre
ud	out
igen	again
at spørge* om vej	to ask the way
nyheder	news
chef (**-en, -er**)	boss
bakke (**-n, -r**)	tray
firma (**-et, -er**)	firm
kartoffel (**kartof(fe)len**)	potato
da	when
at gå* fallit	to go bankrupt
om dagen	per day
helt	completely, altogether
at tage* på i vægt	to put on weight
kilo (**-et, -**)	kilo
et til	one more
topsælger (**-en, -e**)	top salesman

Exercise 16

Translate:

1 Far har gået ti kilometer, og nu er gået ud igen.
2 Jeg bad ham spørge om vej til biografen.
3 De har bragt gode nyheder.
4 Chefen har fået pengene.
5 De lagde brødet på bakken, da de havde smurt det.
6 Firmaet handlede med kartofler, indtil det gik fallit.
7 Jeg plejede at ryge 40 cigaretter om dagen, men så opgav jeg det helt – og tog 10 kilo på i vægt!
8 Når du har solgt et hus til, er du blevet topsælger.

Vocabulary

Australien	Australia
en masse	a lot
tilbage	back
vej (-en, -e)	road
kabel (-et, kabler)	cable
ven (-nen, -ner)	friend
at ankomme*	to arrive
klokken ti	(at) ten o'clock
fair	fair
kamp (-en, -e)	fight
at tabe (-te, -t)	to lose
uærlig	dishonest
borgmester (-en, -tre)	mayor
at lave	to make
pakke (-n, -r)	packet
mellemmad (-en, -der)	sandwich
til	for
tyv (-en, -e)	thief
sølvtøj(-et)	silverware

Exercise 17

Translate into Danish:

1 The American has sailed to Australia – he has sailed a lot.
2 I found thirty-eight mice when (**da**) I came back.
3 We laid cable from the road to the house.
4 Peter's friend arrived at 10 o'clock and they have already gone.
5 They gave the team a fair fight – and lost.
6 The town has got a dishonest new mayor.
7 Mother made a packet of sandwiches for us and we have already eaten them all.
8 Thieves have taken all the silverware.

Vocabulary

er født	was born
at søge (-te, -t)	to look for
arbejde (-t, -r)	work
Danmark	Denmark
skotsk	Scottish
elsket	beloved
stilling (-en, -er)	job, position
løn (-nen)	pay, salary
herover	over here
så . . . som	as . . . as
mulig	possible
derfor	therefore
på dansk	in Danish
herlig	splendid
drøm (-men, -me)	dream
udkant (-en, -er)	edge, outskirts
indbygger (-en, -e)	inhabitant
frodig	fertile
egn (-en, -e)	area
Østjylland	East Jutland
arbejdsplads (-en, -er)	place of work

stuehus (-et, -e)	farmhouse
jord (-en)	land
ikke længere	no longer
landmand (-en, landmænd)	farmer
ca. (cirka)	approximately
halvdel (-en, -e)	half
plæne (-n, -r)	lawn
springvand (-et, -)	fountain
flagstang (-en, -stænger)	flagpole
lejlighed (-en, -er)	opportunity, occasion
blomsterbed (-et, -e)	flower bed
velholdt	well-kept
køkkenhave (-n, -r)	kitchen/vegetable garden
drivhus (-et, -e)	greenhouse
rest (-en, -er)	remainder
hjørne (-t, -r)	corner
busk (-en, -e)	bush
egetræ (-et, -)	oak tree
hytte (-n, -r)	hut
stald (-en, -e)	stable
at holde*	to keep
hest (-en, -e)	horse
at indrette	to install
sauna (-en, -er)	sauna
rum (-met, -)	room
nabo (-en, -er)	neighbour
at udleje	to let out, hire out
mark (-en, -er)	field
kærlig hilsen	with love from
at savne	to miss

READING

George fra Conventry er født i England, af danske forældre, og har søgt arbejde i Danmark. Hans skotske kone forstår noget dansk.

Min elskede Mary,
Hurra!
Nu har jeg fået stillingen, med en meget fin løn, så vi flytter herover til lille Danmark så snart som muligt, og det er derfor, jeg nu skriver til dig på dansk! Er det ikke herligt?! . . . Jeg har set vores drømmehus, i udkanten af Randers (60.000 indbyggere) i en smuk, frodig egn af Østjylland, kun 20 km fra min arbejdsplads. Det er stuehuset på en gård, men ejeren har solgt jorden og vil ikke være landmand længere. Haven er på ca. 100 x 50 meter, halvdelen er plæne med et lille springvand, flagstang – alle danske huse har flagstang og bruger den ved enhver lejlighed – og blomsterbede, og der er en velholdt køkkenhave med et drivhus, mens resten er et hjørne med træer og buske. I toppen af et egetræ er der en Tarzan-hytte – dejligt for Mark og Susan. Vi kan også købe stalden og holde heste dér – eller indrette sauna og bordtennisrum. En nabo vil udleje en mark, hvis vi virkelig vil have heste.
Kærlig hilsen og kys til jer alle, jeg savner jer meget.
Din George

TRANSLATION

George from Coventry was born in England of Danish parents, and has applied for work in Denmark. His Scottish wife understands some Danish.

My beloved Mary,
Hooray!
I have now got the job, with a very fine salary, so we are moving over (here) to little Denmark as soon as possible, and that is why I am now writing to you in Danish. Isn't it splendid?! . . . I have seen our dream house, on the outskirts of Randers (60,000 inhabitants) in a beautiful, fertile area of East Jutland, only 20 kilometres from my place of work.
It is the (farm)house on a farm but the owner has sold the land and does not want to be (will not be) a farmer any longer. The garden is approximately 100 x 50 metres, half is lawn with a small fountain, flagpole – all Danish houses have (a) flagpole and use it on any occasion – and flower beds, and there is a well-kept vegetable garden with a greenhouse, while the remainder is a corner with trees and bushes. In the top of an oak tree (there) is a Tarzan hut – lovely for Mark and Susan. We can also buy the stable and keep horses there – or install a sauna and tabletennis room. A neighbour will let a field (to us) if we really want to have horses.
With love (loving greeting) and kisses to all of you, I miss you very much.
Your George.

Chapter 6

This chapter deals with:

- *telling the time and expressions for talking about periods of time*
- *the past tense forms of the auxiliary verbs*
- *the most important prepositions, words for 'of,' 'through', 'before' and so on.*

19 Hours of the day – Periods of time

Danes invariably use the 24-hour system in anything written and the 'a.m.' and 'p.m.' method is not known. In talking they tend, as in English-speaking countries, to describe 3 a.m. as three o'clock, **klokken tre**, adding **i nat** ('last night' or 'tonight') or **om natten** ('in the night') as appropriate to make it clear. When speaking in timetable or programme terms they often use the 24-hour clock terminology. So if you are in doubt, do the same.

In describing the half-way mark between hours, correct Danish uses what sounds like the colloquial English 'half two', but be careful: **halv to** in Danish is 'half past one'. The Danes think ahead to the next hour, not back to the last one. After about twenty past and until around twenty to the hour, they mostly use the half hour as their basis for telling the time. Here, the Speaking Clock style is given in square brackets:

Hvad (or **Hvor mange**) **er klokken?**	What's the time?
Den er (klokken) ét [klokken tretten].	It's one o'clock.
kalv to [ét tredive]	1.30 a.m.
kvart (or et kvarter) over seks [atten-femten]	6.15 p.m.
fem minutter i halv tre [fjorten-femogtyve]	2.25 p.m.
tretten minutter i tre [fjorten-syvogfyrre]	2.47 p.m.

Toget går fjorten treogtredive or **tre minutter over halv tre.**
The train leaves at 2.33 p.m.
Uret går for hurtigt/langsomt.
The clock is (goes too) fast/slow.

Denmark used to be a very agricultural country, and this still has a strong influence on Danish mealtimes and divisions of the day:

morgen	6-9
formiddag	9-12
middag	12
frokost/frokosttid	noon-13
eftermiddag	12-18
aften	18-24
nat	24-6

The hot main meal is eaten at around 18.00 and is called **middagsmad** or **aftensmad** – **mad** meaning food. **Frokost** is 'lunch' and its use as a time indicator does not differ from English. Breakfast is **morgenmad** – and a very popular end to an evening after a dinner party is to serve a (relatively) light **natmad** around midnight!

om morgenen/om formiddagen	in the morning (forenoon)
om dagen	in the daytime, by day
om aftenen/om natten	in the evening, at night
i (går) aftes	last night (up to bedtime)
i aften	this evening, tonight

i nat	last night, tonight
ved femtiden	about five
ved middagstid	at noon
i forgårs	the day before yesterday
i går	yesterday
i dag	today
i morges/ i formiddags	this morning (looking back)
tidligt i morges or **i morges tidligt**	early this morning
i morgen	tomorrow
i morgen eftermiddag	tomorrow afternoon
i overmorgen	the day after tomorrow
tidligt på aftenen	in the early evening
sent på eftermiddagen	in the late afternoon
et sekund	a second
et minut	one minute
ti minutter	ten minutes
et kvarter	a quarter of an hour
en halv time	half an hour
tre kvarter	three quarters of an hour
en time	an hour
halvanden time	1½ hours
et døgn	24 hours
om dagen or **i døgnet**	a day (per day)
per dag/døgn	per day/24 hours
daglig(t)	daily
en uge	one week
i sidste/næste uge	last/next week
i forrige uge	the week before last
på fredag otte dage	Friday week
i morgen fjorten dage	a fortnight tomorrow
en måned	a month
et år	a year
et århundrede (yearhundred)	a century
for . . . siden	. . . ago
for to år siden	two years ago
i fjor (rarely: **sidste år**)	last year

Storm P.

– Vi har set de første krokus i år, de kommer sent.
– Ja, klokken er snart halv et.

– We have seen the first crocuses of this year, they are late.
– Yes, it's nearly half past twelve.

Exercise 18

Read through the following conversation. Then insert the words of the vocabulary, which are arranged alphabetically, in the appropriate spaces, and read it through again.

1	**afgår**	departs
2	**enkeltbillet (-ten, -ter)**	single ticket
3	**gælder**	is valid
4	**jernbanestation (-en, -er)**	railway station
5	**klippekort (-et, -)**	punchcard
6	**måde: på den måde**	in that way
7	**pensionist (-en, -er)**	pensioner
8	**perron (-en, -er)**	platform
9	**rabat (-ten)**	discount
10	**rejser (en rejse)**	journeys
11	**ret: have ret til**	be entitled to
12	**returbillet (-ten, -ter)**	return ticket
13	**stedet: i stedet for**	instead of
14	**tid: lang tid**	long (time)
15	**vil sige**	means, is the same as

Ved ..... en

Gammel dame	**Jeg vil gerne have en ..... til Roskilde. Hvor meget koster den, og hvornår går det næste tog?**
Billetsælger	**Den koster atten kroner. Og det næste tog .... kokken fjorten-femogtyve fra .... fire.**
Damen	**Men jeg er ..... og har ..... til ..... Sparer jeg noget, hvis jeg køber en ..... i .. ... for to enkeltbilletter?**
Billetsælger	**Ja, men så skal De gøre noget helt andet og købe et .... Det ..... for flere ..... De sparer meget på den .....**
Damen	**Ja, jeg vil gerne have det klippekort. Sig mig, hvor lang ..... tager rejsen til Roskilde?**
Billetsælger	**De ankommer klokken fjorten-treoghalvtres.**
Damen	**Det .... syv minutter i tre, ikke sandt?**

20 Past tense auxiliaries – 'could, 'should'

The simple past tense of the auxiliariy verbs you met in Section 14 is easy to remember, being exactly the same as the infinitive. Unlike their English counterparts, they have a past participle, so can be used in the perfect tense (**har kunnet**), where in English you need to use different words ('have been able to').

	Past	*Past participle*
could	**kunne**	**kunnet**
should	**skulle**	**skullet**
would	**ville**	**villet**
might, had to	**måtte**	**måttet**

ought	**burde**	**burdet**
dared	**turde**	**turdet**

Han har kunnet springe 2 meter og ville have kunnet komme op på 2,10 ned træning.
He has been able to jump 2 metres and would have been capable of getting up to 2.10 with training.
Familien har måttet sælge alt.
The family has had to sell everything.
Jeg har ikke kunnet drikke kaffe i mange år.
I haven't been able to drink coffee for many years.
For to år siden kunne jeg løbe meget hurtigere – jeg bør/skulle træne.
Two years ago I could run much faster – I ought to train.
Engang ville jeg være lokomotivfører.
Once I wanted to be a train driver.
Mor sagde, jeg måtte, ikke, at jeg skulle.
Mummy said I could, not that I had to.

As in English, auxiliaries are used very freely in an endless number of expressions which makes it impossible to produce an exhaustive list of their uses in Danish. However, here are some more examples:

Jeg må gå nu, Mor kunne blive nervøs.
I must/have to go now, Mummy could/might get nervous.
Det kunne være blevet til noget meget specielt.
It could have become something very special.
Det ville være have været en dejlig overraskelse.
It would have been a lovely surprise.
Vi skulle være gået.
We should have left.
De burde have været der.
They ought to have been there.
Hvad det var, jeg ville sige . . .
What I was going to say . . .
Hvad var det nu, jeg skulle til at gøre?
What *was* it I was about to do?
Du skulle bare prøve min hjemmelavede vin.
You should really try my homemade wine.

Vocabulary

i tykt og tyndt	through thick and thin
ting (-en, -)	thing
at mærke	to notice, sense
at klare	to manage, succeed in
at smile	to smile
karakter (-en, -er)	mark
finger (-en, -gre)	finger
at kunne lide	to like
dessert (-en, -er)	dessert
fugl (-en, -e)	bird
om at	to
at holde mund	to keep one's mouth shut
mindre	less
kritisk	critical
nationalistisk	nationalistic
selvglad	self-satisfied
bedre	better
grund (-en, -e)	reason

Exercise 19

Translate:

1 Vi skulle have fulgt dem i tykt og tyndt.
2 Én ting er, hvad vi burde gøre, en helt anden er, hvad vi kan gøre.
3 Kunne I mærke, at han kunne klare det?
4 Jeg måtte smile, da jeg så politibetjenten.
5 Jeg kunne tælle elevens gode karakterer på én finger!
6 Du plejede at kunne lide desserter – kunne du ikke lide denne her?
7 Jeg ville have kunnet høre fuglene synge, hvis jeg havde turdet bede Maggie om at holde mund.
8 Burde danskerne ikke være noget mindre kritiske?
9 Jo, og hvis de kunne, skulle de også være mindre nationalistiske og selvglade!
10 Jamen, hvem kunne have bedre grund til at være det?

21 Prepositions – 'of', 'through'

Prepositions are used to show the relationship between various words in a sentence: **Mor er *i* køkkenet** 'Mummy is *in* the kitchen'. The most important of them are:

ad (moving) by, along
af of
bag, bagved behind
(i)blandt among
efter after
for for
foran in front of/before
forbi past
før before
fra from, off
(i)gennem through
hos with, at
i in
inden before
inden for inside
indtil until
langs (med) along
med with
(i)mellem among, between
(i)mod towards, against
nær(ved) near
om about, on
omkring around
over over, above
over for opposite
på on
til to
uden without
uden for outside
under under, during
ved by, at

Those prepositions with **(i)** at the beginning often appear with this traditional prefix but it does not change their meaning.

These are the very basic translations, but in fact their use, just as in English, is much wider, frequently with a meaning far removed from the basic. Furthermore, the use of prepositions in combination with nouns, verbs, adverbs and so on is often quite different to English. There is no pattern to this, and the variants have to be learnt through practice. Here are just a few examples of the use of some of the Danish prepositions, and you'll find more in Section 35:

Ad (along, through, by, at)
Kom med mig op ad vejen.
Come with me up the road.
Tyven så ind ad vinduet, og klatrede så ind ad det.
The burglar looked in through the window and then climbed in through it.

ud ad vinduet
out of the window
To ad gangen, sagde Noah.
Two at a time, said Noah.

Af (of)
En af dem er morderen.
One of them is the murderer.
et hjerte af sten a heart of stone
ud af badet out of the bath
Jeg er klog af skade.
I am wise from experience (hurt).
Dansk har lånt mange ord af engelsk.
Danish has borrowed many words from English.
Jeg er ked af det.
I am sorry (about it).

Efter (after)
Efter vinter følger forår.
After winter follows spring.
Jeg starter efter dig.
I start after you.
De kaster snebold efter hinanden.
They're throwing snowballs at each other.
efter min mening in my opinion

I (in)
Forretningen ligger i Fiolstræde.
The shop is (lies) in Fiolstræde (street name).
I aften vil jeg tidligt i seng.
Tonight I am going to bed early.
glasset i drivhuset the glass of the greenhouse
i mandags on Monday (i.e. last Monday)
i tolv år for twelve years
at gå i skole/teater to go to school/the theatre *but*
at gå i biografen to go to the cinema

Om (round, about)
om hjørnet round the corner
Om lidt fortæller jeg dig en historie om en moder.
In a little (while) I'll tell you a story about a mother.

Hvad beder du om?
What are you asking for?
Om mandagen sejler jeg altid, men dog ikke om julen.
On Mondays I always sail, but not at Christmas.

På (on)
De danser på bordene!
They are dancing on the tables!
På fredag skal jeg på ferie.
On Friday I'm going on holiday.
Folk på torvet ser på taleren.
People in the square are looking at the speaker.
Jeg tror på Gud.
I believe in God.
på restaurant to the/a restaurant
på universitetet at university
på højre/venstre side on the right/left side

Vocabulary

at skrive*	to write
bank (-en, -er)	bank
posthus (-et, -e)	post office
jul (-en)	Christmas
tante (-n, -r)	aunt
charmerende	charming
bakke (-n, -r)	hill
at tage* til	to go to

Exercise 20

Translate into Danish:

1 I have written a long letter to Holger and Lise.
2 The bank is (lies!) opposite the post office.
3 May I visit you before Christmas?
4 Two of them have left.
5 In my opinion the aunt is a charming woman.
6 Tell me about the journey.
7 The children went up the hill.
8 Without money you cannot buy food.
9 Does the train to Roskilde go from this platform?
10 On Saturday I am going to Herning.

Vocabulary

telefon (-en, -er)	telephone
min	my
ukendt	unknown
herre (-n, -r)	gentleman
undskyld	sorry
at forestille	to introduce
sig selv	themselves
som	as
med mindre	unless
meget	very
feminin	feminine
stemme (-n, -r)	voice
Deres	your
navn (-et, -e)	name
at tage* telefonen	to answer the telephone
nummer (-et, numre)	number
lige med det samme	straight away
mere	more
sikker	safe
lejer (-en, -e)	lodger
at være* ude at fiske	to be out fishing
bro (-en, -er)	bridge

heller ikke	nor, neither
galt nummer	wrong number
både	both
vittighed (-en, -er)	joke
ulejlighed (-en)	inconvenience

CONVERSATION

I telefonen

Birgitte Strøm	**Ja, det er 89 30 60.**
Vagn Klods	**Hallo, hvem taler jeg med?**
Birgitte Strøm	**Fru Strøm, men synes De ikke, De skulle sige, hvem *De* er, min ukendte herre?**
Vagn Klods	**Jo, undskyld, jeg er hr. Klods.**
Birgitte Strøm	**Jeg kan aldrig forstå, hvorfor mænd forestiller sig selv som 'hr.' – med mindre de har en meget feminin stemme.**
Vagn Klods	**Nå, men hvorfor sagde De så ikke Deres navn, da De tog telefonen, fru Strand?**
Birgitte Strøm	**Vi siger altid kun nummeret, når vi tager telefonen, og ikke navnet lige med det samme. Og vi hedder Strøm, ikke Strand. Men hvem ville De tale med?**
Vagn Klods	**Med Deres lejer Frederik, tak. Se, vi skulle have været ude at fiske, og jeg har ventet på broen i over en time.**
Birgitte Strøm	**Jamen, vi har ingen lejer, og heller ikke nogen Frederik i huset. Så De har fået galt nummer.**
Vagn Klods	**Haha, hvorfor tog De så telefonen? Undskyld, både for den dumme vittighed og for ulejligheden. Farvel.**

TRANSLATION

On the telephone

Birgitte Strøm	**Yes, 893060.**
Vagn Klods	**Hello, who am I talking to?**
Birgitte Strøm	**Mrs Strøm, but don't you think you should say who *you* are, my unknown gentleman?**
Vagn Klods	**Yes, sorry, I am Mr Klods.**
Birgitte Strøm	**I never understand why men introduce themselves as 'Mister' – unless they have a very feminine voice.**
Vagn Klods	**Well, but why then did you not say your name when you answered (took) the telephone, Mrs Strand?**
Birgitte Strøm	**We always say the number only when we answer (take) the telephone, and not the name right away. And our name is Strøm, not Strand. But who did you want to talk to?**
Vagn Klods	**With your lodger, Frederik, please (thank you). You see, we should have been out fishing and I have been waiting on the bridge for more than an hour.**
Birgitte Strøm	**Yes, but we haven't a lodger, nor a Frederik in the house. So you've got the wrong number.**
Vagn Klods	**Haha, why did you answer (take) the phone, then? Sorry, both for the bad joke and for the inconvenience. Goodbye.**

Chapter 7

This chapter builds on your knowledge of adjectives and pronouns. You will find out:

- *how to use the possessive pronouns 'my', 'mine', 'your', 'yours' and so on*
- *how to form the comparative ('better', 'wiser') and superlative ('best', 'wisest') of adjectives*
- *how to use the pronoun* ***man*** *to express an impersonal 'one' or 'you'.*

22 The possessive of pronouns – 'mine', 'yours', 'his'

Here is the possessive form ('my/mine', 'your(s)') of the personal pronouns dealt with in Chapter 1. In some cases the gender and number (singular or plural) of the object of the possession influences the form of the possessive.

	Singular c/n	*Plural*
my/mine	**min/mit**	**mine**
your(s) **(du)**	**din/dit**	**dine**
your(s) **(De)**	**Deres**	**Deres**
his	**hans**	**hans**
her(s)	**hendes**	**hendes**
its **(den)**	**dens**	**dens**
its **(det)**	**dets**	**dets**

our(s)	**vor/vort***	**vore***
your(s) **(I)**	**jeres**	**jeres**
your(s) **(De)**	**Deres**	**Deres**
their(s)	**deres**	**deres**

*In common use, both 'our' and 'ours' are **vores**. However, if you wish to be strictly correct, and in formal letters, you may use **vor, vort, vore.**

Giv mig din hånd og dit hjerte, og jeg giver dig brugen af mit kreditkort.
Give me your hand and your heart and I'll give you the use of my credit card.
Vore hjerters skæbne er i dine hænder.
The fate of our hearts is in your hands.
Se på huset, dets vinduer er knust – og bilen, dens tag er beskadiget.
Look at the house, its windows are shattered – and the car, its roof is damaged.
Vore(s) drenge har mistet vor(es) fodbold, den ligger i jeres drivhus.
Our boys have lost our football, it is in your greenhouse.

So far, so good. Now there comes the tricky, but sometimes useful, bit: if the possessor is third person singular, e.g. 'he', 'she' or 'it', and is the subject of the clause in which it appears, then Danish instead of using **hans, hendes, dens** or **dets** uses **sin** *(c)*, **sit** *(n)* or **sine** *(plural)*.

So, where in English you might say 'Peter gave Jens his hat', and it would be unclear whether the hat belonged to Peter or to Jens, in Danish there could be no mistake. If the hat is Peter's, the Danish will be:

Peter gav Jens sin hat.

but if it had belonged to Jens in the first place:

Peter gav Jens hans hat.

Jensen lånte sin søn sin bil.
Jensen lent his son his (Jensen's) car.
Han havde givet sin søn hans bil.
He had given his son his car
Det er hendes pligt.
It is her duty.
Hun gør sin pligt.
She does her duty.
Hønen kunne ikke finde sine æg.
The hen couldn't find her eggs.
Glasset er hans.
The glass is his.
Han gav mig sit glas.
He gave me his glass (his own).
Han gav mig hans glas.
He gave me his glass (someone else's).
Bed ham give dig sit glas.
Ask him to give you his glass.

Remember this applies to singular subjects only.
Det/Den har sit formål.
It has its purpose.
De har deres formål.
They have their purpose.

Be careful not to confuse **deres** (plural subject) and **sine** (singular subject but plural object):

Spillerne tog deres fodboldstøvler af.
The players took their football boots off.
Spilleren tog sine støvler af.
The player took off his boots.

When referring to clothes and parts of the body, though, Danes often don't use the possessive:

Han brækkede benet.
He broke his leg.
Hun gik fra forstanden.
She went out of her mind (from the intelligence).
Han tog hatten af.
He took off his hat.

Vocabulary

egen (eget, egne)	own
stol (-en, -e)	chair
appelsin (-en, -er)	orange
hat (-ten, -te)	hat
højre	right
lomme (-n, -r)	pocket
flag (-et, -)	flag
tur (-en, -e)	turn
grønsager	vegetables
fod (-en, fødder)	foot
sofa (-en, -er)	sofa, settee
mørk	dark
at passe på	to mind, pay attention to
skarp	sharp
tunge (-n, -r)	tongue

Exercise 21

Delete the wrong alternative:

1 Manden flyttede hans/sin egen stol.
2 Appelsinen er i hans/sin hat.
3 Du har pengene i din/dit højre lomme.
4 Amerikanerne elsker deres/sit flag.
5 Vi går vort/vores vej nu, og så er det din/dit tur.
6 Køber du dine/din grønsager hos hr. Bang?
7 Sig til dem, at de skal sælge sit/deres hus nu.
8 Bed ham flytte sine/hans fødder fra sofaen.
9 Vores have har sine/deres mørke hjørner.
10 Hun skal passe på sin/sit skarpe tunge.

23 Comparison of adjectives – good, better, best

When you wish to say how sweet your lady or how good your man is in comparison with others, you mostly do it in a way not far removed from English: 'good', 'better', 'best', **god, bedre, bedst;** 'sweet', 'sweeter', 'sweetest', **sød, sødere,**

sødest. In other words, the comparative ending ('er' in English) is **(e)re** and the superlative ('est' in English) is **(e)st.**

The superlative form adds an **e** in the indefinite plural and in all definite forms (**den sødeste sang, de sødeste sange,** 'the sweetest song', 'the sweetest songs').

Starting with some regular comparisons:

		Comparative	*Superlative*
soft	**blød**	**blødere**	**blødest**
expensive	**dyr**	**dyrere**	**dyrest**
rich	**rig**	**rigere**	**rigest**
wise	**klog**	**klogere**	**klogest**
high	**høj**	**højere**	**højest**
low	**lav**	**lavere**	**lavest**
wide	**bred**	**bredere**	**bredest**

The consonant-doubling which you have met before occurs here too:

narrow	**smal**	**smallere**	**smallest**
smart	**flot**	**flottere**	**flottest**
beautiful	**smuk**	**smukkere**	**smukkest**
stupid	**dum**	**dummere**	**dummest**

Adjectives that end in **ig** (but not **rig**), or **som** add only **st** in the superlative:

lovely	**dejlig**	**dejligere**	**dejligst**
cheap	**billlig**	**billigere**	**billigst**
poor	**fattig**	**fattigere**	**fattigst**
happy	**lykkelig**	**lykkeligere**	**lykkeligst**
slow	**langsom**	**langsommere**	**langsomst**

If an adjective ends with **el, en or er**, you normally drop the **e** before adding the **ere** or **est** endings. In double-consonant words, one consonant is dropped in the process:

noble	**ædel**	**ædlere**	**ædlest**
lazy	**doven**	**dovnere**	**dovnest**

cheerful	**munter**	**muntrere**	**muntrest**
delicious	**lækker**	**lækrere**	**lækrest**

Some adjectives change completely irregularly, though still with the same endings:

good	**god**	**bedre**	**bedst**
bad	**dårlig**	**værre**	**værst**
large	**stor**	**større**	**størst**
small	**lille**	**mindre**	**mindst**
old	**gammel**	**ældre**	**ældst**
young	**ung**	**yngre**	**yngst**
many	**mange**	**flere**	**flest**
few	**få**	**færre**	**færrest**
much	**meget/megen**	**mere**	**mest**
little	**lidt**	**mindre**	**mindst**
long	**lang**	**længere**	**længst**

'Much' as a quantitative term may be formed according to gender: **meget vand** *(n)*, 'much water', **megen vin** *(c)*, 'much wine'.

Notice that 'more/most' is **mere/mest** when it applies to quantity or degree, but **flere/flest** for numbers of items:

Svend har den største samling og har brug for mere plads til endnu flere ting.
Svend has the largest collection and needs (has need for) more space for even more things.
De har spist det meste af osten.
They have eaten (the) most of the cheese.
De fleste butikker holder åbent idag.
(The) Most shops are open (keep open) today.

Mindre/mindst means both 'less/least' (quantity) and 'smaller/smallest'. Be careful not to use it in place of **færre/færrest,** 'fewer/fewest'.

Den lille busk har mindre blomster end den mindste potteplante.

The little bush has smaller flowers than the smallest pot plant.

Kun de færreste skatteydere ønsker mindre socialforsorg, men de vil have færre arbejdsløse.

Only the fewest tax payers want (wish) less social welfare, but they want fewer unemployed.

As in English, some adjectives, usually the longer ones, tend not to take the comparative and superlative endings, but use **mere** and **mest** when they compare. This applies as well to all adjectives ending with **fuld, ende, et** or **s.**

mere samvittighedsfuld	more conscientious
mere charmerende	more charming
mere jaloux	more jealous
mest buttet	plumpest
mere komfortabel	more comfortable
mest gammeldags	most old-fashioned

On the other hand, just as in English, many adjectives can be made comparative in either of the two ways. 'More beautiful', for instance, can be either **smukkere** or **mere smuk.**

Not surprisingly, 'less' and 'least' with adjectives are **mindre** and **mindst:**

mindre misundelig	less envious
mindst ondskabsfuld	least vicious

'More/less . . . than' in Danish is **mere/mindre . . . end**. 'Even' as in 'even better' is **endnu (endnu bedre)** and 'very' as in 'very best' is **aller** added to the beginning of the word **(allerbedst, allermest).**

Mors store frokost er endnu større end den allerstørste appetit.

Mother's big lunch is even bigger than the very biggest appetite.

Vocabulary

dygtig	able
beskeden	modest
bøgetræ (-et, -er)	beech tree
land (-et, -e)	country
Grønland	Greenland
verden ((en), verd(e)ner)	world
ø (-en, -er)	island
at gå* klædt i	to wear
modern	modern
tøj (-et)	clothes
smidig	flexible
tolerant	tolerant
udlænding (-en, -e)	foreigner
par (-ret, -)	couple
deltager (-en, -e)	participant

Exercise 22

Translate:

1. He is the ablest but also the most modest man in the town.
2. That beech tree is old but the other is even older.
3. Denmark is one of the very smallest countries – but Greenland is the world's largest island.
4. They are the loveliest people.
5. It is best to obey if the other is stronger than you are.
6. There are fewer days in February than any other month.
7. More people wear more modern clothes now.
8. Can't you be a little more flexible – and far more tolerant?
9. Danes like most foreigners.
10. The most charming and happy couple are also the very richest of all the participants.

24 The impersonal Danish 'man' (one, you)

The Danish word **man** covers the meaning of the English 'one' and 'you' as used in the impersonal, or general, sense, but is much more widely used:

Man ved (det) aldrig.
One never knows./You never know.
Hvordan skal man gøre det?
How is one to do that?/How is that to be done?
Sådan noget gør man ikke.
That kind of thing is not done.
Skal man ikke dreje til højre her?
Don't you/Doesn't one have to turn right here?
Man kan ikke gøre for, at man stammer.
You can't help it if you stutter.

The possessive, referring back to **man**, is **sin**, **sit** or **sine.**

Man har sin stolthed. One has one's pride.

Rather like the English 'one', the word **en** used to be applied in Danish the way **man** now is, and has not lost its role completely. **Man** is used only when it is the subject, the one 'doing' or 'being' as in the examples. **En** is used when it is the object (and since it is stressed, you will often see it with the accent):

Motion er godt for én. Exercise is good for one/you.

Ens is the possessive where there is no **man** to refer back to:

Det sårer ens stolthed. It hurts one's pride.
. . . godt for ens helbred . . . good for one's health

Storm P.

Filosofisk mand på bænk i parken:
– Man kan lære umådelig meget af de gamle ordsprog – men man gør det ikke.

Philosophical man on park bench:
– We can learn a great deal from the old proverbs – but we don't.

– Man har ment, at oldtiden ikke vedkommer os, men havde vi ikke haft den, havde vi heller ikke haft nutiden!

– It has been said that antiquity does not concern us, but had we not had it, we would not have had the present either.

Vocabulary

grønthandel (-en)	greengrocer's (shop)
vejr (-et)	weather
tomat (-en, -er)	tomato
kilo (-et, -)	kilo
umuligt	not possibly, impossibly
der	which
øre (-n, -(r))	Danish coin, worth 1/100 of a **krone**
moden	ripe
at skynde (-te, -t) sig	to hurry
at forbedre	to improve
salat (-en, -er)	salad
gulerod (-en, -rødder)	carrot
langt	far
kær	dear
at smage (-te, -t)	to taste
at sammenligne	to compare
at stole på	to trust
at skuffe	to disappoint
at emigrere	to emigrate
hurtigt	quickly
blot	only
køn	pretty
kunde (-n, -r)	customer
sans for humor	sense of humour
at håbe	to hope
melon (-en, -er)	melon
gratis	free (of charge)
det bliver	that comes to
uforbederlig	incorrigible

CONVERSATION

I grønthandelen

Fru Frandsen **Goddag, hr. Bang, dejligt vejr i dag. Og De har nogle fine tomater i vinduet, men de koster nitten kroner kiloet.**

Bang **Ja, fru Frandsen, men man kan umuligt få dem bedre i dag! Jeg har lige for et øjeblik siden fået nogle andre, der kun koster fjorten kroner og halvtreds øre, og de er faktisk lige så gode, men lidt mere modne, så man skal skynde sig at spise dem. Se her . . .**

Fru Frandsen **Godt, lad mig få et halvt kilo af dem. De forbedrer altid en salat, ikke? Jeg vil også gerne have et kilo gulerødder, helst små, og halvandet kilo nye kartofler, hvis man kan få dem nu. Jeg har set langt billigere appelsiner, end dem, De har til enogtyve kroner, og mindst lige så gode.**

Bang **Kære fru Frandsen, det ved man kun, når man har smagt dem. Køb nogle af mine, og sammenlign dem med de andre, og hvis mine ikke er langt de bedste, vil jeg give Dem pengene tilbage.**

Fru Frandsen **Nej, jeg stoler på Dem – og hvis De skuffer mig, er det sikreste for Dem at emigrere hurtigt! Min mand er slagter.**

Bang **Haha, De er ikke blot den allerkønneste af alle mine kunder, De har også den bedste sans for humor . . . håber jeg! Det får De denne lækre melon for, gratis. Det bliver fireoghalvtreds kroner og femogfyrre øre i alt, tak.**

Fru Frandsen **Tusind tak, hr. Bang, man kan sige meget om Dem – og man gør det – men uforbederlig er De! Farvel, og på gensyn.**

TRANSLATION

At the greengrocer's

Mrs Frandsen **Good morning (day), Mr Bang, lovely weather today. And you have some fine tomatoes in the window but they cost nineteen kroner a kilo.**

Bang **Yes, Mrs Frandsen, but you won't find (one can't possibly get them) better today! I have just a moment ago received some others which cost only fourteen kroner and fifty øre and they are in fact just as good, but a little riper, so you have to eat them quickly (hurry to eat them). Look . . .**

Mrs Frandsen **Good, let me have half a kilo of them. They always improve a salad, don't they? I would also like (to have) a kilo of carrots, preferably small – and one and a half kilos of new potatoes, if one can get them now. I have seen far cheaper oranges than those you have at twenty-one kroner, and at least just as good.**

Bang **Dear Mrs Frandsen, one only knows that when one has tasted them. Buy some of mine and compare them with the others and if mine are not by far the best, I'll give you your money back.**

Mrs Frandsen **No, I trust you – and if you disappoint me, the safest (thing) for you is to emigrate quickly! My husband is a butcher.**

Bang **Haha, you are not only the very prettiest of all my customers, you also have the best sense of humour . . . I hope! For that you get this delicious melon, free. That'll be fifty-four kroner and forty-five øre in all, thank you.**

Mrs Frandsen **Thank you very much, Mr Bang, they (one) can say a lot about you – and they do – but you *are* incorrigible! Goodbye, see you again.**

Chapter 8

Chapter 8 looks at:

- *the reflexive pronouns, the equivalents of 'myself', 'yourself', etc., and how they are used to form reflexive verbs*
- *frequently used adverbs, such as 'almost', 'especially', and how they are used to modify the meaning of verbs, adjectives and other adverbs*
- *how to link phrases and sentences by means of conjunctions, including 'and', 'but', 'when', 'because'.*

25 Reflexive pronouns: 'myself', 'themselves'

Since Section 7, you have known the Danish for 'me, you, him' etc. – the object pronoun. The same pronouns are used in reflexive constructions – meaning 'myself' etc. – except that 'himself', 'herself' and 'themselves' are all **sig**. Here they are all applied to the verb **skære*** 'to cut'.

jeg skærer	**mig**	(I cut)	myself
du skærer	**dig**		yourself
De skærer	**Dem**		yourself
han/hun skærer	**sig**		him/herself
den/det skærer	**sig**		itself
vi skærer	**os**		ourselves
I skærer	**jer**		yourselves
De skærer	**Dem**		yourselves
de skærer	**sig**		themselves

Jeg vasker mig.
I get washed (wash myself).
Vi morer os.
We are enjoying (amusing) ourselves.
De varmer sig ved ilden.
They are warming themselves by the fire.
Mor, jeg skar mig/har skåret mig!
Mummy, I (have) cut myself!
Man kan more sig over det.
It can be amusing (one can amuse oneself over it).

Some verbs are used with the reflexive pronoun in Danish, though not in English, including:

at gifte sig	to get married
at kede sig	to be bored
at bekymre sig	to worry
at glæde sig over	to be pleased with, enjoy
at glæde sig til	to look forward to
at skabe (-te, -t) sig	to be silly (**at skabe** 'create')
at skynde (-te, -t) sig	to hurry
at komme* sig	to recover
at bryde* sig om	to care for, like
at forandre sig	to change
at rejse (-te, -t) sig	to get up
at klæde sig på	to get dressed

Vi gifter os i morgen.
We're getting married tomorrow.
I bryder jer ikke om Jens.
You don't care for/like Jens.
I har noget at glæde jer til.
You have something to look forward to.
Jeg skynder mig hjem.
I am hurrying home.

To stress the personal aspect ('he did it himself'), Danes use the word **selv** 'self', as follows:

Han gjorde det selv.
He did it himself.

Vi reparerede det selv.
We repaired it ourselves.
Pas jer selv.
Mind your own business (look after yourselves).
Hvis du er gammel nok til at barbere dig selv, kan du også klæde dig selv på.
If you are old enough to shave yourself, you can also dress yourself.
Hun holdt sig for sig selv.
She kept herself to herself.
Jeg lavede mad til mig selv.
I cooked (made food) for myself.
Det kan du selv gøre!
You can do that yourself!

These reflexive pronouns take exactly the same position in the sentence as any other object pronoun.

Vocabulary

at passe sig selv	to mind one's own business
bare	just, only
fordi	because
at blive* færdig	to finish
patient (-en, -er)	patient
ulykke (-n, -r)	accident
selv	even
nu om dage	these days
folk	people
i radioen	on the radio
at behøve	to need
ind	in
mens	while
alder: i deres alder	at their age
at lære (-te, -t)	to learn
at opføre (-te, -t) sig	to behave
ordentligt	properly
læge (-n, -r)	doctor
at skamme sig	to be ashamed

Exercise 23

Translate:

1 They should mind their own business.
2 You must not worry about me just because I have cut myself.
3 He is bored, but she is not hurrying to finish.
4 The patient is now recovering after the accident.
5 Even these days people are getting married!
6 Christmas is really something to look forward to.
7 I get dressed while I listen to the news on the radio.
8 You don't need to get up when I come in.
9 They are only being silly – at their age they should have learnt to behave properly.
10 That lazy doctor ought to be ashamed.

26 Adverbs – 'almost', 'already'

You have already come across a number of adverbs throughout this course: **ikke, gerne, allerede, aldrig, noget** and so on. Adverbs in one way or another *modify* verbs, adjectives, or other adverbs to which they are added – be it by way of adding, detracting, changing or whatever:

Han trækker sig tilbage allerede i år.
He is retiring (already) this year.
i en næsten uhørlig hvisken
in an almost inaudible whisper
Måske vil de kun acceptere dette.
Perhaps they will only accept this.
Dette er ret mistænkeligt.
This is somewhat suspicious.
Selv Søren er lidt træt.
Even Søren is a bit tired.
Selv ikke det gjorde dem helt tilfreds.
Not even that satisfied them completely (made them completely satisfied).

Just as in English some adverbs are made by adding '-ly' to an adjective ('rapidly', 'shortly'), adverbs can be made from adjectives in Danish by adding **t** (**godt** 'well', **langt** 'far'), **vis** (**heldigvis** 'fortunately', **naturligvis** 'naturally, of course'), and sometimes adjectives are used unchanged as adverbs (**let** 'lightly').

Here are some common adverbs:

aldrig never
alligevel all the same, anyway
altid always
bare, blot, kun only
da then
desuden besides, furthermore
desværre unfortunately
dog yet, however
ellers otherwise
endnu still, yet
for too
ganske quite, rather
gerne willingly
heldigvis fortunately
ikke not
især especially
langt far
længe (for a) long (time)
muligvis perhaps
måske perhaps
naturligvis of course
nu now
næsten almost
ofte, tit often
også also
selvfølgelig of course
sommetider sometimes
straks immediately
så then
undertiden occasionally

Adverbs indicating where something is, or where it is going, are dealt with in Section 37.

Some adverbs can be compared. Those derived from adjectives use the same comparative forms as the adjective from which they come, while others follow the same kind of pattern:

willingly	**gerne**	**hellere**	**helst**
frequently	**tit**	**tiere**	**tiest**
often	**ofte**	**oftere**	**oftest**
long (time)	**længe**	**længere**	**længst**
seldom	**sjælden**	**sjældnere**	**sjældnest**

Vocabulary

uanset	regardless, no matter
at øve sig	to practise
at ramme (-te, -t)	to hit
forkert	wrong
at minde om	to remind of
krig (-en, -e)	war
ret (-ten, -ter)	right
at strejke	to (go on) strike
at ringe til	to ring, telephone
alene	alone
bestemt	certainly
almindelig	ordinary

Exercise 24

Translate:

1 Uanset hvor længe Ole øver sig, rammer han tit forkert.
2 Det er langt fra at være helt færdigt, og dog er det allerede smukt.
3 Sangen mindede mig straks om dig og endnu mere om krig.
4 De vil blot have deres ret - ellers strejker de.
5 Hun ringer næsten altid til ham, når hun er alene.
6 Han er bestemt ikke helt almindelig!
7 Bedre sent end aldrig!
8 Undertiden går vi i biografen, men vi går oftere i teater.
9 Selvfølgelig arbejdede de længe, men så kunne de ikke længere.
10 Det er desværre for gammelt, og heller ikke for stærkt.

27 Conjunctions

Words, phrases and sentences can be linked together by conjunctions, such as **og** 'and', **eller** 'or', **men** 'but', **samt** 'plus', **såvel som** 'as well as', **for** 'for', 'because', and **så** 'so'.

Amongst other conjunctions you will recognise several which are also prepositions:

Those dealing with *time:*

da, dengang, når	when
før, inden	before
(i)mens	while
indtil	until
siden	since

Da and **dengang** ('when', 'that time' or 'on the occasion when') are both used in talking about the past, while **når** deals with the present and future and repeated incidents in the past:

Da Mozart levede, var der rigtige komponister til!
When Mozart lived, there were real composers!
Det var dengang vi så det fem-mastede skoleskib, ikke sandt?
It was (the time) when we saw the five-masted training ship, wasn't it?
Det er først rigtig jul, når vi går i kæde om juletræet.
It is only really Christmas when we join hands and walk (walk in chain) around the Christmas tree.
Vi havde det bedst, når vi var hjemme.
We were happiest when we were at home.

Others are used in *comparisons:*

som	as
ligesom	like, just as
end	than
(lige) så . . . som	(just) as . . . as

Tandlægen er (lige) så klodset som han altid har været.
The dentist is (just) as clumsy as he has always been.
Danmark er mindre end Irland.
Denmark is smaller than Ireland.

Cause:

fordi	because
da	since
eftersom	as

Eftersom/Da du ikke har tabt vægt, må det være fordi du ikke har taget motion siden jeres ferie.

Since/As you have not lost weight, it must be because you have not taken any exercise since your holiday.

Condition:

hvis, om	if
såfremt, hvis	provided
ifald, i tilfælde af at	in case of
bare, blot	if only
med mindre	unless

I tilfælde af brand skal man bruge nødudgangen.

In case of fire you must use the emergency exit.

Bare/Blot hun dog ville holde mund.

If only she would keep her mouth shut. (If you must know: 'shut up!' = **hold kæft!**)

Concession:

selvom, skønt	although

Purpose:

for at	in order that, so that

Asking and telling:

at	that
om	if, whether

Vocabulary

berømt	famous
prinsesse (-n, -r)	princess
hovedpine (-n, -r)	headache
at gå* en tur	to go for a walk
slot (-tet, -te)	palace
sol (-en, -e)	sun

ned	down
endelig	finally
at standse	to stop
sø (-en, -er)	lake
at drømme (-te, -t)	to dream
at dreje	to turn
kostbar	costly, precious
ring (-en, -e)	ring
pludselig	suddenly
vand (-et, -e)	water
chock (-et, -)	shock
tåre (-n, -r)	tear
at begynde (-te, -t)	to begin
at flyde*	to flow
tudse (-n, -r)	toad
mund (-en, -e)	mouth
at sove*	to sleep
modbydeligt	repulsive
at protestere	to protest
at give* efter	to give way, acquiesce
at samle op	to pick up
at bære*	to carry
soveværelse (-t, -r)	bedroom
at vågne	to wake up
at opdage	to discover
klodset	clumsy
at ske (-te, -t)	to happen
at forvandle sig til	to turn into
nej, vel?	no, you don't, do you?
konge (-n, -r)	king

Exercise 25

Fit appropriate conjunctions into the spaces:

Som du ved – eller burde vide – er Danmark berømt som eventyrenes land, 1) . . . vi må have denne historie med: Prinsessen havde hovedpine, 2) . . . hun gik en tur i slottets have, 3) . . . solen gik ned. Endelig standsede hun ved søen og stod dér og drømte, 4) . . . hun drejede sin kostbare ring. Pludselig tabte hun ringen, 5) . . . den faldt i vandet. Det var et chok, 6) . . . allerede 7) . . . hendes tårer begyndte at flyde, så hun en stor tudse, 8) . . . den havde hendes ring i munden! "Åh, tak, kære tudse, jeg har ikke været så lykkelig, 9) . . . min far gav mig ringen."
"Jamen, du får den først, 10) . . . jeg kan sove i din seng i nat." "Uh, hvor modbydeligt," tænkte prinsessen, og først protesterede hun, 11) . . . endelig gav hun efter, samlede tudsen op og bar den til sit soveværelse. "12) . . . jeg vågner i morgen, får jeg ringen, 13) . . . min far opdager ikke, hvor klodset jeg har været."
14) . . . næste morgen var der sket noget fantastisk: 15) . . . hun sov, havde tudsen forvandlet sig til en flot, ung mand!
Kære læser, tror DU på eventyr?
Nej, vel? Det gjorde hendes far, kongen, heller ikke!

Vocabulary

taxa (-en, -er)	taxi
at prøve	to try
at rette	to correct
fejl (-en, -)	mistake
taxachauffør (-en, -er)	taxi driver
udtale (-n)	pronunciation
Europa	Europe
præmie (-n, -r)	prize

fransk	French
klar	clear
havfrue (-n, -r)	mermaid
at reparere	to repair
pragtfuld	splendid, wonderful
at forestille sig	to imagine
fjernsyn (-et)	television
frisør (-en, -er)	hairdresser
dronning (-en, -er)	queen
sommerresidens (-en)	summer residence
at mene (-te, -t)	to mean
skønhedsdronning (-en, -er)	beauty queen
at fortjene (-te, -t)	to deserve
ærlig	honest
engang	once (upon a time)

CONVERSATION

I en taxa i København

Miss Canada	**Jeg prøver at lære dansk, for min mor er dansker. Vær venlig at tale langsomt og at rette mig, hvis jeg laver fejl.**
Taxachauffør	**Det er meget fint, så er det derfor, din udtale er god. Jeg læste i avisen, at du er her, fordi du fik en Europarejse i præmie for at være den smukkeste kvinde i Canada, ikke?**
Miss Canada	**Det siger de. Min far er fransk-canadisk, men selvom jeg ikke har været her før, har jeg hørt meget om København.**
Taxachauffør	**Det er klart, at du lærer let. Se nu, før vi kommer til Den lille havfrue, bør du se Gefionspringvandet – selvom det er uden vand lige nu, mens man reparerer det. Alligevel er det pragtfuldt, synes du ikke?**
Miss Canada	**Jo, jeg kan forestille mig, hvordan det ser ud. Men da jeg skal på jeres fjernsyn i aften, må vi skynde os, så jeg ikke kommer for sent til frisøren klokken fem.**
Taxachauffør	**Selvfølgelig, men vil du ikke se, hvor den anden dronning bor, indtil hun flytter ud til sin sommerresidens? Se, dér er Amalienborg.**
Miss Canada	**Hvad mener du, når du siger den anden dronning?**
Taxachauffør	**Ha, du er jo skønhedsdronning. Og du fortjener det, når jeg skal være ærlig! Engang var min kone lige så smuk – der var engang, som der står i eventyret!**

TRANSLATION

In a taxi in Copenhagen

Miss Canada	**I'm trying to learn Danish, because my mother is Danish. Please speak slowly and correct me if I make mistakes.**
Taxi driver	**That is very fine, so that is why your pronunciation is good. I read in the paper that you are here because you were given a trip to Europe as a prize for being the most beautiful woman in Canada, isn't that right?**
Miss Canada	**That's what they say. My father is a French-Canadian but, even though I have not been here before, I have heard a lot about Copenhagen.**
Taxi driver	**It is clear that you learn easily. Look now, before we come to The Little Mermaid you ought to see the Gefion Fountain – even though there is no water in it while they are (one is) repairing it. It is splendid all the same, don't you think?**
Miss Canada	**Yes, I can imagine what it looks like. But since I am going on your television tonight, we must hurry so that I won't be (come too) late for the hairdresser at five o'clock.**
Taxi driver	**Of course, but don't you want to see where the other queen lives until she moves out to her summer residence? Look, there is Amalienborg.**
Miss Canada	**What do you mean when you say 'the other queen'?**
Taxi driver	**Ha, after all, you are a beauty queen. And you deserve it, if I have to be honest! Once my wife was just as beautiful – (there was) once upon a time, as it says (there stands) in the fairy-tale!**

Chapter 9

> *This chapter introduces the words for describing colours. It also deals with building longer and more complex sentences. You will learn about:*
>
> - *the relative pronouns* **som** *and* **der** *('who', 'that', 'which'), and how they join two clauses to form a sentence*
> - *how conjunctions can be used to join clauses, and the effect they have on the order of words.*

28 Relative pronouns – 'that', 'which', 'who'

Yet another Danish word which covers several different English ones: 'who', 'whom', 'that' or 'which' as relative pronouns ('the boy who did it', 'the ship which/that sank') can *all* be represented in Danish by **som**. In many instances, you can equally well use **der**. Both remain the same for both genders and in the plural!

bankbestyreren, som/der sagde nej
the bank manager who said no

De bukser, som/der var i udsalget, kostede kun det halve.
The trousers which were in the sale cost only half as much ('the half').

Mureren, der/som byggede huset, gik fallit.
The mason who built the house went bankrupt.

Enhver, der/som kan svømme, kan være med.
Anyone who can swim can take part.

Notice that sometimes the demonstrative article is used in such sentences (**de bukser**), though this is not essential.

In the examples above, **som** or **der** is the subject of the verb immediately following it (**sagde, var, byggede, kan**). When the relative pronoun is the object of the verb (illustrated by the use of 'whom' rather than 'who'), it can only be **som**, never **der**. Just as in English, though, it is often left out altogether.

mureren, (som) vi ansatte
    the mason (whom) we engaged
Jeg vasker de bukser, (som) vi købte.
    I am washing the trousers (which/that) we bought.
enhver svømmer, (som) klubben har valgt
    any swimmer (whom) the club has chosen
pigen, (som) du flirtede med
    the girl with whom you were flirting/the girl you were flirting with
Jeg kan lide det, (som) fjernsynet viser nu.
    I like what is on TV (that which the TV is showing) now.

Where, as in the last example, the usual English is 'I like what', the same short cut is often used in Danish:

Jeg kan lide, hvad . . .

The possessive form of **som** and **der** is **hvis** 'whose'.

Manden, hvis skyld det var, tilstod.
    The man whose fault it was confessed.

Der is also needed to go with **hvad** and **hvem** when they are the subject of a verb in such sentences as:

Fortæl mig, hvem der gjorde dette her.
    Tell me who (it was that) did this.
Hvad der så skete, ved jeg ikke.
    What happened then, I don't know.
Ved hun, hvad der er nødvendigt?
    Does she know what is necessary?

Vocabulary

nøgle (-n, -r)	key
job (-bet, -)	job
at efterligne	to copy
at rulle	to roll
at samle	to gather
mos (-set)	moss
lærerinde (-n, -r)	(female) teacher
abe (-n, -r)	monkey
blind	blind
væk	away
at hade	to hate
champagne (-n)	champagne
at vaske	to wash
skjorte (-n, -r)	shirt
hård	hard

Exercise 26

Translate into Danish:

1 Give the key to the American who asked for it.
2 The Australian who did the job did it himself.
3 We should copy the method that they use.
4 The stone that rolls gathers no moss.
5 I know a teacher who is a lovely lady.
6 It was the monkey that had one blind eye that ran away.
7 I hate what they are playing.
8 The champagne which they have chosen is far too expensive.
9 Now wash the shirts I gave you two weeks ago!
10 He lost his money, for which he had worked so hard.

29 Sentence building – more complex sentences

Hans har tid nu. Han skriver et brev til Grete.
Hans has time now. He is writing a letter to Grete.

Here we have two perfectly straightforward sentences, each consisting of one clause. Now, if you wish to link them together in one sentence, which will then have two clauses, and the two clauses are equally important, you use simple linking conjunctions such as **og, men, for** and **så** – and the word order does not change:

Hans har tid nu, så han skriver et brev til Grete.
Hans has time now, so he is writing a letter to Grete.
Det er mørkt, men vi har en lygte, og vi kan læse.
It is dark, but we have a lamp, and we can read.

However, if one sentence is dependent on the other, things start to be different. We'll insert conditions with 'if' and 'when':

Hvis Hans har tid, skriver han et brev til Grete.
If Hans has time, he will write a letter to Grete.
Når vi får en lygte, kan vi læse.
When we get a light, we can read.

In these sentences, the first clause is – to use the grammatical term – subordinate to the second, which is known as the main clause because it could stand alone as a sentence. Notice that when a sentence begins with a subordinate clause, there is automatically inversion in the main clause. This inversion does not happen in the subordinate clause, even if the main clause comes first:

Når du kalder, kommer jeg.
When you call I come.
Jeg kommer, når du kalder.
I come when you call.
Du skal vande græsplænen, før du kører til Ålborg.
You must water the lawn before you drive to Ålborg.

Før du kører til Ålborg, skal du vande græsplænen.
Before you drive to Ålborg, you must water the lawn.

Note: Correct Danish punctuation is more regulated than English and a comma should normally be inserted between two clauses. This can sometimes be helpful to understanding.

There is one other extremely important difference in the word order of subordinate clauses. **Ikke, aldrig, altid** and other common adverbs, and negatives such as **ingenting,** instead of following the verb, come between the subject and the verb:

Hvis Hans ikke har tid,
Når vi altid har en lygte,
Siden jeg ikke er rig,
Since I'm not rich,
Selvom han ingenting har gjort i dag.
Even though he hasn't done anything today,
Med mindre du faktisk har tid,
Unless you actually have time,
Hvad jeg ikke har gjort er at skrive det brev.
What I haven't done is to write that letter.
Mureren havde arbejdere, som vi ikke kunne lide.
The mason had workers whom we didn't like.
Den, som/der ikke vil prøve, er en kujon.
He (the one, anyone) who will not try is a coward.

As you see, the same rule applies to the relative clauses we saw in the previous section, since they are also subordinate clauses.

When a question is part of a longer sentence, it has the word order of a subordinate clause, but clauses beginning with **at** meaning 'that' can follow either subordinate clause word order or main clause word order:

Hun spurgte, om vi ikke også ville komme.
She asked whether we wouldn't come too.
Fortæl mig, hvad du synes, og hvad vi skulle gøre.
Tell me what you think, and what we should do.

Han sagde, at han havde ikke tid./Han sagde, at han ikke havde tid.
He said (that) he didn't have time.

One other peculiarity of Danish word order:

Jeg håber ikke, det regner i dag.
I hope it doesn't rain today.
Han håber aldrig, det sker igen.
He hopes it will never happen again.

Naturally, as in any language, emphasis may change the normal word order: **Han sagde, at tid havde han ikke . . .** implying that a 'but' is to follow.

En Storm P. -mand til en anden:
– Hvis De ikke kan huske, hvad jeg hedder, kan De jo bare slå op i telefonbogen.

One Storm P. man to another:
– If you cannot remember my name, all you have to do is look it up in the telephone book.

Tankefuld mand på bænk:
– Nu sidder jeg her, fri som en fugl – men det må være en høne, for flyve kan jeg ikke.

Thoughtful man on bench:
– Now I am sitting here, free as a bird – but it must be a hen, because fly I cannot.

Vocabulary

bukser	trousers
problem (-et, -er)	problem
bil (-en, -er)	car
kvittering (-en, -er)	receipt
at stave	to spell
rigtigt	correctly
supermand (-en, -mænd)	superman
hospital (-et, -er)	hospital

Exercise 27

Translate:

1 De bukser, jeg vaskede i går, er allerede snavsede.
2 Når de arbejder, er der aldrig problemer.
3 Det bliver ikke os to, hvis du ikke er rig.
4 Den mand, du solgte bilen til, vil blot have en kvittering.
5 Selvom du ikke kan stave rigtigt, skulle du skrive tit.
6 Hvem der fulgte efter Frederik den Niende, ved jeg ikke.
7 Fordi du er nummer ét, skal du ikke tro, at du er supermand.
8 Vær venlig at vise mig, hvor hospitalet ligger – hvis du har tid.

30 The colours

hvid	white
grå	grey
sort	black
gul	yellow
grøn	green
blå	blue
brun	brown
rød	red
orangefarvet	orange
violet/purpur	purple

Vocabulary

prins (-en, -er)	prince
at gifte sig med	to marry
at banke	to knock
dør (-en, -e)	door

at lukke op	to open
at fare* vild	to get lost
at byde* ind	to ask in
ægte	genuine
ært (-en, -er)	pea
bund (-en, -e)	bottom
at komme*	to put
madras (-sen, -ser)	mattress
oven på	on top (of)
edderdunsdyne (-n, -r)	eiderdown quilt
forfærdelig	terrible
hel	whole
krop (-pen, -pe)	body
museum (museet, museer)	museum
nutidig	present-day
forfatter (-en, -e)	author
præst (-en, -er)	priest
historie (-n, -r)	story
klasse (-n, -r)	class
opgave (-n, -r)	task
at genfortælle*	to retell
-årig	-year-old
at slutte	to finish
version (-en, -er)	version
over det hele	all over

Exercise 28

Translate:

Hans Christian Andersen fortæller om prinsen, der ikke kunne finde en *rigtig* prinsesse at gifte sig med. En sen aften bankede en pige på slottets dør. Da den gamle konge lukkede op, sagde hun, at hun var en prinsesse og var faret vild. Kongen bød hende ind.
For at undersøge, om hun nu også var en ægte prinsesse, lagde den gamle dronning en ært på bunden af pigens seng, og kom tyve madrasser oven på og oven på dem igen tyve edderdunsdyner.
Om morgenen spurgte de, hvordan pigen havde sovet. Ganske forfærdeligt, svarede hun, for hun havde ligget på noget, der var så hårdt, at hun var brun og blå over hele kroppen. Så det var helt klart, at her var en *rigtig* prinsesse, og prinsen tog hende til kone, mens ærten kom på museum.
Den nutidige danske forfatter og præst Johannes Møllehave skriver, at han fortalte historien til en tredie klasse og gav dem til opgave at genfortælle den. En 9-årig dreng sluttede sin meget korte version med: . . . og da prinsessen vågnede op om morgenen, var hun grøn og gul og blå over *det* hele. Se det var en *rigtig* prins!

31 Politeness

You've already seen several ways of saying 'please' and 'thank you' in Danish. The simple 'Yes, please' or 'No, thank you' in answer to an offer are: **ja tak** and **nej tak** respectively. There are a couple more formal ways of expressing 'please', often used in public announcements: **Vi beder Dem venligst . . . , Vi gør høfligst opmærksom på . . .** The announcer is not describing his or her gentle nature, but using normal Danish courtesy, which means something like

'We ask you to be kind enough to . . .' and 'May we please draw your attention to . . .' .

You will seldom hear **tak** on its own. It is usually **mange tak,** 'many thanks', or, very frequently, **tusind tak** – said with conviction! You respond with **tak i lige måde**, 'and you', **å, jeg beder** 'oh, I beg' or **ikke noget at takke for**, 'not at all'.

At the end of a meal, you are expected to say **tak for mad!** 'thank you for the food', and your host(ess) will reply: **vebekomme!** 'you're welcome'. And the next time you speak to them you must say **tak for sidst!** 'thank you for the last time' or **tak for i går** etc., as appropriate.

Handing something over, you say **værsgo** (literally, 'be so good').

'Sorry!' and 'Excuse me' are basically **undskyld!,** though you will of course also hear other ways of saying it:

Undskyld, De ku' Økunne vel ikke lige sige mig vejen til . . .
Excuse me, I don't suppose you could just tell me the way to. . .
Må jeg godt lige komme forbi?
Excuse me, can I get by?
Undskyld mig bare et øjeblik.
Excuse me a moment.
Undskyld, trådte jeg Dem over tæerne?
Sorry, did I tread on your toes?
Undskyld, må jeg lige se den?
Excuse me, may I just have a look at it?

If your apology is abject, you might say
Åh, jeg er frygteligt ked af det – vil du tilgive mig?
I'm terribly sorry – will you forgive me?

You congratulate with **til lykke (med)** or **må jeg gratulere.** 'Happy birthday' is **til lykke med fødselsdagen,** and 'Merry Christmas and a Happy New Year' would be **glædelig jul og godt nytår!**

'Get well soon' is **god bedring** and 'good luck' **held og lykke!**

To Storm P.-mænd siger farvel til hinanden:
– Hvis vi ikke skulle ses forinden, må jeg så ønske Dem glædelig jul.
– Tak i lige måde, og godt nytår, glædelig påske og pinse og til lykke med fødselsdagen!

Two Storm P. men take leave of each other:
– If we don't see each other before then, may I wish you Happy Christmas.
– Thank you, and to you, and Happy New Year, Happy Easter and Whitsun and Happy Birthday!

Vocabulary

Østtyskland	East Germany
specialitet (-en, -er)	speciality
campingvogn (-en, -e)	caravan
pølse (-n, -r)	sausage
mon	I wonder
kød (-et)	meat
dernede	down there
røget	smoked
skinke (-n, -r)	ham
absolut	absolutely
delikatessedisk (-en, -e)	delicatessen counter
snes (-en, -e)	a score (twenty)
lammerullepølse	rolled lamb sausage
grov	coarse
leverpostej (-en, -er)	liver paté
spegepølse	salami
smør (-ret)	butter
kylling (-en, -er)	chicken
vist	probably, I think
at runde af	to round off
agurk (-en, -er)	gherkin
i orden	all right
lad gå	all right
fristelse (-n, -r)	temptation

CONVERSATION

I slagterforretningen

Slagter **Goddag, fru Pedersen, hvad skal det være i dag?**

Fru Pedersen **Vi skal på ferie i det gamle Østtyskland, så nu vil vi gerne have nogle danske specialiteter med i vores campingvogn.**

Slagter **Mine pølser er meget danske, ikke? Og mon ikke kød er dyrt dernede – hvad med en røget skinke, der kun koster 68 kroner kiloet og absolut er i topklasse?**

Fru Pedersen **Ja, lad mig få halvandet kilo skinke. Men lad mig se på Deres delikatessedisk. Åh ja, og jeg vil gerne have en snes æg. Og må jeg få 500 gram lammerullepølse, grov leverpostej, spegepølse, seks pakker smør, to røgede kyllinger . . . ja, så er der vist ikke mere. Hvor meget bliver det?**

Slagter **Det bli'r – lad mig se . . . trehundredeogfireogtredive kroner – men lad os runde det af til trehundredeogfyrre, hvis jeg giver Dem et stort glas agurker med – er det i orden?**

Fru Pedersen **Lad gå, og jeg siger tak. Opfør Dem ordentligt, mens vi er væk, ikke?**

Slagter **Når De ikke er her, er der ingen fristelser!**

TRANSLATION

In the butcher's shop

Butcher **Good day, Mrs Pedersen, what is it to be today?**

Mrs Pedersen **We are going on holiday in the old East Germany so we would like to take some Danish specialities with us in our caravan.**

Butcher **My sausages are very Danish, aren't they? And I wonder, is meat not expensive down there – what about some smoked ham which costs only 68 kroner a kilo and is absolutely (in) top class?**

Mrs Pedersen **Yes, let me have one and a half kilos of ham. But let me have a look at your delicatessen counter. Oh yes, and I'd like to have a score of eggs. And may I have 500 grammes of rolled lamb, coarse liver paté, salami, six packets of butter, two smoked chickens . . . yes, then I don't think there's any more. How much will that be?**

Butcher **That'll be – let me see . . . 334 kroner – but let's round it off to 340 if I give you a large jar (glass) of gherkins – is that all right?**

Mrs Pedersen **All right, and I say thank you. Behave yourself while we're away, won't you?**

Butcher **When you're not here there are no temptations!**

Chapter 10

Chapter 10 introduces:

- *the passive form of verbs (e.g. 'to be treated') – and how to avoid it by using* ***man***
- *impersonal expressions such as 'it's raining' and 'it is said that'*
- *some more important prepositions.*

It also explains how words are strung together to make longer, 'compound' words.

32 Passive verbs – 'to be treated'

When one does something ('I treat' **jeg behandler**), the verb is said to be 'active'. When something is done to one ('I am [being] treated') or to something ('it is treated'), the verb is dubbed 'passive'. In Danish, the passive is made in one of two ways.

In the first method, an **s** replaces the final **r** of the present tense or is added to the end of the past tense.

to treat	**at behandle**	to be treated	**at behandles**
we treat	**vi behandler**	we are treated	**vi behandles**
I treated	**jeg behandlede**	I was treated	**jeg behandledes**

Den hest behandles dårligt af sin ejer og bruges hårdt.
That horse is treated badly by its owner and is used hard.

Der drikkes for meget alkohol i dag.
There is too much alcohol drunk today.

Applied to the future:

Dyrene vises om et øjeblik.
The animals will be shown in a moment.

However, the **s** ending cannot be used in the other tenses. The other method is to use **blive** with the past participle:

Den bliver behandlet dårligt og (bliver) brugt hårdt.
It is treated badly and used hard.
De bliver vist.
They are shown.

And in the past:

Hun blev husket . . . She was remembered . . .
Hesten blev vist. The horse was shown.

So:

Lyset bliver slukket or **Lyset slukkes.**
The light is turned off.
Lyset blev slukket or **Lyset slukkedes.**
The light was turned off.
Lyset er blevet slukket.
The light has been turned off.
Lyset var blevet slukket.
The light has been turned off.

(Remember that the auxiliary for **blive** is always **være**, never **have**.)

And again moving into the future:

Lyset bliver slukket kl. 23 or **Lyset vil blive slukket . . .**
The light will be turned off at 11 p.m.

And with modal auxiliaries:

Vi ville være blevet straffet.
We would have been punished.
Lyset skulle blive slukket.
The light should be turned off.

If you see **Lyset er/var slukket** 'The light is/was off', don't let it confuse you. In this case **slukket** is being used as an adjective.

In practice, Danes often avoid the passive and resort to the useful **man** – see Section 24:

Man huskede hende. Man spiser for meget i det hjem. Man drikker for meget i dag. Man behandler den hest dårligt. Man havde slukket lyset.

Storm P.

– Ærligt talt, så har jeg ikke megen forstand på opera – men hvis den blev sunget i fri luft, ville hele personalet blive tiltalt for støjende adfærd.

– Frankly speaking, I don't know much about opera – but if it were sung in the open air, the entire cast would be charged with noisy behaviour.

Vocabulary

at køre (-te, -t)	to drive
garage (-n, -r)	garage
at huske	to remember
forsigtig	careful
at omtale (-te, -t)	to talk about
som om	as if
forbryder (-en, -)	criminal
at feje	to sweep
at tænde (-te, -t)	to light
lys (-et, -e)	light, candle
præsentation (-en, -er)	presentation
at drikke*	to drink

Exercise 29

Translate:

1 Kør bilen ud af garagen, men husk, at den skal køres forsigtigt.
2 Han omtales, som om han var en forbryder.
3 Gulvet var aldrig blevet vasket, kun fejet.
4 Man ved ikke altid, hvordan det gøres bedst.
5 Når det er blevet mørkt, tænder man lysene på juletræet.
6 Mit navn staves med 'ph', men du staver det altid med 'f'.
7 Man håber, at præsentationen kan gøres let og hurtigt.
8 Ikke al vinen blev drukket.

33 The impersonal 'it' and 'that': 'it's raining'

Det plays a versatile role in Danish as an *impersonal* – mainly with the meaning of 'it' but frequently meaning 'that' as well.

Det precedes *impersonal verbs:*

Det regner.
It rains/is raining
Det øser ned. It's pouring (down).
Det stormer.
It is blowing a gale.
Det sner.
It is snowing.
Uha, det lyner og tordner.
Ugh, there is lightning and thunder.
Det klør.
I've got an itch.
Det går dårligt.
Things are going badly (it goes badly).

Det er godt – vi trænger til det.
That's good – we need it.
Det er godt, (at) det virker.
It's good that it functions.
Det siges, at vi får en kold vinter.
It is said that we will be getting a cold winter.
Det var mig, som gjorde det.
It was I/me who did it.

The equivalent of the English impersonal 'there' is **der**.

Der skrives så meget sludder.
There is so much nonsense written.
Der er ingen tvivl om hans ærlighed.
There is no doubt about his honesty.

Some expressions which are personal in English are impersonal in Danish:

Det glæder mig at høre det.
I am pleased (It pleases me) to hear that.

Det – or, colloquially, **den** – is used in endless phrases to replace an entire statement, much like 'it', 'so' and 'that' in English.

Hav det sjovt – og rart.
Have fun – and a nice time.
Den går ikke, gamle dreng.
That won't do, old boy.
Er du træt? Det er jeg også.
Are you tired? So am I.
Det skal guderne vide!
Goodness knows (the gods must know it)!

Storm P. demonstrating a couple of points:

– Hvorfor mon sneen er hvid?
– Ellers kan man ikke se, at det er sne.
...
– Tilfældigheder eksisterer ikke, husk det, hvis De tilfældigvis skulle støde på en.

– I wonder why (the) snow is white.
– Otherwise one cannot see that it is snow.
. . .
– Coincidences don't exist – remember that if you happen to (coincidentally) come across one.

34 Compounds

You will already have noticed a few long Danish words which in English require two or more to say the same thing. Basically, when two or more words are used together to mean one thing, in Danish they are 'compounded' into one word: (**brugtvognsforhandleren** 'the used car dealer' from **brugt** = 'used', **vogn** = 'carriage, car', **forhandleren** = 'the dealer'). As a result, there are very many more compounds in Danish than in English, but in all likelihood they will cause you little or no trouble.

The gender of a compounded noun is determined by its last component, as in **bilværksted** ('garage') which, translated literally, is 'car work place'. **Bil** is of common gender (**bilen**), but the neuter **sted** decides the whole: **et bilværksted, bilværkstedet**. Normally only the last component changes in the plural: **bilværksteder.**

When nouns are joined to form compounds, an **s** , **e** or **er** is often inserted as a link:

fabriksarbejdere	factory workers
landbrugsskole	agricultural school
barnevogn	pram
pariserrejserne	the Paris trips
højesteretsdommer	supreme court judge
en tresætskamp	at three-set match
trediveårskrigen	the Thirty Years' War

All kinds of words can be compounded, and we have included only a small selection here. Remember always to make any changes in ending, etc. only in the last component:

mørkegrå	dark grey	**lyseblå**	light blue
blødsøden	sloppy (soft-sweet)	**stenhård**	stone-hard
ungkarl	bachelor	**hurtigtog**	fast train
hjemvendt	returned home	**musikelsker**	music lover
udenfor	outside	**bagved**	behind
underetage	lower floor	**overnatte**	to stay overnight

More members of the family:

lillebror	little brother	**storebror**	big brother
bedstefar	grandfather	**bedstemødre**	grandmothers
oldefædre	great-grandfathers	**oldemødre**	great-grand-mothers
halvsøstrene	the half-sisters	**halvbrødrene**	the half-brothers
svigersøn	son-in-law	**svigerdatter**	daughter-in-law
barnebarn	grandchild	**børnebørn**	grandchildren

(This last example is one of the very few where the plural influences the first part of the compound!)

Vocabulary

Rather than translating the compounds for you, we are providing you with the parts that go to make them up, and you must work out the compounds for yourself.

fart (-en)	motion, speed, (sailing) trip
skib (-et, -e)	ship
passager (-en, -er)	passenger
færge (-n, -r)	ferry
at nyde*	to enjoy
at danse	to dance
orkester (-et, orkestre)	orchestra
en hel del	a lot
told (-en)	(customs) duty
forresten	by the way
at dele (-te, -t)	to share
lærer (-en, -e)	(male) teacher
Fyn	Funen

forlovet	engaged
fanatisk	fanatical
luft (-en)	air
sport (-en)	sport(s)
gal	mad
død	dead
kedelig	boring
indkøb (-et, -)	purchase, shopping
at trække* vejr	to draw breath, breathe

Exercise 30

Translate:

Inge Hoff **Velkommen til Esbjerg og Danmark, var det en god overfart?**

Ted Young **Skibet er den bedste passagerfærge, jeg har været på, og vi nød det ungarske danseorkester.**

Inge Hoff **Ja, og maden var god, men måske lidt dyr, ikke?**

Ted Young **Nej, det synes jeg nu ikke, men vi drak en hel del af den toldfrie vin for at spare! Forresten, ved morgenmaden delte vi bord med en højskolelærer fra Fyn, der kender dig og din mand. Han hed Frank Henriksen.**

Inge Hoff **Ja, jeg var engang forlovet med ham. Men han er fanatisk friluftsmenneske og sportsgal – og dødkedelig. Kom, følg nu efter mig til min indkøbsbil, der har vejrtrækningsproblemer.**

35 More prepositions

Returning to the different uses of key prepositions:

for for
Åbn dåsen for mig.
Open the can for me.
Søg ly for blæsten.
Take shelter from the wind.
Den er god for tandpine.
It is good for/against toothache.
Har du brug for mig lige nu?
Do you need (have use for) me just now?
dag for dag day by day
at bo for sig selv to live on one's own
Hvad er det for noget?
What is that?
Jeg ku' ikke gøre for det.
I couldn't help it/It wasn't my fault.

for at is 'to' in the sense of 'in order to':

Han gik ud for at reparere taget.
He went out to repair the roof.
Jeg kommer for at hente dig.
I'm coming to pick you up (fetch you).

hos with, at
Mor er hos bedstemor.
Mother is at Granny's.
Hos mig er du i sikkerhed.
With me you are safe (in safety).
Man får det bedste brød hos bageren.
You get the best bread at the baker's.

med with
Tag med tog.
Go by train.
Du med dine klager, gå med dig!
You and your complaints, be off with you!
med andre ord in other words

Hun lærer det med tiden.
She will learn, in time.
Skidt med det!
Never mind.

over over, across, about
På kortet over London ser du broen over Themsen.
On the map of London you see the bridge over the Thames.
Klag over det.
Complain about it.
Vi vandt over dem.
We defeated (won over) them.
Er du kommet over din forkølelse?
Have you got over your cold?

til to, for
De kom til byen.
They came to the town.
Der er telefon til dig.
There's a phone call for you.
til gavn for landet for the benefit of the country
Hvad siger du til det?
What do you think of (say to) that?
Til venstre er kirken.
To the left is the church.

til at comes into play with adjectives and verbs:
Nu er du god til at læse dansk.
Now you are good at reading Danish.
Jeg er vant til at blive adlydt.
I am used to being obeyed.
Folk var nødt til at spise bark.
People had to eat bark.
Jeg skulle lige til at gøre det. I was just about to do it.
Har du lagt mærke til, at det er meget dyrere end for ti år siden at leve over evne?
Have you noticed that it is much more expensive than ten years ago to live above your means?
Undskyld, jeg kom til at drikke din champagne.
Sorry, I happened to drink your champagne.

Vocabulary

kold	cold
blæsende	windy
pelskåbe (-n, -r)	fur coat
at betale (-te, -t)	to pay
at betale sig	to pay, be worth it
varm	warm
handske (-n, -r)	glove
ked af det	sorry
dyreven (-nen, -ner)	animal lover
at foretrække*	to prefer
at beholde*	to keep
at hjælpe*	to help
børnehave (-n, -r)	nursery school
samme	same
slankekur (-en, -e)	slimming treatment
nede	down

CONVERSATION

Else **Hvad giver du mig i julegave i år, Henrik?**

Henrik **Det må jeg sige! Du begynder tidligt, Else, det er den tredie maj i dag.**

Else **Jamen, det er koldt og blæsende udenfor, det minder mig om vinteren, og Agnes' mand har købt en pelskåbe til hende nu, fordi det kan betale sig – de er billigere om sommeren.**

Henrik **Det kan godt være, men det er gode, varme handsker også. Jeg er ked af det, men jeg er pludselig blevet en stor dyreven, og pelsdyr foretrækker at beholde deres varme tøj. Hvem er Agnes, forresten?**

Else **Det er en dame, der sommetider hjælper mig i børnehaven, vi er på samme slankekur.**

Henrik **Godt: Du får din pels, når du er nede på den samme vægt, som da du begyndte kuren! Man bør jo betale mindre for en mindre kåbe . . .**

TRANSLATION

Else **What are you giving me as a Christmas present this year, Henrik?**

Henrik **(That) I must say! You're starting early, Else, it is the third of May today.**

Else **Yes, but it is cold and windy outside, that reminds me of the winter, and Agnes' husband has bought a fur coat for her now because it pays – they are cheaper in the summer.**

Henrik **That may well be but so are good, warm gloves. I am sorry but I have suddenly become a great animal lover (friend), and fur-bearing animals prefer to keep their warm clothes. Who is Agnes, by the way?**

Else **She (that) is a lady who sometimes helps me in the nursery school, we are on the same slimming treatment.**

Henrik **Good: you'll get your fur coat when you're down at the same weight as when you began the course! A smaller coat ought to cost less (one ought to pay less for smaller coat) . . .**

Chapter 11

This chapter expands on some earlier topics, introducing:

- *fractions ('a quarter', etc.) and collective numbers ('a dozen', etc.)*
- *adverbs for expressing where something is or which way it is moving*
- *adverbs used in idiomatic ways that have no direct translation in English*
- *conjunctions and adverbs used in pairs, such as 'both . . . and', 'as . . . as'*
- *some pairs of nouns that may catch you out.*

36 Fractions and collective numbers

Fractions follow a pattern close to the English but it must be remembered that **halv** 'half' is an adjective, so is influenced by the gender of the noun.

På en halv dag spiste de et halvt får.
In half a day they ate half a sheep.
Den halve dag brugtes til træning.
Half the day was used for training.

But you can also say **halvdelen** 'the half part':

Grossereren købte halvdelen af beholdningen.
The wholesaler bought half the stock.

As in English, other fractions can also be expressed in different ways:

en kvart or **en fjerdedel**	one fourth/one quarter
trekvart or **tre fjerdedele**	three quarters
en/én trediedel	a/one third

En fjerdedel af appelsinerne var rådne.
One fourth of the oranges were rotten.

Smaller fractions use the **del** ('part') ending:

to femtedele	two fifths

Remember **halvanden/halvandet**, meaning 'one and a half' (or **én og en halv/ét og et halvt**).

to trekvart	two and three quarters
tre en halv	three and a half

Any noun with fractions is in the singular, not the plural: **tre en halv kage** three and a half cakes

Moving into descriptions of groups:

et par	a couple
et dusin	a dozen
en snes	a score

enkelt	single
dobbelt	double
tredobbelt	threefold
seksdobbelt	sixfold

Vocabulary

lektion (-en, -er)	lesson
at huske	to remember
mindst	at least
ret	quite, rather
fremskridt (-et, -)	progress
nok	enough, probably
lydbånd (-et, -)	audiotape
ikke ret	not very
hele tiden	all the time

at bruge (-te, -t)	to use, spend
undersøgelser	investigations, research
rapport (-en, -er)	report
rigtig	really
konklusion (-en, -er)	conclusion
at indbyde*	to invite
at holde* tale	to make a speech
i hvert fald	in any case, at any rate

Exercise 31

Translate:

– Nu har du arbejdet med at lære dansk i to en halv måned, hvordan går det?
– Det går ganske godt, jeg har gjort tre fjerdedele af lektionerne og jeg kan huske mindst treogtyve ord! Nej, jeg gør ret gode fremskridt, men jeg skulle læse mere og øve mig mere. Jeg har bare ikke tid nok.
– Har du ikke et lydbånd, som du kan bruge i bilen?
– Jo, men jeg kører ikke ret tit mere, jeg sidder jo hjemme og skriver hele tiden. Så det er ikke så dårligt, når jeg alligevel bruger tre kvarter om dagen på mit dansk.
– Åh ja, du skriver jo om dine undersøgelser. Er du ikke færdig med din rapport endnu?
– Nej, jeg kan ikke rigtig komme til en konklusion. Men det sker nok snart. Og så skal der være fest, og jeg indbyder selvfølgelig også dig!
– Tak, og så holder du tale på dansk, ikke?
– Det siger du, fordi du ved, at den så i hvert fald bliver kort!

37 Adverbs of place and movement

One intriguing group of adverbs indicates the direction of a movement or, with an **e** added, the place where something is:

gik bort	went away
var borte	was away/gone
gik hjem	went/walked home
blev hjemme	stayed at home
gå frem	walk forward
vi er fremme	we've got there
kom ind!	come in!
vi er lukket inde	we're locked in
ud med dig	out you go
vi er ude	we're out

op(pe)	up(wards)
over/ovre	over, past
hen(ne)	over (to)

The little word **hen** plays a key role when Danes move *to* something. It has no exact equivalent in English, though 'over' comes near:

Hun gik hen til vinduet.
She went (over) to the window.
Gå hen til bageren for mig.
Go to the baker for me.

If you just said **gik til** and **gå til**, it would mean 'walk' rather than using some other means of moving.

When the move requires 'here' or 'there', the little **hen** is required again: **herhen** or **derhen**. 'Where to' is **hvorhen/hvor . . . hen**, and 'where from' is **hvorfra/hvor . . . fra.**

Jeg gik ikke derhen.
I did not go there.
Hvor kommer du fra?
Where do you come/are you coming from?
Hvor skal du hen?
Where are you going?

Hvorfra, sagde du?
From where, did you say?

On the odd occasion, you may want to use 'come over here' **kom herover** or 'go over here' **gå derover** or other combinations with **der/her** and **ud, ind, op, ned.**

Once you've arrived, or if you are speaking of something which is permanently 'over there', 'up here', etc., the **e** ending applies: **derhenne, herovre, herude, herinde, heroppe, hernede.**

derovre på den anden flodbred
over there on the other river bank
Derhenne ligger gården.
Over there is the farm.
Herude er luften ren.
Out here, the air is clean.

Other adverbs describing moves are:

tilbage	back
fremad	forwards

And combinations:

herfra from here	**derfra** from there
hertil to here	**dertil** to there

Vocabulary

hegn (-et, -)	fence
at lukke ind/ud	to let in/out
at lukke inde/ude	to lock in/out, shut in/out
filosofisk	philosophical
at kigge indenfor	to look in, drop in
at mangle	to lack
logik (-ken)	logic

Exercise 32

Translate:

To Storm P.-mænd taler til hinanden gennem et højt hegn:
– De kan vel ikke lukke mig ud?
– Jo, hvis. De kan lukke mig ind.

Men hvis den mand, der er lukket inde, havde svart nej, ville den anden mand være lukket ude.

Filosofisk mand:
– Når man siger 'kig indenfor, når du går forbi', mangler man logik.

38 Some idiomatic uses of adverbs

It is said that Jutlanders – like Yorkshiremen – never overstate and that **Det er ikke for dårligt** ('It's not too bad') is their highest praise. It is certainly in the nature of the down-to-earth Danes to use plenty of weakening adverbs. Though you will recognise many of these adverbs, used in this way they are very hard to translate into English, where the equivalent often lies in the way the sentence is said.

bare (only)
Nu skal du bare se!
Let me really show you something!
Du kan bare prøve!
Don't you dare (You just try!)
BUT **Du skulle bare prøve . . .**
. . . You ought to try . . .

nu (now)
Han gør det nu godt.
He actually does do it well.
Vi har nu ikke taget det hele.
In fact we did not take all of it.
Det ved jeg nu ikke, hvad jeg skal sige til.
Oh, I'm not too sure I agree.

da (then)
Det kan du da ikke!
Surely you can't do that!
Den er da dejlig.
Oh, it *is* lovely.
Kan du da ikke lade være?
Really, *can't* you stop?

jo (after all)
Du kunne jo godt!
So you *were* able to!
Det regner jo hele tiden.
It rains all the time, you see./After all, it does rain all the time.

mon (I wonder)
Hvem mon det er?
I wonder who that is.
Mon ikke vi skulle flyve?
Don't you think we should fly?

nok (enough)
Det lykkes nok for jer.
You will probably succeed.
Det er godt nok farligt.
It is, admittedly, dangerous.
Du er nok meget sikker på dig selv!
You seem to be very sure of yourself!
Det skal nok passe.
I dare say you're right.
Det må du nok sige!
How right you are!

vel (well)
Du er vel ikke gravid?
I hope you're not pregnant?
Det er vel løgn?
It's a lie, I take it?
De er ikke onde, vel?
They are not evil, are they?
Det er vel nok en dejlig flæskesteg.
I dare say it is a lovely pork joint.

nemlig (in fact)
Nej, det er nemlig slet ikke dårligt.
No, it's not bad at all, actually.
De er nemlig de helt rigtige musikere.
They are just the right musicians, you see.

39 Parallel conjunctions and adverbs – 'both . . . and'

Just as in English, conjunctions and adverbs are sometimes used in pairs:

både . . . og	both . . . and
enten . . . eller	either . . . or
hverken . . . eller	neither . . . nor

and in comparisons:

(lige) så . . . som	(just) as . . . as
ikke så . . . som	not as . . . as
jo (mere) . . . des (mere)	the (more) . . . the (more)

Det var både godt og dårligt, at Peter ikke gik i skole i dag. Han lærte ganske vist ikke noget nyt, men han læste meget, og han reddede kanariefuglen fra at blive ædt af en kat! Jo mere jeg tænker over det, des mere overbevist bliver jeg om, at han hverken egner sig til universitetsstudier eller til at blive forretningsmand. Men han er stærk – han er lige så kraftig som sin far – og hans hænder er skruet godt på. Derfor tror jeg, at han enten bliver håndværker eller noget, der har med udendørsliv at gøre.

It was both good and bad that Peter didn't go to school today. He admittedly did not learn anything new but he read a lot and he saved the canary from being eaten by a cat! The more I think about it, the more convinced I am that he is suited neither to university studies nor to becoming a businessman. But he is strong – he is just as strongly built as his father – and his hands are screwed on well. Therefore I think that he will either become a craftsman or something which has to do with outdoor life.

Han er ikke så klog, som han selv tror.
He is not as clever as he thinks (he is).
Jo . . . des can equally well be **jo . . . jo** or **des . . . des.**
Jo/Des mere jeg tjener, jo/des mere bruger jeg.
The more I earn, the more I spend (use).

Vocabulary

grim	ugly
heller ikke	not . . . either
uhøflig	rude
at se på	to look at
frihed (-en, -er)	freedom
religiøs	religious
interesseret	interested
politik (-ken)	politics
fag (-et, -)	trade, subject

Exercise 33

Translate into Danish:

1 Is your friend as rich as he is ugly?
2 No, he is not as rude as you are, either.
3 The more I look at her, the more I love my freedom.
4 That family is neither religious nor interested in politics.
5 Both Romeo and Juliet work in the theatre trade.
6 I neither read nor practise as much (in) Danish as I had wished.

40 Teaser nouns

A limited number of nouns are found in common as well as neuter gender, with a different meaning in each:

en frø (-er) a frog	**et frø (-)** a seed
en nøgle (-r) a key	**et nøgle (-r)** a ball of yarn
en søm (-me) a seam	**et søm (-)** a nail

en øl (-ler) a (bottle of) beer	**øllet** the beer
en øre (-) the smallest coin	**et øre (-r)** an ear

And watch out: whereas **brød** on its own is 'bread', **et brød** is 'a loaf of bread'.

Vocabulary

gade (-n, -r)	street
offentlig	public
toilet (-tet, -ter)	toilet
side (-n, -r)	side
at passe på	to be careful
at stoppe	to stop
midt i	in the middle of
trafik (-ken)	traffic
fortov (-et, -e)	pavement
at fortsætte*	to continue
lige ud	straight on
venstre	left
at hilse (-te, -t)	to greet (give regards to)
længere fremme	further on
parkeringshus (-et, -e)	multi-storey car park
nærmere	closer
meter (-en, -)	metre
at ringe	to ring
lukket	closed
at forklare	to explain
at sende (-te, -t)	to send
at krydse	to cross
park (-en, -er)	park
trappe (-n)	staircase, steps
hånd (-en, hænder)	hand
uha!	oh dear!
må endelig ikke	must be sure not to

CONVERSATION

På gaden

Dame på indkøb **Vær venlig at sige mig, hvor der er et offentligt toilet.**

Avismand **Selvfølgelig, og hurtigt, ikke? Se, du skal lige gå over på den anden side af gaden dér – pas godt på, lad være med at stoppe midt i trafikken. Når du er på det andet fortov, skal du gå til højre. Fortsæt lige ud, til det første hjørne. Drej til venstre – og hils den blomstersælger, der står lidt længere fremme, fra mig. Spørg ham, hvor parkeringshuset er, og dér er der toiletter.**

Damen **Mange tak, men er der ikke et nærmere sted? Og jeg har ikke en bil, så hvordan kan jeg bruge bilparkeringen?**

Manden **Åh, jo, forresten er der en kafé med en rar ejer kun hundrede meter borte. Ring eller bank på, hvis den er lukket, og forklar ham, af Steffen har sendt dig. Kryds over den lille park dér til højre, fortsæt op ad den lille trappe, og på højre hånd ligger 'Eriks Kaffekop'. Skynd dig nu!**

Damen **Uha, ja, farvel, og tak. Nej, giv mig lige "Alt for Damerne".**

Manden **Værsgo, men betal, når du kommer tilbage, du må endelig ikke komme for sent!**

TRANSLATION

In the street

Lady, shopping	**Please tell me where there is a public toilet.**
Newspaper man	**Of course, and quickly, yes? Look, you must just walk over to the other side of the street there – be careful, don't stop in the middle of the traffic. When you are on the other pavement, you must turn right. Continue straight on, to the corner. Turn left – and give my regards to the flower seller who is standing a little further on. Ask him where the multi-storey car park is, there are toilets there.**
Lady	**Many thanks, but is there no place closer? And I haven't got a car, so how can I use the car park?**
The man	**Oh yes, as it happens there is a café with a kind owner only a hundred metres away. Ring or knock if it is closed and explain to him that Steffen has sent you. Cross the little park there on the right and continue up the little staircase and on the right is (lies) 'Erik's Coffee Cup'. Hurry, now!**
The lady	**Oh dear, yes, and thanks. No, just give me "Everything for the ladies" (Danish magazine).**
The man	**There you are, but pay when you come back, you must be sure not to be too late!**

Chapter 12

This final chapter returns to verbs and also gives you some help with writing Danish. It covers:

- *some verbs which are only used in the passive form, or have special meanings in the passive*
- *verbs used as adjectives and as nouns*
- *some features of Danish punctuation*
- *letter-writing conventions*
- *how to expand your vocabulary by means of common prefixes and suffixes, the equivalents of 'un-', 'over-', '-ly' and so on.*

41 More verbs ending in s

A few Danish verbs occur in the passive **s** form only, including:

enes agree
lykkes succeed
længe (efter) long (for)
mislykkes fail

Det enes de aldrig om, selvom de længes efter fred.
They will never agree about that, even though they long for peace.

Notice that **lykkes** and **mislykkes** are impersonal verbs, used with **det:**

Det lykkedes ham at lære dansk.
He succeeded in learning Danish.
Nej, det mislykkedes, han brugte et andet kursus.
No, it was a failure, he used another course.

Other verbs can have the sense of 'each other' when used with the passive **s:**

de ses ofte they see each other often
vi ses! see you (we'll see each other)
de mødes they meet (each other)
drengene slås the boys are fighting (each other)
de skændes they are quarrelling

And some others can have a special meaning with the passive **s:**

der findes they are
det synes it seems
jeg synes I think, I am of the opinion that
synes du om . . . ? do you like . . .?

Learners often confuse **synes** and **tro: at tro** is 'to think' in the sense of 'believe' (**tro på** 'believe in'), whereas **synes** is expressing an opinion. The verb **mene** covers both meanings.

Vocabulary

ret (-ten, -ter)	dish, course
at komme* op at slås	to come to blows
at komme* an på	to depend on
forret (-ten, -ter)	starter, first course
at slå* til	to be enough
spisekort (-et, -)	menu
spændende	exciting
at studere	to study
vinkort (-et, -)	wine list
imens	meanwhile
moms	VAT
betjening (-en)	service
pris (-en, -er)	price
halvgammel	oldish
bagefter	afterwards
begge (dele)	both
at interessere	to interest
lige meget	equally

flødesovs (-en)	cream sauce
citronfromage (-n, -r)	lemon mousse
flødeskum (-men)	whipped cream
jordbær (-ret, -)	strawberry
evig	eternal
laksepaté (-en, -er)	salmon paté

Exercise 34

Translate:

– Kan vi enes om kun at spise to retter? Eller synes du, det er for lidt?
– Det kommer vi ikke op at slås om – eller bare skændes om. Men det kommer noget an på, hvad det er, du vælger – en lille forret og en endnu mindre dessert slår nok ikke til!
– Her er spisekortet, se, om der er noget spændende, så studerer jeg vinkortet imens. Der er både moms og betjening med i prisen.
– Jeg synes ikke, der findes noget bedre end en ung Sauvignon og en halvgammel Rioja – men måske du hellere vil vælge maden først og vinen bagefter?
– Desværre ses det på os begge, at begge dele interesserer os lige meget. Men jeg vil gerne have kylling i flødesovs og citronfromage med masser af flødeskum og jordbær – du bryder dig ikke om dessert, men jeg venter, mens du får din evige laksepaté.
– Tak, og vi mødes igen ved kaffen, om jeg så må sige.
– Du må sige næsten, hvad du vil – du betaler – men husk, at du skal køre, hvis du ved, hvad jeg mener.
– Farvel, vinglas nummer tre og min Drambuie. Vi ses, når det er min kære kones tur til at køre.

42 Verbs used in other ways

Just as in English, verbs can become adjectives in one of two ways. The past participle is often used as an adjective:

et renset gulv a cleaned floor
en nybygget gård a newly built farm
det malede ansigt the painted face
alle hvidkalkede huse all whitewashed houses

In English, the 'ing' form of the verb is often used as an adjective or adverb. Danish has an equivalent: simply add **nde** to the infinitive (or **ende** if the infinitive ends with a stressed vowel):

det blødende hjerte the bleeding heart
Hun er en kommende stjerne.
  She is a rising (coming star).
den eksisterende regel the existing rule
på mine skrivende dage on my writing days
Er det en hårdtarbejdende assistent?
  Is that a hard-working assistant?
det flammende bål the flaming bonfire
det rejsende publikum the travelling public
den voksende utilfredshed the growing dissatisfaction
Han kom løbende over græsplænen.
  He came running across the lawn.

But the **ende** ending is not as common as 'ing' in sentences like the last one. Look at these two:

Hunden ligger ved ilden og slikker sin pote.
  The dog lies by the fire, licking its paw.
Hun gik rundt og spredte rygter.
  She went round spreading rumours.

Adjectives formed from verbs can also act as nouns, in which case they take the separate definite article **den, det, de** rather than the definite ending:

De rejsende standsede.
  The travellers stopped.

De besøgende gik meget stille.
The visitors walked very quietly.
Rejsendes bagage skal afleveres.
Travellers' luggage must be handed over.
Besøgendes indgang er til højre.
The visitors' entrance is to the right.

The infinitive **at . . .** is sometimes used as a noun, where in English the 'ing' ending is common:

Små piger elsker at hoppe.
Little girls love jumping.
Drengene er ude at lege.
The boys are out playing.
Hr. Madsen nyder at arbejde i haven.
Mr Madsen enjoys working in the garden.
At ryge er farligt for helbredet.
Smoking is dangerous to (the) health.
Jeg glæder mig til at se dig.
I am looking forward to seeing you.
Efter at have talt med min kone, . . .
After having talked to my wife . . .

Vocabulary

at restaurere	to restore
at kalke	to whitewash
kostald (-en, -e)	cowshed
at skinne	to shine
centrum (centret, centrer)	centre
at male	to paint
rude (-n, -r)	pane (of glass)
bly (-et)	lead
at indfatte	to frame
at lyse (-te, -t)	to shine
syn (-et, -)	sight

Exercise 35

In the following passage, replace the infinitives (in italics) with the appropriate form of the verb as adjective. In some cases you will need to make compounds. Remember to put the correct endings on all the adjectives.

På min gamle, men *restaurere* (1) gård er den *kalke* (2) kostald et s*kinne* (3) hvidt centrum. Døren er rød*male* (4), ruderne bly*indfatte* (5), og om aftenen er de *lyse* (6) vinduer et dejligt syn.

43 When you write Danish

While correct punctuation matters little unless you wish to use your Danish professionally, it may be helpful in both writing and reading if you learn about a few differences from English.

Punctuation is much more strictly governed by grammatical rules than in English, and the comma in particular is used much more, often to mark separate clauses, which can be helpful.

Vi indbød dem, men de sagde nej tak.
We invited them but they said no, thank you.
De er dygtige, selvom de ikke kan stave.
They are clever although they cannot spell.

In figures, remember that the use of full stop and comma is the reverse of English practice:
10,234.56 in Danish is **10.234,56.**

The date is written like this: **den 8. maj, den 25. december, 8.** being a short form for **ottende.**

There is no equivalent to the traditional English letter opening: 'Dear Sir(s)'. Writing to a firm, you go straight into the text unless you know somebody by their title and name.

Only recently have Danes begun to address someone they don't know with **Kære** 'Dear', and if you are writing to an unknown 'Director Bent Sørensen', you may start with **Hr. direktør Sørensen.** You will sometimes see either form followed by an exclamation mark.

In any case, you end with **Med venlig hilsen** 'kind regards' or, if you want to be extremely formal, **Med højagtelse** 'with high esteem'. In informal letters, you may find phrases like **Mange venlige hils(e)ner, Deres/din hengivne . . . , hengiven** meaning 'devoted'. Friends write phrases such as **Kærlig hilsen,** 'loving greetings'.

On the envelope, you use full title or profession – however 'humble' – and the number of the house follows the name of the street.

'Mr' is **herr** (now in writing normally kept brief: **hr.**). 'Mrs' is **fru** and 'Miss' is **frøken,** abbreviate as **frk.** 'Ms' is **fr** which no one attempts to pronounce!

Vocabulary

at acceptere	to accept
at lede (-te, -t) efter	to look for
lejlighed (-en, -er)	flat
at leje	to rent
hjælp (-en)	help
at takke	to thank
varmt	warmly
at lære (-te, -t) at kende	to get to know

Exercise 36

Translate the following letter into Danish. We have given you a few hints in brackets. Leave out words in square brackets [ ]. Good luck!

Dear Mr Ramsing,
Many thanks for your letter with [the] offer of (**om**) a job in your firm in Copenhagen. After having talked to my wife, I am pleased (it pleases me) to accept and to let you know that I can in fact begin [on] 15 June.
In (**om**) two weeks, from 7 April, I am taking a week's holiday and I would like to fly to Denmark with my wife so that we can begin to look for a flat or a house we can rent – will it be possible for someone in the firm to give us a little help? If it is, I will write a letter to him or her and describe what we are thinking of (**på**) and would prefer.
I thank you again warmly for your offer and look forward very much to getting to know you, your firm and your country.
With kind regards from my wife and myself,

44 Word building – prefixes and suffixes

The most widespread Danish prefix for the negative form of the adjectives is **u** (**ulykkelig**), even more frequently used than the English 'un' (unhappy): **ufarlig, usmuk, usnobbet** ('not dangerous', 'not pretty', 'not snobbish').

uselskabelig unsociable
ulydig disobedient
utilfredsstillende unsatisfactory
ulækker 'unappetizing' but figuratively 'repulsive'

The English 'non-' prefix in Danish is **ikke-**:

De ulærte er som regel ikke-læsere.
The uneducated as a rule are non-readers.

But you will also see the prefix **mis:**

mislykket unsuccessful
misforstået misunderstood
miskredit discredit
mistillid distrust
misinformere misinform (taken from English)

While 'anti' is the same in Danish, the prefix **mod** (against) mostly covers 'counter':

modoffensiv counteroffensive
modarbejde counteract
modforslag counterproposal

Over and **under** are common prefixes, just as in English:

overtræt over-tired
overanstrengt overworked
overbærende indulgent
overmalet painted over
overløber defector (runner-over)
underbetalt underpaid
underernæret undernourished

The English 'ly' ending has a close relative in the Danish **lig.** It is found in indications of time where the ending is added to a noun:

daglig daily
ugentlig weekly
månedlig monthly
årlig yearly

en daglig pligt a daily duty
et årligt marathonløb an annual marathon
min daglige rutine my daily routine

The same suffix, added to the end of a colour, is like 'ish' in English.

rødlig reddish
blålig blueish

The idea of trying to give people the same title whether they are female or male is perhaps less advanced in Denmark than in English-speaking countries. In Danish, **inde** or **ske** added to the end of a position or job description indicates that it is held by a woman, like 'ess' in English:

skuespiller actor	**skuespillerinde** actress
sygeplejer male nurse	**sygeplejerske** nurse
lærer teacher	**lærerinde** schoolmistress
ven male friend, boyfriend	**veninde** female friend, girl-friend
vært host	**værtinde** hostess

Vocabulary

kontinent (-et, -er)	continent
højrekørsel (-en)	driving on the right
fører (-en, -e)	driver
rat (-tet, -)	steering wheel
færdselsregel (-en, -regler)	traffic regulation
påvirket	influenced
heraf	by this
at ligne	to resemble
britisk	British
skilt (-et, -e)	sign
europæisk	European
standard (-en, -er)	standard
køretøj (-et, -er)	vehicle
rundkørsel (-en, -er)	roundabout
overalt	everywhere
at lægge mærke til	to notice, observe
fartgrænse (-n, -r)	speed limit
sprirituskørsel	drinking and driving
at straffe	to punish
streng	strict, severe
uhyre	hugely
selskab (-et, -er)	party
alkoholisk	alcoholic
hundredtusinder	hundreds of thousands
at cykle	to cycle
sti (-en, -er)	path
at skille (-te, -t)	to separate
kørebane (-n, -r)	carriageway, roadway
udbredt	widespread, common
vigtig	important
bilist (-en, -er)	motorist
at respektere	to respect

gadekryds (-et, -)	crossroads
trafiklys (-et, -)	traffic lights
fodgænger (-en, -e)	pedestrian
lastbil (-en, -er)	lorry
varebil (-en, -er)	(goods) van
osv. (og så videre)	etc. (and so on)
respekt (-en)	respect
fodgængerovergang (-en, -e)	pedestrian crossing

READING

I trafikken

I Danmark som på resten af kontinentet har man højrekørsel, så føreren og rattet i en bil sidder i venstre side. Færdselsreglerne er selvfølgelig påvirket heraf, men ligner ellers meget de britiske, og skiltene følger europæisk standard i begge lande. Husk, at køretøjer og cykler, der er i en rundkørsel, kommer fra venstre.

Man bruger kilometer som overalt på kontinentet, og det skal man lægge mærke til, når man lærer fartgrænserne, der er noget lavere end de britiske. Spirituskørsel straffes meget strengt, og det er uhyre almindeligt ved selskaber, at kun den ene af et par drikker noget alkoholisk.

Hundredtusinder af danskere cykler, og cykelstier – helt skilt fra kørebanen – er stærkt udbredt, og det er vigtigt for bilister at respektere dem.

I gadekryds med trafiklys går fodgængere aldrig over for rødt lys, med mindre de er udlændinge – og desværre viser hverken privatbiler, taxaer, lastbiler, varebiler, busser osv. stor respekt for fodgængerovergange.

TRANSLATION

In (the) traffic

In Denmark, as on the rest of the Continent, one drives on the right (there is driving on the right), so the driver and the steering wheel in the car are (sit) on the left side. The traffic regulations are of course influenced by this, but otherwise much resemble the British (ones), and the signs follow European standard(s) in both countries. Remember that vehicles and bicycles which are on a roundabout come from (the) left.

Kilometres are used, as everywhere on the Continent, and you must notice this when you learn the speed limits, which are somewhat lower than the British (ones). Drinking and driving is severely punished and it is hugely common at parties that only one of a couple drinks anything alcoholic.

Hundreds of thousands of Danes cycle, and cycle paths – completely separated from the roadway – are very widespread and it is important for motorists to respect them.

At crossroads with traffic lights pedestrians never cross against the red light unless they are foreigners – and unfortunately, (neither) private cars, taxis, lorries, vans, buses and so on (don't) show great respect for pedestrian crossings.

Storm P.

Storm P. elskede at bruge småforbrydere og vagabonder i sine historier, og de sidste blev normalt udstyret med gamle græske navne som Arkimedes og Sokrates. Hvis alle danskere blev bedt om at fortælle deres to yndlingsvittigheder, ville langt de fleste sikkert bruge to af hans, men den ene ville dog være om en laps, der dovent og uinteresseret – bare for at sige noget – spørger en anden:
– Hvad mener du om verdenssituationen?
– Det ved jeg ikke, jeg har en flue i øjet.

Den anden Flue vender tilbage til vagabonder:
– Er du lykkelig, Herodot?
– Ikke helt – jeg mangler syv øre!

Storm P. loved to use petty criminals and tramps in his stories and the latter were normally equipped with old Greek names such as Archimedes and Socrates. If all Danes were asked to tell their two favourite jokes, by far the most would probably use two of his, though one of them would be about a dandy who, lazily and uninterested – just to say something – asks another:
– What do you think of the world situation?
– I don't know, I've got a fly in my eye.

The other Fly goes back to tramps:
– Are you happy, Herodotus?
– Not completely – I'm seven **øre** short!

Key to exercises

Chapter 1

Exercise 1: 1 vinduet 2 gulvet 3 lampen 4 klubhuset 5 murstenen 6 fabrikken 7 knæet 8 bageren 9 bogen 10 ægget

Exercise 2: 1 dreng – drenge – drengene 2 top – toppe – toppene 3 hund – hunde – hundene 4 by – byer – byerne 5 familie – familier – familierne 6 skotte – skotter – skotterne 7 dansker – danskere – danskerne 8 ske – skeer – skeerne 9 soldat – soldater – soldaterne 10 tag – tage – tagene 11 æg – æg – æggene 12 pas – pas – passene 13 kys – kys – kyssene 14 tæppe – tæpper – tæpperne 15 hold – hold – holdene 16 forsøg – forsøg – forsøgene 17 ideal – idealer – idealerne 18 dyr – dyr – dyrene

Chapter 2

Exercise 3: He talks a lot (much) but says only little. 2 Spring is coming soon. 3 I see the train coming. 4 The dog barks and bites. 5 They tell about the camels in the Zoological Garden. 6 The baker sells Danish pastries (Danish pastry). 7 We sing about a farmer and his animals. 8 I laugh a lot (much) when I see Victor Borge. 9 The hen lays two eggs – there they lie. 10 He falls and hits his knee (the knee).

Exercise 4: 1 mig, dig 2 os 3 mig 4 jer, mig 5 hinanden 6 hende 7 hinanden

Exercise 5: 1 Hans og Grete, vi elsker jer. 2 Hans og Grete elsker hinanden. 3 Jeg kalder dig en kujon. 4 De giver vinen til hende. 5 Jeg spørger dem, og de svarer mig. 6 De bringer os held. 7 De giver hinanden gaver. 8 Jeg forstår dig, ikke hende.

Exercise 6: 1 A Ja, jeg spiser altid morgenmad. B Nej, jeg spiser ikke altid morgenmad *or* Nej, jeg spiser aldrig morgenmad. 2 A Ja, SAS flyver mellem København og Alaska. B Nej, SAS flyver ikke mellem København og Alaska. 3 A Ja, politibetjenten taler engelsk. B Nej, politibetjenten taler ikke engelsk. 4 A Jo, skolen har ferie nu. B Nej, skolen har ikke ferie nu. 5 A Jo, jeg hedder Søren. B Nej, jeg hedder ikke Søren.

Chapter 3

Excercise 7: 1 korte 2 dejlige 3 rare 4 høje 5 tunge 6 farvede 7 grå 8 falske 9 tyske 10 tapre 11 bløde 12 gamle 13 slappe 14 violette 15 private 16 svangre 17 hullede

Exercise 8: 1 kort 2 dejligt 3 tungt 4 farvet 5 gråt 6 tysk 7 tappert 8 blødt 9 violet

Exercise 9: 1 The school is large but good. 2 The house has a green roof. 3 Søren Andersen is a fast runner. 4 The bed is soft, with a fine blanket. 5 MacPherson is a Scot but speaks fluent Danish. 6 There is a delightful little restaurant here. 7 Lars has a wonderful room. 8 They have high ideals. 9 It is a young, clever animal. 10 We have two football teams and there is the new clubhouse.

Exercise 10: 1 sav 2 kopier 3 tro 4 undersøg 5 stop 6 forny 7 hent 8 glo 9 fly 10 fløjt

Exercise 11: 1 slagterens butik *or* slagterbutikken 2 det fremmede holds træner 3 kødets glæder 4 Øjnenes farve er blå. 5 Bogens sider er gule nu. 6 Hans' far er ejer af en gård *or* gårdejer. 7 Dér er forældrenes hjem. 8 resultatet af det stærke angreb 9 en rasende hunds høje gøen 10 Penges magt er stor.

Chapter 4

Exercise 12: 1 Why don't we (Shan't we) go to the cinema, or would you rather go the theatre? 2 You ought to stop talking but you will never hear what I say. 3 You can if you want (will), or if you dare. 4 Where are you sailing to on holiday? 5 I want to go home now, shall we say goodnight? 6 The Sørensen family ought to sell the far too big house. 7 Do you really have to go/leave already? 8 I would like to have the nuts, you are welcome to have (get) the chocolate. 9 They would rather die than give up. 10 I would rather play table tennis.

Exercise 13: 1 There is only a little (some) difference between them. 2 In a few days, all the pupils will be (are) here. 3 They can all see all the animals. 4 Not everyone knows (understands) how to call a halt, but some do. 5 Have you no money left? 6 Not all the tables are occupied, a few are free. 7 None of them know what the others on the team think. 8 We expect them any moment. 9 Nothing else on earth is so beautiful. 10 With the other method you have all the advantages.

Exercise 14: These black bicycles (here) are cheap. 2 Those children have such a good mother. 3 There are such long queues at (by) those two theatres but not at (by) that one. 4 These blue eyes are innocent but how dangerous they are! 5 Such results I'll never achieve! 6 If you choose that career, you must go on that course.

Chapter 5

Exercise 15: 1 We have (a/our) twenty-fifth anniversary in April. 2 Mr Frederiksen, describe them one at a time. 3 He is putting (laying) the paper from the thirteenth of July in your letter box. 4 To you, it costs only 5,954 kroner. 5 This is the 61st time I've warned (I'm warning) you but you never listen to me.

Exercise 16: 1 Father has walked ten kilometres and now he has gone out again. 2 I asked him to ask (about) the way to the cinema. 3 They have brought good news. 4 The boss has received the money. 5 They put the bread on the tray when they had buttered it. 6 The firm traded in (with) potatoes until it went bankrupt. 7 I used to smoke 40 cigarettes a day but then I gave it up altogether – and put on 10 kilos in weight! 8 When you have sold one more house, you will (have) become top salesman.

Exercise 17: 1 Amerikaneren er sejlet til Australien – han har sejlet en masse. 2 Jeg fandt otteogtredive mus, da jeg kom tilbage. 3 Vi lagde kabel fra vejen til huset. 4 Peters venner (an)kom kokken 10, og de er allerede gået. 5 De gav holdet en fair kamp – og tabte. 6 Byen har fået en uærlig ny borgmester. 7 Mor lavede en pakke mellemmadder til os og vi har allerede spist dem alle/allesammen. 8 Tyve har taget alt sølvtøjet.

Chapter 6

Exercise 18: *Correct sequence* 4, 2, 1, 8, 7, 11, 9, 12, 13, 5, 3, 10, 6, 14, 15.

Translation: At the railway station

Old lady: **I would like a single ticket to Roskilde. How much does it cost, and when does the next train go?**

Ticket seller: **It costs eighteen kroner. And the next train departs at 14.25 from platform 4.**

Lady: **But I am a pensioner and am entitled to (a) discount. Do I save anything if I buy a return ticket instead of two single tickets?**

Ticket seller: **Yes, but then you should do something quite different and buy a punchcard. That is valid for several journeys. You save a lot (in) that way.**

Lady: **Yes, I would like that punchcard. Tell me, how long does the journey to Roskilde take?**

Ticket seller: **You arrive at 14.53.**

Lady: **That means seven minutes to three, doesn't it?**

Exercise 19: 1 We should have followed them through thick and thin. 2 One thing is what we ought to do, quite another is what we can do. 3 Could you sense that he would be able to manage it? 4 I had to smile when I saw the policeman. 5 I could count the pupil's good marks on one finger! 6 You used to like desserts – did you not like this one? 7 I would have been able to hear the birds sing if I had dared ask Maggie to keep her mouth shut. 8 Ought the Danes not to be rather less critical? 9 Yes, and if they could, they should also be less nationalistic and self-satisfied! 10 yes, but who could have better reason to be (it)?

Exercise 20: 1 Jeg har skrevet et langt brev til Holger og Lise. 2 Banken ligger over for posthuset. 3 Må jeg besøge jer/dig/Dem før jul? 4 To af dem er gået. 5 Efter min mening er tanten en charmerende kvinde. 6 Fortæl mig om rejsen. 7 Børnene gik op ad bakken. 8 Uden penge kan du ikke købe mad. 9 Går toget til Roskilde fra denne perron? 10 På lørdag tager jeg til Herning.

Chapter 7

Exercise 21: *The correct possesives:* 1 sin 2 hans 3 din 4 deres 5 vores, din 6 dine 7 deres 8 sine 9 sine 10 sin

Exercise 22: 1 Han er den dygtigste, men også den mest beskedne mand i byen. 2 Det bøgetræ er gammelt, men det andet er endnu ældre. 3 Danmark er et af de allermindste lande – men Grønland er verdens største ø. 4 De er de dejligste mennesker. 5 Det er bedst at adlyde, hvis den anden er stærkere end du er. 6 Der er færre dage i februar end i nogen anden måned.7 Flere (mennesker) går klædt i mere moderne tøj nu. 8 Kan du ikke være lidt mere smidig – og langt mere tolerant? 9 Danskere kan lide de fleste udlændinge. 10 Det mest charmerende og lykkelige par er også de allerrigeste af alle deltagerne.

Chapter 8

Exercise 23: 1 De skulle passe sig selv. 2 Du må ikke bekymre dig om mig, bare fordi jeg har skåret mig. 3 Han keder sig, men hun skynder sig ikke at blive færdig. 4 Patienten kommer sig nu efter ulykken. 5 Selv nu om dage gifter folk sig! 6 Julen er virkelig noget at glæde sig til. 7 Jeg klæder mig på, mens jeg lytter til nyhederne i radioen. 8 Du behøver ikke at rejse dig, når jeg kommer ind. 9 De skaber sig bare – i deres alder skulle de have lært at opføre sig ordentligt. 10 Den dovne læge skulle skamme sig.

Exercise 24: 1 Regardless of how/However long Ole practises, he often mishits (hits wrongly). 2 It is far from being completely finished and yet it is already beautiful. 3 The song immediately reminded me of you and even more about war. 4 They only want their right(s) – otherwise they (will) go on strike. 5 She nearly always rings him when she is alone. 6 He is certainly not completely ordinary! 7 Better late than never! 8 Sometimes we go to the cinema, but we go to the theatre more often. 9 Of course they worked for a long time but then they could (work) no longer. 10 It is unfortunately too old, and not too strong either.

Exercise 25: 1) så 2) så 3) mens 4) (i)mens 5) og/så 6) men 7) før 8) og 9) siden 10) såfremt/hvis 11) men 12) når 13) og/så 14) men 15) (i)mens

Translation:
As you know – or ought to know – Denmark is famous as the country of fairy-tales, *so* we must include this story (have this story with):
The princess had a headache, so she went for a walk in the palace garden *while* the sun was going down. Finally she stopped by the lake and stood there dreaming (and dreamt) *while* she turned her costly ring. Suddenly, she lost the ring *and* it fell into the water. It was a shock *but* already *before* her tears began to flow, she saw a large toad *and* it had her ring in its mouth.
"Oh, thank you, dear toad, I have not been so happy *since* my father gave me the ring."
"Yes, but you'll get it only (first) *if* I can sleep in your bed tonight."
"Ugh, how repulsive," thought the princess and at first she protested *but* finally she gave way, picked up the toad and carried it to her bedroom. "*When* I wake up tomorrow, I'll get the ring *and/so* my father won't discover how clumsy I have been."*But* the next morning, something fantastic had happened: *while* she slept, the toad had turned into a handsome young man!
Dear reader, do YOU believe in fairy-tales?
No, you don't, do you? Nor did her father, the king!

Chapter 9

Exercise 26: 1 Giv nøglen til den amerikaner, der/som bad om den. 2 Australieren, der/som gjorde jobbet, gjorde det selv. 3 Vi skulle efterligne den metode, (som) de bruger. 4 Den sten, som/der ruller, samler ikke mos. 5 Jeg kender en lærerinde, der/som er en dejlig dame. 6 Det var den abe, der/som havde et blindt øje, som løb væk. 7 Jeg hader, det/hvad de spiller. 8 Den champagne, (som) de har valgt, er alt for dyr. 9 Vask nu de skjorter, (som) jeg gav dig for to uger siden! 10 Han tabte sine penge, som han havde arbejdet så hårdt for.

Exercise 27: 1 The trousers I washed yesterday are already dirty. 2 When they're working there are never any problems. 3 It won't be the two of us if you are not rich. 4 The man you sold the car to just wants to have a receipt. 5 Even though you cannot spell correctly, you ought to write often. 6 Who followed after Frederik the Ninth, I don't know. 7 (Just) because you are number one you mustn't think that you are a superman. 8 Please show me where the hospital is (lies) – if you have time.

Exercise 28: Hans Christian Andersen tells of the prince who could not find a *true* princess to marry. One late evening, a girl knocked on the door of the palace. When the old king opened (the door), she said that she was a princess and had got lost. The king asked her in.

In order to investigate whether she really was a genuine princess, the old queen laid a pea on the bottom of the girl's bed and put twenty mattresses on top and on top of those again, twenty eiderdown quilts.

In the morning, they asked how the girl had slept. Quite terribly, she replied, for she had been lying on something which was so hard that she was black (brown) and blue over her (the) whole body. So it was quite clear that here was a *true* princess and the prince took her for his wife, while the pea went into a museum.

The present-day Danish author and priest, Johannes Møllehave, writes that he told the story to a third-year (third) class and gave them the task of retelling it. One 9-year-old boy finished his very short version with: . . . and when the princess woke up in the morning, she was green and yellow and blue all over. See, *that* was a *true* prince!

Chapter 10

Exercise 29: 1 Drive the car out of the garage, but remember that it has to be driven carefully. 2 He is being talked about as if he were a criminal. 3 The floor had never been washed, only swept. 4 One doesn't always know how it is best done. 5 When it has got dark, the candles on the Christmas tree are lit. 6 My name is spelt with 'ph' but you always spell it with (an) 'f'. 7 It is hoped that the presentation can be done easily and quickly. 8 Not all the wine was drunk.

Exercise 30:

Inge Hoff: Welcome to Esbjerg and Denmark, was it a good crossing?

Ted Young: The ship is the best passenger ferry I have been on and we enjoyed the Hungarian dance band.

Inge: Yes, and the food was good but perhaps a little expensive, wasn't it?

Ted: No, I don't really think so, but we drank a lot of the duty-free wine in order to save! By the way, at breakfast we shared a table with a high-school teacher from Funen who knows you and your husband. His name was Frank Henriksen.

Inge: Yes, I was once engaged to him. But he is a fanatical open-air person and sports-mad – and deadly boring. Come, follow me to my shopping car, which has breathing problems.

Chapter 11

Exercise 31:

– Now you have worked at learning Danish for two and a half months, how is it going?

– It's going quite well, I have done three quarters of the lessons and I can remember at least twenty-three words! No, I am making quite good progress (progresses), but I should read more and practise more. I just don't have enough time.

– Haven't you got an audiotape that you can use in the car?

– Yes, but I don't drive often any more. I'm sitting at home writing all the time. So it's not so bad when I still spend (use) about three quarters of an hour a day on my Danish.

– Oh yes, you are writing about your research. Haven't you finished your report yet?
– No, I cannot really come to a conclusion. But it will probably happen soon. And then there will be a celebration, and of course I'm inviting you as well!
– Thank you, and then you'll make a speech in Danish, won't you?
– You say that, because you know that then it will be short at any rate!

Exercise 32: Two Storm P. men are talking to each other through a high fence:
– I don't suppose you can let me out?
– Yes, if you can let me in.
But if the man who is shut in had answered no, the other man would be shut out.

Philosophical man:
– When one says 'look in (inside) when you're passing by', one lacks logic.

Exercise 33: 1 Er din ven lige så rig som han er grim? 2 Nej, han er heller ikke så uhøflig, som du er. 3 Jo mere jeg ser på hende, des mere elsker jeg min frihed. 4 Den familie er hverken religiøs eller interesseret i politik. 5 Både Romeo og Juliet arbejder i teaterfaget. 6 Jeg hverken læser eller øver mig så meget i dansk, som jeg havde ønsket.

Chapter 12

Exercise 34:
– Can we agree to eat two courses only? Or do you think that is too little?
– We won't come to blows over that – or even quarrel about it. But it depends somewhat on what it is you choose. A small starter and an even smaller dessert probably won't be enough!
– Here is the menu, see if there is something exciting, then I'll meanwhile study the winelist. Both VAT and service are included in the price.
– I don't think there is anything better (to be found) than a

young Sauvignon and an oldish Rioja – but perhaps you'd rather choose the food first and the wine afterwards?
– Unfortunately, it can be seen on both of us that both parts interest us equally. But I'd like to have chicken in cream sauce and lemon mousse with lots of whipped cream and strawberries – you don't care for dessert but I'll wait while you get your eternal salmon paté.
– Thanks, and we meet again over the coffee, if I may put it like that.
– You may say almost what you like – you're paying – but remember that you have to drive, if you know what I mean.
– Goodbye, glass of wine number three and my Drambuie. We'll meet when it's the turn of my dear wife to drive.

Exercise 35: 1 restaurerede 2 kalkede 3 skinnende 4 rødmalet 5 blyindfattede 6 lysende
Translation: On my old, but restored, farm the whitewashed cowshed is a shining white centre. The door is painted red, the window panes (are) leaded, and in the evening the shining windows are a beautiful sight.

Exercise 36:
Kære hr. Ramsing,
Mange tak for Deres brev med tilbud om et job i Deres firma i København. Efter at have talt med min kone, glæder det mig at acceptere, og at lade Dem vide, at jeg faktisk kan begynde den 15. juni.
Om to uger, fra den 7. april, tager jeg en uges ferie, og jeg vil gerne flyve til Danmark med min kone, så vi kan begynde at lede efter en lejlighed eller et hus, vi kan leje – vil det være muligt for nogen i firmaet at give os lidt hjælp? Hvis det er, vil jeg skrive et brev til ham eller hende og beskrive, hvad vi tænker på og ville foretrække. Jeg takker Dem igen varmt for Deres tilbud og glæder mig meget til at lære Dem, Deres firma og Deres land at kende.
Med venlige hilsener fra min kone og mig selv,

Irregular verbs

Infinitive (at)	(to)	*Present*	*Past*	*Past participle*
bede	pray, ask	**beder**	**bad**	**bedt**
bide	bite	**bider**	**bed**	**bidt**
binde	tie	**binder**	**bandt**	**bundet**
blive	stay/ become	**bliver**	**blev**	**blevet**
bringe	bring	**bringer**	**bragte**	**bragt**
bryde	break	**bryder**	**brød**	**brudt**
burde	ought	**bør**	**burde**	**burdet**
byde	offer	**byder**	**bød**	**budt**
bære	carry	**bærer**	**bar**	**båret**
drikke	drink	**drikker**	**drak**	**drukket**
dø	die	**dør**	**døde**	**(død)**
falde	fall	**falder**	**faldt**	**faldet**
fare	rush	**farer**	**for**	**faret**
finde	find	**finder**	**fandt**	**fundet**
flyde	flow	**flyder**	**flød**	**flydt**
flyve	fly	**flyver**	**fløj**	**fløjet**
forsvinde	disappear	**forsvinder**	**forsvandt**	**forsvundet**
fryse	be cold	**fryser**	**frøs**	**frosset**
følge	follow	**følger**	**fulgte**	**fulgt**
få	get, receive	**får**	**fik**	**fået**
give	give	**giver**	**gav**	**givet**
gribe	catch	**griber**	**greb**	**grebet**
gælde	be valid	**gælder**	**gjaldt**	**gjaldt/gældt**
gøre	do, make	**gør**	**gjorde**	**gjort**
gå	walk, leave	**går**	**gik**	**gået**
have	have	**har**	**havde**	**haft**
hedde	be called	**hedder**	**hed**	**heddet**
hjælpe	help	**hjælper**	**hjalp**	**hjulpet**

Infinitive (at)	(to)	*Present*	*Past*	*Past participle*
holde	hold, keep	**holder**	**holdt**	**holdt**
komme	come/put	**kommer**	**kom**	**kommet**
kunne	be able to	**kan**	**kunne**	**kunnet**
lade	let	**lader**	**lod**	**lad(e)t**
le	laugh	**ler**	**lo**	**le(e)t**
lide	suffer	**lider**	**led**	**lidt**
ligge	lie	**ligger**	**lå**	**ligget**
lyde	sound	**lyder**	**lød**	**lydt**
lyve	tell lies	**lyver**	**løj**	**løjet**
lægge	lay, put	**lægger**	**lagde**	**lagt**
løbe	run	**løber**	**løb**	**løbet**
måtte	may, must	**må**	**måtte**	**måttet**
nyde	enjoy	**nyder**	**nød**	**nydt**
ride	ride	**rider**	**red**	**redet**
ryge	smoke	**ryger**	**røg**	**røget**
række	reach, hand	**rækker**	**rakte**	**rakt**
se	see, look	**ser**	**så**	**set**
sidde	sit	**sidder**	**sad**	**siddet**
sige	say	**siger**	**sagde**	**sagt**
skrige	scream	**skriger**	**skreg**	**skreget**
skrive	write	**skriver**	**skrev**	**skrevet**
skulle	should	**skal**	**skulle**	**skullet**
skyde	shoot	**skyder**	**skød**	**skudt**
skære	cut	**skærer**	**skar**	**skåret**
slide	work hard	**slider**	**sled**	**slidt**
slå	beat, hit	**slår**	**slog**	**slået**
smøre	oil, butter	**smører**	**smurte**	**smurt**
sove	sleep	**sover**	**sov**	**sovet**
springe	jump	**springer**	**sprang**	**sprunget**
spørge	ask	**spørger**	**spurgte**	**spurgt**
stå	stand	**står**	**stod**	**stået**
stjæle	steal	**stjæler**	**stjal**	**stjålet**
strække	stretch	**strækker**	**strakte**	**strakt**
synge	sing	**synger**	**sang**	**sunget**
sælge	sell	**sælger**	**solgte**	**solgt**
sætte	put, set	**sætter**	**satte**	**sat**
tage	take	**tager**	**tog**	**taget**
tie	be quiet	**tier**	**tav**	**tiet**
træde	step	**træder**	**trådte**	**trådt**

Infinitive **(at)**	(to)	*Present*	*Past*	*Past participle*
trække	pull	**trækker**	**trak**	**trukket**
turde	dare	**tør**	**turde**	**turdet**
tælle	count	**tæller**	**talte**	**talt**
vide	know	**ved**	**vidste**	**vidst**
ville	would	**vil**	**ville**	**villet**
vinde	win	**vinder**	**vandt**	**vundet**
vælge	choose	**vælger**	**valgte**	**valgt**
være	be	**er**	**var**	**været**
æde	eat (of animals)	**æder**	**åd**	**ædt**

Mini-dictionary

Danish – English

*Numbers are listed in Section 17. See Section 3 for information about gender and plural of nouns. See Section 18 for information about the past tense of verbs. (Remember that (**-te, -t**) is added to the stem of the verb, not the infinitive.) * indicates that the pattern of that verb will be found in the list of irregular verbs. The past tense of compound verbs is formed according to their last element, so, for instance, for **adlyde** see **lyde.***

abe (-n, -r) monkey
absolut absolutely
acceptere to accept
ad to, by, of, along
adfærd (-en) behaviour
adlyde* to obey
adresse (-n, -r) address
advare to warn
af of
afgå* to depart
aflevere to hand over
aften (-en, -er) evening
aftensmad (-en) dinner
agurk (-en, -er) gherkin, cucumber
al all
alder (-en, aldre) age
  i deres alder at their age
aldrig never
alene alone
alkohol (-en) alcohol
alkoholisk alcoholic
alle all
allé (-en, -er) alley
aller- the very . . .
allerede already
allerhelst most of all
allesammen all
alligevel all the same
almindelig ordinary, common
alt all
alt for far too
altid always
altsammen all (of it)
amerikaner (-en, -e) American
anden, andet, andre other, different, second
anekdote (-n, -r) anecdote
angreb (-et, -) attack
ankomme* to arrive
ansigt (-et, -er) face
appelsin (-en, -er) orange
appetit (-ten) appetite
april (en) April
arbejde to work
arbejde (-t, -r) work
arbejdsløs unemployed
arbejdsplads (-en, -er) place of work
artig well-behaved
assistent (-en, -er) assistant
at to, that

august (en) August
Australien Australia
australier (-en, -e) Australian
avis (-en, -er) newspaper

bad (-et, -) bath
bag/bagved behind, after
bagage (-n) luggage
bager (-en, -e) baker
bakke (-n, -r) tray, hill
bank (-en, -er) bank
bankbestyrer (-en, -e) bank manager
banke to knock
barbere sig to shave
bare only, just, if only
bark (-en) bark
barn (-et, børn) child
barnebarn (-et, børnebørn) grandchild
barnevogn (-en, -e) pram
bede* to pray, ask
bededag, store fourth Friday after Easter
bedre better
bedst best
bedstefar (-en, -fædre) grandfather
bedstemor (-en, -mødre) grandmother
befri to free
begge both
begge to both
begge dele both
begynde (-te, -t) to begin
behandle to treat, handle
behandling (-en, -er) treatment, handling
beholdning (-en, -er) stock
behøve to need
bekymre sig to worry
ben (-et, -) leg, bone
benzinstation (-en, -er) petrol station
berette to report
berømt famous
beskadiget damaged
beskeden modest
beskrive* to describe
bestemt certainly
besøge (-te, -t) to visit
besøgende (en, -) visitor
betale (-te, -t) to pay
betale (-te, -t) sig to be worth it
bide* to bite
bil (-en, -er) car
bilist (-en, -er) motorist
billede (-t, -r) picture
billig cheap
bilværksted (-et, -er) (car) repair shop
biograf (-en, -er) cinema
bjerg (-et, -e) mountain
blad (-et, -e) leaf
blandt amongst
blind blind
blive* to become, remain
det bliver that comes to
blomst (-en, -er) flower
blomsterbed (-et, -e) flower bed
blot only, just, if only
blyindfattet leaded (e.g. windows)
blæsende windy
blæst (-en) wind
blød soft
blødende bleeding
blødsøden sloppy
blå blue
blålig blueish
bo to live, reside
bog (-en, bøger) book
bokser (-en, -e) boxer
bonde (-n, bønder) farmer
bord (-et, -e) table

bordtennis table tennis
bor (-et, -) drill
borgmester (-en, -tre)mayor
bort/borte away
brand (-en, -e) fire
bred wide
brev (-et, -e) letter
brevkasse (-n, -r) letterbox
bringe* to bring
britisk British
bro (-en, -er) bridge
broder, bror (-en, brødre) brother
brug (-en) use **have brug for** to need
bruge (-te, -t) to use
brugtvognsforhandler (-en, -e) used car dealer
brun brown
bryde* sig om to care for, like
bryllupsdag (-en, -e) wedding day/anniversary
brække to break
brød (-et, -) (loaf of) bread
bukser trousers
bund (-en, -e) bottom
burde* ought to
bus (-sen, -ser) bus
busk (-en, -e) bush
butik (-ken, -ker) shop
buttet plump
by (-en, -er) town
bygge to build
bænk (-en, -e) bench
bære* to carry
bøgetræ (-et, -er) beech tree
bør ought to
børn children
børnehave (-n, -r) nursery school
både . . . og both . . . and
bål (-et, -) bonfire

ca. (cirka) approximately
campingvogn (-en, -e) caravan
canadier (-en, -e) Canadian
centrum (centret, centrer) centre
champagne (-n) champagne
charmerende charming
chef (-en, -er) boss
chokolade (-n, -r) chocolate
cigar (-en, -er) cigar
cigaret (-ten, -ter) cigarette
citronfromage (-n, -r) lemon mousse
cykel (-en, cykler) bicycle

da when, since, then
dag (-en, -e) day
daglig daily
dam (-men, -me) pond
dame (-n, -r) lady
Danmark Denmark
danse to dance
danseorkester (-et, -orkestre) dance band
dansk Danish
dansker (-en, -e) Dane
datter (-en, døtre) daughter
dav, davs hello
de they, the, those
De you *pol sing and plur*
december (en) December
dejlig lovely
del (-en, -e) part
dele (-te, -t) to share
deltager (-en, -e) participant
dem them, those
Dem you *pol sing and plur,* yourself, yourselves
demokratisk democratic
den it, the, that
den her this
dengang when
denne this

dens/dets its
der who, which
der, dér there
deres their(s)
Deres your(s) (*pol*)
derfor therefore
derfra from there
derhen(ne) over there
derned(e) down there
derop(pe) up there
derover over (to) there
derovre over there
dertil to there
des . . . des the . . . the
dessert (-en, -er) dessert
desuden besides, furthermore
desværre unfortunately
det it, the, that
det her this
dets its
dette this
dialekt (-en, -er) dialect
dig you, yourself *fam sing*
din, dit, dine your(s) *fam sing*
disse these
dobbelt double
dog yet, however
doven lazy
dreje to turn
dreng (-en, -e) boy
drikke* to drink
drivhus (-et, -e) greenhouse
dronning (-en, -er) queen
drøm (-men, -me) dream
drømme (-te, -t) to dream
du you *fam sing*
dum stupid
dusin (-et, -) dozen
dyne (-n, -r) quilt
dyr expensive
dyr (-et, -) animal
dyreforretning (-en, -er) pet shop
dyreven (-nen, -ner) animal-lover
dygtig able, clever
dø* to die
død dead
dødkedelig dead boring
døgn (-et, -) 24 hours, day and night
dør (-en, -e) door
dårlig bad
dåse (-n, -r) box, can

efter after
efterår (-et, -) autumn
eftermiddag (-en, -e) afternoon
efternavn (-et, -e) surname
efterse* to check
eftersom as
egen, eget, egne own
egetræ (-et, -er) oak tree
egn (-en, -e) area
egne sig til to be suited to
ejer (-en, -e) owner
eksistere to exist
ekspeditrice (-n, -r) saleswoman
elefant (-en, -er) elephant
elev (-en, -er) pupil
eller or
ellers otherwise
elske to love
elsket beloved
embedsmand (-en, -mænd) civil servant
emigrere to emigrate
en a/an, one
en/et til one more
end than
endelig finally
endnu even, still, yet
energi (-en) energy
enes to agree
engang once
engel (englen, engle) angel

engelsk English
englænder (-en, -e) Englishman
enhver, ethvert, each, every, any
enkelt single
enkeltbillet (-ten, -ter) single ticket
ens one's, your
enten . . . eller either . . . or
er am, is, are
et a/an, one
Europa Europe
europæisk European
evig eternal
eventyr (-et, -) fairy tale, adventure
evne (-n, -r) ability

fabrik (-ken, -ker) factory
fabriksarbejder (-en, -e) factory worker
fader, far (-en, fædre) father
fag (-et, -) trade, subject
fair fair
faktisk actually
falde* to fall
fald: i hvert fald in any case
fallit: gå fallit to go bankrupt
falsk false
familie (-n, -r) family
fanatisk fanatical
fantastisk fantastic
far *see* **fader**
fare* vild to get lost
farlig dangerous
fart (-en) speed, motion
fartgrænse (-n, -r) speed limit
farve (-n, -r) colour
farvel goodbye
farverig colourful
farvet coloured
fattig poor
februar (en) February
feje to sweep
fejl (-en, -) mistake
fejre to celebrate
feminin feminine
femtedel (-en, -e) fifth
ferie (-n, -r) holiday
fest (-en, -er) celebration
film (-en, - *or* **-s)** film
filosofisk philosophical
fin fine
finde* to find **der findes** there are
finger (-en, fingre) finger
Firenze Florence
firma (-et, -er) firm
fisk to fish **at være ude at fiske** to be out fishing
fjerdedel (-en, -e) fourth, quarter
fjernsyn (-et) television
fjor: i fjor last year
flag (-et, -) flag
flagstang (-en, -stænger) flagpole
flammende flaming
flaske (-n, -r) bottle
flere several, more
flest most, **de fleste** most
flirte to flirt
flod (-en, er) river
flodbred (-den, -der) river bank
flot smart, handsome
flue (-n, -r) fly
flyde* to flow
flydende fluent
flytte to move
flyve* to fly
flæskesteg (-en, -e) pork joint
fløde (-n) cream
flødesovs (-en) cream sauce
flødeskum (-met) whipped cream
fløjte to whistle

fod (-en, fødder) foot
fodbold (-en, -e) football
fodboldhold (-et, -) soccer team
fodboldstøvle (-n, -r) football boot
fodgænger (-en, -e) pedestrian
fodgængerovergang (-en, -e) pedestrian crossing
fodring (-en) feeding
folk (-et, -) people
for for, too, because
for at in order to, so that
for . . . siden . . . ago
foran before, in front of
forandre (sig) to change (oneself)
forbedre to improve
forbi past
forbryder (-en, -e) criminal
fordel (-en, -e) advantage
fordi because
forestille to introduce
forestille sig to imagine
foretrække* to prefer
forfatter (-en, -e) author
forfærdelig terrible
forinden before (then)
forkert wrong
forklare to explain
forkølelse (-n, -r) cold
forlovet engaged (to be married)
formiddag (-en, -e) morning (9-12)
formål (-et, -) purpose
fornavn (-et, -e) first name
forny to renew
forresten incidentally, by the way
forret (-ten, -ter) first course, starter
forretning (-en, -er) shop, business
forretningsmand (-en, -mænd) businessman
forrig: forrige uge the week before last
forsigtig careful
forskel (-len, -le) difference
forskellig different
forslag (-et, -) suggestion
forsommer (-en, -somre) early summer
forstand (-en) intelligence, mind **have forstand på** to know about
forstå* to understand
forsvinde* to disappear
forsøg (-et, -) attempt
fortjene (-te, -t) to deserve
fortov (-et, -e) pavement
fortsætte* to continue
fortælle* to tell
forvandle (sig) til to turn into, change into
forældre parents
forår (-et, -) spring
fotograf (-en, -er) photographer
fr. Ms
fra from
fransk French
franskmand (-en, -mænd) Frenchman
fred (-en) peace
fredag (-en, -e) Friday
frem, fremad forwards
fremme (further) ahead
fremmed foreign, strange
fremragende outstanding
fremskridt (-et, -) progress
fri free **have fri** to be off (work etc.)
frihed (-en, -er) freedom, liberty

friluftsmenneske (-t, -r) open-air person
frimærke (-t, -r) stamp
fristelse (-n, -r) temptation
frisør (-en, -er) hairdresser
frodig fertile
frokost (-en, -er) lunch
fru Mrs
frue Madam
fræk cheeky
frø (-en, -er) frog
frø (-et, -) seed
frøken (frøk(e)nen, frøk(e)ner) unmarried woman
frøken, frk. Miss
fugl, (-en, -e) bird
fuld full, drunk
fængsel (-et, fængsler) prison
færdig finished **blive* færdig (med)** to finish
færdselsregel (-reg(e)len, -regler) traffic regulation
færge (-n, -r) ferry
færre fewer
færrest fewer
fødselsdag (-en, -e) birthday
fødselsret (-ten) birthright
født: være født to be/have been born
følge* to follow
før before
fører (-en, -e) driver
først first
få* to get, receive
få few
får (-et, -) sheep

gade (-n, -r) street
gadekryds (-et, -) crossroads
gaffel (-en, gafler) fork
gal mad, wrong
gammel old
gammeldags old-fashioned
gang (-en, -e) time
ganske quite, rather
ganske vist admittedly
garage (-n, -r) garage
gardin (-et, -er) curtain
gave (-n, -r) gift
gavn (-en) use, benefit
general (-en, -er) general
genert shy
genfortælle* to retell
geni (-et, -er) genius
gennem through
gensyn: på gensyn see you again
gerne willingly
gerning (-en, -er) deed
gifte sig (med) to get married (to)
give* to give
give* efter to give way, acquiesce
glad happy
glas (-set, -) glass, jar
glat slippery
glemme (-te, -t) to forget
glimrende splendid
glo to stare
glæde (-n, -r) pleasure
glæde to please
glæde sig over to be pleased about
glæde sig til to look forward to
glædelig jul Happy Christmas
god good
godaften good evening
goddag good day
godmorgen good morning
godnat goodnight
godt well, please
grammati(kal)sk grammatical
grammofonplade (-n, -r) gramophone record

gratis free (of charge)
gratulere to congratulate
gravid pregnant
grim ugly
grin (-et, -) grin
grosserer (-en, -e) wholesaler
grov coarse
grund (-en, -e) reason
grundlovsdag
Constitution Day (5 June)
græsk Greek
græsplæne (-n, -r) lawn
grøn green
Grønland Greenland
grønsag (-en, -er) vegetable
grå grey
gud (-en, -er) god
Gud God
gul yellow
guldbryllup (-pet, -per)
golden wedding
gulerod (-en, -rødder) carrot
gulv (-et, -e) floor
gælde* to be valid
gæst (-en, -er) guest
gø to bark
gøen (en) barking
gøre* to do
gøre* for to help (it), do anything (about it)
gøre* opmærksom på
to draw attention to
gå* to go, walk
gå* en tur to go for a walk
gå* fallit to go bankrupt
gård (-en, -e) farm
gås (-en, gæs) goose

hade to hate
hale (-n, -r) tail
halv half
halv to half past one
halvanden one and a half
halvbror (-en, -brødre)
half-brother
halvdel (-en, -e) half
halvgammel elderly
halvsøster (-en, -søstre)
half-sister
ham him
hamre to hammer
han he
handle to act, trade
handske (-n, -r) glove
hans his
hat (-ten, -te) hat
hav (-et, -e) sea
have* to have
have (-n, -r) garden
havrue (-n, -r) mermaid
havn (-en, -e) harbour
hedde* to be called
hegn (-et, -) fence
hej! hi!
helbred (-et) health
held (-et) luck
held og lykke good luck
heldig lucky
heldigvis fortunately
hel whole
hele tiden all the time
over det hele all over
heller ikke nor, neither, not . . . either
hellere rather
helst preferably
helt completely, altogether
hen: hen ad along
hen til over to
hende her
hendes her(s)
hengiven devoted
henne: der henne over there
hente to fetch
her her
heraf by this
herfra from here

herhen (to) here
herind(e) in here
herlig splendid
herned(e) down here
herop(pe) up here
herovre over here
herre, hr. sir, Mr
herre (-n, -r) gentleman
hertil (to) here
herud(e) out here
hest (-en, -e) horse
hilse (-te, -t) to greet
hilsen (-en, -er) greeting
himmel (him(me)len, himle) sky, heaven
hinanden each other
historie (-n, -r) story
hjem (to) home
hjem(-met, -) home
hjemme at home
hjemmelavet home-made
hjemvendt returned home
hjerte (-t, -r) heart
hjælp (-en) help
hjælpe* to help
hjørne (-t, -r) corner
hold (-et, -) team
hold kæft! shut up!
holde* to keep
holde* bryllup med to marry
holde* ferie to spend a holiday
holde* mund to keep one's mouth shut
holde* op med to stop
holde* sig for sig selv to keep oneself to oneself
holde* tale to make a speech
holde* åbent to be open (shops, etc.)
hoppe to jump, hop
hos with, at the house of
hoste to cough
hovedpine (-n, -r) headache
hr. Mr
hul (-let, -ler) hole
hullet holey, full of holes
hun she
hund (-en, -e) dog
hundeelsker (-en, -e) dog lover
hundemad (-en) dog food
hunderace (-n, -r) dog breed
hundredtusinder hundreds of thousands
hurtig fast
hurtigt quickly
hurtigtog (-et, -) express train
hus (-et, -e) house
huske to remember
hvad what
hvad for en/et/nogle which
hvem who
hver, hvert each, every
hverken . . . eller neither . . . nor
hvid white
hvidkalket whitewashed
hvilken/hvilket/hvilke which
hvis whose
hvis if
hvisken (-en) whisper
hvor where
hvor . . . how . . .
hvordan how
hvorfor why
hvorfra from where
hvorhen where to
hvornår when
hytte (-n, -r) hut
høj high, tall, loud
højagtelse (-n) esteem
højre right
højrekørsel (-en) right-hand driving
højskolelærer (-en, -e) high-school teacher
høne (-n, -r) hen
høre (-te, -t) to hear
håbe to hope

hånd (-en, hænder) hand
give hånden på to shake hands on
håndværker (-en, -e) craftsman
hård hard

i in, to, for
I you *fam plur*
i aften this evening
i aftes last night
i alt in all
i dag today
i eftermiddag this afternoon
i fjor last year
i forgårs the day before yesterday
i formiddag this morning
i går yesterday
i hvert fald in any case, at any rate
i lige måde the same to you
i morgen tomorrow
i morges this morning
i nat last night, tonight
i år this year
iblandt among
idé (-en, -er) idea
ideal (-et, -er) ideal
ifald in case of
igen again
igennem through
ikke not
ikke- non-
ikke længere no longer
ikke nogen no, not a, none, nobody
ikke noget no, not a, none, nothing
ikke sandt? not true?
ild (-en) fire
imellem among, between
imens while, meanwhile
imod against, towards
ind(e) in, inside
indbyde* to invite
indbygger (-en, -e) inhabitant
inden before
indenfor inside
indfatte to frame
indgang (-en, -e) entrance
indkøb (-et, -) shopping
indrette to install
indtil until
influenza (-en) influenza
ingen no, not a, none, nobody
ingenting nothing
inspirerende inspiring
intelligens (-en) intelligence
interessere to interest
interesseret interested
intet no, not a, none, nothing
irer (-en, -e) Irishman
især especially
Italien Italy

ja yes
jaloux jealous
jamen well, yes but
januar (en) January
jeg I
jer you *fam plur*
jernbanestation (-en, -er) railway station
jo after all; yes (in answer to negative question)
jo . . . jo/des the . . . the
job (-bet, -) job
jord (-en) earth, land
jordbær (-ret, -) strawberry
journalist (-en, -er) journalist
jubilæum (jubilæet, jubilæer) jubilee
jul (-en) Christmas
juleaften Christmas Eve
juledag Christmas Day
julegave (-n, -r) Christmas present

juletræ (-et, -er) Christmas tree
juli (en) July
juni (en) June
jyde (-n, -r) Jutlander
jysk from/of Jutland, Jutlandish

kabel (-et, kabler) cable
kafé (-en, -er) café
kaffe (-n) coffee
kage (-n, -r) cake
kalde (-te, -t) to call
kamel (-en, -er) camel
kamp (-en, -e) fight
kan can
kanariefugl (-en, -e) canary
karakter (-en, -er) character, marks
karamel (-len, -ler) caramel, toffee
kartoffel (kartof(fe)len, kartofler) potato
kasserer (-en, -e) cashier, treasurer
kaste to throw
kat (-ten, -te) cat
ked af det sorry
kedelig boring
kende (-te, -t) to know
kigge indenfor to look in, drop in
kilo (-et, -) kilo
kilometer (-en, -) kilometre
kirke (-n, -r) church
kirsebær (-ret, -) cherry
klage (-n, -r) complaint
klar clear
klare to manage, succeed in
klarhed (-en) clarity
klasse (-n, -r) class, form
klatre to climb
klippe to cut
klippekort (-et, -) punchcard
klo (-en, kløer) claw
klodset clumsy
klog wise
klokken . . . (at) . . . o'clock
hvad/hvor mange er klokken? what's the time?
klubhus (-et, -e) clubhouse
klud (-en, -e) rag, cloth
klæde (-te, -t) sig på to get dressed **gå* klædt i** to wear
knæ (-et, -) knee
klø to itch
kniv (-en, -e) knife
knust shattered
ko (-en, køer) cow
kok (-ken, -ke) cook
kold cold
komfortabel comfortable
komme* to come, put
komme* op at slås to come to blows
komme* op på to get up to
komme* over to get over
komme* sig over to recover
komme* til at to happen to
kommende coming/future
koncert (-en, -er) concert
kone (-n, -r) woman, wife
konge (-n, -r) king
konklusion (-en, -er) conclusion
kontinent (-et, -er) continent
konto (-en, -er *or* **konti)** account (bank etc.)
kontor (-et, -er) office
kop (-pen, -per) cup
kopiere to copy
kort (-et, -) card, map
kort short
kostald (-en, -e) cowshed
kostbar costly, precious
koste to cost
kraftig hefty, strongly built
kreditkort (-et, -) credit card

krig (-en, -e) war
Kristi himmelfartsdag Ascension Day
kro (-en, -er) inn
krokodille (-n, -r) crocodile
krokus (-sen, -) crocus
krone (-n, -r) crown, main unit of Danish currency
krop (-pen, -pe) body
krydse cross
kujon (-en, -er) coward
kul (-let, -) coal
kun only
kunne* could, to be able to
kunne* lide to like
kunde (-n, -r) customer
kursus (kurset, kurser) course (educ.)
kvart (-en, -er) quarter (of an hour)
kvarter (-et, -er) quarter (of an hour)
kvinde (-n, -r) woman
kvittering (-en, -er) receipt
kylling (-en, -er) chicken
kyllingelår (-et, -) chicken leg
kys (-set, -) kiss
kysse to kiss
kæde (-n, -r) chain
kæreste (-n, -r) sweetheart
kærlig hilsen with love from
kærlighed (-en) love
kø (-en, -er) queue
købe (-te, -t) to buy
København Copenhagen
kød (-et) flesh, meat
køkken (-et, -er) kitchen
køkkenhave (-n, -r) vegetable garden
køn pretty
køre (-te, -t) to drive
kørebane (-n, -r) carriageway, roadway
køretøj (-et, -er) vehicle
kørsel (-en) driving
kåbe (-n, -r) ladies' coat

lad gå all right
lad være med don't (as command)
lade* allow, let
lade (-n, -r) barn
lager (-et, lagre) store, warehouse
laks (-en, -) salmon
lampe (-n, -r) lamp
land (-et, -e) country
landbrugsskole (-n, -r) agricultural school
landmand (-en, -mænd) farmer
lang long i **lang tid** for a long time
langfredag Good Friday
langs (med) along, alongside
langsom slow
langt far
lappe to mend
laps (-en, -e) dandy
lastbil (-en, -er) lorry
lav low
lave to make, produce
lave mad to cook
le* to laugh
lede (-te, -t) efter to look for
leder (-en, -e) leader
lege to play
leje to rent, hire
lejer (-en, -e) lodger, tenant
lejlighed (-en, -er) occasion, opportunity; flat, apartment
lektion (-en, -er) lesson
let light, easy
leve to live
leverpostej (-en, -er) liver paté
lide* suffer
lidt little, a bit
lige just

lige meget equally
lige så . . . som just as . . . as
ligge* to lie
ligne to resemble
lille (små) small, little
lillebroder (-en, små brødre) little brother
liv (-et, -) life
livlig lively
logik (-ken) logic
lokomotivfører (-en, -e) train driver
lomme (-n, -r) pocket
lov (-en, -e) law
love to promise
luft (-en) air **fri luft** open air
lukke to shut
lukke ind/ud to let in/out
lukke inde/ude to shut in/out
lukke op to open
lund (-en, -e) grove
ly (-et) shelter
lydbånd (-et, -) audio tape
lydig obedient
lygte (-n, -r) lamp
lykke: til lykke (med) congratulations (on)
lykkelig happy
lykkes to succeed
lyne to flash with lightning
lys (-et, -) light, candle
lyseblå light blue
lyse (-te, -t) to glow, shine
lytte to listen
læge (-n, -r) doctor
lægge* to put, lay
lægge* mærke til to notice
længe long (time)
længere longer
længere frem(me) further on
længes (-tes) (efter) to long (for)
lækker delicious
lære (-te, -t) to learn, teach
lære . . . at kende to get to know . . .
lærer (-en, -e) teacher
lærerinde (-n, -r) female teacher
læse (-te, -t) to read
løbe* to run
løber (-en, -e) runner
løn (-nen) salary
lørdag (-en, -e) Saturday
løsning (-en, -er) solution
låne (-te, -t) to borrow, lend

mad (-en) food
madras (-sen, -ser) mattress
mager thin, lean
magt (-en, -er) power
maj (en) May
majdag May Day
male to paint
maler (-en, -e) painter
malke to milk
man one, you
mand (-en, mænd) man, husband
mandag (-en, -e) Monday
mange many
mangle to lack
marathonløb (-et, -) marathon
mark (-en, -er) field
marts (en) March
med with
med mindre unless
meget much, very
mellem between, among
melon (-en, -er) melon
men but
mene (-te, -t) to think, be of the opinion
mening (-en, -er) opinion
menneske (-t, -r) human being
mens while
mere more
mest most

meter (-en, -) meter
metode (-n, -r) method
middagstid (-en) noon
midt i in the middle of
mig me, myself
min/mit/mine my, mine
minde (-t, -r) memory
minde om to remind of
mindre smaller, less
mindst smallest, least, at least
minut (-tet, -ter) minute
misforstå* misunderstand
misinformere to misinform
miskredit discredit
mislykkes to fail
mislykket failed, unsuccessful
miste to lose
mistillid distrust
mistænkelig suspicious
misundelig envious
modbydelig repulsive
moden ripe
moder, mor (-en, mødre) mother
modforslag (-et, -) counterproposal
modoffensiv (-en, -er) counteroffensive
moms VAT
mon I wonder
mor *see* **moder**
morder (-en, -e) murderer
more sig to enjoy oneself
morgen (-en, -er) morning
morgenmad (-en) breakfast
morsom amusing
mos (-set, -ser) moss
motion (-en) (physical) exercise
muligvis possibly
mund (-en, -e) mouth
munter cheerful
murer (-en, -e) bricklayer, mason
mursten (-en, -) brick
mus (-en, -) mouse
museum (museet, museer) museum
musiker (-en, -e) musician
musikelsker (-en, -e) music-lover
mælk (-en) milk
mænd men
mærke to notice, sense
mærkelig remarkable, strange
møbel (-et, -bler) (piece of) furniture
møde (-t, -r) meeting
møde (-te, -t) to meet
mødes to meet (together)
møg (-et) rubbish
mørk dark
mørke (-t) darkness
mørkegrå dark grey
må may, must
måltid (-et, -er) meal
måde (-n, -r) way, method, manner
måned (-en, -er) month
månedlig monthly
måske perhaps
måtte* might, to be allowed to, to have to

nabo (-en, -er) neighbour
nat (-ten, nætter) night
nationalistisk nationalistic
natmad (-en) midnight snack
naturligvis of course, naturally
navn (-et, -e) name
ned, nede down
nej no
nemlig in fact
nervøs nervous
nogen some, any, someone, anyone
noget some, any, something, anything, somewhat

nogle some **nogle få** a few
nok enough, probably
nord (-en) north
Nordspanien North Spain
normal normal
november (en) November
nu now
nummer (-et, numre) number
nutid (-en) present (day)
nutidig present-day
ny new
nybygget newly built
nyde* to enjoy, relish
nyhed (-en, -er) news
nytårsaften New Year's Eve
nytårsdag New Year's Day
nær(ved) near(by)
næse (-n, -r) nose
næste next
næsten almost
nød (-den, -der) nut
nødt til: være nødt til to have to
nødudgang (-en, -e) emergency exit
nødvendig necessary
nøgle (-n, -r) key
nøgle (-t, -r) ball of wool
når when

offentlig public
ofte often
og and
og så videre (osv) and so on
også also
oktober (en) October
oldefar (-en, -fædre) great-grandfather
oldemor (-en, -mødre) great-grandmother
oldtid (-en) antiquity
om about, whether, in, on
om dagen per day
omkring around, about
omtale (-te, -t) to talk about
ond evil
ondskabsfuld vicious
onkel (-en, onkler) uncle
onsdag (-en, -e) Wednesday
op, oppe up
opdage to discover
opføre (-te, -t) sig to behave
opgave (-n, -r) task, assignment
oplevelse (-n, -r) experience
opmærksom: gøre opmærksom på to draw attention to
opnå to achieve
optaget occupied, engaged
orangefarvet orange (colour)
ord (-et, -) word
ordbog (-en, -bøger) dictionary
orden: i orden all right
ordentlig proper, ordered
ordsprog (-et, -) proverb
os us, ourselves
ost (-en, -e) cheese
oven på on top
over over, above, past
overalt everywhere
overanstrengt overworked
overbevist convinced
overbærende indulgent
overfart (-en, -er) crossing (sailing)
overfor opposite
overhovedet at all, altogether
overløber (-en, -e) defector
overmale to paint over
overnatte to stay overnight
overraskelse (-n, -r) surprise
overtræt overtired
ovre over

pakke (-n, -r) packet
par (-ret, -) pair, couple
paraply (-en, -er) umbrella

pariserrejse (-n, -r) Paris trip
park (-en, -er) park
parkeringshus (-et, -e) multi-storey car park
pas (-set, -) passport
passagerfærge (-n, -r) ferry
passe ind i to fit into
passe på to mind, be careful (of)
passe sig selv to mind one's own business
patient (-en, -er) patient
pels (-en, -e) fur, fur coat
penge *plur* money
pensionist (-en, -er) pensioner
perron (-en, -er) platform
personale (-t, -r) cast, staff
pige (-n, -r) girl
pinse (-n) Whitsun
plads (-en, -er) space, room
pleje to nurse, take care of
pleje at to be in the habit of
pligt (-en, -er) duty
pludselig suddenly
plæne (-n, -r) lawn
politibetjent (-en, -e) policeman
politik (-ken) policy, politics
pony (-en, -er) pony
posthus (-et, -e) post office
pote (-n, -r) paw
potteplante (-n, -r) pot plant
pragtfuld splendid, wonderful
princip (-pet, -per) principle
prins (-en, -er) prince
prinsesse (-n, -r) princess
pris (-en, -er) price
privat private
problem (-et, -er) problem
program (-met, -mer) programme
protestere to protest
præsentation (-en, -er) presentation
præst (-en, -er) priest
prøve to try
publikum (-met) public
purpur purple
pæl (-en, -e) pole
pølse (-n, -r) sausage
på on
på dansk in Danish
på gensyn see you soon
påske (-n) Easter
påskedag, første og anden Easter Sunday and Monday
påvirke to influence

quiz (-zen/-zet, -zer) quiz

rabat (-ten, -ter) discount, rebate
radio (-en, -er) radio
ramme (-te, -t) to hit
rapport (-en, -er) report
rar kind **have det rart** to have a nice time
rasende furious
rat (-tet, -) steering wheel
redde to rescue
redningshelikopter (-en, -e) rescue helicopter
regel (reg(e)len/regler) rule **som regel** as a rule
regering (-en, -er) government
regn (-en) rain
regne to rain
regning (-en, -er) bill
regulere to regulate
rejse (-n, -r) journey
rejse (-te, -t) to travel, depart
rejse (-te, -t) sig to get up
rejsende (en, -) traveller
religiøs religious
ren clean
rense to clean
reparere to repair

respektere to respect
rest (-en, -er) remainder, rest
restaurant (-en, -er) restaurant
restaurere to restore
resultat (-et, -er) result
ret rather, somewhat
ret (-ten, -ter) dish, course
ret (-ten, -ter) right **have ret til** to be entitled to
rette to correct
returbillet (-ten, -ter) return ticket
ride* to ride
rigtig real, proper, correct, right
ring (-en, -e) ring
ringe til to ring up
rude (-n, -r) windowpane
rulle to roll
rum (-met, -) space, room
runde af to round off
rundkørsel (-s(e)len, -sler) roundabout
rundt around
rutine (-n, -r) routine
rydde op to clear up
ryge* to smoke
rygte (-t, -r) rumour
række* to reach, to hand to
rød red
rødlig reddish
røg (-en) smoke
røget smoked
røver (-en, -e) robber
rå raw, rough
rådden rotten

sag (-en, -er) case, matter
salat (-en, -er) salad
salon (-en, -er) salon, lounge
salt (-et) salt
samle to gather
samle op to pick up
samling (-en, -er) collection
samme same **lige med det samme** straight away
sammenligne to compare
sammenligning (-en, -er) comparison
samt plus, and
samvittighedsfuld conscientious
sand true **ikke sandt?** isn't that right?
sang (-en, -e) song
sanger (-en, -e) singer
sans (-en, -er) for humor sense of humour
saxofon (-en, -er) saxophone
sauna (-en, -er) sauna
save to saw
savne to miss
se* to see, look
sejle to sail
seksdobbelt sixfold
sekund (-et, -er) second
selskab (-et, -er) party
selv self, even
selvfølgelig of course
selvglad self-satisfied
selvom although
sen late
sende (-te, -t) to send
seng (-en, -e) bed
sensommer (-en) late summer
september (en) September
ses (sås) to see each other
sidde* to sit
side (-n, -r) page, side
siden since
sidst last
sig himself, herself, itself, themselves
sige* to say
sige* stop to call a halt
sikke(n) . . . ! what . . . !
sikker safe, sure
sikkerhed (-en) safety

sikkert probably, surely
sin, sit, sine his, her(s), its
sjov: have det sjovt
to have fun
sjældent seldom
skabe (-te, -t) to create
skabe sig
to be silly, show off
(skauda) **skade (-n, -r)** hurt, damage
skal must, shall
skamme sig to be ashamed
skarp sharp
skat (-ten, -te) treasure, darling
skat (-ten, -ter) tax
skatteyder (-en, -e) tax-payer
ske (-te, -t) to happen
ske (-en, -er) spoon
skib (-et, -e) ship
skidt med det never mind
skilt (-et, -e) sign (post)
skilt separated
skinke (-n, -r) ham, gammon
skinne to shine
skjorte (-n, -r) shirt
sko (-en, -) shoe
skole (-n, -r) school
skoleskib (-et, -e) training ship
skomager (-en, -e) shoemaker
skotsk Scottish
skotte (-n, -r) Scot
skov (-en, -e) wood, forest
skrive* to write
skrue (-n, -r) screw
skruet på screwed on
skubbe to push
skuespiller (-en, -e) actor
skuespillerinde (-n, -r) actress
skuffe to disappoint
skulle* should, to have to
skulle* lige til at
to be just about to
skyld (-en) sake, fault
skylle to rinse
skynde (-te, -t) sig to hurry
skæbne (-n, -r) fate
skændes (-tes)
to argue, quarrel
skære* (sig) to cut (oneself)
skærtorsdag
Maundy Thursday
skønhed (-en, -er) beauty
skønt although
skål! cheers!
slags (-en, -) kind, sort
slagter (-en, -e) butcher
slank slim
slankekur (-en, -e) diet, slimming course
slet ikke not at all
slidt worn
slikke to lick
slot (-tet, -te) palace
sludder (-et) nonsense
slukke to turn off, extinguish
slutte to end, finish
slå* to hit, beat
slå* op to look up
(in reference book)
slå* til to suffice
slås (sloges) to fight
smag (-en, -e) taste
smage (-te, -t) to taste
smal narrow
smerte (-n, -r) pain
smil (-et, -)
smile
smile (-ede *or* **-te, -(e)t)** to smile
smuk beautiful
smør (-ret) butter
smøre* to spread (butter etc.)
små *see* **lille**
småforbryder (-en, -e)
petty criminal
snart soon **så snart** as soon as
snavset dirty
sne to snow
snebold (-en, -e) snowball

snes (-en, -) a score
snitte to carve
snu sly, cunning
socialforsorg (-en)
social welfare
sofa (-en, -er) sofa
sol (-en, -e) sun
soldat (-en, -er) soldier
som who(m), which, that
som as **som om** as if
sommer (-en, somre) summer
sommerresidens (-en, -er)
summer residence
sommetider sometimes
sorg (-en, -er) sorrow
sort black
sove* to sleep
soveværelse (-t, -r) bedroom
spare to save
specialitet (-en, -er) speciality
speciel special
spegepølse (-n, -r) salami
spille to play
spiller (-en, -e) player
spirituskørsel (-en) drinking
and driving
spise (-te, -t) to eat
spisekort (-et, -) menu
sport (-en) sport
sportsgal sports-mad
sprede (-te, -t) to spread
springe* to jump
springvand (-et, -) fountain
sprog (-et, -) language
spurv (-en, -e) sparrow
spændende exciting
spørge* to ask, inquire
spørge* om vej to ask the way
spørgsmål (-et, -) question
stakkels poor, pitiable
stald (-en, -e) stable, (cow)shed
stamme to stammer
standard (-en, -er) standard
standse to stop
starte to start
stave to spell
stemme (-n, -r) voice
sten (-en, -) stone
stenhård rock-hard
sti (-en, -er) path
stille quietly
stilling (-en, -er) job, position
stjerne (-n, -r) star
stole på to trust
stol (-en, -e) chair
stolthed (-en) pride
stoppe
to stuff, darn, stop
stor big, large
storebror (-en, -brødre)
big brother
storme to blow a gale
straffe to beach
stram tight
straks immediately
strand (-en, -e) beach
strejke to go on strike
streng strict, severe
studere to study
studerende (en, -) student
stuehus (-et, -e) farmhouse
stærk strong
stød (-et, -) glottal stop, bump
støde (-te, -t) på to come
across
støj (-en) noise
støjende noisy
støvle (-n, -r) boot
stå* to stand
sult (-en) hunger
suppe (-n, -r) soup
svanger pregnant
svar (-et, -) answer, reply
svare to answer, reply
svigerdatter (-en, -døtre)
daughter-in-law
svigerfar (-en, -fædre)
father-in-law

svigermor (-en, -mødre) mother-in-law
svigersøn (-nen, -ner) son-in-law
svømme to swim
sy to sew
syd (-en) south
syg ill, sick
sygeplejer (-en, -e) male nurse
sygeplejerske (-n, -r) (female) nurse
syn (-et, -) sight, vision
synes (-tes, -tes) to seem, to think (be of the opinion)
synge* to sing
sælge* to sell
særligt in particular, especially
sætte* to put, set
sød sweet
søge (-te, -t) to look for
sølvbryllup (-pet, -per) silver wedding
sølvtøj (-et) silverware
søm (-met, -) nail
søm (-men, -me) seam
sømand (-en, -mænd) sailor
søn (-nen, -ner) son
søndag (-en, -e) Sunday
søvnig sleepy
søster (-en, søstre) sister
så so, then
sådan such
såvel som as well as

tabe (-te, -t) to lose
tabe vægt to lose weight
tag (-et, -e) roof
tage* to take
tage* af to take off
tak (-ken, -) thanks
takke to thank
tale (-te, -t) to speak, talk
tale (-n, -r) speech
taler (-en, -e) speaker
tand (-en, tænder) tooth
tandlæge (-n, -r) dentist
tandpine (-n, -r) toothache
tankefuld thoughtful
tante (-n, -r) aunt
tapper brave
taxa (-en, -er) taxi
taxachauffør (-en, -er) taxi driver
te (-en) tea
teater (teat(e)ret), teatre) theatre
telefon (-en, -er) telephone
telefonbog (-en, -bøger) telephone book
Themsen the Thames
tid (-en, -er) time
tidlig early
tie* stille to stop talking, be quiet
til to
til lykke congratulations
tilbage back, left (over)
tilbud (-et, -) offer
tilfreds satisfied
tilfælde (-t, -) case, coincidence
i tilfælde af (at) in case (of)
tilfældighed (-en, -er) coincidence
tilfældigvis by chance
tilgive* to forgive
tilstå* to confess
tiltale (-te, -t) to charge
time (-n, -r) hour
ting (-en, -) thing
tirsdag (-en, -e) Tuesday
tit often
tog (-et, -) train
toilet (-tet, -ter) toilet
toldfri duty-free
tolerant tolerant
tomat (-en, -er) tomato
top (-pen, -pe) top

topsælger (-en, -e) top salesman
tordne to thunder
torsdag (-en, -e) Thursday
torv (-et, -e) square (place)
trafik (-ken) traffic
trafiklys (-et, -) traffic lights
trediedel (-en, -e) third
tredobbelt threefold
trekvart three quarters
trick (-et, - *or* **-s)** trick
trillebør (-en, -e) wheelbarrow
tro to believe
trone (-n, -r) throne
træ (-et, -er) tree
træde* to tread
trække* sig tilbage to retire
trække* vejr to draw breath, breathe
træne to train
træner (-en, -e) trainer, coach
trænge (-te, -t) til to need
træning (-en) training
træt tired
tudse (-n, -r) toad
tung heavy
tunge (-n, -r) tongue
tur (-e, -e) turn, trip
tusind (et, - *or* **-er)** thousand
tusind tak thank you very much
tvivl (-en, -) doubt
tygge to chew
tyggegummi (-et) chewing gum
tyk thick, fat **i tykt og tyndt** through thick and thin
tysk German
tyv (-en, -e) thief
tælle* to count
tænde (-te, -t) to light, turn on lights
tænke (-te, -t) to think
tæppe (-t, -r) carpet, blanket
tøj (-et) clothes
tør dares
tørstig thirsty
tå (-en, tæer) toe
tåre (-n, -r) tear

uanset regardless, no matter
ud(e) out
udbredt widespread
uden without
udendørsliv (-et) outdoor life
udenfor outside
udkant (-en, -er) outskirts
udleje to let out, hire out
udlænding (-en, -er) foreigner
udmattet exhausted
udsalg (-et, -) sales
udstyret equipped
udtale (-n) pronunciation
udtryk (-ket, -) expression
ufarlig safe, harmless
uforbederlig incorrigible
uge (-n, -r) week
ugentlig weekly
uha oh dear
uhyre huge(ly)
uhøflig rude
uhørlig inaudible
ukendt unknown
ulækker repulsive, unappetising
ulært uneducated
ulejlighed (-en) inconvenience
ulydig disobedient
ulykke (-n, -r) accident
umulig impossible
umådelig meget a great deal
under under, below, during
underbetalt underpaid
underernæret undernourished
underetage (-n, -r) lower floor
undersøge (-te, -t) to investigate
undersøgelse (-n, -r) investigation, research

undertiden occasionally
undre (sig) to wonder
undskyld sorry, excuse me
undskyldning (-en, -er) apology, excuse
undtagelse (-n, -r) exception
ung young
ungkarl (-en, -e) bachelor
universitet (-et, -er) university
universitetsstudier university studies
ur (-et, -e) watch, clock
urmager (-en, -e) watchmaker
uselskabelig unsociable
uskyldig innocent
utilfredshed (-en) dissatisfaction
utilfredstillende unsatisfactory
uærlig dishonest

vagabond (-en, -er) tramp
vand (-et, -e) water
vande to water
vant til used/accustomed to
var was, were
varebil (-en, -er) goods van
varm warm
varme to warm
vaske to wash
ved by, at
vedkomme* to concern
vegne: ingen vegne nowhere
vej (-en, -e) road, way, **noget i vejen** something wrong **sige* vejen** to tell (someone) the way
vejr (-et) weather
vel do you think so?, I hope?
velbekomme you're welcome
velhavende well-heeled
velholdt well-kept
velkommen welcome
ven (-nen, -ner) (boy)friend
vende (-te, -t) to turn
vende tilbage to go back
veninde (-n, -r) (girl)friend
venlig friendly **venlig hilsen** best wishes, kind regards
venstre left
vente to wait, expect
verden (-(en), verd(e)ner) world
verdenssituation (-en, -er) world situation
version (-en, -er) version
vest (-en) west
vi we
vide* to know
vidunderlig wonderful
vigtig important
vil will, wants to
vil gerne would like to
vil hellere would rather
vil helst would most like to
vil sige means
vin (-en, -e) wine
vinde* to win **vinde* over** to defeat, beat
vindue (-t, -r) window
vinge (-n, -r) wing
vinkort (-et, -) wine list
vinter (-en, vintre) winter
violet violet, purple
virke to work, function
virkelig real, really
virkning (-en, -er) impact, effect
vise (-te, -t) to show
vissen faded, jaded
vist probably, I think
vittighed (-en, -er) joke
vokse to grow
vor, vort, vores our(s)
vægt (-en, -e) weight
væk away
vække to wake (someone)
vælge* to choose

vær venlig at please, be so good as to
værdi (-en, -er) value
være* to be
være* med to take part
være* til to exist
værelse (-t, -r) room
værre worse
værsgo there you are
værst worst
vært (-en, -er) host
værtinde (-n, -r) hostess
vågne to wake up

waliser (-en, -e) Welshman
wienerbrød (-et, -) Danish pastry

xylofon (-en, -er) xylophone

yndlingsvittighed (-en, -er) favourite joke
yngre younger, youngish
yngst youngest

zebra (-en, -er) zebra
zoologisk have zoo

æde * to eat (of animals)
ædel noble
æg (-get, -) egg
ægte genuine
ældre older, elderly
ældst eldest, oldest
ærlig honest
ærlighed (-en) honesty
ærligt talt frankly (speaking)
ært (-en, -er) pea

ø (-en, -er) island
øje (-t, øjne) eye
øjeblik (-ket, -ke) moment
øl (-let) beer
øl (-len, -ler) (bottle/glass/can of) beer
ønske to wish
øre (-n, -(r)) øre, 1/100 of a krone
øre (-t, -r) ear
øse (-te, -t) ned to pour down
øst (-en) east
Østjylland East Jutland
øve sig to practise

å (-en, -er) stream, rivulet
åben open
åh oh
år (-et, -) year
århundrede (-t, -r) century
årlig annually
årsag (-en, -er) cause
årsdag (-en, -e) anniversary

English – Danish

*Numbers are listed in Section 17. See Section 3 for information about gender and plural of nouns. See Section 18 for information about the past tense of verbs. (Remember that (**-te, -t**) are added to the stem of the verb, not the infinitive.) * indicates that the pattern of that verb will be found in the list of irregular verbs.*

a/an en, et
ability evne (-n, -r)
able dygtig
able: to be a. to *(vb)* kunne*
about *(adv)* om, rundt, rundt om
about *(prep)* om, omkring
above over
absolutely absolut
accept *(vb)* acceptere
accident ulykke (-n, -r)
account (bank etc.) konto (-en, -er *or* konti)
accustomed to vant til
achieve *(vb)* opnå
acquiesce *(vb)* give* efter
act *(vb)* handle, spille, virke
actor skuespiller (-en, -e)
actress skuespillerinde (-n, -r)
actually faktisk
address adresse (-n, -r)
admittedly ganske vist
advantage fordel (-en, -e)
adventure eventyr (-et, -)
after efter
after all alligevel, jo
afternoon eftermiddag (-en, -e)
afternoon: this a. i eftermiddag
again igen
against (i)mod
age alder (-en, aldre)
agree *(vb)* enes
agricultural school landbrugsskole (-n, -r)
ago: . . . a. for . . . siden
ahead foran, fremad, fremme
air luft (-en)
alcohol alkohol (-en)
alcoholic *(adj)* alkoholisk
all al (alt, alle)
all (of it) altsammen
all (of them) allesammen
all: in a. i alt
all over over det hele
all right lad gå, i orden
all the same alligevel
all the time hele tiden
alley allé (-en, -er)
allow *(vb)* lade*
allowed: to be a. to måtte*
almost næsten
alone alene
along hen ad, langs (med)
already allerede
also også
although selvom, skønt
altogether helt
always altid
am (is, are) er
America Amerika
American amerikaner (-en, -e)
American *(adj)* amerikansk
among(st) (i)blandt
amusing morsom

and og
and so on og så videre (osv)
anecdote anekdote (-n, -r)
angel engel (englen, engle)
animal-lover dyreven (-nen,-ner)
anniversary årsdag (-en, -e)
annually årlig
answer svar (-et, -)
answer *(vb)* svare
antiquity oldtid (-en)
any nogen, noget; enhver, ethvert
anyone nogen
anything noget
apology undskyldning (-en, -er)
apartment lejlighed (-en, -er)
appetite appetit (-ten)
approximately ca. (cirka)
April april (en)
are *(vb)* er
area egn (-en, -e)
argue *(vb)* skændes (-tes)
around rundt, om, omkring
arrive *(vb)* ankomme*
as som, eftersom, da
as . . . as så . . . som
as if som om
Ascension Day Kristi himmelfartsdag
ashamed: to be a. *(vb)* skamme sig
ask *(vb)* spørge* (om), bede* (om)
assignment opgave (-n, -r)
assistant assistent (-en, -er)
at i, på, ved, for, over, med, hos
attack angreb (-et, -)
attempt forsøg (-et, -)
attention: to draw a. to *(vb)* gøre* opmærksom på
audio tape lydbånd (-et, -)
August august (en)
aunt tante (-n, -r)
Australia Australien
Australian australier (-en, -e)
Australian *(adj)* australsk
author forfatter (-en, -e)
autumn efterår (-et, -)
away bort(e), af sted, væk

bachelor ungkarl (-en, -e)
back ryg (-gen, -ge)
back *(adv)* tilbage
bad dårlig
baker bager (-en, -e)
ball of wool nøgle (-t, -r)
bank bank (-en, -er)
bank manager bankbestyrer (-en, -e)
bankrupt fallit
bankrupt: to go b. *(vb)* gå* fallit
bark bark (-en)
bark *(vb)* gø
barking gøen (en)
barn lade (-n, -r)
bath bad (-et, -)
be *(vb)*være*
beach strand (-en, -e)
beat *(vb)* slå*
beautiful smuk
beauty skønhed (-en, -er)
because fordi
become blive*
bed seng (-en, -e)
bedroom soveværelse (-t, -r)
beech tree bøgetræ (-et, -er)
beer (substance) øl (-let)
beer (bottle/can/glass of b.) øl (-len, -ler)
before før, foran, inden, forinden
begin *(vb)* begynde (-te, -t)
behave *(vb)* opføre (-te, -t) sig
behaviour adfærd (-en)

behind *(adv)* bagved
behind *(prep)* bag
believe *(vb)* tro
beloved elsket
below under
bench bænk (-en, -e)
benefit gavn (-en)
besides desuden
best bedst
better bedre
between (i)mellem
bicycle cykel (-en, cykler)
big stor
bill regning (-en, -er)
bird fugl (-en, -e)
birthday fødselsdag (-en, -e)
birthright fødselsret (-ten)
bit: a (little) b. lidt
bite *(vb)* bide*
black sort
blanket tæppe (-t, -r)
bleeding blødende
blind blind
blow (a gale) *(vb)* storme
blue blå
blueish blålig
body krop (-pen, -pe)
bone ben (-et, -)
bonfire bål (-et, -)
book bog (-en, bøger)
boot støvle (-n, -r)
boring kedelig
born: to be/have been b. *(vb)* være* født
borrow *(vb)* låne (-te, -t)
boss chef (-en, -er)
both begge (to), begge dele, både
both . . . and både . . . og
bottle flaske (-n, -r)
bottom bund (-en, -e)
box dåse (-n, -r)
boxer bokser (-en, -e)
boy dreng (-en, -e)
brave tapper
bread brød (-et, -)
bread: a loaf of b. brød (-et, -)
break *(vb)* brække
breakfast morgenmad (-en)
breathe *(vb)* trække* vejr
brick mursten (-en, -)
bricklayer murer (-en, -e)
bridge bro (-en, -er)
bring *(vb)* bringe*
British britisk
brother broder, bror (-en, brødre)
brown brun
build *(vb)* bygge
bump stød (-et, -)
bus bus (-sen, -ser)
bush busk (-en, -e)
business forretning (-en, -er)
businessman forretningsmand (-en, -mænd)
but men
butcher slagter (-en, -e)
butter smør (-ret)
buy *(vb)* købe (-te, -t)
by af, ved, forbi

cable kabel (-et, kabler)
café kafé (-en, -er)
cake kage (-n, -r)
call *(vb)* kalde (-te, -t)
called: to be c. *(vb)* hedde*
camel kamel (-en, -er)
can *(n)* dåse (-n, -r)
can *(vb)* kan
Canada Canada
Canadian *(adj)* canadisk
Canadian *(n)* canadier (-en, -e)
canary kanariefugl (-en, -e)
candle lys (-et, -)
car bil (-en, -er)
caramel karamel (-len, -ler)
caravan campingvogn (-en, -e)
card kort (-et, -)

care for *(vb)* bryde* sig om
careful forsigtig
careful: to be c. (of) *(vb)* passe på
carpet tæppe (-t, -r)
carriageway kørebane (-n, -r)
carrot gulerod (-en, -rødder)
carry *(vb)* bære*
carve *(vb)* snitte
case tilfælde (-t, -), sag (-en, -er)
cashier kasserer (-en, -e)
cast personale (-t, -r)
cat kat (-ten, -te)
case: in any c. i hvert fald
case: in c. of ifald, i tilfælde af (at)
cause årsag (-en, -er)
celebrate *(vb)* fejre
celebration fest (-en, -er)
centre centrum (centret, centrer)
century århundrede (-t, -r)
certainly bestemt, sikkert
chain kæde (-n, -r)
chair stol (-en, -e)
champagne champagne (-n)
chance: by chance *(adv)* tilfældigvis
change (oneself) *(vb)* forandre (sig)
change into *(vb)* forvandle (sig) til
character karakter (-en, -er)
charge *(vb)* tiltale (-te, -t)
charming charmerende
cheap billig
check *(vb)* efterse*
cheeky fræk
cheerful munter
cheers! skål!
cheese ost (-en, -e)
cherry kirsebær (-ret, -)
chew *(vb)* tygge
chewing gum tyggegummi (-et)
chicken kylling (-en, -er)
chicken leg kyllingelår (-et, -)
child barn (-et, børn)
chocolate chokolade (-n, -r)
choose *(vb)* vælge*
Christmas jul (-en)
Christmas Day juledag
Christmas Eve juleaften
Christmas: Happy C. glædelig jul
Christmas present julegave (-n, -r)
Christmas tree juletræ (-et, -er)
church kirke (-n, -r)
cigar cigar (-en, -er)
cigarette cigaret (-ten, -ter)
cinema biograf (-en, -er)
civil servant embedsmand (-en, -mænd)
clarity klarhed (-en)
class klasse (-n, -r)
claw klo (-en, kløer)
clean *(adj)* ren
clean *(vb)* rense
clear klar
clear up *(vb)* rydde op
clever dygtig
climb *(vb)* klatre
clock ur (-et, -e)
cloth klud (-en, -e)
clothes tøj (-et)
clubhouse klubhus (-et, -e)
clumsy klodset
coach træner (-en, -e)
coal kul (-let, -)
coarse grov
coffee kaffe (-n)
coincidence tilfældighed (-en, -er), tilfælde (-t, -)
cold *(adj)* kold
cold *(n)* forkølelse (-n, -r)

collection samling (-en, -er)
colour farve (-n, -r)
coloured farvet
colourful farverig
come *(vb)* komme*
come across *(vb)* støde (-te, -t) på
come to blows *(vb)* komme* op at slås
comfortable komfortabel
coming (i.e. future *(adj)***)** kommende
common almindelig
compare *(vb)* sammenligne
comparison sammenligning (-en, -er)
complaint klage (-n, -r)
completely helt
concern *(vb)* vedkomme*
concert koncert (-en, -er)
conclusion konklusion (-en, -er)
confess *(vb)* tilstå*
congratulate *(vb)* gratulere
congratulations (on) til lykke (med)
conscientious samvittighedsfuld
Constitution Day (5 June) grundlovsdag
continent kontinent (-et, -er)
continue *(vb)* fortsætte*
convinced overbevist
cook kok (-ken, -ke)
cook *(vb)* lave mad
Copenhagen København
copy *(vb)* kopiere
corner hjørne (-t, -r)
correct rigtig
correct *(vb)* rette
cost *(vb)* koste
costly kostbar
cough *(vb)* hoste
count *(vb)* tælle*
counteroffensive modoffensiv (-en, -er)
counterproposal modforslag (-et, -)
country land (-et, -e)
couple par (-ret, -)
course (educ.) kursus (kurset, kurser)
course (of meal) ret (-ten, -ter)
cow ko (-en, køer)
coward kujon (-en, -er)
cowshed stald (-en, -e), kostald (-en, -e)
craftsman håndværker (-en, -e)
cream fløde (-n)
cream sauce flødesovs (-en)
create *(vb)* skabe (-te, -t)
credit card kreditkort (-et, -)
criminal forbryder (-en, -e)
crocodile krokodille (-n, -r)
crocus krokus (-sen, -)
cross *(vb)* krydse
crossing (sailing) overfart (-en, -er)
crossroads gadekryds (-et, -)
crown (main unit of Danish currency) krone (-n, -r)
cucumber agurk (-en, -er)
cunning *(adj)* snu
cup kop (-pen, -per)
curtain gardin (-et, -er)
customer kunde (-n, -r)
cut *(vb)* klippe
cut (oneself) *(vb)* skære* (sig)

daily daglig
damage skade (-n, -r)
damaged beskadiget
dance *(vb)* danse
dance band danseorkester (-et, -orkestre)
dandy laps (-en, -e)
Dane dansker (-en, -e)

dangerous farlig
Danish dansk
Danish pastry wienerbrød (-et, -)
dare *(vb)* turde*
dark mørk
dark grey mørkegrå
darkness mørke (-t)
darling skat (-ten, -te)
darn *(vb)* stoppe
daughter datter (-en, døtre)
daughter-in-law svigerdatter (-en, -døtre)
day dag (-en, -e)
day: d. and night, 24 hours døgn (-et, -)
day: per d. om dagen
dead død
dead boring dødkedelig
deal: a great d. umådelig meget
December december (en)
deed gerning (-en, -er)
defeat *(vb)* vinde* over
defector overløber (-en, -e)
delicious lækker
democratic demokratisk
Denmark Danmark
dentist tandlæge (-n, -r)
depart *(vb)* afgå*, rejse (-te, -t)
describe *(vb)* beksrive*
deserve *(vb)* fortjene (-te, -t)
dessert dessert (-en, -er)
devoted hengiven
dialect dialekt (-en, -er)
dictionary ordbog (-en, -bøger)
die *(vb)* dø*
diet slankekur (-en, -e)
difference forskel (-len, -le)
different forskellig; anderledes; anden, andet, andre
dinner aftensmad (-en)
dirty snavset
disappear *(vb)* forsvinde*
disappoint *(vb)* skuffe
discount rabat (-ten, -ter)
discover *(vb)* opdage
discredit miskredit
dish ret (-ten, -ter)
dishonest uærlig
disobedient ulydig
dissatisfaction utilfredshed (-en)
distrust mistillid (-en)
do *(vb)* gøre*
doctor læge (-n, -r)
dog hund (-en, -e)
dog breed hunderace (-n, -r)
dog food hundemad (-en)
dog lover hundeelsker (-en, -e)
don't! (as command) lad være!
door dør (-en, -e)
double dobbelt
doubt tvivl (-en, -)
down ned(e)
down here herned(e)
down there derned(e)
dozen dusin (-et, -)
draw attention to *(vb)* gøre* opmærksom på
draw breath *(vb)* trække* vejr
dream *(n)* drøm (-men, -me)
dream *(vb)* drømme (-te, -t)
dressed: to get d. *(vb)* klæde (-te, -t) sig på
drill bor (-et, -)
drink *(vb)* drikke*
drink driving spirituskørsel (-en)
drive *(vb)* køre (-te, -t)
driver fører (-en, -e)
driving kørsel (-en)
drop in *(vb)* kigge indenfor
drunk fuld
during under
duty pligt (-en, -er), told (-en)
duty-free toldfri

each hver, hvert
each other hinanden
ear øre (-t, -r)
early tidlig
early summer forsommer (-en, -somre)
earth jord (-en)
east øst (-en)
East Jutland Østjylland
Easter påske (-n)
Easter Monday anden påskedag
Easter Sunday første påskedag
easy nem, rolig, let
eat *(vb)* spise (-te, -t)
eat (of animals) *(vb)* æde*
effect virkning (-en, -er)
egg æg (-get, -)
either . . . or enten . . . eller
elderly halvgammel, ældre
eldest ældst
elephant elefant (-en, -er)
emergency exit nødudgang (-en, -e)
emigrate *(vb)* emigrere
end *(vb)* slutte
energy energi (-en)
engaged optaget
engaged (to be married) forlovet
England England
English *(adj)* engelsk
Englishman englænder (-en, -e)
enjoy *(vb)* nyde*
enjoy oneself *(vb)* more sig
enough nok
entitled: to be e. to have* ret til
entrance indgang (-en, -e)
envious misundelig
equally lige meget
equipped udstyret
especially især, særligt
esteem højagtelse (-n)
eternal evig
Europe Europa
European *(adj)* europæisk
even *(adv)* selv, endnu
evening aften (-en, -er)
evening: this e. i aften
every enhver, ethvert; hver, hvert; alle, al mulig
everywhere overalt
evil ond
exception undtagelse (-n, -r)
exciting spændende
excuse undskyldning (-en, -er)
excuse me! undskyld!
exercise: physical e. motion (-en)
exhausted udmattet
exist *(vb)* eksistere, være* til, findes*
expect *(vb)* vente
expensive dyr
experience oplevelse (-n, -r)
explain *(vb)* forklare
express train hurtigtog (-et, -)
expression udtryk (-ket, -)
extinguish *(vb)* slukke
eye øje (-t, øjne)

face ansigt (-et, -er)
fact: in f. nemlig, i virkeligheden, faktisk
factory fabrik (-ken, -ker)
factory worker fabriksarbejder (-en, -e)
faded vissen
fail *(vb)* mislykkes
failed mislykket
fair fair
fairy-tale eventyr (-et, -)
fall *(vb)* falde*
false falsk
family familie (-n, -r)

famous berømt
fanatical fanatisk
fantastic fantastisk
far langt
farm gård (-en, -e)
farmer bonde (-n, bønder), landmand (-en, -mænd)
farmhouse bondegård (-en, -e), stuehus (-et, -e)
fast hurtig
fat tyk
fate skæbne (-n, -r)
father far, fader (-en, fædre)
father-in-law svigerfar (-en, -fædre)
fault fejl (-en, -), skyld (-en)
favourite joke yndlingsvittighed (-en, -er)
February februar (en)
feeding fodring (-en)
feminine feminin
fence hegn (-et, -)
ferry færge (-n, -r)
fertile frodig
fetch *(vb)* hente
few få
few: a f. nogle få
fewer færre
fewest færrest
field mark (-en, -er)
fifth femtedel (-en, -e)
fight *(n)* kamp (-en, -e)
fight *(vb)* slås* (sloges)
film film (-en, - *or* -s)
finally endelig
find *(vb)* finde*
fine fin
finger finger (-en, fingre)
finish *(vb)* blive* færdig (med)
finished færdig
fire brand (-en, -e), ild (-en)
firm firma (-et, -er)
first først
first course (of meal) forret (-ten, -ter)
first name fornavn (-et, -e)
fish *(vb)* fiske
fish: to be out fishing *(vb)* være* ude at fiske
fit into *(vb)* passe ind i
flag flag (-et, -)
flagpole flagstang (-en, -stænger)
flaming flammende
flash (with lightning) *(vb)* lyne
flat *(n)* lejlighed (-en, -er)
flesh kød (-et)
flirt *(vb)* flirte
floor gulv (-et, -e)
Florence Firenze
flow *(vb)* flyde*
flower blomst (-en, -er)
flower bed blomsterbed (-et, -e)
fluent flydende
fly *(n)* flue (-n, -r)
fly *(vb)* flyve*
follow *(vb)* følge*
food mad (-en)
foot fod (-en, fødder)
football fodbold (-en, -e)
football boot fodboldstøvle (-n, -r)
football team fodboldhold (-et, -)
for for
foreign fremmed
foreigner udlænding (-en, -e)
forest skov (-en, -e)
forget *(vb)* glemme (-te, -t)
forgive *(vb)* tilgive*
fork gaffel (-en, gafler)
fortunately heldigvis
forwards frem, fremad
found: to be f. *(vb)* findes*
fountain springvand (-et, -)

fourth fjerdedel (-en, -e)
fourth Friday after Easter store bededag
frame *(vb)* indfatte
France Frankrig
frankly (speaking) ærligt talt
free *(adj)* fri
free (of charge) gratis
free *(vb)* befri
freedom frihed (-en, -er)
French fransk
Frenchman franskmand (-en, -mænd)
Friday fredag (-en, -e)
friend ven (-nen, -ner)
friend: girl/lady f. veninde (-n, -r)
friendly venlig
frog frø (-en, -er)
from fra
from here herfra
from there derfra
from where hvorfra
full fuld
fun *(adj)* sjov
fun: to have f. *(vb)* have* det sjovt
function *(vb)* virke
fur, fur coat pels (-en, -e)
furious rasende
furniture møbler *(plural)*
furniture: a piece of f. møbel (-et, -bler)
further on længere frem(me)
furthermore desuden

gammon skinke (-n, -r)
garage garage (-n, -r), bilværksted (-et, -er)
garden have (-n, -r)
gather *(vb)* samle
general general (-en, -er)
genius geni (-et, -er)
gentleman herre (-n, -r)
genuine ægte
German *(adj)* tysk
German *(n)* tysker (-en, -e)
Germany Tyskland
get *(vb)* få*
get over *(vb)* komme* over
get up *(vb)* rejse (-te, -t) sig
get up to *(vb)* komme* op på
gherkin agurk (-en, -er)
gift gave (-n, -r)
girl pige (-n, -r)
give *(vb)* give*
give way *(vb)* give* efter
glass glas (-set, -)
glottal stop stød (-et, -)
glove handske (-n, -r)
glow *(vb)* lyse (-te, -t)
go *(vb)* gå*
go back *(vb)* vende (-te, -t) tilbage
god gud (-en, -er)
God Gud
golden wedding guldbryllup (-pet, -per)
good god
good day goddag
good evening godaften
Good Friday langfredag
good morning godmorgen
good night godnat
goodbye farvel
goods van varebil (-en, -er)
goose gås (-en, gæs)
government regering (-en, -er)
grammatical grammatikalsk, grammatisk
gramophone record grammofonplade (-n, -r)
grandchild barnebarn (-et, børnebørn)
grandfather bedstefar (-en, -fædre)
grandmother bedstemor (-en, -mødre)

great-grandfather oldefar (-en, -fædre)
great-grandmother oldemor (-en, -mødre)
Greece Grækenland
Greek *(adj)* græsk
Greek *(n)* græker (-en, -e)
green grøn
greenhouse drivhus (-et, -e)
Greenland Grønland
Greenlander grønlænder (-en, -e)
Greenlandic grønlandsk
greet *(vb)* hilse (-te, -t)
greeting hilsen (-en, -er)
grey grå
grin grin (-et, -)
grove lund (-en, -e)
grow *(vb)* vokse
guest gæst (-en, -er)

habit: to be in the h. of *(vb)* pleje at
hairdresser frisør (-en, -er)
half *(adj)* halv
half *(n)* halvdel (-en, -e)
half past . . . (time) halv . . .
half-brother halvbror (-en, -brødre)
half-sister halvsøster (-en, -søstre)
halt: to call a h. *(vb)* sige* stop
ham skinke (-n, -r)
hammer *(vb)* hamre
hand hånd (-en, hænder)
hand over *(vb)* aflevere
hand to *(vb)* række*
handle *(vb)* behandle
handling behandling (-en, -er)
handsome flot, smuk, køn
happen *(vb)* ske (-te, -t)
happen to *(vb)* komme* til at
happy glad, lykkelig
harbour havn (-en, -r)
hard hård
harmless ufarlig
hat hat (-ten, -te)
hate *(vb)* hade
have *(vb)* have*
have to *(vb)* være* nødt til, måtte*, skulle*
he han
headache hovedpine (-n, -r)
health helbred (-et)
hear *(vb)* høre (-te, -t)
heart hjerte (-t, -r)
heaven himmel (him(me)len, himle)
heavy tung
hefty kraftig
hello dav, davs
help *(n)* hjælp (-en)
help *(vb)* hjælpe*
hen høne (-n, -r)
her hende; sig; hendes; sin, sit, sine
here her, herhen, hertil
hers hendes; sin, sit, sine
herself hun selv, hende selv; sig selv; sig; selv
hi! hej!
high høj
high-school teacher højskolelærer (-en, -e)
hill bakke (-n, -r)
him ham; den, det; sig
himself han selv, ham selv; sig selv; sig; selv
hire *(vb)* leje
hire out *(vb)* udleje
his hans; sin, sit, sine
hit *(vb)* ramme (-te, -t), slå*
hole hul (-let, -ler)
holey (full of holes) hullet
holiday ferie (-n, -r)
holiday: to spend a h. *(vb)* holde* ferie
home hjem (-met, -)

home: at h. hjemme
home: (to) h. hjem
home-made hjemmelavet
honest ærlig
honesty ærlighed (-en)
hop *(vb)* hoppe
hope *(vb)* håbe
horse hest (-en, -e)
host vært (-en, -er)
hostess værtinde (-n, -r)
hour time (-n, -r)
house hus (-et, -e)
how hvor, hvordan
however dog
huge uhyre
hugely uhyre
human being menneske (-t, -r)
hunger sult (-en)
hurry *(vb)* skynde (-te, -t) sig
husband mand (-en, mænd)
hut hytte (-n, -r)

I jeg
idea idé (-en, -er)
ideal ideal (-et, -er)
if hvis
ill syg
imagine *(vb)* forestille sig
immediately straks
impact virkning (-en, -er)
important vigtig
impossible umulig
improve *(vb)* forbedre
in *(prep)* i, ind, på
in *(adv)* inde
inaudible uhørlig
incidentally forresten
inconvenience ulejlighed (-en)
incorrigible uforbederlig
indulgent overbærende
influence *(vb)* påvirke
influenza influenza (-en)
inhabitant indbygger (-en, -e)
inn kro (-en, -er)
innocent uskyldig
inside indenfor
inspiring inspirerende
install *(vb)* indrette
intelligence intelligens (-en), forstand (-en)
interest *(vb)* interessere
interested interesseret
introduce *(vb)* forestille
investigate *(vb)* undersøge (-te, -t)
investigation undersøgelse (-n, -r)
invite *(vb)* indbyde*
Ireland Irland
Irish *(adj)* irsk
Irishman irer (-en, -e), irlænder (-en, -e)
is, am, are *(vb)* er
island ø (-en, -er)
isn't it? isn't that right? (etc.) ikke sandt?
it den, det
Italian *(adj)* italiensk
Italian *(n)* italiener (-en, -e)
Italy Italien
itch *(vb)* klø
its dens, dets; sin, sit, sine
itself den/det selv; sig, sig selv; selv; selve

jaded vissen
January januar (en)
jar glas (-set, -)
jealous jaloux
job job (-bet, -), stilling (-en, -er)
joke vittighed (-en, -er)
joke: favourite joke yndlingsvittighed (-en, -er)
journalist journalist (-en, -er)
journey rejse (-n, -r)
jubilee jubilæum (jubilæet, jubilæer)

July juli (en)
jump *(vb)* springe*, hoppe
June juni (en)
just lige; bare, blot
just as . . . as lige så . . . som
Jutland Jylland
Jutlander jyde (-n, -r)
Jutlandish *(adj)* jysk

keep *(vb)* holde*
keep oneself to oneself *(vb)* holde* sig for sig selv
key nøgle (-n, -r)
kilo kilo (-et, -)
kilometre kilometer (-en, -)
kind *(adj)* god, venlig, kærlig, rar
kind *(n)* slags (-en, -)
king konge (-n, -r)
kiss *(n)* kys (-set, -)
kiss *(vb)* kysse
kitchen køkken (-et, -er)
knee knæ (-et, -)
knife kniv (-en, -e)
knock *(vb)* banke
know *(vb)* kende (-te, -t), vide*
know about *(vb)* have* forstand på
know: to get to k. *(vb)* lære (-te, -t) . . . at kende

lack *(vb)* mangle
ladies' coat kåbe (-n, -r)
lady dame (-n, -r)
lamp lampe (-n, -r), lygte (-n, -r)
land jord (-en)
language sprog (-et, -)
large stor
last sidst
last night i aftes, i nat
last year i fjor
late sen
late summer sensommer (-en)
laugh *(vb)* le*
law lov (-en, -e)
lawn (græs)plæne (-n, -r)
lay *(vb)* lægge*
lazy doven
leaded (e.g. windows) blyindfattet
leader leder (-en, -e)
leaf blad (-et, -e)
lean mager
learn *(vb)* lære (-te, -t)
least: at l. mindst
left venstre
left (over) tilbage
leg ben (-et, -)
lemon mousse citronfromage (-n, -r)
lend *(vb)* låne (-te, -t)
lesson lektion (-en, -er)
let *(vb)* lade*
let in/out *(vb)* lukke ind/ud
letter brev (-et, -e)
letterbox brevkasse (-n, -r)
liberty frihed (-en, -er)
lick *(vb)* slikke
lie *(vb)* ligge*; lyve*
life liv (-et, -)
light blue lyseblå
light *(adj)* let
light *(n)* lys (-et, -)
light: to turn on the l.(s) *(vb)* tænde (-te, -t)
lightning lyn (-et)
like *(vb)* kunne* lide, bryde* sig om
like: X would l. to *(vb)* X vil gerne
like: X would most l. to X vil helst
listen *(vb)* lytte
little lille/små

little brother lillebroder (-en, små brødre)
live *(vb)* leve, bo
lively livlig
liver paté leverpostej (-en, -er)
loaf: a l. of bread brød (-et, -)
lodger lejer (-en, -e)
logic logik (-ken)
long lang
long (for) *(vb)* længes (-tes) (efter)
long (time) længe
long: for a l. time i lang tid
look *(vb)* se*
look for *(vb)* lede (-te, -t) efter, søge (-te, -t)
look forward to *(vb)* glæde sig til
look in *(vb)* kigge indenfor
look up (in reference book) (vb) slå* op
lorry lastbil (-en, -er)
lose *(vb)* miste, tabe (-te, -t)
lose weight *(vb)* tabe vægt
lost: to get l. *(vb)* fare* vildt
loud høj
lounge salon (-en, -er)
love *(n)* kærlighed (en)
love *(vb)* elske
love: with l. from kærlig hilsen
lovely dejlig
low lav
lower floor underetage (-n, -r)
luck held (-et)
luck: good l.! held og lykke!
lucky heldig
luggage bagage (-n)
lunch frokost (-en, -er)

mad gal
Madam frue
make *(vb)* lave
male nurse sygeplejer (-en, -e)
man mand (-en, mænd)
manage *(vb)* klare
manner måde (-n, -r)
many mange
map kort (-et, -)
marathon marathonløb (-et, -)
March marts (en)
married: to get m. (to) gifte sig (med)
mark karakter (-en, -er)
marry *(vb)* holde* bryllup med
mason murer (-en, -e)
matter: no m. uanset
mattress madras (-sen, -ser)
Maundy Thursday skærtorsdag
may *(vb)* måtte*, kunne*
May maj (en)
May Day majdag
mayor borgmester (-en, borgmestre)
me mig
meal måltid (-et, -er)
mean *(vb)* ville* sige
meanwhile imens
meat kød (-et)
meet *(vb)* møde (-te, -t)
meet (together) *(vb)* mødes
meeting møde (-t, -r)
melon melon (-en, -er)
memory minde (-t, -r)
mend *(vb)* lappe
menu spisekort (-et, -)
mermaid havfrue (-n, -r)
meter meter (-en, -)
method metode (-n, -r), måde (-n, -r)
middle: in the m. of midt i
midnight snack natmad (-en)
might *(vb)* måtte*
milk *(n)* mælk (-en)
milk *(vb)* malke
mind *(n)* forstand (-en)
mind *(vb)* passe på

mind one's own business *(vb)* passe sig selv
mine min, mit, mine
minute minut (-tet, -ter)
misinform *(vb)* misinformere
miss *(vb)* savne
Miss frøken, frk.
mistake fejl (-en, -)
misunderstand *(vb)* misforstå*
modest beskeden
moment øjeblik (-ket, -ke)
Monday mandag (-en, -e)
money penge *(always plural)*
monkey abe (-n, -r)
month måned (-en, -er)
monthly månedlig
motion fart (-en)
more mere, flere
more: one m. en/et til
morning morgen (-en, -er), formiddag (-en, -e)
morning: this m. i formiddag, i morges
moss mos (-set, -ser)
most mest, flest(e), de fleste
most of all allerhelst
mother mor, moder (-en, mødre)
motorist bilist (-en, -er)
mountain bjerg (-et, -e)
mouse mus (-en, -)
mouth mund (-en, -e)
move *(vb)* flytte
Mr hr.
Mrs fru
Ms fr.
much meget
multi-storey car park parkeringshus (-et, -e)
murderer morder (-en, -e)
museum museum (museet, museer)
musician musiker (-en, -e)
music-lover musikelsker (-en, -e)
must *(vb)* måtte*, skulle*
my min, mit, mine
myself jeg selv, selv; mig selv, mig

nail søm (-met, -)
name navn (-et, -e)
narrow smal
nationalistic nationalistisk
naturally naturligvis
near(by) nær(ved)
necessary nødvendig
need *(vb)* behøve, have* brug for, trænge (-te, -t)
neighbour nabo (-en, -er)
neither . . . nor hverken . . . eller
nervous nervøs
never aldrig
never mind skidt med det
new ny
New Year's Day nytårsdag
New Year's Eve nytårsaften
news nyhed (-en, -er)
newspaper avis (-en, -er)
next næste
nice: to have a n. time *(vb)* have* det rart
night nat (-ten, nætter)
night: day and n., 24 hours døgn (-et, -)
no nej; ikke; ingen, ikke nogen/noget, intet
no longer ikke længere
noble ædel
nobody ingen
noise støj (-en)
noisy støjende
nonsense sludder (-et)
noon middag (-en)
normal normal

north nord (-en)
North Spain Nordspanien
nose næse (-n, -r)
not ikke
not at all slet ikke
nothing ingenting
notice *(vb)* mærke, lægge* mærke til
November november (en)
now nu
nowhere ingen vegne
number nummer (-et, numre)
nurse (female) sygeplejerske (-n, -r)
nurse (male) sygeplejer (-en, -e)
nurse *(vb)* pleje
nursery school børnehave (-n, -r)
nut nød (-den, -der)

oak tree egetræ (-et, -er)
obedient lydig
obey *(vb)* adlyde*
occasion lejlighed (-en, -er)
occasionally undertiden
occupied optaget
o'clock klokken
o'clock: at . . . o'c. klokken . . .
o'clock: it is . . . o'c. klokken er . . .
October oktober (en)
of af
of course naturligvis, selvfølgelig
off: to be o. (work etc.) have* fri
offer tilbud (-et, -)
office kontor (-et, -er)
often ofte, tit
oh! åh!
oh dear! uha!
old gammel
older ældre
oldest ældst
old-fashioned gammeldags
on på
on top oven på
once en gang, engang
one *(pron)* man
one and a half halvanden
one more en/et til
one's ens; sin, sit, sine
only kun, bare, blot
only: if o. bare, blot
open *(adj)* åben
open *(vb)* åbne, lukke op
open: to be o. holde* åbent
open air fri luft
open-air person friluftsmenneske (-t, -r)
opinion mening (-en, -er)
opportunity lejlighed (-en, -er)
opposite overfor
or eller
orange appelsin (-en, -er)
orange (colour) orangefarvet
ordered *(adj)* ordentlig
ordinary almindelig
other anden, andet, andre
otherwise ellers
ought to *(vb)* burde*
our(s) vor, vort, vores
ourselves os
out ud(e)
outdoor life udendørsliv (-et)
outside udenfor
outskirts udkant (-en, -er)
outstanding fremragende
over over, ovre
over here herover, herovre
over there derhen, derhenne; derover, derovre
over to hen til
overtired overtræt
overworked overanstrengt
own egen, eget, egne
owner ejer (-en, -e)

packet pakke (-n, -r)
page side (-n, -r)
pain smerte (-n, -r)
paint *(vb)* male
paint over *(vb)* overmale
painter maler (-en, -e)
pair par (-ret, -)
palace slot (-tet, -te)
parents forældre
Paris trip pariserrejse (-n, -r)
park park (-en, -er)
part del (-en, -e)
participant deltager (-en, -e)
particular: in p. særligt
party selskab (-et, -er)
passport pas (-set, -)
past forbi; over
path sti (-en, -er)
patient patient (-en, -er)
pavement fortov (-et, -e)
paw pote (-n, -r)
pay *(vb)* betale (-te, -t)
pea ært (-en, -er)
peace fred (-en)
pedestrian fodgænger (-en, -e)
pedestrian crossing fodgængerovergang (-en, -e)
pensioner pensionist (-en, -er)
people folk (-et, -)
perhaps måske
pet shop dyreforretning (-en, -er)
petrol station benzinstation (-en, -er)
petty criminal småforbryder (-en, -e)
philosophical filosofisk
photographer fotograf (-en, -er)
pick up *(vb)* samle op
picture billede (-t, -r)
place of work arbejdsplads (-en, -er)
platform (railway) perron (-en, -er)
play *(vb)* lege, spille
player spiller (-en, -e)
please *(vb)* glæde
please (be (so) good as to) vær (så) venlig at
pleased: to be p. about glæde sig over
pleasure glæde (-n, -r)
plump buttet
plus samt
pocket lomme (-n, -r)
pole pæl (-en, -e)
policeman politibetjent (-en, -e)
policy politik (-ken, -ker)
politics politik (-ken)
pond dam (-men, -me)
pony pony (-en, -er)
poor fattig; stakkels
pitiable stakkels
pork joint flæskesteg (-en, -e)
position stilling (-en, -er)
possibly muligvis
post office posthus (-et, -e)
pot plant potteplante (-n, -r)
potato kartoffel (kartoflen, kartofler)
pour down (e.g. rain) *(vb)* øse (-te, -t) ned
power magt (-en, -er)
practise *(vb)* øve sig
pram barnevogn (-en, -e)
pray *(vb)* bede*
precious kostbar
prefer *(vb)* foretrække*
preferably helst
pregnant gravid, svanger
present (day) nutid (-en)
presentation præsentation (-en, -er)
present-day *(adj)* nutidig

pretty køn
price pris (-en, -er)
pride stolthed (-en)
priest præst (-en, -er)
prince prins (-en, -er)
princess prinsesse (-n, -r)
principle princip (-pet, -per)
prison fængsel (-et, fængsler)
private privat
probably vist, sikkert, nok
problem problem (-et, -er)
produce *(vb)* lave
programme program (-met, -mer)
progress fremskridt (-et, -)
promise *(vb)* love
pronunciation udtale (-n)
proper ordentlig, rigtig
protest *(vb)* protestere
proverb ordsprog (-et, -)
public *(adj)* offentlig
public *(n)* publikum (-met)
punchcard klippekort (-et, -)
punish *(vb)* straffe
pupil elev (-en, -er)
purple purpur, violet
purpose formål (-et, -)
push *(vb)* skubbe
put *(vb)* lægge*, sætte*

quarrel *(vb)* skændes (-tes)
quarter fjerdedel (-en, -e)
quarter (of an hour) kvart (-en, -er), kvarter (-et, -er)
queen dronning (-en, -er)
question spørgsmål (-et, -)
queue kø (-en, -er)
quickly hurtigt
quiet: to be q. *(vb)* tie* stille
quietly stille
quilt dyne (-n, -r)
quite ganske
quiz quiz (-zen/zet, -zer)

radio radio (-en, -er)
rag klud (-en, -e)
railway station jernbanestation (-en, -er)
rain *(n)* regn (-en)
rain *(vb)* regne
rate: at any r. i hvert fald
rather hellere, ganske, ret
rather: X would rather X vil hellere
raw rå
reach *(vb)* række*
read *(vb)* læse (-te, -t)
real rigtig, virkelig
really virkelig
reason grund (-en, -e)
rebate rabat (-ten, -ter)
receipt kvittering (-en, -er)
receive *(vb)* få*
recover *(vb)* komme* sig (over)
red rød
reddish rødlig
regardless uanset
regards: kind r. venlig hilsen
regulate *(vb)* regulere
religious religiøs
relish *(vb)* nyde*
remain *(vb)* blive*
remainder rest (-en, -er)
remarkable mærkelig
remember *(vb)* huske
remind of *(vb)* minde om
renew *(vb)* forny
rent *(vb)* leje
repair *(vb)* reparere
repair shop (car) bilværksted (-et, -er)
reply *(n)* svar (-et, -)
reply *(vb)* svare
report *(n)* rapport (-en, -er)
report (vb) berette
repulsive modbydelig, ulækker

research undersøgelse (-n, -r)
rescue *(vb)* redde
rescue helicopter rednings-helikopter (-en, -e)
resemble *(vb)* ligne
reside *(vb)* bo
respect *(vb)* respektere
restaurant restaurant (-en, -er)
restore *(vb)* restaurere
result resultat (-et, -er)
retell *(vb)* genfortælle*
retire *(vb)* trække* sig tilbage
returned home hjemvendt
ride *(vb)* ride*
right højre; rigtig; ret (-ten, -ter)
right-hand driving højrekørsel (-en)
ring ring (-en, -e)
ring up *(vb)* ringe til
rinse *(vb)* skylle
ripe moden
river flod (-en, er)
river bank flodbred (-den, -der)
rivulet å (-en, -er)
road vej (-en, -e)
robber røver (-en, -e)
rock-hard stenhård
roll *(vb)* rulle
roof tag (-et, -e)
room værelse (-t, -r), rum (-met, -), plads (-en, -er)
rotten rådden
rough rå
round off *(vb)* runde af
roundabout rundkørsel (-kørs(e)len, -kørsler)
routine rutine (-n, -r)
rubbish møg (-et)
rude uhøflig
rule regel (reg(e)len, regler)
rule: as a r. som regel
rumour rygte (-t, -r)
run *(vb)* løbe*
runner løber (-en, -e)

safe sikker, ufarlig
safety sikkerhed (-en)
sail *(vb)* sejle
sailor sømand (-en, -mænd)
sake skyld (-en)
salad salat (-en, -er)
salami spegepølse (-n, -r)
salary løn (-nen)
sales udsalg (-et, -)
saleswoman ekspeditrice (-n, -r)
salmon laks (-en, -)
salon salon (-en, -er)
salt salt (-et)
same samme
same: the s. to you i lige måde
satisfied tilfreds
Saturday lørdag (-en, -e)
sauna sauna (-en, -er)
sausage pølse (-n, -r)
save *(vb)* spare
saw *(vb)* save
saxophone saxofon (-en, -er)
say *(vb)* sige*
school skole (-n, -r)
score snes (-en, -)
Scot skotte (-n, -r)
Scotland Skotland
Scottish *(adj)* skotsk
screw skrue (-n, -r)
screwed on skruet på
sea hav (-et, -e)
seam søm (-men, -me)
second (adj) anden, andet, andre
second *(n)* sekund (-et, -er)
see *(vb)* se*
see: s. each other *(vb)* ses (sås)
see: s. you again/soon på gensyn
seed frø (-et, -)

seem *(vb)* synes (-tes, -tes)
seldom sjældent
self selv
self-satisfied selvglad
sell *(vb)* sælge*
send *(vb)* sende (-te, -t)
sense *(vb)* mærke
sense of humour sans (-en, -er) for humor
separated skilt
September september (en)
set *(vb)* sætte*
several adskillige, flere
severe streng
sew *(vb)* sy
shake hands on *(vb)* give* hånden på
shall *(vb)* skulle*, ville*
share *(vb)* dele (-te, -t)
sharp skarp
shattered knust
she hun
sheep får (-et, -)
shelter ly (-et)
shine *(vb)* skinne, lyse (-te, -t)
ship skib (-et, -e)
shirt skjorte (-n, -r)
shoe sko (-en, -)
shoemaker skomager (-en, -e)
shop butik (-ken, -ker), forretning (-en, -er)
shopping indkøb (-et)
short kort
show *(vb)* vise (-te, -t)
show off *(vb)* skabe (-te, -t) sig
shut *(vb)* lukke
shut in/out *(vb)* lukke ind(e)/ud(e)
shut: keep one's mouth s. *(vb)* holde* mund
shut up! hold* kæft!
shy genert
shave *(vb)* barbere sig
sick syg
sight syn (-et, -)
sign(post) skilt (-et, -e)
silly: to be s. skabe (-te, -t) sig
silver wedding sølvbryllup (-pet, -per)
silverware sølvtøj (-et)
since *(adv)* siden
since *(conj)* siden, da
sing *(vb)* synge*
singer sanger (-en, -e)
single enkelt
sir herre, hr.
sister søster (-en, søstre)
sit *(vb)* sidde*
sixfold seksdobbelt
sky himmel (him(me)len, himle)
sleep *(vb)* sove*
sleepy søvnig
slim slank
slimming course slankekur (-en, -e)
slippery glat
sloppy blødsøden
slow langsom
sly snu
small lille/små
smart smart, flot
smile *(n)* smil (-et, -)
smile *(vb)* smile (-de *or* -te, -(e)t)
smoke *(n)* røg (-en)
smoke *(vb)* ryge*
smoked røget
snow *(vb)* sne
snowball snebold (-en, -e)
so så
soccer team fodboldhold (-et, -)
social welfare socialforsorg (-en)
sofa sofa (-en, -er)
soft blød
soldier soldat (-en, -er)
solution løsning (-en, -er)

some nogen, noget, nogle
something noget
sometimes sommetider
somewhat noget, ret
son søn (-nen, -ner)
son-in-law svigersøn (-nen, -ner)
song sang (-en, -e)
soon snart
sorrow sorg (-en, -er)
sorry ked af det
sorry: I'm s.! undskyld!
sort slags (-en, -)
soup suppe (-n, -r)
south syd (-en)
space plads (-en, -er), rum (-met, -)
sparrow spurv (-en, -e)
speak *(vb)* tale (-te, -t)
speaker taler (-en, -e)
special speciel
speciality specialitet (-en, -er)
speech tale (-n, -r)
speech: to give/make a s. holde* tale
speed fart (-en)
speed limit fartgrænse (-n, -r)
spell *(vb)* stave
splendid glimrende, herlig, pragtfuld
spoon ske (-en, -er)
sport sport (-en)
sports-mad sportsgal
spread *(vb)* sprede (-te, -t); (**butter etc.**) smøre*
spring forår (-et, -)
square torv (-et, -e)
stable stald (-en, -e)
staff personale (-t, -r)
stammer *(vb)* stamme
stamp frimærke (-t, -r)
stand *(vb)* stå*
standard standard (-en, -er)
star stjerne (-n, -r)
stare *(vb)* glo
start *(vb)* starte
starter (of meal) forret (-ten, -ter)
stay overnight *(vb)* overnatte
steering wheel rat (-tet, -)
step *(vb)* træde*
still endnu
stock beholdning (-en, -er)
stone sten (-en, -)
stop *(vb)* holde* op med, standse
stop talking *(vb)* tie* stille
store lager (-et, lagre)
story historie (-n, -r)
straight away lige med det samme
strange fremmed
strawberry jordbær (-ret, -)
stream å (-en, -er)
street gade (-n, -r)
strict streng
strike: to go on s. *(vb)* strejke
strong stærk
student studerende (en, -)
study *(vb)* studere
stuff *(vb)* stoppe
stupid dum
subject fag (-et, -)
succeed *(vb)* lykkes
such sådan
suddenly pludselig
suffer *(vb)* lide*
suffice *(vb)* slå* til
suggestion forslag (-et, -)
suited: to be s. to *(vb)* egne sig til
summer sommer (-en, somre)
summer residence sommerresidens (-en, -er)
sun sol (-en, -e)
Sunday søndag (-en, -e)
sure sikker

surely sikkert
surname efternavn (-et, -e)
surprise overraskelse (-n, -r)
suspicious mistænkelig
sweep *(vb)* feje
sweet sød
sweetheart kæreste (-n, -r)
swim *(vb)* svømme

table bord (-et, -e)
table tennis bordtennis
tail hale (-n, -r)
take *(vb)* tage*
take off *(vb)* tage* af
take part *(vb)* være* med
talk *(vb)* tale (-te, -t)
talk about *(vb)* omtale (-te, -t)
tall høj
tape: audio t. lydbånd (-et, -)
task opgave (-n, -r)
taste *(n)* smag (-en, -e)
taste *(vb)* smage (-te, -t)
tax skat (-ten, -ter)
tax-payer skatteyder (-en, -e)
taxi taxa (-en, -er)
taxi driver taxachauffør (-en, -er)
tea te (-en)
teach *(vb)* lære (-te, -t)
teacher lærer (-en, -e)
teacher (female) lærerinde (-n, -r)
team hold (-et, -)
tear tåre (-n, -r)
telephone telefon (-en, -er)
telephone book telefonbog (-en, -bøger)
television fjernsyn (-et)
tell *(vb)* fortælle*
tell (someone) the way *(vb)* sige* vejen
temptation fristelse (-n, -r)
tenant lejer (-en, -e)
terrible forfærdelig
Thames: the T. Themsen
than end
thank *(vb)* takke
thank you very much tusind tak
thanks tak (-ken, -)
that *(conj)* at, så at, for at
that *(pron)* den, det, denne, dette
that *(rel. pron)* der, som
the den, det, de
the . . . the des . . . des, jo . . . jo/des
theatre teater (teat(e)ret, teatre)
their(s) deres
them dem
themselves sig, sig selv, dem selv
then (adv) så, da
there der, dér
there you are! værsgo!
therefore derfor
these disse
they de
thick tyk
thief tyv (-en, -e)
thin mager
thing ting (-en, -)
think *(vb)* tænke (-te, -t), mene (-te, -t),synes (-tes, -tes)
third trediedel (-en, -e)
thirsty tørstig
this denne, dette, det her
those dem
thoughtful tankefuld
thousand tusind (et, - *or* -er)
three quarters trekvart
threefold tredobbelt
throne trone (-n, -r)
through **(i)**gennem
through thick and thin i tykt og tyndt
throw *(vb)* kaste

thunder *(vb)* tordne
Thursday torsdag (-en, -e)
ticket billet (-ten, -ter)
ticket: return t. returbillet (-ten, -ter)
ticket: single t. enkeltbillet (-ten, -ter)
tight stram
time tid (-en, -er), gang (-en, -e)
time: for a long t. i lang tid
time: what's the t.? hvad/hvor mange er klokken?
tired træt
to til, mod, at
toad tudse (-n, -r)
today i dag
toe tå (-en, tæer)
toffee karamel (-len, -ler)
toilet toilet (-tet, -ter)
tolerant tolerant
tomato tomat (-en, -er)
tomorrow i morgen
tongue tunge (-n, -r)
tonight i nat
too for
tooth tand (-en, tænder)
toothache tandpine (-n, -r)
top top (-pen, -pe)
top salesman topsælger (-en, -e)
towards imod
town by (-en, -er)
trade *(n)* fag (-et, -)
trade *(vb)* handle
traffic trafik (-ken)
traffic lights trafiklys (-et, -)
traffic regulation færdselsregel (-reg(e)len, -regler)
train *(n)* tog (-et, -)
train *(vb)* træne
train driver lokomotivfører (-en, -e)
trainer træner (-en, -e)
training træning (-en)
training ship skoleskib (-et, -e)
tramp vagabond (-en, -er)
travel *(vb)* rejse (-te, -t)
traveller rejsende (en, -)
tray bakke (-n, -r)
tread *(vb)* træde*
treasure skat (-ten, -te)
treasurer kasserer (-en, -e)
treat *(vb)* behandle
treatment behandling (-en, -er)
tree træ (-et, -er)
trick trick (-et, - *or* -s)
trip tur (-en, -e)
trousers bukser
true sand
trust *(vb)* stole på
try *(vb)* prøve
Tuesday tirsdag (-en, -e)
turn *(n)* tur (-en, -e)
turn *(vb)* dreje, vende (-te, -t)
turn into *(vb)* forvandle (sig) til
turn off *(vb)* slukke

ugly grim
unappetising ulækker
umbrella paraply (-en, -er)
uncle onkel (-en, onkler)
under under
undernourished underernæret
underpaid underbetalt
understand *(vb)* forstå*
uneducated ulært
unemployed arbejdsløs
unfortunately desværre
university universitet (-et, -er)
university studies universitetsstudier
unknown ukendt
unless med mindre
unmarried woman frøken (frøk(e)nen, frøk(e)ner)

unsatisfactory utilfredsstillende
unsociable uselskabelig
unsuccessful mislykket
until indtil
up op(pe)
up here herop(pe)
up there derop(pe)
us os
use *(n)* brug (-en), gavn (-en)
use *(vb)* bruge (-te, -t)
used car dealer brugtvogns forhandler (-en, -e)
used to vant til

valid: to be v. *(vb)* gælde*
value værdi (-en, -er)
VAT moms (en)
vegetable grønsag (-en, -er)
vegetable garden køkkenhave (-n, -r)
vehicle køretøj (-et, -er)
version version (-en, -er)
very meget
very: the v. . . . alle-
vicious ondskabsfuld
violet (colour) violet
vision syn (-et, -)
visit *(vb)* besøge (-te, -t)
visitor besøgende (en, -)
voice stemme (-n, -r)

wait *(vb)* vente
wake (someone) *(vb)* vække
wake up *(vb)* vågne
walk *(vb)* gå*
walk: to go for a w. *(vb)* gå* en tur
want to *(vb)* ville*
war krig (-en, -e)
warehouse lager (-et, lagre)
warm *(adj)* varm
warm *(vb)* varme
warn *(vb)* advare
was *(vb)* var
wash *(vb)* vaske
watch ur (-et, -e)
watchmaker urmager (-en, -e)
water *(n)* vand (-et, -e)
water *(vb)* vande
way vej (-en, -e); måde (-n, -r)
way: by the w. forresten
we vi
wear *(vb)* gå* klædt i
weather vejr (-et)
wedding day/anniversary bryllupsdag (-en, -e)
Wednesday onsdag (-en, -e)
week uge (-n, -r)
week: the w. before last forrige uge
weekly ugentlig
weight vægt (-en, -e)
welcome velkommen
welcome: you're w.! velbekomme!
well *(adj)* godt
well-behaved artig
well-heeled velhavende
well-kept velholdt
Welsh walisisk
Welshman waliser (-en, -e)
were *(vb)* var
west vest (-en)
what hvad
what . . . ! sikke(n) . . .!
wheelbarrow trillebør (-en, -e)
when hvornår, når; da, når; dengang
where hvor
where to hvorhen
whether om
which *(int. pron)* hvad for en/et/nogle, hvilken/hvilket/hvilke
which *(rel. pron)* der, som; hvad der
while mens, imens

whipped cream flødeskum (-met)
whisper hvisken (-en)
whistle *(vb)* fløjte
white hvid
whitewashed hvidkalket
Whitsun pinse (-n, -r)
who(m) *(int. pron)* hvem
who(m) *(rel. pron)* der, som
whole hel
wholesaler grosserer (-en, -e)
whose hvis
why hvorfor
wide bred
widespread udbredt
wife kone (-n, -r)
will *(vb)* ville*
willingly gerne
win *(vb)* vinde*
wind blæst (-en)
window vindue (-t, -e)
windowpane rude (-n, -r)
windy blæsende
wine vin (-en, -e)
wine list vinkort (-et, -)
wing vinge (-n, -r)
winter vinter (-en, vintre)
wise klog
wish *(vb)* ønske
wishes: best w. venlig hilsen
with med, hos
without uden
woman kvinde (-n, -r), kone (-n, -r)
woman: unmarried w. frøken (frøk(e)nen, frøk(e)ner)
wonder *(vb)* undre (sig)
wonder: I w. (if) mon
wonderful pragtfuld, vidunderlig
wood skov (-en, -e)
word ord (-et, -)
work *(n)* arbejde (-t, -r)
work (vb) arbejde
work (function) *(vb)* virke
world verden ((-en), verd(e)ner)
world situation verdens-situation (-en, -er)
worn slidt
worry *(vb)* bekymre sig
worse værre
worst værst
worth: to be w. it *(vb)* betale (-te, -t) sig
write *(vb)* skrive*
wrong forkert, gal
wrong: something w. noget i vejen

xylophone xylofon (-en, -er)

year år (-et, -)
year: this y. i år
yellow gul
yes ja, jo
yes but jamen
yesterday i går
yesterday: the day before y. i forgårs
yet dog, endnu
you I, jer; De, Dem, du, dig; man, en
young ung
younger, youngish yngre
youngest yngst
yours din, dit, dine; jeres; Deres
yourself du (dig, De, Dem) selv
yourselves I (jer, De, Dem) selv

zebra zebra (-en, -er)
zoo zoologisk have

Index

Numbers refer to sections, unless otherwise indicated.

The Maltese Falcon

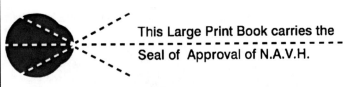

The Maltese Falcon

Dashiell Hammett

GALE
CENGAGE Learning

Detroit • New York • San Francisco • New Haven, Conn • Waterville, Maine • London

GALE
CENGAGE Learning

Superior Collection.
The text of this Large Print edition is unabridged.
Other aspects of the book may vary from the original edition.
Set in 16 pt. Plantin.
Printed on permanent paper.

LIBRARY OF CONGRESS CATALOGING-IN-PUBLICATION DATA

Hammett, Dashiell, 1894–1961.
The Maltese falcon / by Dashiell Hammett.
p. cm.
ISBN-13: 978-1-59722-898-5 (hardcover : alk. paper)
ISBN-10: 1-59722-898-2 (hardcover : alk. paper)
1. Spade, Sam (Fictitious character)—Fiction. 2. Private investigators—California—San Francisco—Fiction. 3. San Francisco (Calif.)—Fiction. 4. Large type books. I. Title.
PS3515.A4347M3 2009
813'.52—dc22 2008042566

Published in 2009 by arrangement with Alfred A. Knopf, Inc.

Printed in the United States of America
2 3 4 5 6 16 15 14 13 12

FD131

To Jose

1
Spade & Archer

Samuel Spade's jaw was long and bony, his chin a jutting v under the more flexible v of his mouth. His nostrils curved back to make another, smaller, v. His yellow-gray eyes were horizontal. The v *motif* was picked up again by thickish brows rising outward from twin creases above a hooked nose, and his pale brown hair grew down — from high flat temples — in a point on his forehead. He looked rather pleasantly like a blond satan.

He said to Effie Perine: "Yes, sweetheart?"

She was a lanky sunburned girl whose tan dress of thin woolen stuff clung to her with an effect of dampness. Her eyes were brown and playful in a shiny boyish face. She finished shutting the door behind her, leaned against it, and said: "There's a girl wants to see you. Her name's Wonderly."

"A customer?"

"I guess so. You'll want to see her anyway:

she's a knockout."

"Shoo her in, darling," said Spade. "Shoo her in."

Effie Perine opened the door again, following it back into the outer office, standing with a hand on the knob while saying: "Will you come in, Miss Wonderly?"

A voice said, "Thank you," so softly that only the purest articulation made the words intelligible, and a young woman came through the doorway. She advanced slowly, with tentative steps, looking at Spade with cobalt-blue eyes that were both shy and probing.

She was tall and pliantly slender, without angularity anywhere. Her body was erect and high-breasted, her legs long, her hands and feet narrow. She wore two shades of blue that had been selected because of her eyes. The hair curling from under her blue hat was darkly red, her full lips more brightly red. White teeth glistened in the crescent her timid smile made.

Spade rose bowing and indicating with a thick-fingered hand the oaken armchair beside his desk. He was quite six feet tall. The steep rounded slope of his shoulders made his body seem almost conical — no broader than it was thick — and kept his freshly pressed gray coat from fitting very well.

Miss Wonderly murmured, "Thank you," softly as before and sat down on the edge of the chair's wooden seat.

Spade sank into his swivel-chair, made a quarter-turn to face her, smiled politely. He smiled without separating his lips. All the v's in his face grew longer.

The tappity-tap-tap and the thin bell and muffled whir of Effie Perine's typewriting came through the closed door. Somewhere in a neighboring office a power-driven machine vibrated dully. On Spade's desk a limp cigarette smoldered in a brass tray filled with the remains of limp cigarettes. Ragged gray flakes of cigarette-ash dotted the yellow top of the desk and the green blotter and the papers that were there. A buff-curtained window, eight or ten inches open, let in from the court a current of air faintly scented with ammonia. The ashes on the desk twitched and crawled in the current.

Miss Wonderly watched the gray flakes twitch and crawl. Her eyes were uneasy. She sat on the very edge of the chair. Her feet were flat on the floor, as if she were about to rise. Her hands in dark gloves clasped a flat dark handbag in her lap.

Spade rocked back in his chair and asked: "Now what can I do for you, Miss Wonderly?"

She caught her breath and looked at him. She swallowed and said hurriedly: "Could you — ? I thought — I — that is —" Then she tortured her lower lip with glistening teeth and said nothing. Only her dark eyes spoke now, pleading.

Spade smiled and nodded as if he understood her, but pleasantly, as if nothing serious were involved. He said: "Suppose you tell me about it, from the beginning, and then we'll know what needs doing. Better begin as far back as you can."

"That was in New York."

"Yes."

"I don't know where she met him. I mean I don't know where in New York. She's five years younger than I — only seventeen — and we didn't have the same friends. I don't suppose we've ever been as close as sisters should be. Mama and Papa are in Europe. It would kill them. I've got to get her back before they come home."

"Yes," he said.

"They're coming home the first of the month."

Spade's eyes brightened. "Then we've two weeks," he said.

"I didn't know what she had done until her letter came. I was frantic." Her lips trembled. Her hands mashed the dark handbag in her lap. "I was too afraid she had done something like this to go to the police, and the fear that something had happened to her kept urging me to go. There wasn't anyone I could go to for advice. I didn't know what to do. What could I do?"

"Nothing, of course," Spade said, "but then her letter came?"

"Yes, and I sent her a telegram asking her to come home. I sent it to General Delivery here. That was the only address she gave me. I waited a whole week, but no answer came, not another word from her. And Mama and Papa's return was drawing nearer and nearer. So I came to San Francisco to get her. I wrote her I was coming. I shouldn't have done that, should I?"

"Maybe not. It's not always easy to know what to do. You haven't found her?"

"No, I haven't. I wrote her that I would go to the St. Mark, and I begged her to come and let me talk to her even if she didn't intend to go home with me. But she didn't come. I waited three days, and she didn't come, didn't even send me a message of any sort."

Spade nodded his blond satan's head,

frowned sympathetically, and tightened his lips together.

"It was horrible," Miss Wonderly said, trying to smile. "I couldn't sit there like that — waiting — not knowing what had happened to her, what might be happening to her." She stopped trying to smile. She shuddered. "The only address I had was General Delivery. I wrote her another letter, and yesterday afternoon I went to the Post Office. I stayed there until after dark, but I didn't see her. I went there again this morning, and still didn't see Corinne, but I saw Floyd Thursby."

Spade nodded again. His frown went away. In its place came a look of sharp attentiveness.

"He wouldn't tell me where Corinne was," she went on, hopelessly. "He wouldn't tell me anything, except that she was well and happy. But how can I believe that? That is what he would tell me anyhow, isn't it?"

"Sure," Spade agreed. "But it might be true."

"I hope it is. I do hope it is," she exclaimed. "But I can't go back home like this, without having seen her, without even having talked to her on the phone. He wouldn't take me to her. He said she didn't want to see me. I can't believe that. He promised to tell her he had seen me, and to bring her to see me — if she would come — this evening at the hotel. He said he knew she wouldn't. He promised to come himself if she wouldn't. He —"

She broke off with a startled hand to her mouth as the door opened.

The man who had opened the door came in a step, said, "Oh, excuse me!" hastily took his brown hat from his head, and backed out.

"It's all right, Miles," Spade told him. "Come in. Miss Wonderly, this is Mr. Archer, my partner."

Miles Archer came into the office again, shutting the door behind him, ducking his head and smiling at Miss Wonderly, making a vaguely polite gesture with the hat in his hand. He was of medium height, solidly built, wide in the shoulders, thick in the neck, with a jovial heavy-jawed red face and some gray in his close-trimmed hair. He was apparently as many years past forty as Spade was past thirty.

Spade said: "Miss Wonderly's sister ran away from New York with a fellow named Floyd Thursby. They're here. Miss Wonderly has seen Thursby and has a date with him tonight. Maybe he'll bring the sister with him. The chances are he won't. Miss Wonderly wants us to find the sister and get her away from him and back home." He looked at Miss Wonderly. "Right?"

"Yes," she said indistinctly. The embarrassment that had gradually been driven away by Spade's ingratiating smiles and nods and assurances was pinkening her face again. She looked at the bag in her lap and picked nervously at it with a gloved finger.

Spade winked at his partner.

Miles Archer came forward to stand at a corner of the desk. While the girl looked at her bag he looked at her. His little brown eyes ran their bold appraising gaze from her lowered face to her feet and up to her face again. Then he looked at Spade and made a silent whistling mouth of appreciation.

Spade lifted two fingers from the arm of his chair in a brief warning gesture and said:

"We shouldn't have any trouble with it. It's simply a matter of having a man at the hotel this evening to shadow him away when he leaves, and shadow him until he leads us to your sister. If she comes with him, and you persuade her to return with you, so much the better. Otherwise — if she doesn't want to leave him after we've found her — well, we'll find a way of managing that."

Archer said: "Yeh." His voice was heavy, coarse.

Miss Wonderly looked up at Spade, quickly, puckering her forehead between her eyebrows.

"Oh, but you must be careful!" Her voice shook a little, and her lips shaped the words with nervous jerkiness. "I'm deathly afraid of him, of what he might do. She's so young and his bringing her here from New York is such a serious — Mightn't he — mightn't he do — something to her?"

Spade smiled and patted the arms of his chair.

"Just leave that to us," he said. "We'll know how to handle him."

"But mightn't he?" she insisted.

"There's always a chance." Spade nodded judicially. "But you can trust us to take care of that."

"I do trust you," she said earnestly, "but I want you to know that he's a dangerous man. I honestly don't think he'd stop at anything. I don't believe he'd hesitate to — to kill Corinne if he thought it would save him. Mightn't he do that?"

"You didn't threaten him, did you?"

"I told him that all I wanted was to get her home before Mama and Papa came so they'd never know what she had done. I promised him I'd never say a word to them about it if he helped me, but if he didn't Papa would certainly see that he was punished. I — I don't suppose he believed me, altogether."

"Can he cover up by marrying her?" Archer asked.

The girl blushed and replied in a confused voice: "He has a wife and three children in England. Corinne wrote me that, to explain why she had gone off with him."

"They usually do," Spade said, "though not always in England." He leaned forward to reach for pencil and pad of paper. "What does he look like?"

"Oh, he's thirty-five years old, perhaps, and as tall as you, and either naturally dark or quite sunburned. His hair is dark too, and he has thick eyebrows. He talks in a rather loud, blustery way and has a nervous, irritable manner. He gives the impression of being — of violence."

Spade, scribbling on the pad, asked without looking up: "What color eyes?"

"They're blue-gray and watery, though not in a weak way. And — oh, yes — he has a marked cleft in his chin."

"Thin, medium, or heavy build?"

"Quite athletic. He's broad-shouldered and carries himself erect, has what could be called a decidedly military carriage. He was wearing a light gray suit and a gray hat when I saw him this morning."

"What does he do for a living?" Spade asked as he laid down his pencil.

"I don't know," she said. "I haven't the slightest idea."

"What time is he coming to see you?"

"After eight o'clock."

"All right, Miss Wonderly, we'll have a man there. It'll help if —"

"Mr. Spade, could either you or Mr. Archer?" She made an appealing gesture with both hands. "Could either of you look after it personally? I don't mean that the man you'd send wouldn't be capable, but — oh! — I'm so afraid of what might happen to Corinne. I'm afraid of him. Could you? I'd be — I'd expect to be charged more, of course." She opened her handbag with nervous fingers and put two hundred-dollar bills on Spade's desk. "Would that be enough?"

"Yeh," Archer said, "and I'll look after it myself."

Miss Wonderly stood up, impulsively holding a hand out to him.

"Thank you! Thank you!" she exclaimed, and then gave Spade her hand, repeating: "Thank you!"

"Not at all," Spade said over it. "Glad to. It'll help some if you either meet Thursby downstairs or let yourself be seen in the lobby with him at some time."

"I will," she promised, and thanked the partners again.

"And don't look for me," Archer cautioned her. "I'll see you all right."

Spade went to the corridor-door with Miss Wonderly. When he returned to his desk Archer nodded at the hundred-dollar bills there, growled complacently, "They're right enough," picked one up, folded it, and tucked it into a vest-pocket. "And they had brothers in her bag."

Spade pocketed the other bill before he sat down. Then he said: "Well, don't dynamite her too much. What do you think of her?"

"Sweet! And you telling me not to dynamite her." Archer guffawed suddenly without merriment. "Maybe you saw her first, Sam, but I spoke first." He put his hands in his trousers-pockets and teetered on his heels.

"You'll play hell with her, you will." Spade grinned wolfishly, showing the edges of teeth far back in his jaw. "You've got brains, yes you have." He began to make a cigarette.

2
Death in the Fog

A telephone-bell rang in darkness. When it had rung three times bed-springs creaked, fingers fumbled on wood, something small and hard thudded on a carpeted floor, the springs creaked again, and a man's voice said:

"Hello. . . . Yes, speaking. . . . Dead? . . . Yes. . . . Fifteen minutes. Thanks."

A switch clicked and a white bowl hung on three gilded chains from the ceiling's center filled the room with light. Spade, bare-footed in green and white checked pajamas, sat on the side of his bed. He scowled at the telephone on the table while his hands took from beside it a packet of brown papers and a sack of Bull Durham tobacco.

Cold steamy air blew in through two open windows, bringing with it half a dozen times a minute the Alcatraz foghorn's dull moaning. A tinny alarm-clock, insecurely mounted on a corner of Duke's *Celebrated Criminal Cases of America* — face down on the table — held its hands at five minutes past two.

Spade's thick fingers made a cigarette with deliberate care, sifting a measured quantity of tan flakes down into curved paper, spreading the flakes so that they lay equal at the ends with a slight depression in the middle, thumbs rolling the paper's inner edge down and up under the outer edge as forefingers pressed it over, thumbs and fingers sliding to the paper cylinder's ends to hold it even while tongue licked the flap, left forefinger and thumb smoothed the damp seam, right forefinger and thumb twisting their end and lifting the other to Spade's mouth.

He picked up the pigskin and nickel lighter that had fallen to the floor, manipulated it, and with the cigarette burning in a corner of his mouth stood up. He took off his pajamas. The smooth thickness of his arms, legs, and body, the sag of his big rounded shoulders, made his body like a bear's. It was like a shaved bear's: his chest was hairless. His skin was childishly soft and pink.

He scratched the back of his neck and began to dress. He put on a thin white union-suit, gray socks, black garters, and dark brown shoes. When he had fastened his shoes he picked up the telephone, called Graystone 4500, and ordered a taxicab. He put on a green-striped white shirt, a soft white collar, a green necktie, the gray suit he had worn that day, a loose tweed overcoat, and a dark gray hat. The street-doorbell rang as he stuffed tobacco, keys, and money into his pockets.

Where Bush Street roofed Stockton before slipping downhill to Chinatown, Spade paid his fare and left the taxicab. San Francisco's night-fog, thin, clammy, and penetrant, blurred the street. A few yards from where Spade had dismissed the taxicab a small group of men stood looking up an alley. Two women stood with a man on the other side of Bush Street, looking at the alley. There were faces at windows.

Spade crossed the sidewalk between iron-railed hatchways that opened above bare ugly stairs, went to the parapet, and, resting his hands on the damp coping, looked down into Stockton Street.

An automobile popped out of the tunnel beneath him with a roaring swish, as if it had been blown out, and ran away. Not far from the tunnel's mouth a man was hunkered on his heels before a billboard that held advertisements of a moving picture and a gasoline across the front of a gap between two store-buildings. The hunkered man's head was bent almost to the sidewalk so he could look under the billboard. A hand flat on the paving, a hand clenched on the billboard's green frame, held him in this grotesque position. Two other men stood awkwardly together at one end of the billboard, peeping through the few inches of space between it and the building at that end. The building at the other end had a blank gray sidewall that looked down on the lot behind the billboard. Lights flickered on the sidewall, and the shadows of men moving among lights.

Spade turned from the parapet and walked up Bush Street to the alley where men were grouped. A uniformed policeman chewing gum under an enameled sign that said *Burritt St.* in white against dark blue put out an arm and asked:

"What do you want here?"

"I'm Sam Spade. Tom Polhaus phoned me."

"Sure you are." The policeman's arm went down. "I didn't know you at first. Well, they're back there." He jerked a thumb over his shoulder. "Bad business."

"Bad enough," Spade agreed, and went up the alley.

Half-way up it, not far from the entrance, a dark ambulance stood. Behind the ambulance, to the left, the alley was bounded by a waist-high fence, horizontal strips of rough boarding. From the fence dark ground fell away steeply to the billboard on Stockton Street below.

A ten-foot length of the fence's top rail had been torn from a post at one end and hung dangling from the other. Fifteen feet down the slope a flat boulder stuck out. In the notch between boulder and slope Miles Archer lay on his back. Two men stood over him. One of them held the beam of an electric torch on the dead man. Other men with lights moved up and down the slope.

One of them hailed Spade, "Hello, Sam," and clambered up to the alley, his shadow running up the slope before him. He was a barrel-bellied tall man with shrewd small eyes, a thick mouth, and carelessly shaven dark jowls. His shoes, knees, hands, and chin were daubed with brown loam.

"I figured you'd want to see it before we took him away," he said as he stepped over the broken fence.

"Thanks, Tom," Spade said. "What happened?" He put an elbow on a fence-post and looked down at the men below, nodding to those who nodded to him.

Tom Polhaus poked his own left breast with a dirty finger. “Got him right through the pump — with this.” He took a fat revolver from his coat-pocket and held it out to Spade. Mud inlaid the depressions in the revolver’s surface. “A Webley. English, ain’t it?”

Spade took his elbow from the fence-post and leaned down to look at the weapon, but he did not touch it.

“Yes,” he said, “Webley-Fosbery automatic revolver. That’s it. Thirty-eight, eight shot. They don’t make them any more. How many gone out of it?”

“One pill.” Tom poked his breast again. “He must’ve been dead when he cracked the fence.” He raised the muddy revolver. “Ever seen this before?”

Spade nodded. “I’ve seen Webley-Fosberys,” he said without interest, and then spoke rapidly: “He was shot up here, huh? Standing where you are, with his back to the fence. The man that shot him stands here.” He went around in front of Tom and raised a hand breast-high with leveled forefinger. “Lets him have it and Miles goes back, taking the top off the fence and going on through and down till the rock catches him. That it?"

"That's it," Tom replied slowly, working his brows together. "The blast burnt his coat."

"Who found him?"

"The man on the beat, Shilling. He was coming down Bush, and just as he got here a machine turning threw headlights up here, and he saw the top off the fence. So he came up to look at it, and found him."

"What about the machine that was turning around?"

"Not a damned thing about it, Sam. Shilling didn't pay any attention to it, not knowing anything was wrong then. He says nobody didn't come out of here while he was coming down from Powell or he'd've seen them. The only other way out would be under the billboard on Stockton. Nobody went that way. The fog's got the ground soggy, and the only marks are where Miles slid down and where this here gun rolled."

"Didn't anybody hear the shot?"

"For the love of God, Sam, we only just got here. Somebody must've heard it, when we find them." He turned and put a leg over the fence. "Coming down for a look at him before he's moved?"

Spade said: "No."

Tom halted astride the fence and looked

back at Spade with surprised small eyes.

Spade said: "You've seen him. You'd see everything I could."

Tom, still looking at Spade, nodded doubtfully and withdrew his leg over the fence.

"His gun was tucked away on his hip," he said. "It hadn't been fired. His overcoat was buttoned. There's a hundred and sixty-some bucks in his clothes. Was he working, Sam?"

Spade, after a moment's hesitation, nodded.

Tom asked: "Well?"

"He was supposed to be tailing a fellow named Floyd Thursby," Spade said, and described Thursby as Miss Wonderly had described him.

"What for?"

Spade put his hands into his overcoat-pockets and blinked sleepy eyes at Tom.

Tom repeated impatiently: "What for?"

"He was an Englishman, maybe. I don't know what his game was, exactly. We were trying to find out where he lived." Spade grinned faintly and took a hand from his pocket to pat Tom's shoulder. "Don't crowd me." He put the hand in his pocket again. "I'm going out to break the news to Miles's wife." He turned away.

Tom, scowling, opened his mouth, closed

it without having said anything, cleared his throat, put the scowl off his face, and spoke with a husky sort of gentleness:

"It's tough, him getting it like that. Miles had his faults same as the rest of us, but I guess he must've had some good points too."

"I guess so," Spade agreed in a tone that was utterly meaningless, and went out of the alley.

In an all-night drug-store on the corner of Bush and Taylor Streets, Spade used a telephone.

"Precious," he said into it a little while after he had given a number, "Miles has been shot. . . . Yes, he's dead. . . . Now don't get excited. . . . Yes. . . . You'll have to break it to Iva. . . . No, I'm damned if I will. You've got to do it. . . . That's a good girl. . . . And keep her away from the office. . . . Tell her I'll see her — uh — some time. . . . Yes, but don't tie me up to anything. . . . That's the stuff. You're an angel. 'Bye."

Spade's tinny alarm-clock said three-forty when he turned on the light in the suspended bowl again. He dropped his hat and overcoat on the bed and went into his kitchen, returning to the bedroom with a wine-glass and a tall bottle of Bacardi. He poured a drink and drank it standing. He put bottle and glass on the table, sat on the side of the bed facing them, and rolled a cigarette. He had drunk his third glass of Bacardi and was lighting his fifth cigarette when the street-door-bell rang. The hands of the alarm-clock registered four-thirty.

Spade sighed, rose from the bed, and went to the telephone-box beside his bathroom-door. He pressed the button that released the street-door-lock. He muttered, "Damn her," and stood scowling at the black telephone-box, breathing irregularly while a dull flush grew in his cheeks.

The grating and rattling of the elevator-door opening and closing came from the corridor. Spade sighed again and moved towards the corridor-door. Soft heavy footsteps sounded on the carpeted floor outside, the footsteps of two men. Spade's face brightened. His eyes were no longer harassed. He opened the door quickly.

"Hello, Tom," he said to the barrel-bellied tall detective with whom he had talked in Burritt Street, and, "Hello, Lieutenant," to the man beside Tom. "Come in."

They nodded together, neither saying anything, and came in. Spade shut the door and ushered them into his bedroom. Tom sat on an end of the sofa by the windows. The Lieutenant sat on a chair beside the table.

The Lieutenant was a compactly built man with a round head under short-cut grizzled hair and a square face behind a short-cut grizzled mustache. A five-dollar gold-piece was pinned to his necktie and there was a small elaborate diamond-set secret-society-emblem on his lapel.

Spade brought two wine-glasses in from the kitchen, filled them and his own with Bacardi, gave one to each of his visitors, and sat down with his on the side of the bed. His face was placid and uncurious. He raised his glass, and said, "Success to crime," and drank it down.

Tom emptied his glass, set it on the floor beside his feet, and wiped his mouth with a muddy forefinger. He stared at the foot of the bed as if trying to remember something of which it vaguely reminded him.

The Lieutenant looked at his glass for a dozen seconds, took a very small sip of its contents, and put the glass on the table at his elbow. He examined the room with hard deliberate eyes, and then looked at Tom.

Tom moved uncomfortably on the sofa and, not looking up, asked: "Did you break the news to Miles's wife, Sam?"

Spade said: “Uh-huh.”

“How’d she take it?”

Spade shook his head. “I don’t know anything about women.”

Tom said softly: “The hell you don’t.”

The Lieutenant put his hands on his knees and leaned forward. His greenish eyes were fixed on Spade in a peculiarly rigid stare, as if their focus were a matter of mechanics, to be changed only by pulling a lever or pressing a button.

“What kind of gun do you carry?” he asked.

“None. I don’t like them much. Of course there are some in the office.”

“I’d like to see one of them,” the Lieutenant said. “You don’t happen to have one here?”

“No.”

“You sure of that?”

“Look around.” Spade smiled and waved his empty glass a little. “Turn the dump upside-down if you want. I won’t squawk — if you’ve got a search-warrant.”

Tom protested: “Oh, hell, Sam!”

Spade set his glass on the table and stood up facing the Lieutenant.

“What do you want, Dundy?” he asked in a voice hard and cold as his eyes.

Lieutenant Dundy’s eyes had moved to

maintain their focus on Spade's. Only his eyes had moved.

Tom shifted his weight on the sofa again, blew a deep breath out through his nose, and growled plaintively: "We're not wanting to make any trouble, Sam."

Spade, ignoring Tom, said to Dundy: "Well, what do you want? Talk turkey. Who in hell do you think you are, coming in here trying to rope me?"

"All right," Dundy said in his chest, "sit down and listen."

"I'll sit or stand as I damned please," said Spade, not moving.

"For Christ's sake be reasonable," Tom begged. "What's the use of us having a row? If you want to know why we didn't talk turkey it's because when I asked you who this Thursby was you as good as told me it was none of my business. You can't treat us that way, Sam. It ain't right and it won't get you anywheres. We got our work to do."

Lieutenant Dundy jumped up, stood close to Spade, and thrust his square face up at the taller man's.

"I've warned you your foot was going to slip one of these days," he said.

Spade made a depreciative mouth, raising his eyebrows. "Everybody's foot slips sometime," he replied with derisive mildness.

"And this is yours."

Spade smiled and shook his head. "No, I'll do nicely, thank you." He stopped smiling. His upper lip, on the left side, twitched over his eyetooth. His eyes became narrow and sultry. His voice came out deep as the Lieutenant's. "I don't like this. What are you sucking around for? Tell me, or get out and let me go to bed."

"Who's Thursby?" Dundy demanded.

"I told Tom what I knew about him."

"You told Tom damned little."

"I knew damned little."

"Why were you tailing him?"

"I wasn't. Miles was — for the swell reason that we had a client who was paying good United States money to have him tailed."

"Who's the client?"

Placidity came back to Spade's face and voice. He said reprovingly: "You know I can't tell you that until I've talked it over with the client."

"You'll tell it to me or you'll tell it in court," Dundy said hotly. "This is murder and don't you forget it."

"Maybe. And here's something for you to not forget, sweetheart. I'll tell it or not as I damned please. It's a long while since I burst out crying because policemen didn't like me."

Tom left the sofa and sat on the foot of the bed. His carelessly shaven mud-smeared face was tired and lined.

"Be reasonable, Sam," he pleaded. "Give us a chance. How can we turn up anything on Miles's killing if you won't give us what you've got?"

"You needn't get a headache over that," Spade told him. "I'll bury my dead."

Lieutenant Dundy sat down and put his hands on his knees again. His eyes were warm green discs.

"I thought you would," he said. He smiled with grim content. "That's just exactly why we came to see you. Isn't it, Tom?"

Tom groaned, but said nothing articulate.

Spade watched Dundy warily.

"That's just exactly what I said to Tom," the Lieutenant went on. "I said: 'Tom, I've got a hunch that Sam Spade's a man to keep the family-troubles in the family.' That's just what I said to him."

The wariness went out of Spade's eyes. He made his eyes dull with boredom. He turned his face around to Tom and asked with great carelessness: "What's itching your boyfriend now?"

Dundy jumped up and tapped Spade's chest with the ends of two bent fingers.

"Just this," he said, taking pains to make each word distinct, emphasizing them with his tapping finger-ends: "Thursby was shot down in front of his hotel just thirty-five minutes after you left Burritt Street."

Spade spoke, taking equal pains with his words: "Keep your God-damned paws off me."

Dundy withdrew the tapping fingers, but there was no change in his voice: "Tom says you were in too much of a hurry to even stop for a look at your partner."

Tom growled apologetically: "Well, damn it, Sam, you did run off like that."

"And you didn't go to Archer's house to tell his wife," the Lieutenant said. "We called up and that girl in your office was there, and she said you sent her."

Spade nodded. His face was stupid in its calmness.

Lieutenant Dundy raised his two bent fingers towards Spade's chest, quickly lowered them, and said: "I give you ten minutes to get to a phone and do your talking to the girl. I give you ten minutes to get to Thursby's joint — Geary near Leavenworth — you could do it easy in that time, or fifteen at the most. And that gives you ten or fifteen minutes of waiting before he showed up."

"I knew where he lived?" Spade asked. "And I knew he hadn't gone straight home from killing Miles?"

"You knew what you knew," Dundy replied stubbornly. "What time did you get home?"

"Twenty minutes to four. I walked around thinking things over."

The Lieutenant wagged his round head up and down. "We knew you weren't home at three-thirty. We tried to get you on the phone. Where'd you do your walking?"

"Out Bush Street a way and back."

"Did you see anybody that — ?"

"No, no witnesses," Spade said and laughed pleasantly. "Sit down, Dundy. You haven't finished your drink. Get your glass, Tom."

Tom said: "No, thanks, Sam."

Dundy sat down, but paid no attention to his glass of rum.

Spade filled his own glass, drank, set the empty glass on the table, and returned to his bedside-seat.

"I know where I stand now," he said, looking with friendly eyes from one of the police-detectives to the other. "I'm sorry I got up on my hind legs, but you birds coming in and trying to put the work on me made me nervous. Having Miles knocked off bothered me, and then you birds cracking foxy. That's all right now, though, now that I know what you're up to."

Tom said: "Forget it."

The Lieutenant said nothing.

Spade asked: "Thursby die?"

While the Lieutenant hesitated Tom said: "Yes."

Then the Lieutenant said angrily: "And you might just as well know it — if you don't — that he died before he could tell anybody anything."

Spade was rolling a cigarette. He asked, not looking up: "What do you mean by that? You think I did know it?"

"I meant what I said," Dundy replied bluntly.

Spade looked up at him and smiled, holding the finished cigarette in one hand, his lighter in the other.

"You're not ready to pinch me yet, are you, Dundy?" he asked.

Dundy looked with hard green eyes at Spade and did not answer him.

"Then," said Spade, "there's no particular reason why I should give a damn what you think, is there, Dundy?"

Tom said: "Aw, be reasonable, Sam."

Spade put the cigarette in his mouth, set fire to it, and laughed smoke out.

"I'll be reasonable, Tom," he promised. "How did I kill this Thursby? I've forgotten."

Tom grunted disgust. Lieutenant Dundy said: "He was shot four times in the back, with a forty-four or forty-five, from across the street, when he started to go in the hotel. Nobody saw it, but that's the way it figures."

"And he was wearing a Luger in a shoulder-holster," Tom added. "It hadn't been fired."

"What do the hotel-people know about him?" Spade asked.

"Nothing except that he'd been there a week."

"Alone?"

"Alone."

"What did you find on him? or in his room?"

Dundy drew his lips in and asked: "What'd you think we'd find?"

Spade made a careless circle with his limp cigarette. "Something to tell you who he was, what his story was. Did you?"

"We thought you could tell us that."

Spade looked at the Lieutenant with yellow-gray eyes that held an almost exaggerated amount of candor. "I've never seen Thursby, dead or alive."

Lieutenant Dundy stood up looking dissatisfied. Tom rose yawning and stretching.

"We've asked what we came to ask," Dundy said, frowning over eyes hard as green pebbles. He held his mustached upper lip tight to his teeth, letting his lower lip push the words out. "We've told you more than you've told us. That's fair enough. You know me, Spade. If you did or you didn't you'll get a square deal out of me, and most of the breaks. I don't know that I'd blame you a hell of a lot — but that wouldn't keep me from nailing you."

"Fair enough," Spade replied evenly. "But I'd feel better about it if you'd drink your drink."

Lieutenant Dundy turned to the table, picked up his glass, and slowly emptied it. Then he said, "Good night," and held out his hand. They shook hands ceremoniously. Tom and Spade shook hands ceremoniously. Spade let them out. Then he undressed, turned off the lights, and went to bed.

3
Three Women

When Spade reached his office at ten o'clock the following morning Effie Perine was at her desk opening the morning's mail. Her boyish face was pale under its sunburn. She put down the handful of envelopes and the brass paper-knife she held and said: "She's in there." Her voice was low and warning.

"I asked you to keep her away," Spade complained. He too kept his voice low.

Effie Perine's brown eyes opened wide and her voice was irritable as his: "Yes, but you didn't tell me how." Her eyelids went together a little and her shoulders drooped. "Don't be cranky, Sam," she said wearily. "I had her all night."

Spade stood beside the girl, put a hand on her head, and smoothed her hair away from its parting. "Sorry, angel, I haven't —" He broke off as the inner door opened. "Hello,

Iva," he said to the woman who had opened it.

"Oh, Sam!" she said.

She was a blonde woman of a few more years than thirty. Her facial prettiness was perhaps five years past its best moment. Her body for all its sturdiness was finely modeled and exquisite. She wore black clothes from hat to shoes. They had as mourning an impromptu air. Having spoken, she stepped back from the door and stood waiting for Spade.

He took his hand from Effie Perine's head and entered the inner office, shutting the door. Iva came quickly to him, raising her sad face for his kiss. Her arms were around him before his held her. When they had kissed he made a little movement as if to release her, but she pressed her face to his chest and began sobbing.

He stroked her round back, saying: "Poor darling." His voice was tender. His eyes, squinting at the desk that had been his partner's, across the room from his own, were angry. He drew his lips back over his teeth in an impatient grimace and turned his chin aside to avoid contact with the crown of her hat. "Did you send for Miles's brother?" he asked.

"Yes, he came over this morning." The

words were blurred by her sobbing and his coat against her mouth.

He grimaced again and bent his head for a surreptitious look at the watch on his wrist. His left arm was around her, the hand on her left shoulder. His cuff was pulled back far enough to leave the watch uncovered. It showed ten-ten.

The woman stirred in his arms and raised her face again. Her blue eyes were wet, round, and white-ringed. Her mouth was moist.

"Oh, Sam," she moaned, "did you kill him?"

Spade stared at her with bulging eyes. His bony jaw fell down. He took his arms from her and stepped back out of her arms. He scowled at her and cleared his throat.

She held her arms up as he had left them. Anguish clouded her eyes, partly closed them under eyebrows pulled up at the inner ends. Her soft damp red lips trembled.

Spade laughed a harsh syllable, "Ha!" and went to the buff-curtained window. He stood there with his back to her looking through the curtain into the court until she started towards him. Then he turned quickly and went to his desk. He sat down, put his elbows on the desk, his chin between his fists, and looked at her. His yellowish eyes glittered between narrowed lids.

"Who," he asked coldly, "put that bright idea in your head?"

"I thought —" She lifted a hand to her mouth and fresh tears came to her eyes. She came to stand beside the desk, moving with easy sure-footed grace in black slippers whose smallness and heel-height were extreme. "Be kind to me, Sam," she said humbly.

He laughed at her, his eyes still glittering. "You killed my husband, Sam, be kind to me." He clapped his palms together and said: "Jesus Christ."

She began to cry audibly, holding a white handkerchief to her face.

He got up and stood close behind her. He put his arms around her. He kissed her neck between ear and coat-collar. He said: "Now, Iva, don't." His face was expressionless. When she had stopped crying he put his mouth to her ear and murmured: "You shouldn't have come here today, precious. It wasn't wise. You can't stay. You ought to be home."

She turned around in his arms to face him and asked: "You'll come tonight?"

He shook his head gently. "Not tonight."

"Soon?"

"Yes."

"How soon?"

"As soon as I can."

He kissed her mouth, led her to the door, opened it, said, "Good-bye, Iva," bowed her out, shut the door, and returned to his desk.

He took tobacco and cigarette-papers from his vest-pockets, but did not roll a cigarette. He sat holding the papers in one hand, the tobacco in the other, and looked with brooding eyes at his dead partner's desk.

Effie Perine opened the door and came in. Her brown eyes were uneasy. Her voice was careless. She asked: "Well?"

Spade said nothing. His brooding gaze did not move from his partner's desk.

The girl frowned and came around to his side. "Well," she asked in a louder voice, "how did you and the widow make out?"

"She thinks I shot Miles," he said. Only his lips moved.

"So you could marry her?"

Spade made no reply to that.

The girl took his hat from his head and put it on the desk. Then she leaned over and took the tobacco-sack and the papers from his inert fingers.

"The police think I shot Thursby," he said.

"Who is he?" she asked, separating a

cigarette-paper from the packet, sifting tobacco into it.

"Who do you think I shot?" he asked.

When she ignored that question he said: "Thursby's the guy Miles was supposed to be tailing for the Wonderly girl."

Her thin fingers finished shaping the cigarette. She licked it, smoothed it, twisted its ends, and placed it between Spade's lips. He said, "Thanks, honey," put an arm around her slim waist, and rested his cheek wearily against her hip, shutting his eyes.

"Are you going to marry Iva?" she asked, looking down at his pale brown hair.

"Don't be silly," he muttered. The unlighted cigarette bobbed up and down with the movement of his lips.

"She doesn't think it's silly. Why should she — the way you've played around with her?"

He sighed and said: "I wish to Christ I'd never seen her."

"Maybe you do now." A trace of spitefulness came into the girl's voice. "But there was a time."

"I never know what to do or say to women except that way," he grumbled, "and then I didn't like Miles."

"That's a lie, Sam," the girl said. "You know I think she's a louse, but I'd be a louse too if it would give me a body like hers."

Spade rubbed his face impatiently against her hip, but said nothing.

Effie Perine bit her lip, wrinkled her forehead, and, bending over for a better view of his face, asked: "Do you suppose she could have killed him?"

Spade sat up straight and took his arm from her waist. He smiled at her. His smile held nothing but amusement. He took out his lighter, snapped on the flame, and applied it to the end of his cigarette. "You're an angel," he said tenderly through smoke, "a nice rattle-brained angel."

She smiled a bit wryly. "Oh, am I? Suppose I told you that your Iva hadn't been home many minutes when I arrived to break the news at three o'clock this morning?"

"Are you telling me?" he asked. His eyes had become alert though his mouth continued to smile.

"She kept me waiting at the door while she undressed or finished undressing. I saw her clothes where she had dumped them on a chair. Her hat and coat were underneath. Her singlette, on top, was still warm. She said she had been asleep, but she hadn't. She had wrinkled up the bed, but the wrinkles weren't mashed down."

Spade took the girl's hand and patted it.

"You're a detective, darling, but" — he shook his head — "she didn't kill him."

Effie Perine snatched her hand away. "That louse wants to marry you, Sam," she said bitterly.

He made an impatient gesture with his head and one hand.

She frowned at him and demanded: "Did you see her last night?"

"No."

"Honestly?"

"Honestly. Don't act like Dundy, sweetheart. It ill becomes you."

"Has Dundy been after you?"

"Uh-huh. He and Tom Polhaus dropped in for a drink at four o'clock."

"Do they really think you shot this what's-his-name?"

"Thursby." He dropped what was left of his cigarette into the brass tray and began to roll another.

"Do they?" she insisted.

"God knows." His eyes were on the cigarette he was making. "They did have some such notion. I don't know how far I talked them out of it."

"Look at me, Sam."

He looked at her and laughed so that for the moment merriment mingled with the anxiety in her face.

"You worry me," she said, seriousness returning to her face as she talked. "You always think you know what you're doing, but you're too slick for your own good, and some day you're going to find it out."

He sighed mockingly and rubbed his cheek against her arm. "That's what Dundy says, but you keep Iva away from me, sweet, and I'll manage to survive the rest of my troubles." He stood up and put on his hat. "Have the *Spade & Archer* taken off the door and *Samuel Spade* put on. I'll be back in an hour, or phone you."

Spade went through the St. Mark's long purplish lobby to the desk and asked a red-haired dandy whether Miss Wonderly was in. The red-haired dandy turned away, and then back shaking his head. "She checked out this morning, Mr. Spade."

"Thanks."

Spade walked past the desk to an alcove off the lobby where a plump young-middle-aged man in dark clothes sat at a flat-topped mahogany desk. On the edge of the desk facing the lobby was a triangular prism of mahogany and brass inscribed *Mr. Freed.*

The plump man got up and came around the desk holding out his hand.

"I was awfully sorry to hear about Archer,

Spade," he said in the tone of one trained to sympathize readily without intrusiveness. "I've just seen it in the *Call.* He was in here last night, you know."

"Thanks, Freed. Were you talking to him?"

"No. He was sitting in the lobby when I came in early in the evening. I didn't stop. I thought he was probably working and I know you fellows like to be left alone when you're busy. Did that have anything to do with his — ?"

"I don't think so, but we don't know yet. Anyway, we won't mix the house up in it if it can be helped."

"Thanks."

"That's all right. Can you give me some dope on an ex-guest, and then forget that I asked for it?"

"Surely."

"A Miss Wonderly checked out this morning. I'd like to know the details."

"Come along," Freed said, "and we'll see what we can learn."

Spade stood still, shaking his head. "I don't want to show in it."

Freed nodded and went out of the alcove. In the lobby he halted suddenly and came back to Spade.

"Harriman was the house-detective on duty last night," he said. "He's sure to have seen Archer. Shall I caution him not to mention it?"

Spade looked at Freed from the corners of his eyes. "Better not. That won't make any difference as long as there's no connection shown with this Wonderly. Harriman's all right, but he likes to talk, and I'd as lief not have him think there's anything to be kept quiet."

Freed nodded again and went away. Fifteen minutes later he returned.

"She arrived last Tuesday, registering from New York. She hadn't a trunk, only some bags. There were no phone-calls charged to her room, and she doesn't seem to have received much, if any, mail. The only one anybody remembers having seen her with was a tall dark man of thirty-six or so. She went out at half-past nine this morning, came back an hour later, paid her bill, and had her bags carried out to a car. The boy who carried them says it was a Nash touring car, probably a hired one. She left a forwarding address — the Ambassador, Los Angeles."

Spade said, "Thanks a lot, Freed," and left the St. Mark.

When Spade returned to his office Effie Perine stopped typing a letter to tell him: "Your friend Dundy was in. He wanted to look at your guns."

"And?"

"I told him to come back when you were here."

"Good girl. If he comes back again let him look at them."

"And Miss Wonderly called up."

"It's about time. What did she say?"

"She wants to see you." The girl picked up a slip of paper from her desk and read the memorandum penciled on it: "She's at the Coronet, on California Street, apartment one thousand and one. You're to ask for Miss Leblanc."

Spade said, "Give me," and held out his hand. When she had given him the memorandum he took out his lighter, snapped on the frame, set it to the slip of paper, held the paper until all but one corner was curling black ash, dropped it on the linoleum floor, and mashed it under his shoe-sole.

The girl watched him with disapproving eyes.

He grinned at her, said, "That's just the way it is, dear," and went out again.

4
The Black Bird

Miss Wonderly, in a belted green crêpe silk dress, opened the door of apartment 1001 at the Coronet. Her face was flushed. Her dark red hair, parted on the left side, swept back in loose waves over her right temple, was somewhat tousled.

Spade took off his hat and said: "Good morning."

His smile brought a fainter smile to her face. Her eyes, of blue that was almost violet, did not lose their troubled look. She lowered her head and said in a hushed, timid voice: "Come in, Mr. Spade."

She led him past open kitchen-, bathroom-, and bedroom-doors into a cream and red living-room, apologizing for its confusion: "Everything is upside-down. I haven't even finished unpacking."

She laid his hat on a table and sat down on a walnut settee. He sat on a brocaded oval-backed chair facing her.

She looked at her fingers, working them together, and said: “Mr. Spade, I’ve a terrible, terrible confession to make.”

Spade smiled a polite smile, which she did not lift her eyes to see, and said nothing.

“That — that story I told you yesterday was all — a story,” she stammered, and looked up at him now with miserable frightened eyes.

“Oh, that,” Spade said lightly. “We didn’t exactly believe your story.”

“Then — ?” Perplexity was added to the misery and fright in her eyes.

“We believed your two hundred dollars.”

“You mean — ?” She seemed to not know what he meant.

“I mean that you paid us more than if you’d been telling the truth,” he explained blandly, “and enough more to make it all right.”

Her eyes suddenly lighted up. She lifted herself a few inches from the settee, settled down again, smoothed her skirt, leaned forward, and spoke eagerly: “And even now you’d be willing to — ?”

Spade stopped her with a palm-up motion of one hand. The upper part of his face frowned. The lower part smiled. “That depends,” he said. “The hell of it is, Miss — Is your name Wonderly or Leblanc?”

She blushed and murmured: "It's really O'Shaughnessy — Brigid O'Shaughnessy."

"The hell of it is, Miss O'Shaughnessy, that a couple of murders" — she winced — "coming together like this get everybody stirred up, make the police think they can go the limit, make everybody hard to handle and expensive. It's not —"

He stopped talking because she had stopped listening and was waiting for him to finish.

"Mr. Spade, tell me the truth." Her voice quivered on the verge of hysteria. Her face had become haggard around desperate eyes. "Am I to blame for — for last night?"

Spade shook his head. "Not unless there are things I don't know about," he said. "You warned us that Thursby was dangerous. Of course you lied to us about your sister and all, but that doesn't count: we didn't believe you." He shrugged his sloping shoulders. "I wouldn't say it was your fault."

She said, "Thank you," very softly, and then moved her head from side to side. "But I'll always blame myself." She put a hand to her throat. "Mr. Archer was so — so alive yesterday afternoon, so solid and hearty and —"

"Stop it," Spade commanded. "He knew

what he was doing. They're the chances we take."

"Was — was he married?"

"Yes, with ten thousand insurance, no children, and a wife who didn't like him."

"Oh, please don't!" she whispered.

Spade shrugged again. "That's the way it was." He glanced at his watch and moved from his chair to the settee beside her. "There's no time for worrying about that now." His voice was pleasant but firm. "Out there a flock of policemen and assistant district attorneys and reporters are running around with their noses to the ground. What do you want to do?"

"I want you to save me from — from it all," she replied in a thin tremulous voice. She put a timid hand on his sleeve. "Mr. Spade, do they know about me?"

"Not yet. I wanted to see you first."

"What — what would they think if they knew about the way I came to you — with those lies?"

"It would make them suspicious. That's why I've been stalling them till I could see you. I thought maybe we wouldn't have to let them know all of it. We ought to be able to fake a story that will rock them to sleep, if necessary."

"You don't think I had anything to do

with the — the murders — do you?"

Spade grinned at her and said: "I forgot to ask you that. Did you?"

"No."

"That's good. Now what are we going to tell the police?"

She squirmed on her end of the settee and her eyes wavered between heavy lashes, as if trying and failing to free their gaze from his. She seemed smaller, and very young and oppressed.

"Must they know about me at all?" she asked. "I think I'd rather die than that, Mr. Spade. I can't explain now, but can't you somehow manage so that you can shield me from them, so I won't have to answer their questions? I don't think I could stand being questioned now. I think I would rather die. Can't you, Mr. Spade?"

"Maybe," he said, "but I'll have to know what it's all about."

She went down on her knees at his knees. She held her face up to him. Her face was wan, taut, and fearful over tight-clasped hands.

"I haven't lived a good life," she cried. "I've been bad — worse than you could know — but I'm not all bad. Look at me, Mr. Spade. You know I'm not all bad, don't you? You can see that, can't you? Then can't you trust me a little? Oh, I'm so alone and afraid, and I've got nobody to help me if you won't help me. I know I've no right to ask you to trust me if I won't trust you. I do trust you, but I can't tell you. I can't tell you now. Later I will, when I can. I'm afraid, Mr. Spade. I'm afraid of trusting you. I don't mean that. I do trust you, but — I trusted Floyd and — I've nobody else, nobody else, Mr. Spade. You can help me. You've said you can help me. If I hadn't believed you could save me I would have run away today instead of sending for you. If I thought anybody else could save me would I be down on my knees like this? I know this isn't fair of me. But be generous, Mr. Spade, don't ask me to be fair. You're strong, you're resourceful, you're brave. You can spare me some of that strength and resourcefulness and courage, surely. Help me, Mr. Spade. Help me because I need help so badly, and because if you don't where will I find anyone who can, no matter how willing? Help me. I've no right to ask you to help me blindly, but I do ask you. Be generous, Mr. Spade. You can help me. Help me."

Spade, who had held his breath through much of this speech, now emptied his lungs with a long sighing exhalation between pursed lips and said: "You won't need much of anybody's help. You're good. You're very good. It's chiefly your eyes, I think, and that throb you get into your voice when you say things like 'Be generous, Mr. Spade.' "

She jumped up on her feet. Her face crimsoned painfully, but she held her head erect and she looked Spade straight in the eyes.

"I deserve that," she said. "I deserve it, but — oh! — I did want your help so much. I do want it, and need it, so much. And the lie was in the way I said it, and not at all in what I said." She turned away, no longer holding herself erect. "It is my own fault that you can't believe me now."

Spade's face reddened and he looked down at the floor, muttering: "Now you are dangerous."

Brigid O'Shaughnessy went to the table and picked up his hat. She came back and stood in front of him holding the hat, not offering it to him, but holding it for him to take if he wished. Her face was white and thin.

Spade looked at his hat and asked: "What happened last night?"

"Floyd came to the hotel at nine o'clock, and we went out for a walk. I suggested that so Mr. Archer could see him. We stopped at a restaurant in Geary Street, I think it was, for supper and to dance, and came back to the hotel at about half-past twelve. Floyd left me at the door and I stood inside and watched Mr. Archer follow him down the street, on the other side."

"Down? You mean towards Market Street?"

"Yes."

"Do you know what they'd be doing in the neighborhood of Bush and Stockton, where Archer was shot?"

"Isn't that near where Floyd lived?"

"No. It would be nearly a dozen blocks out of his way if he was going from your hotel to his. Well, what did you do after they had gone?"

"I went to bed. And this morning when I went out for breakfast I saw the headlines in the papers and read about — you know. Then I went up to Union Square, where I had seen automobiles for hire, and got one and went to the hotel for my luggage. After I found my room had been searched yesterday I knew I would have to move, and I had found this place yesterday afternoon. So I came up here and then telephoned your office."

"Your room at the St. Mark was searched?" he asked.

"Yes, while I was at your office." She bit

her lip. "I didn't mean to tell you that."

"That means I'm not supposed to question you about it?"

She nodded shyly.

He frowned.

She moved his hat a little in her hands.

He laughed impatiently and said: "Stop waving the hat in my face. Haven't I offered to do what I can?"

She smiled contritely, returned the hat to the table, and sat beside him on the settee again.

He said: "I've got nothing against trusting you blindly except that I won't be able to do you much good if I haven't some idea of what it's all about. For instance, I've got to have some sort of a line on your Floyd Thursby."

"I met him in the Orient." She spoke slowly, looking down at a pointed finger tracing eights on the settee between them. "We came here from Hongkong last week. He was — he had promised to help me. He took advantage of my helplessness and dependence on him to betray me."

"Betray you how?"

She shook her head and said nothing.

Spade, frowning with impatience, asked: "Why did you want him shadowed?"

"I wanted to learn how far he had gone.

He wouldn't even let me know where he was staying. I wanted to find out what he was doing, whom he was meeting, things like that."

"Did he kill Archer?"

She looked up at him, surprised. "Yes, certainly," she said.

"He had a Luger in a shoulder-holster. Archer wasn't shot with a Luger."

"He had a revolver in his overcoat-pocket," she said.

"You saw it?"

"Oh, I've seen it often. I know he always carries one there. I didn't see it last night, but I know he never wears an overcoat without it."

"Why all the guns?"

"He lived by them. There was a story in Hongkong that he had come out there, to the Orient, as a bodyguard to a gambler who had had to leave the States, and that the gambler had since disappeared. They said Floyd knew about his disappearing. I don't know. I do know that he always went heavily armed and that he never went to sleep without covering the floor around his bed with crumpled newspaper so nobody could come silently into his room."

"You picked a nice sort of playmate."

"Only that sort could have helped me,"

she said simply, "if he had been loyal."

"Yes, if." Spade pinched his lower lip between finger and thumb and looked gloomily at her. The vertical creases over his nose deepened, drawing his brows together. "How bad a hole are you actually in?"

"As bad," she said, "as could be."

"Physical danger?"

"I'm not heroic. I don't think there's anything worse than death."

"Then it's that?"

"It's that as surely as we're sitting here" — she shivered — "unless you help me."

He took his fingers away from his mouth and ran them through his hair. "I'm not Christ," he said irritably. "I can't work miracles out of thin air." He looked at his watch. "The day's going and you're giving me nothing to work with. Who killed Thursby?"

She put a crumpled handkerchief to her mouth and said, "I don't know," through it.

"Your enemies or his?"

"I don't know. His, I hope, but I'm afraid — I don't know."

"How was he supposed to be helping you? Why did you bring him here from Hongkong?"

She looked at him with frightened eyes and shook her head in silence. Her face was haggard and pitifully stubborn.

Spade stood up, thrust his hands into the pockets of his jacket, and scowled down at her. “This is hopeless,” he said savagely. “I can’t do anything for you. I don’t know what you want done. I don’t even know if you know what you want.”

She hung her head and wept.

He made a growling animal noise in his throat and went to the table for his hat.

“You won’t,” she begged in a small choked voice, not looking up, “go to the police?”

“Go to them!” he exclaimed, his voice loud with rage. “They’ve been running me ragged since four o’clock this morning. I’ve made myself God knows how much trouble standing them off. For what? For some crazy notion that I could help you. I can’t. I won’t try.” He put his hat on his head and pulled it down tight. “Go to them? All I’ve got to do is stand still and they’ll be swarming all over me. Well, I’ll tell them what I know and you’ll have to take your chances.”

She rose from the settee and held herself straight in front of him though her knees were trembling, and she held her white panic-stricken face up high though she couldn’t hold the twitching muscles of mouth and chin still. She said: “You’ve been patient. You’ve tried to help me. It is hopeless, and useless, I suppose." She stretched out her right hand. "I thank you for what you have done. I — I'll have to take my chances."

Spade made the growling animal noise in his throat again and sat down on the settee. "How much money have you got?" he asked.

The question startled her. Then she pinched her lower lip between her teeth and answered reluctantly: "I've about five hundred dollars left."

"Give it to me."

She hesitated, looking timidly at him. He made angry gestures with mouth, eyebrows, hands, and shoulders. She went into her bedroom, returning almost immediately with a sheaf of paper money in one hand.

He took the money from her, counted it, and said: "There's only four hundred here."

"I had to keep some to live on," she explained meekly, putting a hand to her breast.

"Can't you get any more?"

"No."

"You must have something you can raise money on," he insisted.

"I've some rings, a little jewelry."

"You'll have to hock them," he said, and held out his hand. "The Remedial's the best place — Mission and Fifth."

She looked pleadingly at him. His yellow-gray eyes were hard and implacable. Slowly she put her hand inside the neck of her dress, brought out a slender roll of bills, and put them in his waiting hand.

He smoothed the bills out and counted them — four twenties, four tens, and a five. He returned two of the tens and the five to her. The others he put in his pocket. Then he stood up and said: "I'm going out and see what I can do for you. I'll be back as soon as I can with the best news I can manage. I'll ring four times — long, short, long, short — so you'll know it's me. You needn't go to the door with me. I can let myself out."

He left her standing in the center of the floor looking after him with dazed blue eyes.

Spade went into a reception-room whose door bore the legend *Wise, Merican & Wise.* The red-haired girl at the switchboard said: "Oh, hello, Mr. Spade."

"Hello, darling," he replied. "Is Sid in?"

He stood beside her with a hand on her plump shoulder while she manipulated a plug and spoke into the mouthpiece: "Mr. Spade to see you, Mr. Wise." She looked up at Spade. "Go right in."

He squeezed her shoulder by way of

acknowledgment, crossed the reception-room to a dully lighted inner corridor, and passed down the corridor to a frosted glass door at its far end. He opened the frosted glass door and went into an office where a small olive-skinned man with a tired oval face under thin dark hair dotted with dandruff sat behind an immense desk on which bales of paper were heaped.

The small man flourished a cold cigar-stub at Spade and said: "Pull a chair around. So Miles got the big one last night?" Neither his tired face nor his rather shrill voice held any emotion.

"Uh-huh, that's what I came in about." Spade frowned and cleared his throat. "I think I'm going to have to tell a coroner to go to hell, Sid. Can I hide behind the sanctity of my clients' secrets and identities and what-not, all the same priest or lawyer?"

Sid Wise lifted his shoulders and lowered the ends of his mouth. "Why not? An inquest is not a court-trial. You can try, anyway. You've gotten away with more than that before this."

"I know, but Dundy's getting snotty, and maybe it is a little bit thick this time. Get your hat, Sid, and we'll go see the right people. I want to be safe."

Sid Wise looked at the papers massed on

his desk and groaned, but he got up from his chair and went to the closet by the window. "You're a son of a gun, Sammy," he said as he took his hat from its hook.

Spade returned to his office at ten minutes past five that evening. Effie Perine was sitting at his desk reading *Time.* Spade sat on the desk and asked: "Anything stirring?"

"Not here. You look like you'd swallowed the canary."

He grinned contentedly. "I think we've got a future. I always had an idea that if Miles would go off and die somewhere we'd stand a better chance of thriving. Will you take care of sending flowers for me?"

"I did."

"You're an invaluable angel. How's your woman's intuition today?"

"Why?"

"What do you think of Wonderly?"

"I'm for her," the girl replied without hesitation.

"She's got too many names," Spade mused. "Wonderly, Leblanc, and she says the right one's O'Shaughnessy."

"I don't care if she's got all the names in the phone-book. That girl is all right, and you know it."

"I wonder." Spade blinked sleepily at Effie Perine. He chuckled. "Anyway she's given up seven hundred smacks in two days, and that's all right."

Effie Perine sat up straight and said: "Sam, if that girl's in trouble and you let her down, or take advantage of it to bleed her, I'll never forgive you, never have any respect for you, as long as I live."

Spade smiled unnaturally. Then he frowned. The frown was unnatural. He opened his mouth to speak, but the sound of someone's entrance through the corridor-door stopped him.

Effie Perine rose and went into the outer office. Spade took off his hat and sat in his chair. The girl returned with an engraved card — *Mr. Joel Cairo.*

"This guy is queer," she said.

"In with him, then, darling," said Spade.

Mr. Joel Cairo was a small-boned dark man of medium height. His hair was black and smooth and very glossy. His features were Levantine. A square-cut ruby, its sides paralleled by four baguette diamonds, gleamed against the deep green of his cravat. His black coat, cut tight to narrow shoulders, flared a little over slightly plump hips. His trousers fitted his round legs more snugly than was the current fashion. The uppers of his patent-leather shoes were hidden by fawn spats. He held a black derby hat in a chamois-gloved hand and came towards Spade with short, mincing, bobbing steps. The fragrance of *chypre* came with him.

Spade inclined his head at his visitor and then at a chair, saying: "Sit down, Mr. Cairo."

Cairo bowed elaborately over his hat, said, "I thank you," in a high-pitched thin voice and sat down. He sat down primly, crossing his ankles, placing his hat on his knees, and began to draw off his yellow gloves.

Spade rocked back in his chair and asked: "Now what can I do for you, Mr. Cairo?" The amiable negligence of his tone, his motion in the chair, were precisely as they had been when he had addressed the same question to Brigid O'Shaughnessy on the previous day.

Cairo turned his hat over, dropping his gloves into it, and placed it bottom-up on the corner of the desk nearest him. Diamonds twinkled on the second and fourth fingers of his left hand, a ruby that matched the one in his tie even to the surrounding diamonds on the third finger of his right hand. His hands were soft and well cared for. Though they were not large their flaccid bluntness made them seem clumsy. He rubbed his palms together and said over the whispering sound they made: "May a stranger offer condolences for your partner's unfortunate death?"

"Thanks."

"May I ask, Mr. Spade, if there was, as the newspapers inferred, a certain — ah — relationship between that unfortunate happening and the death a little later of the man Thursby?"

Spade said nothing in a blank-faced definite way.

Cairo rose and bowed. "I beg your pardon." He sat down and placed his hands side by side, palms down, on the corner of the desk. "More than idle curiosity made me ask that, Mr. Spade. I am trying to recover an — ah — ornament that has been — shall we say? — mislaid. I thought, and hoped, you could assist me."

Spade nodded with eyebrows lifted to indicate attentiveness.

"The ornament is a statuette," Cairo went on, selecting and mouthing his words carefully, "the black figure of a bird."

Spade nodded again, with courteous interest.

"I am prepared to pay, on behalf of the figure's rightful owner, the sum of five thousand dollars for its recovery." Cairo raised one hand from the desk-corner and touched a spot in the air with the broad-nailed tip of an ugly forefinger. "I am prepared to promise that — what is the phrase? — no questions will be asked." He put his hand on the desk again beside the other and smiled blandly over them at the private detective.

"Five thousand is a lot of money," Spade commented, looking thoughtfully at Cairo. "It —"

Fingers drummed lightly on the door.

When Spade had called, "Come in," the door opened far enough to admit Effie Perine's head and shoulders. She had put on a small dark felt hat and a dark coat with a gray fur collar.

"Is there anything else?" she asked.

"No. Good night. Lock the door when you go, will you?"

Spade turned in his chair to face Cairo again, saying: "It's an interesting figure."

The sound of the corridor-door's closing behind Effie Perine came to them.

Cairo smiled and took a short compact flat black pistol out of an inner pocket. "You will please," he said, "clasp your hands together at the back of your neck."

5
THE LEVANTINE

Spade did not look at the pistol. He raised his arms and, leaning back in his chair, intertwined the fingers of his two hands behind his head. His eyes, holding no particular expression, remained focused on Cairo's dark face.

Cairo coughed a little apologetic cough and smiled nervously with lips that had lost some of their redness. His dark eyes were humid and bashful and very earnest. "I intend to search your offices, Mr. Spade. I warn you that if you attempt to prevent me I shall certainly shoot you."

"Go ahead." Spade's voice was as empty of expression as his face.

"You will please stand," the man with the pistol instructed him at whose thick chest the pistol was aimed. "I shall have to make sure that you are not armed."

Spade stood up pushing his chair back with his calves as he straightened his legs.

Cairo went around behind him. He transferred the pistol from his right hand to his left. He lifted Spade's coat-tail and looked under it. Holding the pistol close to Spade's back, he put his right hand around Spade's side and patted his chest. The Levantine face was then no more than six inches below and behind Spade's right elbow.

Spade's elbow dropped as Spade spun to the right. Cairo's face jerked back not far enough: Spade's right heel on the patent-leathered toes anchored the smaller man in the elbow's path. The elbow struck him beneath the cheek-bone, staggering him so that he must have fallen had he not been held by Spade's foot on his foot. Spade's elbow went on past the astonished dark face and straightened when Spade's hand struck down at the pistol. Cairo let the pistol go the instant that Spade's fingers touched it. The pistol was small in Spade's hand.

Spade took his foot off Cairo's to complete his about-face. With his left hand Spade gathered together the smaller man's coat-lapels — the ruby-set green tie bunching out over his knuckles — while his right hand stowed the captured weapon away in a coat-pocket. Spade's yellow-gray eyes were somber. His face was wooden, with a trace of sullenness around the mouth.

Cairo's face was twisted by pain and chagrin. There were tears in his dark eyes. His skin was the complexion of polished lead except where the elbow had reddened his cheek.

Spade by means of his grip on the Levantine's lapels turned him slowly and pushed him back until he was standing close in front of the chair he had lately occupied. A puzzled look replaced the look of pain in the lead-colored face. Then Spade smiled. His smile was gentle, even dreamy. His right shoulder raised a few inches. His bent right arm was driven up by the shoulder's lift. Fist, wrist, forearm, crooked elbow, and upper arm seemed all one rigid piece, with only the limber shoulder giving them motion. The fist struck Cairo's face, covering for a moment one side of his chin, a corner of his mouth, and most of his cheek between cheek-bone and jawbone.

Cairo shut his eyes and was unconscious.

Spade lowered the limp body into the chair, where it lay with sprawled arms and legs, the head lolling back against the chair's back, the mouth open.

Spade emptied the unconscious man's pockets one by one, working methodically, moving the lax body when necessary, making a pile of the pockets' contents on the desk. When the last pocket had been turned out he returned to his own chair, rolled and lighted a cigarette, and began to examine his spoils. He examined them with grave unhurried thoroughness.

There was a large wallet of dark soft leather. The wallet contained three hundred and sixty-five dollars in United States bills of several sizes; three five-pound notes; a much-visaed Greek passport bearing Cairo's name and portrait; five folded sheets of pinkish onion-skin paper covered with what seemed to be Arabic writing; a raggedly clipped newspaper-account of the finding of Archer's and Thursby's bodies; a post-card photograph of a dusky woman with bold cruel eyes and a tender drooping mouth; a large silk handkerchief, yellow with age and somewhat cracked along its folds; a thin sheaf of Mr. Joel Cairo's engraved cards; and a ticket for an orchestra seat at the Geary Theatre that evening.

Besides the wallet and its contents there were three gaily colored silk handkerchiefs fragrant of *chypre;* a platinum Longines watch on a platinum and red gold chain, attached at the other end to a small pear-shaped pendant of some white metal; a handful of United States, British, French, and Chinese coins; a ring holding half a dozen keys; a silver and onyx fountain-pen; a metal comb in a leatherette case; a nail-file in a leatherette case; a small street-guide to San Francisco; a Southern Pacific baggage-check; a half-filled package of violet pastilles; a Shanghai insurance-broker's business-card; and four sheets of Hotel Belvedere writing paper, on one of which was written in small precise letters Samuel Spade's name and the addresses of his office and his apartment.

Having examined these articles carefully — he even opened the back of the watch-case to see that nothing was hidden inside — Spade leaned over and took the unconscious man's wrist between finger and thumb, feeling his pulse. Then he dropped the wrist, settled back in his chair, and rolled and lighted another cigarette. His face while he smoked was, except for occasional slight and aimless movements of his lower lip, so still and reflective that it seemed stupid; but when Cairo presently moaned and fluttered his eyelids Spade's face became bland, and he put the beginning of a friendly smile into his eyes and mouth.

Joel Cairo awakened slowly. His eyes opened first, but a full minute passed before they fixed their gaze on any definite part of the ceiling. Then he shut his mouth and swallowed, exhaling heavily through his nose afterward. He drew in one foot and turned a hand over on his thigh. Then he raised his head from the chair-back, looked around the office in confusion, saw Spade, and sat up. He opened his mouth to speak, started, clapped a hand to his face where Spade's fist had struck and where there was now a florid bruise.

Cairo said through his teeth, painfully: "I could have shot you, Mr. Spade."

"You could have tried," Spade conceded.

"I did not try."

"I know."

"Then why did you strike me after I was disarmed?"

"Sorry," Spade said, and grinned wolfishly, showing his jaw-teeth, "but imagine my embarrassment when I found that five-thousand-dollar offer was just hooey."

"You are mistaken, Mr. Spade. That was, and is, a genuine offer."

"What the hell?" Spade's surprise was genuine.

"I am prepared to pay five thousand dollars for the figure's return." Cairo took his hand away from his bruised face and sat up prim and business-like again. "You have it?"

"No."

"If it is not here" — Cairo was very politely skeptical — "why should you have risked serious injury to prevent my searching for it?"

"I should sit around and let people come in and stick me up?" Spade flicked a finger at Cairo's possessions on the desk. "You've got my apartment-address. Been up there yet?"

"Yes, Mr. Spade. I am ready to pay five thousand dollars for the figure's return, but surely it is natural enough that I should try first to spare the owner that expense if possible."

"Who is he?"

Cairo shook his head and smiled. "You will have to forgive my not answering that question."

"Will I?" Spade leaned forward smiling with tight lips. "I've got you by the neck, Cairo. You've walked in and tied yourself up, plenty strong enough to suit the police, with last night's killings. Well, now you'll have to play with me or else."

Cairo's smile was demure and not in any way alarmed. "I made somewhat extensive inquiries about you before taking any action," he said, "and was assured that you were far too reasonable to allow other considerations to interfere with profitable business relations."

Spade shrugged. "Where are they?" he asked.

"I have offered you five thousand dollars for —"

Spade thumped Cairo's wallet with the backs of his fingers and said: "There's nothing like five thousand dollars here. You're betting your eyes. You could come in and say you'd pay me a million for a purple elephant, but what in hell would that mean?"

"I see, I see," Cairo said thoughtfully, screwing up his eyes. "You wish some assurance of my sincerity." He brushed his red lower lip with a fingertip. "A retainer, would that serve?"

"It might."

Cairo put his hand out towards his wallet, hesitated, withdrew the hand, and said: "You will take, say, a hundred dollars?"

Spade picked up the wallet and took out a hundred dollars. Then he frowned, said, "Better make it two hundred," and did.

Cairo said nothing.

"Your first guess was that I had the bird," Spade said in a crisp voice when he had put the two hundred dollars into his pocket and had dropped the wallet on the desk again.

"There's nothing in that. What's your second?"

"That you know where it is, or, if not exactly that, that you know it is where you can get it."

Spade neither denied nor affirmed that: he seemed hardly to have heard it. He asked: "What sort of proof can you give me that your man is the owner?"

"Very little, unfortunately. There is this, though: nobody else can give you any authentic evidence of ownership at all. And if you know as much about the affair as I suppose — or I should not be here — you know that the means by which it was taken from him shows that his right to it was more valid than anyone else's — certainly more valid than Thursby's."

"What about his daughter?" Spade asked.

Excitement opened Cairo's eyes and mouth, turned his face red, made his voice shrill. "*He* is not the owner!"

Spade said, "Oh," mildly and ambiguously.

"Is he here, in San Francisco, now?" Cairo asked in a less shrill, but still excited, voice.

Spade blinked his eyes sleepily and suggested: "It might be better all around if we put our cards on the table."

Cairo recovered composure with a little

jerk. "I do not think it would be better." His voice was suave now. "If you know more than I, I shall profit by your knowledge, and so will you to the extent of five thousand dollars. If you do not then I have made a mistake in coming to you, and to do as you suggest would be simply to make that mistake worse."

Spade nodded indifferently and waved his hand at the articles on the desk, saying: "There's your stuff"; and then, when Cairo was returning them to his pockets: "It's understood that you're to pay my expenses while I'm getting this black bird for you, and five thousand dollars when it's done?"

"Yes, Mr. Spade; that is, five thousand dollars less whatever moneys have been advanced to you — five thousand in all."

"Right. And it's a legitimate proposition." Spade's face was solemn except for wrinkles at the corners of his eyes. "You're not hiring me to do any murders or burglaries for you, but simply to get it back if possible in an honest and lawful way."

"If possible," Cairo agreed. His face also was solemn except for the eyes. "And in any event with discretion." He rose and picked up his hat. "I am at the Hotel Belvedere when you wish to communicate with me — room six-thirty-five. I confidently expect the greatest mutual benefit from our association, Mr. Spade." He hesitated. "May I have my pistol?"

"Sure. I'd forgotten it."

Spade took the pistol out of his coat-pocket and handed it to Cairo.

Cairo pointed the pistol at Spade's chest.

"You will please keep your hands on the top of the desk," Cairo said earnestly. "I intend to search your offices."

Spade said: "I'll be damned." Then he laughed in his throat and said: "All right. Go ahead. I won't stop you."

6
The Undersized Shadow

For half an hour after Joel Cairo had gone Spade sat alone, still and frowning, at his desk. Then he said aloud in the tone of one dismissing a problem, "Well, they're paying for it," and took a bottle of Manhattan cocktail and a paper drinking-cup from a desk-drawer. He filled the cup two-thirds full, drank, returned the bottle to the drawer, tossed the cup into the wastebasket, put on his hat and overcoat, turned off the lights, and went down to the night-lit street.

An undersized youth of twenty or twenty-one in neat gray cap and overcoat was standing idly on the corner below Spade's building.

Spade walked up Sutter Street to Kearny, where he entered a cigar-store to buy two sacks of Bull Durham. When he came out the youth was one of four people waiting for a street-car on the opposite corner.

Spade ate dinner at Herbert's Grill in

Powell Street. When he left the Grill, at a quarter to eight, the youth was looking into a nearby haberdasher's window.

Spade went to the Hotel Belvedere, asking at the desk for Mr. Cairo. He was told that Cairo was not in. The youth sat in a chair in a far corner of the lobby.

Spade went to the Geary Theatre, failed to see Cairo in the lobby, and posted himself on the curb in front, facing the theatre. The youth loitered with other loiterers before Marquard's restaurant below.

At ten minutes past eight Joel Cairo appeared, walking up Geary Street with his little mincing bobbing steps. Apparently he did not see Spade until the private detective touched his shoulder. He seemed moderately surprised for a moment, and then said: "Oh, yes, of course you saw the ticket."

"Uh-huh. I've got something I want to show you." Spade drew Cairo back towards the curb a little away from the other waiting theatre-goers. "The kid in the cap down by Marquard's."

Cairo murmured, "I'll see," and looked at his watch. He looked up Geary Street. He looked at a theatre-sign in front of him on which George Arliss was shown costumed as Shylock, and then his dark eyes crawled sidewise in their sockets until they were looking at the kid in the cap, at his cool pale face with curling lashes hiding lowered eyes.

"Who is he?" Spade asked.

Cairo smiled up at Spade. "I do not know him."

"He's been tailing me around town."

Cairo wet his lower lip with his tongue and asked: "Do you think it was wise, then, to let him see us together?"

"How do I know?" Spade replied. "Anyway, it's done."

Cairo removed his hat and smoothed his hair with a gloved hand. He replaced his hat carefully on his head and said with every appearance of candor: "I give you my word I do not know him, Mr. Spade. I give you my word I have nothing to do with him. I have asked nobody's assistance except yours, on my word of honor."

"Then he's one of the others?"

"That may be."

"I just wanted to know, because if he gets to be a nuisance I may have to hurt him."

"Do as you think best. He is not a friend of mine."

"That's good. There goes the curtain. Good night," Spade said, and crossed the street to board a westbound street-car.

The youth in the cap boarded the same car.

Spade left the car at Hyde Street and went up to his apartment. His rooms were not greatly upset, but showed unmistakable signs of having been searched. When Spade had washed and had put on a fresh shirt and collar he went out again, walked up to Sutter Street, and boarded a westbound car. The youth boarded it also.

Within half a dozen blocks of the Coronet Spade left the car and went into the vestibule of a tall brown apartment-building. He pressed three bell-buttons together. The street-door-lock buzzed. He entered, passed the elevator and stairs, went down a long yellow-walled corridor to the rear of the building, found a back door fastened by a Yale lock, and let himself out into a narrow court. The court led to a dark back street, up which Spade walked for two blocks. Then he crossed over to California Street and went to the Coronet. It was not quite half-past nine o'clock.

The eagerness with which Brigid O'Shaughnessy welcomed Spade suggested that she had been not entirely certain of his coming. She had put on a satin gown of the blue shade called Artoise that season, with chalcedony shoulder-straps, and her stockings and slippers were Artoise.

The red and cream sitting-room had been brought to order and livened with flowers in squat pottery vases of black and silver. Three small rough-barked logs burned in the fireplace. Spade watched them burn while she put away his hat and coat.

"Do you bring me good news?" she asked when she came into the room again. Anxiety looked through her smile, and she held her breath.

"We won't have to make anything public that hasn't already been made public."

"The police won't have to know about me?"

"No."

She sighed happily and sat on the walnut settee. Her face relaxed and her body relaxed. She smiled up at him with admiring eyes. "However did you manage it?" she asked more in wonder than in curiosity.

"Most things in San Francisco can be bought, or taken."

"And you won't get into trouble? Do sit down." She made room for him on the settee.

"I don't mind a reasonable amount of trouble," he said with not too much complacence.

He stood beside the fireplace and looked at her with eyes that studied, weighed, judged her without pretense that they were not studying, weighing, judging her. She flushed slightly under the frankness of his scrutiny, but she seemed more sure of herself than before, though a becoming shyness had not left her eyes. He stood there until it seemed plain that he meant to ignore her invitation to sit beside her, and then crossed to the settee.

"You aren't," he asked as he sat down, "exactly the sort of person you pretend to be, are you?"

"I'm not sure I know what you mean," she said in her hushed voice, looking at him with puzzled eyes.

"Schoolgirl manner," he explained, "stammering and blushing and all that."

She blushed and replied hurriedly, not looking at him: "I told you this afternoon that I've been bad — worse than you could know."

"That's what I mean," he said. "You told me that this afternoon in the same words, same tone. It's a speech you've practiced."

After a moment in which she seemed confused almost to the point of tears she laughed and said: "Very well, then, Mr. Spade, I'm not at all the sort of person I pretend to be. I'm eighty years old, incredibly wicked, and an iron-molder by trade.

But if it's a pose it's one I've grown into, so you won't expect me to drop it entirely, will you?"

"Oh, it's all right," he assured her. "Only it wouldn't be all right if you were actually that innocent. We'd never get anywhere."

"I won't be innocent," she promised with a hand on her heart.

"I saw Joel Cairo tonight," he said in the manner of one making polite conversation.

Gaiety went out of her face. Her eyes, focused on his profile, became frightened, then cautious. He had stretched his legs out and was looking at his crossed feet. His face did not indicate that he was thinking about anything.

There was a long pause before she asked uneasily:

"You — you know him?"

"I saw him tonight." Spade did not look up and he maintained his light conversational tone. "He was going to see George Arliss."

"You mean you talked to him?"

"Only for a minute or two, till the curtain-bell rang."

She got up from the settee and went to the fireplace to poke the fire. She changed slightly the position of an ornament on the mantelpiece, crossed the room to get a box of cigarettes from a table in a corner, straightened a curtain, and returned to her seat. Her face now was smooth and unworried.

Spade grinned sidewise at her and said: "You're good. You're very good."

Her face did not change. She asked quietly: "What did he say?"

"About what?"

She hesitated. "About me."

"Nothing." Spade turned to hold his lighter under the end of her cigarette. His eyes were shiny in a wooden satan's face.

"Well, what did he say?" she asked with half-playful petulance.

"He offered me five thousand dollars for the black bird."

She started, her teeth tore the end of her cigarette, and her eyes, after a swift alarmed glance at Spade, turned away from him.

"You're not going to go around poking at the fire and straightening up the room again, are you?" he asked lazily.

She laughed a clear merry laugh, dropped the mangled cigarette into a tray, and looked at him with clear merry eyes. "I won't," she promised. "And what did you say?"

"Five thousand dollars is a lot of money."

She smiled, but when, instead of smiling, he looked gravely at her, her smile became faint, confused, and presently vanished. In its place came a hurt, bewildered look. "Surely you're not really considering it," she said.

"Why not? Five thousand dollars is a lot of money."

"But, Mr. Spade, you promised to help me." Her hands were on his arm. "I trusted you. You can't —" She broke off, took her hands from his sleeve and worked them together.

Spade smiled gently into her troubled eyes. "Don't let's try to figure out how much you've trusted me," he said. "I promised to help you — sure — but you didn't say anything about any black birds."

"But you must've known or — or you wouldn't have mentioned it to me. You do know now. You won't — you can't — treat me like that." Her eyes were cobalt-blue prayers.

"Five thousand dollars is," he said for the third time, "a lot of money."

She lifted her shoulders and hands and let them fall in a gesture that accepted defeat. "It is," she agreed in a small dull voice. "It is far more than I could ever offer you, if I must bid for your loyalty."

Spade laughed. His laughter was brief and somewhat bitter. "That is good," he said, "coming from you. What have you given me besides money? Have you given me any of your confidence? any of the truth? any help in helping you? Haven't you tried to buy my loyalty with money and nothing else? Well, if I'm peddling it, why shouldn't I let it go to the highest bidder?"

"I've given you all the money I have." Tears glistened in her white-ringed eyes. Her voice was hoarse, vibrant. "I've thrown myself on your mercy, told you that without your help I'm utterly lost. What else is there?" She suddenly moved close to him on the settee and cried angrily: "Can I buy you with my body?"

Their faces were a few inches apart. Spade took her face between his hands and he kissed her mouth roughly and contemptuously. Then he sat back and said: "I'll think it over." His face was hard and furious.

She sat still holding her numbed face where his hands had left it.

He stood up and said: "Christ! there's no sense to this." He took two steps towards the fireplace and stopped, glowering at the burning logs, grinding his teeth together.

She did not move.

He turned to face her. The two vertical lines above his nose were deep clefts between red wales. "I don't give a damn about your honesty," he told her, trying to make himself speak calmly. "I don't care what kind of tricks you're up to, what your secrets are, but I've got to have something to show that you know what you're doing."

"I do know. Please believe that I do, and that it's all for the best, and —"

"Show me," he ordered. "I'm willing to help you. I've done what I could so far. If necessary I'll go ahead blindfolded, but I can't do it without more confidence in you than I've got now. You've got to convince me that you know what it's all about, that you're not simply fiddling around by guess and by God, hoping it'll come out all right somehow in the end."

"Can't you trust me just a little longer?"

"How much is a little? And what are you waiting for?"

She bit her lip and looked down. "I must talk to Joel Cairo," she said almost inaudibly.

"You can see him tonight," Spade said, looking at his watch. "His show will be out soon. We can get him on the phone at his hotel."

She raised her eyes, alarmed. "But he can't come here. I can't let him know where I am. I'm afraid."

"My place," Spade suggested.

She hesitated, working her lips together,

then asked: "Do you think he'd go there?"

Spade nodded.

"All right," she exclaimed, jumping up, her eyes large and bright. "Shall we go now?"

She went into the next room. Spade went to the table in the corner and silently pulled the drawer out. The drawer held two packs of playing-cards, a pad of score-cards for bridge, a brass screw, a piece of red string, and a gold pencil. He had shut the drawer and was lighting a cigarette when she returned wearing a small dark hat and a grey kidskin coat, carrying his hat and coat.

Their taxicab drew up behind a dark sedan that stood directly in front of Spade's street-door. Iva Archer was alone in the sedan, sitting at the wheel. Spade lifted his hat to her and went indoors with Brigid O'Shaughnessy. In the lobby he halted beside one of the benches and asked: "Do you mind waiting here a moment? I won't be long."

"That's perfectly all right," Brigid O'Shaughnessy said, sitting down. "You needn't hurry."

Spade went out to the sedan. When he had opened the sedan's door Iva spoke quickly: "I've got to talk to you, Sam. Can't I come in?" Her face was pale and nervous.

"Not now."

Iva clicked her teeth together and asked sharply: "Who is she?"

"I've only a minute, Iva," Spade said patiently. "What is it?"

"Who is she?" she repeated, nodding at the street-door.

He looked away from her, down the street. In front of a garage on the next corner an undersized youth of twenty or twenty-one in neat gray cap and overcoat loafed with his back against a wall. Spade frowned and returned his gaze to Iva's insistent face. "What is the matter?" he asked. "Has anything happened? You oughtn't to be here at this time of night."

"I'm beginning to believe that," she complained. "You told me I oughtn't to come to the office, and now I oughtn't to come here. Do you mean I oughtn't to chase after you? If that's what you mean why don't you say it right out?"

"Now, Iva, you've got no right to take that attitude."

"I know I haven't. I haven't any rights at all, it seems, where you're concerned. I thought I did. I thought your pretending to love me gave me —"

Spade said wearily: "This is no time to be

arguing about that, precious. What was it you wanted to see me about?"

"I can't talk to you here, Sam. Can't I come in?"

"Not now."

"Why can't I?"

Spade said nothing.

She made a thin line of her mouth, squirmed around straight behind the wheel, and started the sedan's engine, staring angrily ahead.

When the sedan began to move Spade said, "Good night, Iva," shut the door, and stood at the curb with his hat in his hand until it had been driven away. Then he went indoors again.

Brigid O'Shaughnessy rose smiling cheerfully from the bench and they went up to his apartment.

7
G in the Air

In his bedroom that was a living-room now the wall-bed was up, Spade took Brigid O'Shaughnessy's hat and coat, made her comfortable in a padded rocking chair, and telephoned the Hotel Belvedere. Cairo had not returned from the theatre. Spade left his telephone-number with the request that Cairo call him as soon as he came in.

Spade sat down in the armchair beside the table and without any preliminary, without an introductory remark of any sort, began to tell the girl about a thing that had happened some years before in the Northwest. He talked in a steady matter-of-fact voice that was devoid of emphasis or pauses, though now and then he repeated a sentence slightly rearranged, as if it were important that each detail be related exactly as it had happened.

At the beginning Brigid O'Shaughnessy listened with only partial attentiveness, obviously more surprised by his telling the story than interested in it, her curiosity more engaged with his purpose in telling the story than with the story he told; but presently, as the story went on, it caught her more and more fully and she became still and receptive.

A man named Flitcraft had left his real-estate-office, in Tacoma, to go to luncheon one day and had never returned. He did not keep an engagement to play golf after four that afternoon, though he had taken the initiative in making the engagement less than half an hour before he went out to luncheon. His wife and children never saw him again. His wife and he were supposed to be on the best of terms. He had two children, boys, one five and the other three. He owned his house in a Tacoma suburb, a new Packard, and the rest of the appurtenances of successful American living.

Flitcraft had inherited seventy thousand dollars from his father, and, with his success in real estate, was worth something in the neighborhood of two hundred thousand dollars at the time he vanished. His affairs were in order, though there were enough loose ends to indicate that he had not been setting them in order preparatory to vanishing. A deal that would have brought him an attractive profit, for instance, was to have been concluded the day after the one on which he disappeared. There was nothing to suggest that he had more than fifty or sixty dollars in his immediate possession at the time of his going. His habits for months past could be accounted for too thoroughly to justify any suspicion of secret vices, or even of another woman in his life, though either was barely possible.

"He went like that," Spade said, "like a fist when you open your hand."

When he had reached this point in his story the telephone-bell rang.

"Hello," Spade said into the instrument. "Mr. Cairo? . . . This is Spade. Can you come up to my place — Post Street — now? . . . Yes, I think it is." He looked at the girl, pursed his lips, and then said rapidly: "Miss O'Shaughnessy is here and wants to see you."

Brigid O'Shaughnessy frowned and stirred in her chair, but did not say anything.

Spade put the telephone down and told her: "He'll be up in a few minutes. Well, that was in 1922. In 1927 I was with one of the big detective agencies in Seattle. Mrs. Flitcraft came in and told us somebody had seen a man in Spokane who looked a lot like her husband. I went over there. It was

Flitcraft, all right. He had been living in Spokane for a couple of years as Charles — that was his first name — Pierce. He had an automobile-business that was netting him twenty or twenty-five thousand a year, a wife, a baby son, owned his home in a Spokane suburb, and usually got away to play golf after four in the afternoon during the season."

Spade had not been told very definitely what to do when he found Flitcraft. They talked in Spade's room at the Davenport. Flitcraft had no feeling of guilt. He had left his first family well provided for, and what he had done seemed to him perfectly reasonable. The only thing that bothered him was a doubt that he could make that reasonableness clear to Spade. He had never told anybody his story before, and thus had not had to attempt to make its reasonableness explicit. He tried now.

"I got it all right," Spade told Brigid O'Shaughnessy, "but Mrs. Flitcraft never did. She thought it was silly. Maybe it was. Anyway, it came out all right. She didn't want any scandal, and, after the trick he had played on her — the way she looked at it — she didn't want him. So they were divorced on the quiet and everything was swell all around.

"Here's what had happened to him. Going to lunch he passed an office-building that was being put up — just the skeleton. A beam or something fell eight or ten stories down and smacked the sidewalk alongside him. It brushed pretty close to him, but didn't touch him, though a piece of the sidewalk was chipped off and flew up and hit his cheek. It only took a piece of skin off, but he still had the scar when I saw him. He rubbed it with his finger — well, affectionately — when he told me about it. He was scared stiff of course, he said, but he was more shocked than really frightened. He felt like somebody had taken the lid off life and let him look at the works."

Flitcraft had been a good citizen and a good husband and father, not by any outer compulsion, but simply because he was a man who was most comfortable in step with his surroundings. He had been raised that way. The people he knew were like that. The life he knew was a clean orderly sane responsible affair. Now a falling beam had shown him that life was fundamentally none of these things. He, the good citizen-husband-father, could be wiped out between office and restaurant by the accident of a falling beam. He knew then that men died at haphazard like that, and lived only while blind chance spared them.

It was not, primarily, the injustice of it that disturbed him: he accepted that after the first shock. What disturbed him was the discovery that in sensibly ordering his affairs he had got out of step, and not into step, with life. He said he knew before he had gone twenty feet from the fallen beam that he would never know peace again until he had adjusted himself to this new glimpse of life. By the time he had eaten his luncheon he had found his means of adjustment. Life could be ended for him at random by a falling beam: he would change his life at random by simply going away. He loved his family, he said, as much as he supposed was usual, but he knew he was leaving them adequately provided for, and his love for them was not of the sort that would make absence painful.

"He went to Seattle that afternoon," Spade said, "and from there by boat to San Francisco. For a couple of years he wandered around and then drifted back to the Northwest, and settled in Spokane and got married. His second wife didn't look like the first, but they were more alike than they were different. You know, the kind of women that play fair games of golf and bridge and like new salad-recipes. He wasn't sorry for what he had done. It seemed reasonable enough to him. I don't think he even knew he had settled back naturally into the same groove he had jumped out of in Tacoma. But that's the part of it I always liked. He adjusted himself to beams falling, and then no more of them fell, and he adjusted himself to them not falling."

"How perfectly fascinating," Brigid O'Shaughnessy said. She left her chair and stood in front of him, close. Her eyes were wide and deep. "I don't have to tell you how utterly at a disadvantage you'll have me, with him here, if you choose."

Spade smiled slightly without separating his lips. "No, you don't have to tell me," he agreed.

"And you know I'd never have played myself in this position if I hadn't trusted you completely." Her thumb and forefinger twisted a black button on his blue coat.

Spade said, "That again!" with mock resignation.

"But you know it's so," she insisted.

"No, I don't know it." He patted the hand that was twisting the button. "My asking for reasons why I should trust you brought us here. Don't let's confuse things. You don't have to trust me, anyhow, as long as you can persuade me to trust you."

She studied his face. Her nostrils quivered.

Spade laughed. He patted her hand again and said: "Don't worry about that now. He'll be here in a moment. Get your business with him over, and then we'll see how we'll stand."

"And you'll let me go about it — with him — in my own way?"

"Sure."

She turned her hand under his so that her fingers pressed his. She said softly: "You're a God-send."

Spade said: "Don't overdo it."

She looked reproachfully at him, though smiling, and returned to the padded rocker.

Joel Cairo was excited. His dark eyes seemed all irises and his high-pitched thin-voiced words were tumbling out before Spade had the door half-open.

"That boy is out there watching the house, Mr. Spade, that boy you showed me, or to whom you showed me, in front of the theatre. What am I to understand from that, Mr. Spade? I came here in good faith, with no thought of tricks or traps."

"You were asked in good faith." Spade frowned thoughtfully. "But I ought to've guessed he might show up. He saw you come in?"

"Naturally. I could have gone on, but that

seemed useless, since you had already let him see us together."

Brigid O'Shaughnessy came into the passageway behind Spade and asked anxiously: "What boy? What is it?"

Cairo removed his black hat from his head, bowed stiffly, and said in a prim voice: "If you do not know, ask Mr. Spade. I know nothing about it except through him."

"A kid who's been trying to tail me around town all evening," Spade said carelessly over his shoulder, not turning to face the girl. "Come on in, Cairo. There's no use standing here talking for all the neighbors."

Brigid O'Shaughnessy grasped Spade's arm above the elbow and demanded: "Did he follow you to my apartment?"

"No. I shook him before that. Then I suppose he came back here to try to pick me up again."

Cairo, holding his black hat to his belly with both hands, had come into the passageway. Spade shut the corridor-door behind him and they went into the living-room. There Cairo bowed stiffly over his hat once more and said: "I am delighted to see you again, Miss O'Shaughnessy."

"I was sure you would be, Joe," she replied, giving him her hand.

He made a formal bow over her hand and

released it quickly.

She sat in the padded rocker she had occupied before. Cairo sat in the armchair by the table. Spade, when he had hung Cairo's hat and coat in the closet, sat on an end of the sofa in front of the windows and began to roll a cigarette.

Brigid O'Shaughnessy said to Cairo: "Sam told me about your offer for the falcon. How soon can you have the money ready?"

Cairo's eyebrows twitched. He smiled. "It is ready." He continued to smile at the girl for a little while after he had spoken, and then looked at Spade.

Spade was lighting his cigarette. His face was tranquil.

"In cash?" the girl asked.

"Oh, yes," Cairo replied.

She frowned, put her tongue between her lips, withdrew it, and asked: "You are ready to give us five thousand dollars, now, if we give you the falcon?"

Cairo held up a wriggling hand. "Excuse me," he said. "I expressed myself badly. I did not mean to say that I have the money in my pockets, but that I am prepared to get it on a very few minutes' notice at any time during banking hours."

"Oh!" She looked at Spade.

Spade blew cigarette-smoke down the

front of his vest and said: "That's probably right. He had only a few hundred in his pockets when I frisked him this afternoon."

When her eyes opened round and wide he grinned.

The Levantine bent forward in his chair. He failed to keep eagerness from showing in his eyes and voice. "I can be quite prepared to give you the money at, say, half-past ten in the morning. Eh?"

Brigid O'Shaughnessy smiled at him and said: "But I haven't got the falcon."

Cairo's face was darkened by a flush of annoyance. He put an ugly hand on either arm of his chair, holding his small-boned body erect and stiff between them. His dark eyes were angry. He did not say anything.

The girl made a mock-placatory face at him. "I'll have it in a week at the most, though," she said.

"Where is it?" Cairo used politeness of mien to express skepticism.

"Where Floyd hid it."

"Floyd? Thursby?"

She nodded.

"And you know where that is?" he asked.

"I think I do."

"Then why must we wait a week?"

"Perhaps not a whole week. Whom are you buying it for, Joe?"

Cairo raised his eyebrows. "I told Mr. Spade. For its owner."

Surprise illuminated the girl's face. "So you went back to him?"

"Naturally I did."

She laughed softly in her throat and said: "I should have liked to have seen that."

Cairo shrugged. "That was the logical development." He rubbed the back of one hand with the palm of the other. His upper lids came down to shade his eyes. "Why, if I in turn may ask a question, are you willing to sell to me?"

"I'm afraid," she said simply, "after what happened to Floyd. That's why I haven't it now. I'm afraid to touch it except to turn it over to somebody else right away."

Spade, propped on an elbow on the sofa, looked at and listened to them impartially. In the comfortable slackness of his body, in the easy stillness of his features, there was no indication of either curiosity or impatience.

"Exactly what," Cairo asked in a low voice, "happened to Floyd?"

The tip of Brigid O'Shaughnessy's right forefinger traced a swift G in the air.

Cairo said, "I see," but there was something doubting in his smile. "Is he here?"

"I don't know." She spoke impatiently.

"What difference does it make?"

The doubt in Cairo's smile deepened. "It might make a world of difference," he said, and rearranged his hands in his lap so that, intentionally or not, a blunt forefinger pointed at Spade.

The girl glanced at the pointing finger and made an impatient motion with her head. "Or me," she said, "or you."

"Exactly, and shall we add more certainly the boy outside?"

"Yes," she agreed and laughed. "Yes, unless he's the one you had in Constantinople."

Sudden blood mottled Cairo's face. In a shrill enraged voice he cried: "The one you couldn't make?"

Brigid O'Shaughnessy jumped up from her chair. Her lower lip was between her teeth. Her eyes were dark and wide in a tense white face. She took two quick steps towards Cairo. He started to rise. Her right hand went out and cracked sharply against his cheek, leaving the imprint of fingers there.

Cairo grunted and slapped her cheek, staggering her sidewise, bringing from her mouth a brief muffled scream.

Spade, wooden of face, was up from the sofa and close to them by then. He caught

Cairo by the throat and shook him. Cairo gurgled and put a hand inside his coat. Spade grasped the Levantine's wrist, wrenched it away from the coat, forced it straight out to the side, and twisted it until the clumsy flaccid fingers opened to let the black pistol fall down on the rug.

Brigid O'Shaughnessy quickly picked up the pistol.

Cairo, speaking with difficulty because of the fingers on his throat, said: "This is the second time you've put your hands on me." His eyes, though the throttling pressure on his throat made them bulge, were cold and menacing.

"Yes," Spade growled. "And when you're slapped you'll take it and like it." He released Cairo's wrist and with a thick open hand struck the side of his face three times, savagely.

Cairo tried to spit in Spade's face, but the dryness of the Levantine's mouth made it only an angry gesture. Spade slapped the mouth, cutting the lower lip.

The door-bell rang.

Cairo's eyes jerked into focus on the passageway that led to the corridor-door. His eyes had become unangry and wary. The girl had gasped and turned to face the passageway. Her face was frightened. Spade stared gloomily for a moment at the blood trickling from Cairo's lip, and then stepped back, taking his hand from the Levantine's throat.

"Who is it?" the girl whispered, coming close to Spade; and Cairo's eyes jerked back to ask the same question.

Spade gave his answer irritably: "I don't know."

The bell rang again, more insistently.

"Well, keep quiet," Spade said, and went out of the room, shutting the door behind him.

Spade turned on the light in the passageway and opened the door to the corridor. Lieutenant Dundy and Tom Polhaus were there.

"Hello, Sam," Tom said. "We thought maybe you wouldn't've gone to bed yet."

Dundy nodded, but said nothing.

Spade said good-naturedly: "Hello. You guys pick swell hours to do your visiting in. What is it this time?"

Dundy spoke then, quietly: "We want to talk to you, Spade."

"Well?" Spade stood in the doorway, blocking it. "Go ahead and talk."

Tom Polhaus advanced saying: "We don't have to do it standing here, do we?"

Spade stood in the doorway and said:

"You can't come in." His tone was very slightly apologetic.

Tom's thick-featured face, even in height with Spade's, took on an expression of friendly scorn, though there was a bright gleam in his small shrewd eyes. "What the hell, Sam?" he protested and put a big hand playfully on Spade's chest.

Spade leaned against the pushing hand, grinned wolfishly, and asked: "Going to strong-arm me, Tom?"

Tom grumbled, "Aw, for God's sake," and took his hand away.

Dundy clicked his teeth together and said through them: "Let us in."

Spade's lip twitched over his eyetooth. He said: "You're not coming in. What do you want to do about it? Try to get in? Or do your talking here? Or go to hell?"

Tom groaned.

Dundy, still speaking through his teeth, said: "It'd pay you to play along with us a little, Spade. You've got away with this and you've got away with that, but you can't keep it up forever."

"Stop me when you can," Spade replied arrogantly.

"That's what I'll do." Dundy put his hands behind him and thrust his hard face up towards the private detective's. "There's talk going around that you and Archer's wife were cheating on him."

Spade laughed. "That sounds like something you thought up yourself."

"Then there's not anything to it?"

"Not anything."

"The talk is," Dundy said, "that she tried to get a divorce out of him so's she could put in with you, but he wouldn't give it to her. Anything to that?"

"No."

"There's even talk," Dundy went on stolidly, "that that's why he was put on the spot."

Spade seemed mildly amused. "Don't be a hog," he said. "You oughtn't try to pin more than one murder at a time on me. Your first idea that I knocked Thursby off because he'd killed Miles falls apart if you blame me for killing Miles too."

"You haven't heard me say you killed anybody," Dundy replied. "You're the one that keeps bringing that up. But suppose I did. You could have blipped them both. There's a way of figuring it."

"Uh-huh. I could've butchered Miles to get his wife, and then Thursby so I could hang Miles's killing on him. That's a hell of a swell system, or will be when I can give somebody else the bump and hang Thursby's on them. How long am I supposed to keep that up? Are you going to put your hand on my shoulder for all the killings in San Francisco from now on?"

Tom said: "Aw, cut the comedy, Sam. You know damned well we don't like this any more than you do, but we got our work to do."

"I hope you've got something to do besides pop in here early every morning with a lot of damned fool questions."

"And get damned lying answers," Dundy added deliberately.

"Take it easy," Spade cautioned him.

Dundy looked him up and down and then looked him straight in the eyes. "If you say there was nothing between you and Archer's wife," he said, "you're a liar, and I'm telling you so."

A startled look came into Tom's small eyes.

Spade moistened his lips with the tip of his tongue and asked: "Is that the hot tip that brought you here at this ungodly time of night?"

"That's one of them."

"And the others?"

Dundy pulled down the corners of his mouth. "Let us in." He nodded significantly at the doorway in which Spade stood.

Spade frowned and shook his head.

Dundy's mouth-corners lifted in a smile of grim satisfaction. "There must've been something to it," he told Tom.

Tom shifted his feet and, not looking at either man, mumbled: "God knows."

"What's this?" Spade asked. "Charades?"

"All right, Spade, we're going." Dundy buttoned his overcoat. "We'll be in to see you now and then. Maybe you're right in bucking us. Think it over."

"Uh-huh," Spade said, grinning. "Glad to see you any time, Lieutenant, and whenever I'm not busy I'll let you in."

A voice in Spade's living-room screamed: "Help! Help! Police! Help!" The voice, high and thin and shrill, was Joel Cairo's.

Lieutenant Dundy stopped turning away from the door, confronted Spade again, and said decisively: "I guess we're going in."

The sounds of a brief struggle, of a blow, of a subdued cry, came to them.

Spade's face twisted into a smile that held little joy. He said, "I guess you are," and stood out of the way.

When the police-detectives had entered he shut the corridor-door and followed them back to the living-room.

8
Horse Feathers

Brigid O'Shaughnessy was huddled in the armchair by the table. Her forearms were up over her cheeks, her knees drawn up until they hid the lower part of her face. Her eyes were white-circled and terrified.

Joel Cairo stood in front of her, bending over her, holding in one hand the pistol Spade had twisted out of his hand. His other hand was clapped to his forehead. Blood ran through the fingers of that hand and down under them to his eyes. A smaller trickle from his cut lip made three wavy lines across his chin.

Cairo did not heed the detectives. He was glaring at the girl huddled in front of him. His lips were working spasmodically, but no coherent sound came from between them.

Dundy, the first of the three into the living-room, moved swiftly to Cairo's side, put a hand on his own hip under his overcoat, a hand on the Levantine's wrist, and growled: "What are you up to here?"

Cairo took the red-smeared hand from his head and flourished it close to the Lieutenant's face. Uncovered by the hand, his forehead showed a three-inch ragged tear. "This is what she has done," he cried. "Look at it."

The girl put her feet down on the floor and looked warily from Dundy, holding Cairo's wrist, to Tom Polhaus, standing a little behind them, to Spade, leaning against the door-frame. Spade's face was placid. When his gaze met hers his yellow-gray eyes glinted for an instant with malicious humor and then became expressionless again.

"Did you do that?" Dundy asked the girl, nodding at Cairo's cut head.

She looked at Spade again. He did not in any way respond to the appeal in her eyes. He leaned against the door-frame and observed the occupants of the room with the polite detached air of a disinterested spectator.

The girl turned her eyes up to Dundy's. Her eyes were wide and dark and earnest. "I had to," she said in a low throbbing voice. "I was all alone in here with him when he attacked me. I couldn't — I tried to keep him off. I — I couldn't make myself shoot him."

"Oh, you liar!" Cairo cried, trying unsuccessfully to pull the arm that held his pistol out of Dundy's grip. "Oh, you dirty filthy liar!" He twisted himself around to face Dundy. "She's lying awfully. I came here in good faith and was attacked by both of them, and when you came he went out to talk to you, leaving her here with this pistol, and then she said they were going to kill me after you left, and I called for help, so you wouldn't leave me here to be murdered, and then she struck me with the pistol."

"Here, give me this thing," Dundy said, and took the pistol from Cairo's hand. "Now let's get this straight. What'd you come here for?"

"He sent for me." Cairo twisted his head around to stare defiantly at Spade. "He called me up on the phone and asked me to come here."

Spade blinked sleepily at the Levantine and said nothing.

Dundy asked: "What'd he want you for?"

Cairo withheld his reply until he had mopped his bloody forehead and chin with a lavender-barred silk handkerchief. By then some of the indignation in his manner had been replaced by caution. "He said he wanted — they wanted — to see me. I didn't know what about."

Tom Polhaus lowered his head, sniffed the odor of *chypre* that the mopping handkerchief had released in the air, and turned his head to scowl interrogatively at Spade. Spade winked at him and went on rolling a cigarette.

Dundy asked: "Well, what happened then?"

"Then they attacked me. She struck me first, and then he choked me and took the pistol out of my pocket. I don't know what they would have done next if you hadn't arrived at that moment. I dare say they would have murdered me then and there. When he went out to answer the bell he left her here with the pistol to watch over me."

Brigid O'Shaughnessy jumped out of the armchair crying, "Why don't you make him tell the truth?" and slapped Cairo on the cheek.

Cairo yelled inarticulately.

Dundy pushed the girl back into the chair with the hand that was not holding the Levantine's arm and growled: "None of that now."

Spade, lighting his cigarette, grinned softly through smoke and told Tom: "She's impulsive."

"Yeah," Tom agreed.

Dundy scowled down at the girl and

asked: "What do you want us to think the truth is?"

"Not what he said," she replied. "Not anything he said." She turned to Spade. "Is it?"

"How do I know?" Spade responded. "I was out in the kitchen mixing an omelette when it all happened, wasn't I?"

She wrinkled her forehead, studying him with eyes that perplexity clouded.

Tom grunted in disgust.

Dundy, still scowling at the girl, ignored Spade's speech and asked her: "If he's not telling the truth, how come he did the squawking for help, and not you?"

"Oh, he was frightened to death when I struck him," she replied, looking contemptuously at the Levantine.

Cairo's face flushed where it was not blood-smeared. He exclaimed: "Pfoo! Another lie!"

She kicked his leg, the high heel of her blue slipper striking him just below the knee. Dundy pulled him away from her while big Tom came to stand close to her, rumbling: "Behave, sister. That's no way to act."

"Then make him tell the truth," she said defiantly.

"We'll do that all right," he promised.

"Just don't get rough."

Dundy, looking at Spade with green eyes hard and bright and satisfied, addressed his subordinate: "Well, Tom, I don't guess we'll go wrong pulling the lot of them in."

Tom nodded gloomily.

Spade left the door and advanced to the center of the room, dropping his cigarette into a tray on the table as he passed it. His smile and manner were amiably composed. "Don't be in a hurry," he said. "Everything can be explained."

"I bet you," Dundy agreed, sneering.

Spade bowed to the girl. "Miss O'Shaughnessy," he said, "may I present Lieutenant Dundy and Detective-sergeant Polhaus." He bowed to Dundy. "Miss O'Shaughnessy is an operative in my employ."

Joel Cairo said indignantly: "That isn't so. She —"

Spade interrupted him in a quite loud, but still genial, voice: "I hired her just recently, yesterday. This is Mr. Joel Cairo, a friend — an acquaintance, at any rate — of Thursby's. He came to me this afternoon and tried to hire me to find something Thursby was supposed to have on him when he was bumped off. It looked funny, the way he put it to me, so I wouldn't touch it. Then he pulled a gun — well, never mind that unless it comes to a point of laying charges against each other. Anyway, after talking it over with Miss O'Shaughnessy, I thought maybe I could get something out of him about Miles's and Thursby's killings, so I asked him to come up here. Maybe we put the questions to him a little rough, but he wasn't hurt any, not enough to have to cry for help. I'd already had to take his gun away from him again."

As Spade talked anxiety came into Cairo's reddened face. His eyes moved jerkily up and down, shifting their focus uneasily between the floor and Spade's bland face.

Dundy confronted Cairo and bruskly demanded: "Well, what've you got to say to that?"

Cairo had nothing to say for nearly a minute while he stared at the Lieutenant's chest. When he lifted his eyes they were shy and wary. "I don't know what I should say," he murmured. His embarrassment seemed genuine.

"Try telling the facts," Dundy suggested.

"The facts?" Cairo's eyes fidgeted, though their gaze did not actually leave the Lieutenant's. "What assurance have I that the facts will be believed?"

"Quit stalling. All you've got to do is swear

to a complaint that they took a poke at you and the warrant-clerk will believe you enough to issue a warrant that'll let us throw them in the can."

Spade spoke in an amused tone: "Go ahead, Cairo. Make him happy. Tell him you'll do it, and then we'll swear to one against you, and he'll have the lot of us."

Cairo cleared his throat and looked nervously around the room, not into the eyes of anyone there.

Dundy blew breath through his nose in a puff that was not quite a snort and said: "Get your hats."

Cairo's eyes, holding worry and a question, met Spade's mocking gaze. Spade winked at him and sat on the arm of the padded rocker. "Well, boys and girls," he said, grinning at the Levantine and at the girl with nothing but delight in his voice and grin, "we put it over nicely."

Dundy's hard square face darkened the least of shades. He repeated peremptorily: "Get your hats."

Spade turned his grin on the Lieutenant, squirmed into a more comfortable position on the chair-arm, and asked lazily: "Don't you know when you're being kidded?"

Tom Polhaus's face became red and shiny.

Dundy's face, still darkening, was immobile except for lips moving stiffly to say: "No, but we'll let that wait till we get down to the Hall."

Spade rose and put his hands in his trousers-pockets. He stood erect so he might look that much farther down at the Lieutenant. His grin was a taunt and self-certainty spoke in every line of his posture.

"I dare you to take us in, Dundy," he said. "We'll laugh at you in every newspaper in San Francisco. You don't think any of us is going to swear to any complaints against the others, do you? Wake up. You've been kidded. When the bell rang I said to Miss O'Shaughnessy and Cairo: 'It's those damned bulls again. They're getting to be nuisances. Let's play a joke on them. When you hear them going one of you scream, and then we'll see how far we can string them along before they tumble.' And —"

Brigid O'Shaughnessy bent forward in her chair and began to laugh hysterically.

Cairo started and smiled. There was no vitality in his smile, but he held it fixed on his face.

Tom, glowering, grumbled: "Cut it out, Sam."

Spade chuckled and said: "But that's the way it was. We —"

"And the cuts on his head and mouth?"

Dundy asked scornfully. "Where'd they come from?"

"Ask him," Spade suggested. "Maybe he cut himself shaving."

Cairo spoke quickly, before he could be questioned, and the muscles of his face quivered at the strain of holding his smile in place while he spoke. "I fell. We intended to be struggling for the pistol when you came in, but I fell. I tripped on the end of the rug and fell while we were pretending to struggle."

Dundy said: "Horse feathers."

Spade said: "That's all right, Dundy, believe it or not. The point is that that's our story and we'll stick to it. The newspapers will print it whether they believe it or not, and it'll be just as funny one way as the other, or more so. What are you going to do about it? It's no crime to kid a copper, is it? You haven't got anything on anybody here. Everything we told you was part of the joke. What are you going to do about it?"

Dundy put his back to Spade and gripped Cairo by the shoulders. "You can't get away with that," he snarled, shaking the Levantine. "You belched for help and you've got to take it."

"No, sir," Cairo sputtered. "It was a joke. He said you were friends of his and would understand."

Spade laughed.

Dundy pulled Cairo roughly around, holding him now by one wrist and the nape of his neck. "I'll take you along for packing the gun, anyway," he said. "And I'll take the rest of you along to see who laughs at the joke."

Cairo's alarmed eyes jerked sidewise to focus on Spade's face.

Spade said: "Don't be a sap, Dundy. The gun was part of the plant. It's one of mine." He laughed. "Too bad it's only a thirty-two, or maybe you could find it was the one Thursby and Miles were shot with."

Dundy released Cairo, spun on his heel, and his right fist clicked on Spade's chin.

Brigid O'Shaughnessy uttered a short cry.

Spade's smile flickered out at the instant of the impact, but returned immediately with a dreamy quality added. He steadied himself with a short backward step and his thick sloping shoulders writhed under his coat. Before his fist could come up Tom Polhaus had pushed himself between the two men, facing Spade, encumbering Spade's arms with the closeness of his barrel-like belly and his own arms.

"No, no, for Christ's sake!" Tom begged.

After a long moment of motionlessness

Spade's muscles relaxed. "Then get him out of here quick," he said. His smile had gone away again, leaving his face sullen and somewhat pale.

Tom, staying close to Spade, keeping his arms on Spade's arms, turned his head to look over his shoulder at Lieutenant Dundy. Tom's small eyes were reproachful.

Dundy's fists were clenched in front of his body and his feet were planted firm and a little apart on the floor, but the truculence in his face was modified by thin rims of white showing between green irises and upper eyelids.

"Get their names and addresses," he ordered.

Tom looked at Cairo, who said quickly: "Joel Cairo, Hotel Belvedere."

Spade spoke before Tom could question the girl. "You can always get in touch with Miss O'Shaughnessy through me."

Tom looked at Dundy. Dundy growled: "Get her address."

Spade said: "Her address is in care of my office."

Dundy took a step forward, halting in front of the girl. "Where do you live?" he asked.

Spade addressed Tom: "Get him out of here. I've had enough of this."

Tom looked at Spade's eyes — hard and glittering — and mumbled: "Take it easy, Sam." He buttoned his coat and turned to Dundy, asking, in a voice that aped casualness, "Well, is that all?" and taking a step towards the door.

Dundy's scowl failed to conceal indecision.

Cairo moved suddenly towards the door, saying: "I'm going too, if Mr. Spade will be kind enough to give me my hat and coat."

Spade asked: "What's the hurry?"

Dundy said angrily: "It was all in fun, but just the same you're afraid to be left here with them."

"Not at all," the Levantine replied, fidgeting, looking at neither of them, "but it's quite late and — and I'm going. I'll go out with you if you don't mind."

Dundy put his lips together firmly and said nothing. A light was glinting in his green eyes.

Spade went to the closet in the passageway and fetched Cairo's hat and coat. Spade's face was blank. His voice held the same blankness when he stepped back from helping the Levantine into his coat and said to Tom: "Tell him to leave the gun."

Dundy took Cairo's pistol from his overcoat-pocket and put it on the table. He went out first, with Cairo at his heels. Tom halted in front of Spade, muttering, "I hope to God you know what you're doing," got no response, sighed, and followed the others out. Spade went after them as far as the bend in the passageway, where he stood until Tom had closed the corridor-door.

9
Brigid

Spade returned to the living-room and sat on an end of the sofa, elbows on knees, cheeks in hands, looking at the floor and not at Brigid O'Shaughnessy smiling weakly at him from the armchair. His eyes were sultry. The creases between brows over his nose were deep. His nostrils moved in and out with his breathing.

Brigid O'Shaughnessy, when it became apparent that he was not going to look up at her, stopped smiling and regarded him with growing uneasiness.

Red rage came suddenly into his face and he began to talk in a harsh guttural voice. Holding his maddened face in his hands, glaring at the floor, he cursed Dundy for five minutes without break, cursed him obscenely, blasphemously, repetitiously, in a harsh guttural voice.

Then he took his face out of his hands, looked at the girl, grinned sheepishly, and said: "Childish, huh? I know, but, by God, I do hate being hit without hitting back." He touched his chin with careful fingers. "Not that it was so much of a sock at that." He laughed and lounged back on the sofa, crossing his legs. "A cheap enough price to pay for winning." His brows came together in a fleeting scowl. "Though I'll remember it."

The girl, smiling again, left her chair and sat on the sofa beside him. "You're absolutely the wildest person I've ever known," she said. "Do you always carry on so high-handed?"

"I let him hit me, didn't I?"

"Oh, yes, but a police official."

"It wasn't that," Spade explained. "It was that in losing his head and slugging me he overplayed his hand. If I'd mixed it with him then he couldn't've backed down. He'd've had to go through with it, and we'd've had to tell that goofy story at headquarters." He stared thoughtfully at the girl, and asked: "What did you do to Cairo?"

"Nothing." Her face became flushed. "I tried to frighten him into keeping still until they had gone and he either got too frightened or stubborn and yelled."

"And then you smacked him with the gun?"

"I had to. He attacked me."

"You don't know what you're doing." Spade's smile did not hide his annoyance. "It's just what I told you: you're fumbling along by guess and by God."

"I'm sorry," she said, face and voice soft with contrition, "Sam."

"Sure you are." He took tobacco and papers from his pockets and began to make a cigarette. "Now you've had your talk with Cairo. Now you can talk to me."

She put a fingertip to her mouth, staring across the room at nothing with widened eyes, and then, with narrower eyes, glanced quickly at Spade. He was engrossed in the making of his cigarette. "Oh, yes," she began, "of course —" She took the finger away from her mouth and smoothed her blue dress over her knees. She frowned at her knees.

Spade licked his cigarette, sealed it, and asked, "Well?" while he felt for his lighter.

"But I didn't," she said, pausing between words as if she were selecting them with great care, "have time to finish talking to him." She stopped frowning at her knees and looked at Spade with clear candid eyes. "We were interrupted almost before we had begun."

Spade lighted his cigarette and laughed

his mouth empty of smoke. “Want me to phone him and ask him to come back?”

She shook her head, not smiling. Her eyes moved back and forth between her lids as she shook her head, maintaining their focus on Spade’s eyes. Her eyes were inquisitive.

Spade put an arm across her back, cupping his hand over the smooth bare white shoulder farthest from him. She leaned back into the bend of his arm. He said: “Well, I’m listening.”

She twisted her head around to smile up at him with playful insolence, asking: “Do you need your arm there for that?”

“No.” He removed his hand from her shoulder and let his arm drop down behind her.

“You’re altogether unpredictable,” she murmured.

He nodded and said amiably: “I’m still listening.”

“Look at the time!” she exclaimed, wriggling a finger at the alarm-clock perched atop the book saying two-fifty with its clumsily shaped hands.

“Uh-huh, it’s been a busy evening.”

“I must go.” She rose from the sofa. “This is terrible.”

Spade did not rise. He shook his head and said: “Not until you’ve told me about it.”

"But look at the time," she protested, "and it would take hours to tell you."

"It'll have to take them then."

"Am I a prisoner?" she asked gaily.

"Besides, there's the kid outside. Maybe he hasn't gone home to sleep yet."

Her gaiety vanished. "Do you think he's still there?"

"It's likely."

She shivered. "Could you find out?"

"I could go down and see."

"Oh, that's — will you?"

Spade studied her anxious face for a moment and then got up from the sofa saying: "Sure." He got a hat and overcoat from the closet. "I'll be gone about ten minutes."

"Do be careful," she begged as she followed him to the corridor-door.

He said, "I will," and went out.

Post Street was empty when Spade issued into it. He walked east a block, crossed the street, walked west two blocks on the other side, recrossed it, and returned to his building without having seen anyone except two mechanics working on a car in a garage.

When he opened his apartment-door Brigid O'Shaughnessy was standing at the bend in the passageway, holding Cairo's pistol straight down at her side.

"He's still there," Spade said.

She bit the inside of her lip and turned slowly, going back into the living-room. Spade followed her in, put his hat and overcoat on a chair, said, "So we'll have time to talk," and went into the kitchen.

He had put the coffee-pot on the stove when she came to the door, and was slicing a slender loaf of French bread. She stood in the doorway and watched him with preoccupied eyes. The fingers of her left hand idly caressed the body and barrel of the pistol her right hand still held.

"The table-cloth's in there," he said, pointing the breadknife at a cupboard that was one breakfast-nook partition.

She set the table while he spread liverwurst on, or put cold corned beef between, the small ovals of bread he had sliced. Then he poured the coffee, added brandy to it from a squat bottle, and they sat at the table. They sat side by side on one of the benches. She put the pistol down on the end of the bench nearer her.

"You can start now, between bites," he said.

She made a face at him, complained, "You're the most insistent person," and bit a sandwich.

"Yes, and wild and unpredictable. What's

this bird, this falcon, that everybody's all steamed up about?"

She chewed the beef and bread in her mouth, swallowed it, looked attentively at the small crescent its removal had made in the sandwich's rim, and asked: "Suppose I wouldn't tell you? Suppose I wouldn't tell you anything at all about it? What would you do?"

"You mean about the bird?"

"I mean about the whole thing."

"I wouldn't be too surprised," he told her, grinning so that the edges of his jaw-teeth were visible, "to know what to do next."

"And that would be?" She transferred her attention from the sandwich to his face. "That's what I wanted to know: what would you do next?"

He shook his head.

Mockery rippled in a smile on her face. "Something wild and unpredictable?"

"Maybe. But I don't see what you've got to gain by covering up now. It's coming out bit by bit anyhow. There's a lot of it I don't know, but there's some of it I do, and some more that I can guess at, and, give me another day like this, I'll soon be knowing things about it that you don't know."

"I suppose you do now," she said, looking at her sandwich again, her face serious. "But

— oh! — I'm so tired of it, and I do so hate having to talk about it. Wouldn't it — wouldn't it be just as well to wait and let you learn about it as you say you will?"

Spade laughed. "I don't know. You'll have to figure that out for yourself. My way of learning is to heave a wild and unpredictable monkey-wrench into the machinery. It's all right with me, if you're sure none of the flying pieces will hurt you."

She moved her bare shoulders uneasily, but said nothing. For several minutes they ate in silence, he phlegmatically, she thoughtfully. Then she said in a hushed voice: "I'm afraid of you, and that's the truth."

He said: "That's not the truth."

"It is," she insisted in the same low voice. "I know two men I'm afraid of and I've seen both of them tonight."

"I can understand your being afraid of Cairo," Spade said. "He's out of your reach."

"And you aren't?"

"Not that way," he said and grinned.

She blushed. She picked up a slice of bread encrusted with grey liverwurst. She put it down on her plate. She wrinkled her white forehead and she said: "It's a black figure, as you know, smooth and shiny, of a bird, a hawk or falcon, about that high." She held her hands a foot apart.

"What makes it important?"

She sipped coffee and brandy before she shook her head. "I don't know," she said. "They'd never tell me. They promised me five hundred pounds if I helped them get it. Then Floyd said afterward, after we'd left Joe, that he'd give me seven hundred and fifty."

"So it must be worth more than seventy-five hundred dollars?"

"Oh, much more than that," she said. "They didn't pretend that they were sharing equally with me. They were simply hiring me to help them."

"To help them how?"

She lifted her cup to her lips again. Spade, not moving the domineering stare of his yellow-gray eyes from her face, began to make a cigarette. Behind them the percolator bubbled on the stove.

"To help them get it from the man who had it," she said slowly when she had lowered her cup, "a Russian named Kemidov."

"How?"

"Oh, but that's not important," she objected, "and wouldn't help you" — she smiled impudently — "and is certainly none of your business."

"This was in Constantinople?"

She hesitated, nodded, and said: "Marmora."

He waved his cigarette at her, saying: "Go ahead, what happened then?"

"But that's all. I've told you. They promised me five hundred pounds to help them and I did and then we found that Joe Cairo meant to desert us, taking the falcon with him and leaving us nothing. So we did exactly that to him, first. But then I wasn't any better off than I had been before, because Floyd hadn't any intention at all of paying me the seven hundred and fifty pounds he had promised me. I had learned that by the time we got here. He said we would go to New York, where he would sell it and give me my share, but I could see he wasn't telling me the truth." Indignation had darkened her eyes to violet. "And that's why I came to you to get you to help me learn where the falcon was."

"And suppose you'd got it? What then?"

"Then I'd have been in a position to talk terms with Mr. Floyd Thursby."

Spade squinted at her and suggested: "But you wouldn't have known where to take it to get more money than he'd give you, the larger sum that you knew he expected to sell it for?"

"I did not know," she said.

Spade scowled at the ashes he had dumped on his plate. "What makes it worth all that money?" he demanded. "You must have some idea, at least be able to guess."

"I haven't the slightest idea."

He directed the scowl at her. "What's it made of?"

"Porcelain or black stone. I don't know. I've never touched it. I've only seen it once, for a few minutes. Floyd showed it to me when we'd first got hold of it."

Spade mashed the end of his cigarette in his plate and made one draught of the coffee and brandy in his cup. His scowl had gone away. He wiped his lips with his napkin, dropped it crumpled on the table, and spoke casually: "You *are* a liar."

She got up and stood at the end of the table, looking down at him with dark abashed eyes in a pinkening face. "I am a liar," she said. "I have always been a liar."

"Don't brag about it. It's childish." His voice was good-humored. He came out from between table and bench. "Was there any truth at all in that yarn?"

She hung her head. Dampness glistened on her dark lashes. "Some," she whispered.

"How much?"

"Not — not very much."

Spade put a hand under her chin and lifted her head. He laughed into her wet eyes and said: "We've got all night before us. I'll put some more brandy in some more coffee and we'll try again."

Her eyelids drooped. "Oh, I'm so tired," she said tremulously, "so tired of it all, of myself, of lying and thinking up lies, and of not knowing what is a lie and what is the truth. I wish I —"

She put her hands up to Spade's cheeks, put her open mouth hard against his mouth, her body flat against his body.

Spade's arms went around her, holding her to him, muscles bulging his blue sleeves, a hand cradling her head, its fingers half lost among red hair, a hand moving groping fingers over her slim back. His eyes burned yellowly.

10
The Belvedere Divan

Beginning day had reduced night to a thin smokiness when Spade sat up. At his side Brigid O'Shaughnessy's soft breathing had the regularity of utter sleep. Spade was quiet leaving bed and bedroom and shutting the bedroom-door. He dressed in the bathroom. Then he examined the sleeping girl's clothes, took a flat brass key from the pocket of her coat, and went out.

He went to the Coronet, letting himself into the building and into her apartment with the key. To the eye there was nothing furtive about his going in: he entered boldly and directly. To the ear his going in was almost unnoticeable: he made as little sound as might be.

In the girl's apartment he switched on all the lights. He searched the place from wall to wall. His eyes and thick fingers moved without apparent haste, and without ever lingering or fumbling or going back, from one inch of their fields to the next, probing, scrutinizing, testing with expert certainty. Every drawer, cupboard, cubbyhole, box, bag, trunk — locked or unlocked — was opened and its contents subjected to examination by eyes and fingers. Every piece of clothing was tested by hands that felt for telltale bulges and ears that listened for the crinkle of paper between pressing fingers. He stripped the bed of bedclothes. He looked under rugs and at the under side of each piece of furniture. He pulled down blinds to see that nothing had been rolled up in them for concealment. He leaned through windows to see that nothing hung below them on the outside. He poked with a fork into powder and cream-jars on the dressing-table. He held atomizers and bottles up against the light. He examined dishes and pans and food and food-containers. He emptied the garbage-can on spread sheets of newspaper. He opened the top of the flush-box in the bathroom, drained the box, and peered down into it. He examined and tested the metal screens over the drains of bathtub, wash-bowl, sink, and laundry-tub.

He did not find the black bird. He found nothing that seemed to have any connection with a black bird. The only piece of writing he found was a week-old receipt for the month's apartment-rent Brigid O'Shaughnessy had paid. The only thing he found that interested him enough to delay his search while he looked at it was a double-handful of rather fine jewelry in a polychrome box in a locked dressing-table-drawer.

When he had finished he made and drank a cup of coffee. Then he unlocked the kitchen-window, scarred the edge of its lock a little with his pocket-knife, opened the window — over a fire-escape — got his hat and overcoat from the settee in the living-room, and left the apartment as he had come.

On his way home he stopped at a store that was being opened by a puffy-eyed shivering plump grocer and bought oranges, eggs, rolls, butter, and cream.

Spade went quietly into his apartment, but before he had shut the corridor-door behind him Brigid O'Shaughnessy cried: "Who is that?"

"Young Spade bearing breakfast."

"Oh, you frightened me!"

The bedroom-door he had shut was open. The girl sat on the side of the bed, trembling, with her right hand out of sight under a pillow.

Spade put his packages on the kitchen-table and went into the bedroom. He sat on the bed beside the girl, kissed her smooth shoulder, and said: "I wanted to see if that kid was still on the job, and to get stuff for breakfast."

"Is he?"

"No."

She sighed and leaned against him. "I awakened and you weren't here and then I heard someone coming in. I was terrified."

Spade combed her red hair back from her face with his fingers and said: "I'm sorry, angel. I thought you'd sleep through it. Did you have that gun under your pillow all night?"

"No. You know I didn't. I jumped up and got it when I was frightened."

He cooked breakfast — and slipped the flat brass key into her coat-pocket again — while she bathed and dressed.

She came out of the bathroom whistling *En Cuba.* "Shall I make the bed?" she asked.

"That'd be swell. The eggs need a couple of minutes more."

Their breakfast was on the table when she returned to the kitchen. They sat where they had sat the night before and ate heartily.

"Now about the bird?" Spade suggested presently as they ate.

She put her fork down and looked at him. She drew her eyebrows together and made her mouth small and tight. "You can't ask me to talk about that this morning of all mornings," she protested. "I don't want to and I won't."

"It's a stubborn damned hussy," he said sadly and put a piece of roll into his mouth.

The youth who had shadowed Spade was not in sight when Spade and Brigid O'Shaughnessy crossed the sidewalk to the waiting taxicab. The taxicab was not followed. Neither the youth nor another loiterer was visible in the vicinity of the Coronet when the taxicab arrived there.

Brigid O'Shaughnessy would not let Spade go in with her. "It's bad enough to be coming home in evening dress at this hour without bringing company. I hope I don't meet anybody."

"Dinner tonight?"

"Yes."

They kissed. She went into the Coronet. He told the chauffeur: "Hotel Belvedere."

When he reached the Belvedere he saw the youth who had shadowed him sitting in the lobby on a divan from which the elevators could be seen. Apparently the youth was reading a newspaper.

At the desk Spade learned that Cairo was not in. He frowned and pinched his lower lip. Points of yellow light began to dance in his eyes. "Thanks," he said softly to the clerk and turned away.

Sauntering, he crossed the lobby to the divan from which the elevators could be seen and sat down beside — not more than a foot from — the young man who was apparently reading a newspaper.

The young man did not look up from his newspaper. Seen at this scant distance, he seemed certainly less than twenty years old. His features were small, in keeping with his stature, and regular. His skin was very fair. The whiteness of his cheeks was as little blurred by any considerable growth of beard as by the glow of blood. His clothing was neither new nor of more than ordinary quality, but it, and his manner of wearing it, was marked by a hard masculine neatness.

Spade asked casually, "Where is he?" while shaking tobacco down into a brown paper curved to catch it.

The boy lowered his paper and looked around, moving with a purposeful sort of slowness, as of a more natural swiftness restrained. He looked with small hazel eyes under somewhat long curling lashes at Spade's chest. He said, in a voice as colorless and composed and cold as his young face: "What?"

"Where is he?" Spade was busy with his cigarette.

"Who?"

"The fairy."

The hazel eyes' gaze went up Spade's chest to the knot of his maroon tie and rested there. "What do you think you're doing, Jack?" the boy demanded. "Kidding me?"

"I'll tell you when I am." Spade licked his cigarette and smiled amiably at the boy. "New York, aren't you?"

The boy stared at Spade's tie and did not speak. Spade nodded as if the boy had said yes and asked: "Baumes rush?"

The boy stared at Spade's tie for a moment longer, then raised his newspaper and returned his attention to it. "Shove off," he said from the side of his mouth.

Spade lighted his cigarette, leaned back comfortably on the divan, and spoke with good-natured carelessness: "You'll have to talk to me before you're through, sonny — some of you will — and you can tell G. I said so."

The boy put his paper down quickly and faced Spade, staring at his necktie with bleak hazel eyes. The boy's small hands were spread flat over his belly. "Keep asking for it and you're going to get it," he said, "plenty." His voice was low and flat and menacing. "I told you to shove off. Shove off."

Spade waited until a bespectacled pudgy man and a thin-legged blonde girl had passed out of hearing. Then he chuckled and said: "That would go over big back on Seventh Avenue. But you're not in Romeville now. You're in my burg." He inhaled cigarette-smoke and blew it out in a long pale cloud. "Well, where is he?"

The boy spoke two words, the first a short guttural verb, the second "you."

"People lose teeth talking like that." Spade's voice was still amiable though his face had become wooden. "If you want to hang around you'll be polite."

The boy repeated his two words.

Spade dropped his cigarette into a tall stone jar beside the divan and with a lifted hand caught the attention of a man who had been standing at an end of the cigar-stand for several minutes. The man nodded and came towards them. He was a middle-aged man of medium height, round and sallow of face, compactly built, tidily dressed in dark clothes.

"Hello, Sam," he said as he came up.

"Hello, Luke."

They shook hands and Luke said: "Say, that's too bad about Miles."

"Uh-huh, a bad break." Spade jerked his head to indicate the boy on the divan beside him. "What do you let these cheap gunmen hang out in your lobby for, with their tools bulging their clothes?"

"Yes?" Luke examined the boy with crafty brown eyes set in a suddenly hard face. "What do you want here?" he asked.

The boy stood up. Spade stood up. The boy looked at the two men, at their neckties, from one to the other. Luke's necktie was black. The boy looked like a schoolboy standing in front of them.

Luke said: "Well, if you don't want anything, beat it, and don't come back."

The boy said, "I won't forget you guys," and went out.

They watched him go out. Spade took off his hat and wiped his damp forehead with a handkerchief.

The hotel-detective asked: "What is it?"

"Damned if I know," Spade replied. "I just happened to spot him. Know anything about Joel Cairo — six-thirty-five?"

"Oh, that one!" The hotel-detective leered.

"How long's he been here?"

"Four days. This is the fifth."

"What about him?"

"Search me, Sam. I got nothing against him but his looks."

"Find out if he came in last night?"

"Try to," the hotel-detective promised and went away. Spade sat on the divan until he returned. "No," Luke reported, "he didn't sleep in his room. What is it?"

"Nothing."

"Come clean. You know I'll keep my clam shut, but if there's anything wrong we ought to know about it so's we can collect our bill."

"Nothing like that," Spade assured him. "As a matter of fact, I'm doing a little work for him. I'd tell you if he was wrong."

"You'd better. Want me to kind of keep an eye on him?"

"Thanks, Luke. It wouldn't hurt. You can't know too much about the men you're working for these days."

It was twenty-one minutes past eleven by the clock over the elevator-doors when Joel Cairo came in from the street. His forehead was bandaged. His clothes had the limp unfreshness of too many hours' consecutive wear. His face was pasty, with sagging mouth and eyelids.

Spade met him in front of the desk. "Good morning," Spade said easily.

Cairo drew his tired body up straight and the drooping lines of his face tightened. "Good morning," he responded without enthusiasm.

There was a pause.

Spade said: "Let's go some place where we can talk."

Cairo raised his chin. "Please excuse me," he said. "Our conversations in private have not been such that I am anxious to continue them. Pardon my speaking bluntly, but it is the truth."

"You mean last night?" Spade made an impatient gesture with head and hands. "What in hell else could I do? I thought you'd see that. If you pick a fight with her, or let her pick one with you, I've got to throw in with her. I don't know where that damned bird is. You don't. She does. How in hell are we going to get it if I don't play along with her?"

Cairo hesitated, said dubiously: "You have always, I must say, a smooth explanation ready."

Spade scowled. "What do you want me to do? Learn to stutter? Well, we can talk over here." He led the way to the divan. When they were seated he asked: "Dundy take you down to the Hall?"

"Yes."

"How long did they work on you?"

"Until a very little while ago, and very much against my will." Pain and indignation were mixed in Cairo's face and voice. "I shall certainly take the matter up with the Consulate General of Greece and with an attorney."

"Go ahead, and see what it gets you. What did you let the police shake out of you?"

There was prim satisfaction in Cairo's smile. "Not a single thing. I adhered to the course you indicated earlier in your rooms." His smile went away. "Though I certainly wished you had devised a more reasonable story. I felt decidedly ridiculous repeating it."

Spade grinned mockingly. "Sure," he said, "but its goofiness is what makes it good. You sure you didn't give them anything?"

"You may rely upon it, Mr. Spade, I did not."

Spade drummed with his fingers on the leather seat between them. "You'll be hearing from Dundy again. Stay dummied-up on him and you'll be all right. Don't worry about the story's goofiness. A sensible one would've had us all in the cooler." He rose to his feet. "You'll want sleep if you've been standing up under a police-storm all night. See you later."

■ ■ ■ ■

Effie Perine was saying, "No, not yet," into the telephone when Spade entered his outer office. She looked around at him and her lips shaped a silent word: "Iva." He shook his head. "Yes, I'll have him call you as soon as he comes in," she said aloud and replaced the receiver on its prong. "That's the third time she's called up this morning," she told Spade.

He made an impatient growling noise.

The girl moved her brown eyes to indicate the inner office. "Your Miss O'Shaughnessy's in there. She's been waiting since a few minutes after nine."

Spade nodded as if he had expected that and asked: "What else?"

"Sergeant Polhaus called up. He didn't leave any message."

"Get him for me."

"And G. called up."

Spade's eyes brightened. He asked: "Who?"

"G. That's what he said." Her air of personal indifference to the subject was flawless. "When I told him you weren't in he said: 'When he comes in, will you please tell him that G., who got his message, phoned and will phone again?' "

Spade worked his lips together as if tasting something he liked. "Thanks, darling," he said. "See if you can get Tom Polhaus." He opened the inner door and went into his private office, pulling the door to behind him.

Brigid O'Shaughnessy, dressed as on her first visit to the office, rose from a chair beside his desk and came quickly towards him. "Somebody has been in my apartment," she explained. "It is all upside-down, every which way."

He seemed moderately surprised. "Anything taken?"

"I don't think so. I don't know. I was afraid to stay. I changed as fast as I could and came down here. Oh, you must've let that boy follow you there!"

Spade shook his head. "No, angel." He took an early copy of an afternoon paper from his pocket, opened it, and showed her a quarter-column headed SCREAM ROUTS BURGLAR.

A young woman named Carolin Beale, who lived alone in a Sutter Street apartment, had been awakened at four that morning by the sound of somebody moving in her bedroom. She had screamed. The mover had run away. Two other women who lived alone in the same building had discovered, later in the morning, signs of the burglar's having visited their apartments. Nothing had been taken from any of the three.

"That's where I shook him," Spade explained. "I went into that building and ducked out the back door. That's why all three were women who lived alone. He tried the apartments that had women's names in the vestibule-register, hunting for you under an alias."

"But he was watching your place when we were there," she objected.

Spade shrugged. "There's no reason to think he's working alone. Or maybe he went to Sutter Street after he had begun to think you were going to stay all night in my place. There are a lot of maybes, but I didn't lead him to the Coronet."

She was not satisfied. "But he found it, or somebody did."

"Sure." He frowned at her feet. "I wonder if it could have been Cairo. He wasn't at his hotel all night, didn't get in till a few minutes ago. He told me he had been standing up under a police-grilling all night. I wonder." He turned, opened the door, and asked Effie Perine: "Got Tom yet?"

"He's not in. I'll try again in a few minutes."

"Thanks." Spade shut the door and faced Brigid O'Shaughnessy.

She looked at him with cloudy eyes. "You went to see Joe this morning?" she asked.

"Yes."

She hesitated. "Why?"

"Why?" He smiled down at her. "Because, my own true love, I've got to keep in some sort of touch with all the loose ends of this dizzy affair if I'm ever going to make heads or tails of it." He put an arm around her shoulders and led her over to his swivel-chair. He kissed the tip of her nose lightly and set her down in the chair. He sat on the desk in front of her. He said: "Now we've got to find a new home for you, haven't we?"

She nodded with emphasis. "I won't go back there."

He patted the desk beside his thighs and made a thoughtful face. "I think I've got it," he said presently. "Wait a minute." He went into the outer office, shutting the door.

Effie Perine reached for the telephone, saying: "I'll try again."

"Afterwards. Does your woman's intuition still tell you that she's a madonna or something?"

She looked sharply up at him. "I still

believe that no matter what kind of trouble she's gotten into she's all right, if that's what you mean."

"That's what I mean," he said. "Are you strong enough for her to give her a lift?"

"How?"

"Could you put her up for a few days?"

"You mean at home?"

"Yes. Her joint's been broken into. That's the second burglary she's had this week. It'd be better for her if she wasn't alone. It would help a lot if you could take her in."

Effie Perine learned forward, asking earnestly: "Is she really in danger, Sam?"

"I think she is."

She scratched her lip with a fingernail. "That would scare Ma into a green hemorrhage. I'll have to tell her she's a surprise-witness or something that you're keeping under cover till the last minute."

"You're a darling," Spade said. "Better take her out there now. I'll get her key from her and bring whatever she needs over from her apartment. Let's see. You oughtn't to be seen leaving here together. You go home now. Take a taxi, but make sure you aren't followed. You probably won't be, but make sure. I'll send her out in another in a little while, making sure she isn't followed."

11
The Fat Man

The telephone-bell was ringing when Spade returned to his office after sending Brigid O'Shaughnessy off to Effie Perine's house. He went to the telephone.

"Hello . . . Yes, this is Spade. . . . Yes, I got it. I've been waiting to hear from you. . . . Who? . . . Mr. Gutman? Oh, yes, sure! . . . Now — the sooner the better. . . . Twelve C. . . . Right. Say fifteen minutes. . . . Right."

Spade sat on the corner of his desk beside the telephone and rolled a cigarette. His mouth was a hard complacent v. His eyes, watching his fingers make the cigarette, smoldered over lower lids drawn up straight.

The door opened and Iva Archer came in.

Spade said, "Hello, honey," in a voice as lightly amiable as his face had suddenly become.

"Oh, Sam, forgive me! forgive me!" she cried in a choked voice. She stood just inside the door, wadding a black-bordered handkerchief in her small gloved hands, peering into his face with frightened red and swollen eyes.

He did not get up from his seat on the desk-corner. He said: "Sure. That's all right. Forget it."

"But, Sam," she wailed, "I sent those policemen there. I was mad, crazy with jealousy, and I phoned them that if they'd go there they'd learn something about Miles's murder."

"What made you think that?"

"Oh, I didn't! But I was mad, Sam, and I wanted to hurt you."

"It made things damned awkward." He put his arm around her and drew her nearer. "But it's all right now, only don't get any more crazy notions like that."

"I won't," she promised, "ever. But you weren't nice to me last night. You were cold and distant and wanted to get rid of me, when I had come down there and waited so long to warn you, and you —"

"Warn me about what?"

"About Phil. He's found out about — about you being in love with me, and Miles had told him about my wanting a divorce, though of course *he* never knew what for, and now Phil thinks we — you killed his brother because he wouldn't give me the divorce so we could get married. He told me he believed that, and yesterday he went and told the police."

"That's nice," Spade said softly. "And you came to warn me, and because I was busy you got up on your ear and helped this damned Phil Archer stir things up."

"I'm sorry," she whimpered, "I know you won't forgive me. I — I'm sorry, sorry, sorry."

"You ought to be," he agreed, "on your own account as well as mine. Has Dundy been to see you since Phil did his talking? Or anybody from the bureau?"

"No." Alarm opened her eyes and mouth.

"They will," he said, "and it'd be just as well to not let them find you here. Did you tell them who you were when you phoned?"

"Oh, no! I simply told them that if they'd go to your apartment right away they'd learn something about the murder and hung up."

"Where'd you phone from?"

"The drug-store up above your place. Oh, Sam, dearest, I —"

He patted her shoulder and said pleasantly: "It was a dumb trick, all right, but it's done now. You'd better run along home and think up things to tell the police. You'll be hearing from them. Maybe it'd be best to say 'no' right across the board." He frowned at something distant. "Or maybe you'd better see Sid Wise first." He removed his arm from around her, took a card out of his pocket, scribbled three lines on its back, and gave it to her. "You can tell Sid everything." He frowned. "Or almost everything. Where were you the night Miles was shot?"

"Home," she replied without hesitating.

He shook his head, grinning at her.

"I was," she insisted.

"No," he said, "but if that's your story it's all right with me. Go see Sid. It's up on the next corner, the pinkish building, room eight-twenty-seven."

Her blue eyes tried to probe his yellow-gray ones. "What makes you think I wasn't home?" she asked slowly.

"Nothing except that I know you weren't."

"But I was, I was." Her lips twisted and anger darkened her eyes. "Effie Perine told you that," she said indignantly. "I saw her looking at my clothes and snooping around. You know she doesn't like me, Sam. Why do you believe things she tells you when you know she'd do anything to make trouble for me?"

"Jesus, you women," Spade said mildly. He looked at the watch on his wrist. "You'll have to trot along, precious. I'm late for an appointment now. You do what you want, but if I were you I'd tell Sid the truth or nothing. I mean leave out the parts you don't want to tell him, but don't make up anything to take its place."

"I'm not lying to you, Sam," she protested.

"Like hell you're not," he said and stood up.

She strained on tiptoe to hold her face nearer his. "You don't believe me?" she whispered.

"I don't believe you."

"And you won't forgive me for — for what I did?"

"Sure I do." He bent his head and kissed her mouth. "That's all right. Now run along."

She put her arms around him. "Won't you go with me to see Mr. Wise?"

"I can't, and I'd only be in the way." He patted her arms, took them from around his body, and kissed her left wrist between glove and sleeve. He put his hands on her shoulders, turned her to face the door, and released her with a little push. "Beat it," he ordered.

The mahogany door of suite 12-C at the Alexandria Hotel was opened by the boy Spade had talked to in the Belvedere lobby.

Spade said, "Hello," good-naturedly. The boy did not say anything. He stood aside holding the door open.

Spade went in. A fat man came to meet him.

The fat man was flabbily fat with bulbous pink cheeks and lips and chins and neck, with a great soft egg of a belly that was all his torso, and pendant cones for arms and legs. As he advanced to meet Spade all his bulbs rose and shook and fell separately with each step, in the manner of clustered soap-bubbles not yet released from the pipe through which they had been blown. His eyes, made small by fat puffs around them, were dark and sleek. Dark ringlets thinly covered his broad scalp. He wore a black cutaway coat, black vest, black satin Ascot tie holding a pinkish pearl, striped grey worsted trousers, and patent-leather shoes.

His voice was a throaty purr. "Ah, Mr. Spade," he said with enthusiasm and held out a hand like a fat pink star.

Spade took the hand and smiled and said: "How do you do, Mr. Gutman?"

Holding Spade's hand, the fat man turned beside him, put his other hand to Spade's elbow, and guided him across a green rug to a green plush chair beside a table that held a siphon, some glasses, and a bottle of

Johnnie Walker whiskey on a tray, a box of cigars — Coronas del Ritz — two newspapers, and a small and plain yellow soapstone box.

Spade sat in the green chair. The fat man began to fill two glasses from bottle and siphon. The boy had disappeared. Doors set in three of the room's walls were shut. The fourth wall, behind Spade, was pierced by two windows looking out over Geary Street.

"We begin well, sir," the fat man purred, turning with a proffered glass in his hand. "I distrust a man that says when. If he's got to be careful not to drink too much it's because he's not to be trusted when he does."

Spade took the glass and, smiling, made the beginning of a bow over it.

The fat man raised his glass and held it against a window's light. He nodded approvingly at the bubbles running up in it. He said: "Well, sir, here's to plain speaking and clear understanding."

They drank and lowered their glasses.

The fat man looked shrewdly at Spade and asked: "You're a close-mouthed man?"

Spade shook his head. "I like to talk."

"Better and better!" the fat man exclaimed. "I distrust a close-mouthed man. He generally picks the wrong time to talk and says the wrong things. Talking's something you can't do judiciously unless you keep in practice." He beamed over his glass. "We'll get along, sir, that we will." He set his glass on the table and held the box of Coronas del Ritz out to Spade. "A cigar, sir."

Spade took a cigar, trimmed the end of it, and lighted it. Meanwhile the fat man pulled another green plush chair around to face Spade's within convenient distance and placed a smoking-stand within reach of both chairs. Then he took his glass from the table, took a cigar from the box, and lowered himself into his chair. His bulbs stopped jouncing and settled into flabby rest. He sighed comfortably and said: "Now, sir, we'll talk if you like. And I'll tell you right out that I'm a man who likes talking to a man that likes to talk."

"Swell. Will we talk about the black bird?"

The fat man laughed and his bulbs rode up and down on his laughter. "Will we?" he asked and, "We will," he replied. His pink face was shiny with delight. "You're the man for me, sir, a man cut along my own lines. No beating about the bush, but right to the point. 'Will we talk about the black bird?' We will. I like that, sir. I like that way of doing business. Let us talk about the black bird by all means, but first, sir, answer me a question, please, though maybe it's an unnecessary one, so we'll understand each other from the beginning. You're here as Miss O'Shaughnessy's representative?"

Spade blew smoke above the fat man's head in a long slanting plume. He frowned thoughtfully at the ash-tipped end of his cigar. He replied deliberately: "I can't say yes or no. There's nothing certain about it either way, yet." He looked up at the fat man and stopped frowning. "It depends."

"It depends on — ?"

Spade shook his head. "If I knew what it depends on I could say yes or no."

The fat man took a mouthful from his glass, swallowed it, and suggested: "Maybe it depends on Joel Cairo?"

Spade's prompt "Maybe" was noncommittal. He drank.

The fat man leaned forward until his belly stopped him. His smile was ingratiating and so was his purring voice. "You could say, then, that the question is which one of them you'll represent?"

"You could put it that way."

"It will be one or the other?"

"I didn't say that."

The fat man's eyes glistened. His voice sank to a throaty whisper asking: "Who else is there?"

Spade pointed his cigar at his own chest. "There's me," he said.

The fat man sank back in his chair and let his body go flaccid. He blew his breath out in a long contented gust. "That's wonderful, sir," he purred. "That's wonderful. I do like a man that tells you right out he's looking out for himself. Don't we all? I don't trust a man that says he's not. And the man that's telling the truth when he says he's not I distrust most of all, because he's an ass and an ass that's going contrary to the laws of nature."

Spade exhaled smoke. His face was politely attentive. He said: "Uh-huh. Now let's talk about the black bird."

The fat man smiled benevolently. "Let's," he said. He squinted so that fat puffs crowding together left nothing of his eyes but a dark gleam visible. "Mr. Spade, have you any conception of how much money can be made out of that black bird?"

"No."

The fat man leaned forward again and put a bloated pink hand on the arm of Spade's chair. "Well, sir, if I told you — by Gad, if I told you half! — you'd call me a liar."

Spade smiled. "No," he said, "not even if I thought it. But if you won't take the risk just tell me what it is and I'll figure out the profits."

The fat man laughed. "You couldn't do it, sir. Nobody could do it that hadn't had a world of experience with things of that sort, and" — he paused impressively — "there aren't any other things of that sort." His bulbs jostled one another as he laughed again. He stopped laughing, abruptly. His fleshy lips hung open as laughter had left them. He stared at Spade with an intentness that suggested myopia. He asked: "You mean you don't know what it is?" Amazement took the throatiness out of his voice.

Spade made a careless gesture with his cigar. "Oh, hell," he said lightly, "I know what it's supposed to look like. I know the value in life you people put on it. I don't know what it is."

"She didn't tell you?"

"Miss O'Shaughnessy?"

"Yes. A lovely girl, sir."

"Uh-huh. No."

The fat man's eyes were dark gleams in ambush behind pink puffs of flesh. He said indistinctly, "She must know," and then, "And Cairo didn't either?"

"Cairo is cagey. He's willing to buy it, but he won't risk telling me anything I don't know already."

The fat man moistened his lips with his tongue. "How much is he willing to buy it for?" he asked.

"Ten thousand dollars."

The fat man laughed scornfully. "Ten thousand, and dollars, mind you, not even pounds. That's the Greek for you. Humph! And what did you say to that?"

"I said if I turned it over to him I'd expect the ten thousand."

"Ah, yes, *if!* Nicely put, sir." The fat man's forehead squirmed in a flesh-blurred frown. "They must know," he said only partly aloud, then: "Do they? Do they know what the bird is, sir? What was your impression?"

"I can't help you there," Spade confessed. "There's not much to go by. Cairo didn't say he did and he didn't say he didn't. She said she didn't, but I took it for granted that she was lying."

"That was not an injudicious thing to do," the fat man said, but his mind was obviously not on his words. He scratched his head. He frowned until his forehead was marked by raw red creases. He fidgeted in his chair as much as his size and the size of the chair permitted fidgeting. He shut his eyes, opened them suddenly — wide — and said to Spade: "Maybe they don't." His bulbous pink face slowly lost its worried frown and then, more quickly, took on an expression of ineffable happiness. "If they don't," he cried, and again: "If they don't I'm the only one in the whole wide sweet world who does!"

Spade drew his lips back in a tight smile. "I'm glad I came to the right place," he said.

The fat man smiled too, but somewhat vaguely. Happiness had gone out of his face, though he continued to smile, and caution had come into his eyes. His face was a watchful-eyed smiling mask held up between his thoughts and Spade. His eyes, avoiding Spade's, shifted to the glass at Spade's elbow. His face brightened. "By Gad, sir," he said, "your glass is empty." He got up and went to the table and clattered glasses and siphon and bottle mixing two drinks.

Spade was immobile in his chair until the fat man, with a flourish and a bow and a jocular "Ah, sir, this kind of medicine will never hurt you!" had handed him his refilled glass. Then Spade rose and stood close to the fat man, looking down at him, and Spade's eyes were hard and bright. He raised his glass. His voice was deliberate, challenging: "Here's to plain speaking and clear understanding."

The fat man chuckled and they drank. The

fat man sat down. He held his glass against his belly with both hands and smiled up at Spade. He said: "Well, sir, it's surprising, but it well may be a fact that neither of them does know exactly what that bird is, and that nobody in all this whole wide sweet world knows what it is, saving and excepting only your humble servant, Casper Gutman, Esquire."

"Swell." Spade stood with legs apart, one hand in his trousers-pocket, the other holding his glass. "When you've told me there'll only be two of us who know."

"Mathematically correct, sir" — the fat man's eyes twinkled — "but" — his smile spread — "I don't know for certain that I'm going to tell you."

"Don't be a damned fool," Spade said patiently. "You know what it is. I know where it is. That's why we're here."

"Well, sir, where is it?"

Spade ignored the question.

The fat man bunched his lips, raised his eyebrows, and cocked his head a little to the left. "You see," he said blandly, "I must tell you what I know, but you will not tell me what you know. That is hardly equitable, sir. No, no, I do not think we can do business along those lines."

Spade's face became pale and hard. He

spoke rapidly in a low furious voice: "Think again and think fast. I told that punk of yours that you'd have to talk to me before you got through. I'll tell you now that you'll do your talking today or you are through. What are you wasting my time for? You and your lousy secret! Christ! I know exactly what that stuff is that they keep in the subtreasury vaults, but what good does that do me? I can get along without you. God damn you! Maybe you could have got along without me if you'd kept clear of me. You can't now. Not in San Francisco. You'll come in or you'll get out — and you'll do it today."

He turned and with angry heedlessness tossed his glass at the table. The glass struck the wood, burst apart, and splashed its contents and glittering fragments over table and floor. Spade, deaf and blind to the crash, wheeled to confront the fat man again.

The fat man paid no more attention to the glass's fate than Spade did: lips pursed, eyebrows raised, head cocked a little to the left, he had maintained his pink-faced blandness throughout Spade's angry speech, and he maintained it now.

Spade, still furious, said: "And another thing, I don't want —"

The door to Spade's left opened. The boy who had admitted Spade came in. He shut the door, stood in front of it with his hands flat against his flanks, and looked at Spade. The boy's eyes were wide open and dark with wide pupils. Their gaze ran over Spade's body from shoulders to knees, and up again to settle on the handkerchief whose maroon border peeped from the breast-pocket of Spade's brown coat.

"Another thing," Spade repeated, glaring at the boy: "Keep that gunsel away from me while you're making up your mind. I'll kill him. I don't like him. He makes me nervous. I'll kill him the first time he gets in my way. I won't give him an even break. I won't give him a chance. I'll kill him."

The boy's lips twitched in a shadowy smile. He neither raised his eyes nor spoke.

The fat man said tolerantly: "Well, sir, I must say you have a most violent temper."

"Temper?" Spade laughed crazily. He crossed to the chair on which he had dropped his hat, picked up the hat, and set it on his head. He held out a long arm that ended in a thick forefinger pointing at the fat man's belly. His angry voice filled the room. "Think it over and think like hell. You've got till five-thirty to do it in. Then you're either in or out, for keeps." He let his arm drop, scowled at the bland fat man for a moment, scowled at the boy, and went to the door through which he had entered. When he opened the door he turned and said harshly: "Five-thirty — then the curtain."

The boy, staring at Spade's chest, repeated the two words he had twice spoken in the Belvedere lobby. His voice was not loud. It was bitter.

Spade went out and slammed the door.

12
Merry-Go-Round

Spade rode down from Gutman's floor in an elevator. His lips were dry and rough in a face otherwise pale and damp. When he took out his handkerchief to wipe his face he saw his hand trembling. He grinned at it and said, "Whew!" so loudly that the elevator-operator turned his head over his shoulder and asked: "Sir?"

Spade walked down Geary Street to the Palace Hotel, where he ate luncheon. His face had lost its pallor, his lips their dryness, and his hand its trembling by the time he had sat down. He ate hungrily without haste, and then went to Sid Wise's office.

When Spade entered, Wise was biting a fingernail and staring at the window. He took his hand from his mouth, screwed his chair around to face Spade, and said: " 'Lo. Push a chair up."

Spade moved a chair to the side of the big paper-laden desk and sat down. "Mrs.

Archer come in?" he asked.

"Yes." The faintest of lights flickered in Wise's eyes. "Going to marry the lady, Sammy?"

Spade sighed irritably through his nose. "Christ, now you start that!" he grumbled.

A brief tired smile lifted the corners of the lawyer's mouth. "If you don't," he said, "you're going to have a job on your hands."

Spade looked up from the cigarette he was making and spoke sourly: "You mean you are? Well, that's what you're for. What did she tell you?"

"About you?"

"About anything I ought to know."

Wise ran fingers through his hair, sprinkling dandruff down on his shoulders. "She told me she had tried to get a divorce from Miles so she could —"

"I know all that," Spade interrupted him. "You can skip it. Get to the part I don't know."

"How do I know how much she — ?"

"Quit stalling, Sid." Spade held the flame of his lighter to the end of his cigarette. "What did she tell you that she wanted kept from me?"

Wise looked reprovingly at Spade. "Now, Sammy," he began, "that's not —"

Spade looked heavenward at the ceiling

and groaned: "Dear God, he's my own lawyer that's got rich off me and I have to get down on my knees and beg him to tell me things!" He lowered at Wise. "What in hell do you think I sent her to you for?"

Wise made a weary grimace. "Just one more client like you," he complained, "and I'd be in a sanitarium — or San Quentin."

"You'd be with most of your clients. Did she tell you where she was the night he was killed?"

"Yes."

"Where?"

"Following him."

Spade sat up straight and blinked. He exclaimed incredulously: "Jesus, these women!" Then he laughed, relaxed, and asked: "Well, what did she see?"

Wise shook his head. "Nothing much. When he came home for dinner that evening he told her he had a date with a girl at the St. Mark, ragging her, telling her that was her chance to get the divorce she wanted. She thought at first he was just trying to get under her skin. He knew —"

"I know the family history," Spade said. "Skip it. Tell me what she did."

"I will if you'll give me a chance. After he had gone out she began to think that maybe he might have had that date. You know

Miles. It would have been like him to —"

"You can skip Miles's character too."

"I oughtn't to tell you a damned thing," the lawyer said. "So she got their car from the garage and drove to the St. Mark, sitting in the car across the street. She saw him come out of the hotel and she saw that he was shadowing a man and a girl — she says she saw the same girl with you last night — who had come out just ahead of him. She knew then that he was working, had been kidding her. I suppose she was disappointed, and mad — she sounded that way when she told me about it. She followed Miles long enough to make sure he was shadowing the pair, and then she went up to your apartment. You weren't home."

"What time was that?" Spade asked.

"When she got to your place? Between half-past nine and ten the first time."

"The first time?"

"Yes. She drove around for half an hour or so and then tried again. That would make it, say, ten-thirty. You were still out, so she drove back downtown and went to a movie to kill time until after midnight, when she thought she'd be more likely to find you in."

Spade frowned. "She went to a movie at ten-thirty?"

"So she says — the one on Powell Street that stays open till one in the morning. She didn't want to go home, she said, because she didn't want to be there when Miles came. That always made him mad, it seems, especially if it was around midnight. She stayed in the movie till it closed." Wise's words came out slower now and there was a sardonic glint in his eye. "She says she had decided by then not to go back to your place again. She says she didn't know whether you'd like having her drop in that late. So she went to Tait's — the one on Ellis Street — had something to eat and then went home — alone." Wise rocked back in his chair and waited for Spade to speak.

Spade's face was expressionless. He asked: "You believe her?"

"Don't you?" Wise replied.

"How do I know? How do I know it isn't something you fixed up between you to tell me?"

Wise smiled. "You don't cash many checks for strangers, do you, Sammy?"

"Not basketfuls. Well, what then? Miles wasn't home. It was at least two o'clock by then — must've been — and he was dead."

"Miles wasn't home," Wise said. "That seems to have made her mad again — his not being home first to be made mad by her not being home. So she took the car out of the garage again and went back to your place."

"And I wasn't home. I was down looking at Miles's corpse. Jesus, what a swell lot of merry-go-round riding. Then what?"

"She went home, and her husband still wasn't there, and while she was undressing your messenger came with the news of his death."

Spade didn't speak until he had with great care rolled and lighted another cigarette. Then he said: "I think that's an all right spread. It seems to click with most of the known facts. It ought to hold."

Wise's fingers, running through his hair again, combed more dandruff down on his shoulders. He studied Spade's face with curious eyes and asked: "But you don't believe it?"

Spade plucked his cigarette from between his lips. "I don't believe it or disbelieve it, Sid. I don't know a damned thing about it."

A wry smile twisted the lawyer's mouth. He moved his shoulders wearily and said: "That's right — I'm selling you out. Why don't you get an honest lawyer — one you can trust?"

"That fellow's dead." Spade stood up. He sneered at Wise. "Getting touchy, huh? I haven't got enough to think about: now I've got to remember to be polite to you. What did I do? Forget to genuflect when I came in?"

Sid Wise smiled sheepishly. "You're a son of a gun, Sammy," he said.

Effie Perine was standing in the center of Spade's outer office when he entered. She looked at him with worried brown eyes and asked: "What happened?"

Spade's face grew stiff. "What happened where?" he demanded.

"Why didn't she come?"

Spade took two long steps and caught Effie Perine by the shoulders. "She didn't get there?" he bawled into her frightened face.

She shook her head violently from side to side. "I waited and waited and she didn't come, and I couldn't get you on the phone, so I came down."

Spade jerked his hands away from her shoulders, thrust them far down in his trousers-pockets, said, "Another merry-go-round," in a loud enraged voice, and strode into his private office. He came out again. "Phone your mother," he commanded. "See if she's come yet."

He walked up and down the office while the girl used the telephone. "No," she said when she had finished. "Did — did you send her out in a taxi?"

His grunt probably meant yes.

"Are you sure she — Somebody must have followed her!"

Spade stopped pacing the floor. He put his hands on his hips and glared at the girl. He addressed her in a loud savage voice: "Nobody followed her. Do you think I'm a God-damned schoolboy? I made sure of it before I put her in the cab, I rode a dozen blocks with her to be more sure, and I checked her another half-dozen blocks after I got out."

"Well, but —"

"But she didn't get there. You've told me that. I believe it. Do you think I think she did get there?"

Effie Perine sniffed. "You certainly act like a God-damned schoolboy," she said.

Spade made a harsh noise in his throat and went to the corridor-door. "I'm going out and find her if I have to dig up sewers," he said. "Stay here till I'm back or you hear from me. For Christ's sake let's do something right."

He went out, walked half the distance to the elevators, and retraced his steps. Effie Perine was sitting at her desk when he opened the door. He said: "You ought to know better than to pay any attention to me when I talk like that."

"If you think I pay any attention to you you're crazy," she replied, "only" — she crossed her arms and felt her shoulders, and her mouth twitched uncertainly — "I won't be able to wear an evening gown for two weeks, you big brute."

He grinned humbly, said, "I'm no damned good, darling," made an exaggerated bow, and went out again.

Two yellow taxicabs were at the corner-stand to which Spade went. Their chauffeurs were standing together talking. Spade asked: "Where's the red-faced blond driver that was here at noon?"

"Got a load," one of the chauffeurs said.

"Will he be back here?"

"I guess so."

The other chauffeur ducked his head to the east. "Here he comes now."

Spade walked down to the corner and stood by the curb until the red-faced blond chauffeur had parked his cab and got out. Then Spade went up to him and said: "I got into your cab with a lady at noontime. We went out Stockton Street and up Sacramento to Jones, where I got out."

"Sure," the red-faced man said. "I remember that."

"I told you to take her to a Ninth-Avenue-number. You didn't take her there. Where did you take her?"

The chauffeur rubbed his cheek with a grimy hand and looked doubtfully at Spade. "I don't know about this."

"It's all right," Spade assured him, giving him one of his cards. "If you want to play safe, though, we can ride up to your office and get your superintendent's OK."

"I guess it's all right. I took her to the Ferry Building."

"By herself?"

"Yeah. Sure."

"Didn't take her anywhere else first?"

"No. It was like this: after we dropped you I went on out Sacramento, and when we got to Polk she rapped on the glass and said she wanted to get a newspaper, so I stopped at the corner and whistled for a kid, and she got her paper."

"Which paper?"

"The *Call.* Then I went on out Sacramento some more, and just after we'd crossed Van Ness she knocked on the glass again and said take her to the Ferry Building."

"Was she excited or anything?"

"Not so's I noticed."

"And when you got to the Ferry Building?"

"She paid me off, and that was all."

"Anybody waiting for her there?"

"I didn't see them if they was."

"Which way did she go?"

"At the Ferry? I don't know. Maybe upstairs, or towards the stairs."

"Take the newspaper with her?"

"Yeah, she had it tucked under her arm when she paid me."

"With the pink sheet outside, or one of the white?"

"Hell, Cap, I don't remember that."

Spade thanked the chauffeur, said, "Get yourself a smoke," and gave him a silver dollar.

Spade bought a copy of the *Call* and carried it into an office-building-vestibule to examine it out of the wind.

His eyes ran swiftly over the front-page-headlines and over those on the second and third pages. They paused for a moment under SUSPECT ARRESTED AS COUNTERFEITER on the fourth page, and again on page five under BAY YOUTH SEEKS DEATH WITH BULLET. Pages six and seven held nothing to interest him. On eight 3 BOYS ARRESTED AS S.F. BURGLARS

AFTER SHOOTING held his attention for a moment, and after that nothing until he reached the thirty-fifth page, which held news of the weather, shipping, produce, finance, divorce, births, marriages, and deaths. He read the list of the dead, passed over pages thirty-six and thirty-seven — financial news — found nothing to stop his eyes on the thirty-eighth and last page, sighed, folded the newspaper, put it in his coat-pocket, and rolled a cigarette.

For five minutes he stood there in the office-building-vestibule smoking and staring sulkily at nothing. Then he walked up to Stockton Street, hailed a taxicab, and had himself driven to the Coronet.

He let himself into the building and into Brigid O'Shaughnessy's apartment with the key she had given him. The blue gown she had worn the previous night was hanging across the foot of her bed. Her blue stockings and slippers were on the bedroom floor. The polychrome box that had held jewelry in her dressing-table-drawer now stood empty on the dressing-table-top. Spade frowned at it, ran his tongue across his lips, strolled through the rooms, looking around but not touching anything, then left the Coronet and went downtown again.

In the doorway of Spade's office-building

he came face to face with the boy he had left at Gutman's. The boy put himself in Spade's path, blocking the entrance, and said: "Come on. He wants to see you."

The boy's hands were in his overcoat-pockets. His pockets bulged more than his hands need have made them bulge.

Spade grinned and said mockingly: "I didn't expect you till five-twenty-five. I hope I haven't kept you waiting."

The boy raised his eyes to Spade's mouth and spoke in the strained voice of one in physical pain: "Keep on riding me and you're going to be picking iron out of your navel."

Spade chuckled. "The cheaper the crook, the gaudier the patter," he said cheerfully. "Well, let's go."

They walked up Sutter Street side by side. The boy kept his hands in his overcoat-pockets. They walked a little more than a block in silence. Then Spade asked pleasantly: "How long have you been off the goose-berry lay, son?"

The boy did not show that he had heard the question.

"Did you ever — ?" Spade began, and stopped. A soft light began to glow in his yellowish eyes. He did not address the boy again.

They went into the Alexandria, rode up to the twelfth floor, and walked down the corridor towards Gutman's suite. Nobody else was in the corridor.

Spade lagged a little, so that, when they were within fifteen feet of Gutman's door, he was perhaps a foot and a half behind the boy. He leaned sidewise suddenly and grasped the boy from behind by both arms, just beneath the boy's elbows. He forced the boy's arms forward so that the boy's hands, in his overcoat-pockets, lifted the overcoat up before him. The boy struggled and squirmed, but he was impotent in the big man's grip. The boy kicked back, but his feet went between Spade's spread legs.

Spade lifted the boy straight up from the floor and brought him down hard on his feet again. The impact made little noise on the thick carpet. At the moment of impact Spade's hands slid down and got a fresh grip on the boy's wrists. The boy, teeth set hard together, did not stop straining against the man's big hands, but he could not tear himself loose, could not keep the man's hands from crawling down over his own hands. The boy's teeth ground together audibly, making a noise that mingled with the noise of Spade's breathing as Spade crushed the boy's hands.

They were tense and motionless for a long moment. Then the boy's arms became limp. Spade released the boy and stepped back. In each of Spade's hands, when they came out of the boy's overcoat-pockets, there was a heavy automatic pistol.

The boy turned and faced Spade. The boy's face was a ghastly white blank. He kept his hands in his overcoat-pockets. He looked at Spade's chest and did not say anything.

Spade put the pistols in his own pockets and grinned derisively. "Come on," he said. "This will put you in solid with your boss."

They went to Gutman's door and Spade knocked.

13
The Emperor's Gift

Gutman opened the door. A glad smile lighted his fat face. He held out a hand and said: "Ah, come in, sir! Thank you for coming. Come in."

Spade shook the hand and entered. The boy went in behind him. The fat man shut the door. Spade took the boy's pistols from his pockets and held them out to Gutman. "Here. You shouldn't let him run around with these. He'll get himself hurt."

The fat man laughed merrily and took the pistols. "Well, well," he said, "what's this?" He looked from Spade to the boy.

Spade said: "A crippled newsie took them away from him, but I made him give them back."

The white-faced boy took the pistols out of Gutman's hands and pocketed them. The boy did not speak.

Gutman laughed again. "By Gad, sir," he told Spade, "you're a chap worth knowing, an amazing character. Come in. Sit down. Give me your hat."

The boy left the room by the door to the right of the entrance.

The fat man installed Spade in a green plush chair by the table, pressed a cigar upon him, held a light to it, mixed whiskey and carbonated water, put one glass in Spade's hand, and, holding the other, sat down facing Spade.

"Now, sir," he said, "I hope you'll let me apologize for —"

"Never mind that," Spade said. "Let's talk about the black bird."

The fat man cocked his head to the left and regarded Spade with fond eyes. "All right, sir," he agreed. "Let's." He took a sip from the glass in his hand. "This is going to be the most astounding thing you've ever heard of, sir, and I say that knowing that a man of your caliber in your profession must have known some astounding things in his time."

Spade nodded politely.

The fat man screwed up his eyes and asked: "What do you know, sir, about the Order of the Hospital of St. John of Jerusalem, later called the Knights of Rhodes and other things?"

Spade waved his cigar. "Not much — only

what I remember from history in school — Crusaders or something."

"Very good. Now you don't remember that Suleiman the Magnificent chased them out of Rhodes in 1523?"

"No."

"Well, sir, he did, and they settled in Crete. And they stayed there for seven years until 1530 when they persuaded the Emperor Charles V to give them" — Gutman held up three puffy fingers and counted them — "Malta, Gozo, and Tripoli."

"Yes?"

"Yes, sir, but with these conditions: they were to pay the Emperor each year the tribute of one" — he held up a finger — "falcon in the acknowledgment that Malta was still under Spain, and if they ever left the island it was to revert to Spain. Understand? He was giving it to them, but not unless they used it, and they couldn't give or sell it to anybody else."

"Yes."

The fat man looked over his shoulders at the three closed doors, hunched his chair a few inches nearer Spade's, and reduced his voice to a husky whisper: "Have you any conception of the extreme, the immeasurable, wealth of the Order at that time?"

"If I remember," Spade said, "they were

pretty well fixed."

Gutman smiled indulgently. "Pretty well, sir, is putting it mildly." His whisper became lower and more purring. "They were rolling in wealth, sir. You've no idea. None of us has any idea. For years they had preyed on the Saracens, had taken nobody knows what spoils of gems, precious metals, silks, ivories — the cream of the cream of the East. That is history, sir. We all know that the Holy Wars to them, as to the Templars, were largely a matter of loot.

"Well, now, the Emperor Charles has given them Malta, and all the rent he asks is one insignificant bird per annum, just as a matter of form. What could be more natural than for these immeasurably wealthy Knights to look around for some way of expressing their gratitude? Well, sir, that's exactly what they did, and they hit on the happy thought of sending Charles for the first year's tribute, not an insignificant live bird, but a glorious golden falcon encrusted from head to foot with the finest jewels in their coffers. And — remember, sir — they had fine ones, the finest out of Asia." Gutman stopped whispering. His sleek dark eyes examined Spade's face, which was placid. The fat man asked: "Well, sir, what do you think of that?"

"I don't know."

The fat man smiled complacently. "These are facts, historical facts, not schoolbook history, not Mr. Wells's history, but history nevertheless." He leaned forward. "The archives of the Order from the twelfth century on are still at Malta. They are not intact, but what is there holds no less than three" — he held up three fingers — "references that can't be to anything else but this jeweled falcon. In J. Delaville Le Roulx's *Les Archives de l'Ordre de Saint-Jean* there is a reference to it — oblique to be sure, but a reference still. And the unpublished — because unfinished at the time of his death — supplement to Paoli's *Dell' origine ed instituto del sacro militar ordine* has a clear and unmistakable statement of the facts I am telling you."

"All right," Spade said.

"All right, sir. Grand Master Villiers de l'Isle d'Adam had this foot-high jeweled bird made by Turkish slaves in the castle of St. Angelo and sent it to Charles, who was in Spain. He sent it in a galley commanded by a French knight named Cormier or Corvere, a member of the Order." His voice dropped to a whisper again. "It never reached Spain." He smiled with compressed lips and asked: "You know of Barbarossa,

Red-beard, Khair-ed-Din? No? A famous admiral of buccaneers sailing out of Algiers then. Well, sir, he took the Knights' galley and he took the bird. The bird went to Algiers. That's a fact. That's a fact that the French historian Pierre Dan put in one of his letters from Algiers. He wrote that the bird had been there for more than a hundred years, until it was carried away by Sir Francis Verney, the English adventurer who was with the Algerian buccaneers for a while. Maybe it wasn't, but Pierre Dan believed it was, and that's good enough for me.

"There's nothing said about the bird in Lady Frances Verney's *Memoirs of the Verney Family during the Seventeenth Century,* to be sure. I looked. And it's pretty certain that Sir Francis didn't have the bird when he died in a Messina hospital in 1615. He was stony broke. But, sir, there's no denying that the bird *did* go to Sicily. It was there and it came into the possession there of Victor Amadeus II some time after he became king in 1713, and it was one of his gifts to his wife when he married in Chambery after abdicating. That is a fact, sir. Carutti, the author of *Storia del Regno di Vittorio Amadeo II,* himself vouched for it.

"Maybe they — Amadeo and his wife —

took it along with them to Turin when he tried to revoke his abdication. Be that as it may, it turned up next in the possession of a Spaniard who had been with the army that took Naples in 1734 — the father of Don José Monino y Redondo, Count of Floridablanca, who was Charles III's chief minister. There's nothing to show that it didn't stay in that family until at least the end of the Carlist War in '40. Then it appeared in Paris at just about the time that Paris was full of Carlists who had had to get out of Spain. One of them must have brought it with him, but, whoever he was, it's likely he knew nothing about its real value. It had been — no doubt as a precaution during the Carlist trouble in Spain — painted or enameled over to look like nothing more than a fairly interesting black statuette. And in that disguise, sir, it was, you might say, kicked around Paris for seventy years by private owners and dealers too stupid to see what it was under the skin."

The fat man paused to smile and shake his head regretfully. Then he went on: "For seventy years, sir, this marvelous item was, as you might say, a football in the gutters of Paris — until 1911 when a Greek dealer named Charilaos Konstantinides found it in an obscure shop. It didn't take Charilaos long to learn what it was and to acquire it. No thickness of enamel could conceal value from his eyes and nose. Well, sir, Charilaos was the man who traced most of its history and who identified it as what it actually was. I got wind of it and finally forced most of the history out of him, though I've been able to add a few details since.

"Charilaos was in no hurry to convert his find into money at once. He knew that — enormous as its intrinsic value was — a far higher, a terrific, price could be obtained for it once its authenticity was established beyond doubt. Possibly he planned to do business with one of the modern descendants of the old Order — the English Order of St. John of Jerusalem, the Prussian Johanniterorden, or the Italian or German *langues* of the Sovereign Order of Malta — all wealthy orders."

The fat man raised his glass, smiled at its emptiness, and rose to fill it and Spade's. "You begin to believe me a little?" he asked as he worked the siphon.

"I haven't said I didn't."

"No," Gutman chuckled. "But how you looked." He sat down, drank generously, and patted his mouth with a white handkerchief. "Well, sir, to hold it safe while pursuing his researches into its history, Charilaos had re-enameled the bird, apparently just as it is now. One year to the very day after he had acquired it — that was possibly three months after I'd made him confess to me — I picked up the *Times* in London and read that his establishment had been burglarized and him murdered. I was in Paris the next day." He shook his head sadly. "The bird was gone. By Gad, sir, I was wild. I didn't believe anybody else knew what it was. I didn't believe he had told anybody but me. A great quantity of stuff had been stolen. That made me think that the thief had simply taken the bird along with the rest of his plunder, not knowing what it was. Because I assure you that a thief who knew its value would not burden himself with anything else — no, sir — at least not anything less than crown jewels."

He shut his eyes and smiled complacently at an inner thought. He opened his eyes and said: "That was seventeen years ago. Well, sir, it took me seventeen years to locate that bird, but I did it. I wanted it, and I'm not a man that's easily discouraged when he wants something." His smile grew broad. "I wanted it and I found it. I want it and I'm going to have it." He drained his glass, dried his lips again, and returned his handkerchief to his pocket. "I traced it to the home of a

Russian general — one Kemidov — in a Constantinople suburb. He didn't know a thing about it. It was nothing but a black enameled figure to him, but his natural contrariness — the natural contrariness of a Russian general — kept him from selling it to me when I made him an offer. Perhaps in my eagerness I was a little unskillful, though not very. I don't know about that. But I did know I wanted it and I was afraid this stupid soldier might begin to investigate his property, might chip off some of the enamel. So I sent some — ah — agents to get it. Well, sir, they got it and I haven't got it." He stood up and carried his empty glass to the table. "But I'm going to get it. Your glass, sir."

"Then the bird doesn't belong to any of you?" Spade asked, "but to a General Kemidov?"

"Belong?" the fat man said jovially. "Well, sir, you might say it belonged to the King of Spain, but I don't see how you can honestly grant anybody else clear title to it — except by right of possession." He clucked. "An article of that value that has passed from hand to hand by such means is clearly the property of whoever can get hold of it."

"Then it's Miss O'Shaughnessy's now?"

"No, sir, except as my agent."

Spade said, "Oh," ironically.

Gutman, looking thoughtfully at the stopper of the whiskey-bottle in his hand, asked: "There's no doubt that she's got it now?"

"Not much."

"Where?"

"I don't know exactly."

The fat man set the bottle on the table with a bang. "But you said you did," he protested.

Spade made a careless gesture with one hand. "I meant to say I know where to get it when the time comes."

The pink bulbs of Gutman's face arranged themselves more happily. "And you do?" he asked.

"Yes."

"Where?"

Spade grinned and said: "Leave that to me. That's my end."

"When?"

"When I'm ready."

The fat man pursed his lips and, smiling with only slight uneasiness, asked: "Mr. Spade, where is Miss O'Shaughnessy now?"

"In my hands, safely tucked away."

Gutman smiled with approval. "Trust you for that, sir," he said. "Well now, sir, before we sit down to talk prices, answer me this: how soon can you — or how soon are you willing to — produce the falcon?"

"A couple of days."

The fat man nodded. "That is satisfactory. We — But I forgot our nourishment." He turned to the table, poured whiskey, squirted charged water into it, set a glass at Spade's elbow and held his own aloft. "Well, sir, here's to a fair bargain and profits large enough for both of us."

They drank. The fat man sat down. Spade asked: "What's your idea of a fair bargain?"

Gutman held his glass up to the light, looked affectionately at it, took another long drink, and said: "I have two proposals to make, sir, and either is fair. Take your choice. I will give you twenty-five thousand dollars when you deliver the falcon to me, and another twenty-five thousand as soon as I get to New York; or I will give you one quarter — twenty-five per cent — of what I realize on the falcon. There you are, sir: an almost immediate fifty thousand dollars or a vastly greater sum within, say, a couple of months."

Spade drank and asked: "How much greater?"

"Vastly," the fat man repeated. "Who knows how much greater? Shall I say a hundred thousand, or a quarter of a million? Will you believe me if I name the sum that seems the probable minimum?"

"Why not?"

The fat man smacked his lips and lowered his voice to a purring murmur. "What would you say, sir, to half a million?"

Spade narrowed his eyes. "Then you think the dingus is worth two million?"

Gutman smiled serenely. "In your own words, why not?" he asked.

Spade emptied his glass and set it on the table. He put his cigar in his mouth, took it out, looked at it, and put it back in. His yellow-gray eyes were faintly muddy. He said: "That's a hell of a lot of dough."

The fat man agreed: "That's a hell of a lot of dough." He leaned forward and patted Spade's knee. "That is the absolute rock-bottom minimum — or Charilaos Konstantinides was a blithering idiot — and he wasn't."

Spade removed the cigar from his mouth again, frowned at it with distaste, and put it on the smoking-stand. He shut his eyes hard, opened them again. Their muddiness had thickened. He said: "The — the minimum, huh? And the maximum?" An unmistakable *sh* followed the x in maximum as he said it.

"The maximum?" Gutman held his empty hand out, palm up. "I refuse to guess. You'd think me crazy. I don't know. There's no telling how high it could go, sir, and that's the one and only truth about it."

Spade pulled his sagging lower lip tight against the upper. He shook his head impatiently. A sharp frightened gleam awoke in his eyes — and was smothered by the deepening muddiness. He stood up, helping himself up with his hands on the arms of his chair. He shook his head again and took an uncertain step forward. He laughed thickly and muttered: "God damn you."

Gutman jumped up and pushed his chair back. His fat globes jiggled. His eyes were dark holes in an oily pink face.

Spade swung his head from side to side until his dull eyes were pointed at — if not focused on — the door. He took another uncertain step.

The fat man called sharply: "Wilmer!"

A door opened and the boy came in.

Spade took a third step. His face was gray now, with jaw-muscles standing out like tumors under his ears. His legs did not straighten again after his fourth step and his muddy eyes were almost covered by their lids. He took his fifth step.

The boy walked over and stood close to Spade, a little in front of him, but not directly between Spade and the door. The boy's right hand was inside his coat over his heart. The corners of his mouth twitched.

Spade essayed his sixth step.

The boy's leg darted out across Spade's leg, in front. Spade tripped over the interfering leg and crashed face-down on the floor. The boy, keeping his right hand under his coat, looked down at Spade. Spade tried to get up. The boy drew his right foot far back and kicked Spade's temple. The kick rolled Spade over on his side. Once more he tried to get up, could not, and went to sleep.

14
La Paloma

Spade, coming around the corner from the elevator at a few minutes past six in the morning, saw yellow light glowing through the frosted glass of his office-door. He halted abruptly, set his lips together, looked up and down the corridor, and advanced to the door with swift quiet strides.

He put his hand on the knob and turned it with care that permitted neither rattle nor click. He turned the knob until it would turn no farther: the door was locked. Holding the knob still, he changed hands, taking it now in his left hand. With his right hand he brought his keys out of his pocket, carefully, so they could not jingle against one another. He separated the office-key from the others and, smothering the others together in his palm, inserted the office-key in the lock. The insertion was soundless. He balanced himself on the balls of his feet, filled his lungs, clicked the door open, and went in.

Effie Perine sat sleeping with her head on her forearms, her forearms on her desk. She wore her coat and had one of Spade's overcoats wrapped cape-fashion around her.

Spade blew his breath out in a muffled laugh, shut the door behind him, and crossed to the inner door. The inner office was empty. He went over to the girl and put a hand on her shoulder.

She stirred, raised her head drowsily, and her eyelids fluttered. Suddenly she sat up straight, opening her eyes wide. She saw Spade, smiled, leaned back in her chair, and rubbed her eyes with her fingers. "So you finally got back?" she said. "What time is it?"

"Six o'clock. What are you doing here?"

She shivered, drew Spade's overcoat closer around her, and yawned. "You told me to stay till you got back or phoned."

"Oh, you're the sister of the boy who stood on the burning deck?"

"I wasn't going to —" She broke off and stood up, letting his coat slide down on the chair behind her. She looked with dark excited eyes at his temple under the brim of his hat and exclaimed: "Oh, your head! What happened?"

His right temple was dark and swollen.

"I don't know whether I fell or was slugged. I don't think it amounts to much, but it hurts like hell." He barely touched it with his fingers, flinched, turned his grimace into a grim smile, and explained: "I went visiting, was fed knockout-drops, and came to twelve hours later all spread out on a man's floor."

She reached up and removed his hat from his head. "It's terrible," she said. "You'll have to get a doctor. You can't walk around with a head like that."

"It's not as bad as it looks, except for the headache, and that might be mostly from the drops." He went to the cabinet in the corner of the office and ran cold water on a handkerchief. "Anything turn up after I left?"

"Did you find Miss O'Shaughnessy, Sam?"

"Not yet. Anything turn up after I left?"

"The District Attorney's office phoned. He wants to see you."

"Himself?"

"Yes, that's the way I understood it. And a boy came in with a message — that Mr. Gutman would be delighted to talk to you before five-thirty."

Spade turned off the water, squeezed the handkerchief, and came away from the cabinet holding the handkerchief to his temple. "I got that," he said. "I met the boy downstairs, and talking to Mr. Gutman got me this."

"Is that the G. who phoned, Sam?"

"Yes."

"And what — ?"

Spade stared through the girl and spoke as if using speech to arrange his thoughts: "He wants something he thinks I can get. I persuaded him I could keep him from getting it if he didn't make the deal with me before five-thirty. Then — uh-huh — sure — it was after I'd told him he'd have to wait a couple of days that he fed me the junk. It's not likely he thought I'd die. He'd know I'd be up and around in ten or twelve hours. So maybe the answer's that he figured he could get it without my help in that time if I was fixed so I couldn't butt in." He scowled. "I hope to Christ he was wrong." His stare became less distant. "You didn't get any word from the O'Shaughnessy?"

The girl shook her head no and asked: "Has this got anything to do with her?"

"Something."

"This thing he wants belongs to her?"

"Or to the King of Spain. Sweetheart, you've got an uncle who teaches history or something over at the University?"

"A cousin. Why?"

"If we brightened his life with an alleged historical secret four centuries old could we trust him to keep it dark awhile?"

"Oh, yes, he's good people."

"Fine. Get your pencil and book."

She got them and sat in her chair. Spade ran more cold water on his handkerchief and, holding it to his temple, stood in front of her and dictated the story of the falcon as he had heard it from Gutman, from Charles V's grant to the Hospitallers up to — but no further than — the enameled bird's arrival in Paris at the time of the Carlist influx. He stumbled over the names of authors and their works that Gutman had mentioned, but managed to achieve some sort of phonetic likeness. The rest of the history he repeated with the accuracy of a trained interviewer.

When he had finished the girl shut her notebook and raised a flushed smiling face to him. "Oh, isn't this thrilling?" she said. "It's —"

"Yes, or ridiculous. Now will you take it over and read it to your cousin and ask him what he thinks of it? Has he ever run across anything that might have some connection with it? Is it probable? Is it possible — even barely possible? Or is it the bunk? If he wants more time to look it up, OK, but get some sort of opinion out of him now. And for God's sake make him keep it under his hat."

"I'll go right now," she said, "and you go see a doctor about that head."

"We'll have breakfast first."

"No, I'll eat over in Berkeley. I can't wait to hear what Ted thinks of this."

"Well," Spade said, "don't start boo-hooing if he laughs at you."

After a leisurely breakfast at the Palace, during which he read both morning papers, Spade went home, shaved, bathed, rubbed ice on his bruised temple, and put on fresh clothes.

He went to Brigid O'Shaughnessy's apartment at the Coronet. Nobody was in the apartment. Nothing had been changed in it since his last visit.

He went to the Alexandria Hotel. Gutman was not in. None of the other occupants of Gutman's suite was in. Spade learned that these other occupants were the fat man's secretary, Wilmer Cook, and his daughter Rhea, a brown-eyed fair-haired smallish girl of seventeen who the hotel-staff said was beautiful. Spade was told that the Gutman party had arrived at the hotel, from New York, ten days before, and had not checked out.

Spade went to the Belvedere and found the hotel-detective eating in the hotel-café.

"Morning, Sam. Set down and bite an egg." The hotel-detective stared at Spade's temple. "By God, somebody maced you plenty!"

"Thanks, I've had mine," Spade said as he sat down, and then, referring to his temple: "It looks worse than it is. How's my Cairo's conduct?"

"He went out not more than half an hour behind you yesterday and I ain't seen him since. He didn't sleep here again last night."

"He's getting bad habits."

"Well, a fellow like that alone in a big city. Who put the slug to you, Sam?"

"It wasn't Cairo." Spade looked attentively at the small silver dome covering Luke's toast. "How's chances of giving his room a casing while he's out?"

"Can do. You know I'm willing to go all the way with you all the time." Luke pushed his coffee back, put his elbows on the table, and screwed up his eyes at Spade. "But I got a hunch you ain't going all the way with me. What's the honest-to-God on this guy, Sam? You don't have to kick back on me. You know I'm regular."

Spade lifted his eyes from the silver dome. They were clear and candid. "Sure, you are," he said. "I'm not holding out. I gave you it straight. I'm doing a job for him, but he's got some friends that look wrong to me and I'm a little leery of him."

"The kid we chased out yesterday was one of his friends."

"Yes, Luke, he was."

"And it was one of them that shoved Miles across."

Spade shook his head. "Thursby killed Miles."

"And who killed him?"

Spade smiled. "That's supposed to be a secret, but, confidentially, I did," he said, "according to the police."

Luke grunted and stood up saying: "You're a tough one to figure out, Sam. Come on, we'll have that look-see."

They stopped at the desk long enough for Luke to "fix it so we'll get a ring if he comes in," and went up to Cairo's room. Cairo's bed was smooth and trim, but paper in the wastebasket, unevenly drawn blinds, and a couple of rumpled towels in the bathroom showed that the chambermaid had not yet been in that morning.

Cairo's luggage consisted of a square trunk, a valise, and a gladstone bag. His bathroom-cabinet was stocked with cosmetics — boxes, cans, jars, and bottles of powders, creams, unguents, perfumes, lotions, and tonics. Two suits and an overcoat hung in the closet over three pairs of carefully treed shoes.

The valise and smaller bag were unlocked. Luke had the trunk unlocked by the time Spade had finished searching elsewhere.

"Blank so far," Spade said as they dug down into the trunk.

They found nothing there to interest them.

"Any particular thing we're supposed to be looking for?" Luke asked as he locked the trunk again.

"No. He's supposed to have come here from Constantinople. I'd like to know if he did. I haven't seen anything that says he didn't."

"What's his racket?"

Spade shook his head. "That's something else I'd like to know." He crossed the room and bent down over the wastebasket. "Well, this is our last shot."

He took a newspaper from the basket. His eyes brightened when he saw it was the previous day's *Call*. It was folded with the classified-advertising page outside. He opened it, examined that page, and nothing there stopped his eyes.

He turned the paper over and looked at the page that had been folded inside, the page that held financial and shipping news, the weather, births, marriages, divorces, and deaths. From the lower left-hand corner, a little more than two inches of the bottom of the second column had been torn out.

Immediately above the tear was a small caption *Arrived Today* followed by:

12:20 a.m. — Capac from Astoria.
5:05 a.m. — Helen P. Drew from Greenwood.
5:06 a.m. — Albarado from Bandon.

The tear passed through the next line, leaving only enough of its letters to *make from Sydney* inferable.

Spade put the *Call* down on the desk and looked into the wastebasket again. He found a small piece of wrapping-paper, a piece of string, two hosiery tags, a haberdasher's sale-ticket for half a dozen pairs of socks, and, in the bottom of the basket, a piece of newspaper rolled in a tiny ball.

He opened the ball carefully, smoothed it out on the desk, and fitted it into the torn part of the *Call*. The fit at the sides was exact, but between the top of the crumpled fragment and the inferable *from Sydney* half an inch was missing, sufficient space to have held announcement of six or seven boats' arrival. He turned the sheet over and saw that the other side of the missing portion could have held only a meaningless corner of a stockbroker's advertisement.

Luke, leaning over his shoulder, asked: "What's this all about?"

"Looks like the gent's interested in a boat."

"Well, there's no law against that, or is there?" Luke said while Spade was folding the torn page and the crumpled fragment together and putting them into his coat-pocket. "You all through here now?"

"Yes. Thanks a lot, Luke. Will you give me a ring as soon as he comes in?"

"Sure."

Spade went to the Business Office of the *Call,* bought a copy of the previous day's issue, opened it to the shipping-news-page, and compared it with the page taken from Cairo's wastebasket. The missing portion had read:

5:17 a.m. — Tahiti from Sydney and Papeete.

6:05 a.m. — Admiral Peoples from Astoria.
8:07 a.m. — Caddopeak from San Pedro.
8:17 a.m. — Silverado from San Pedro.
8:05 a.m. — La Paloma from Hongkong.
9:03 a.m. — Daisy Gray from Seattle.

He read the list slowly and when he had finished he underscored *Hongkong* with a fingernail, cut the list of arrivals from the paper with his pocket-knife, put the rest of the paper and Cairo's sheet into the waste-basket, and returned to his office.

He sat down at his desk, looked up a number in the telephone-book, and used the telephone.

"Kearny one four o one, please. . . . Where is the *Paloma,* in from Hongkong yesterday morning docked?" He repeated the question. "Thanks."

He held the receiver-hook down with his thumb for a moment, released it, and said: "Davenport two o two o, please. . . . Detective bureau, please. . . . Is Sergeant Polhaus there? . . . Thanks. . . . Hello, Tom, this is Sam Spade. . . . Yes, I tried to get you yesterday afternoon. . . . Sure, suppose you go to lunch with me. . . . Right."

He kept the receiver to his ear while his thumb worked the hook again.

"Davenport o one seven o, please. . . . Hello, this is Samuel Spade. My secretary got a message yesterday that Mr. Bryan wanted to see me. Will you ask him what time's the most convenient for him? . . . Yes, Spade, S-p-a-d-e." A long pause. "Yes. . . . Two-thirty? All right. Thanks."

He called a fifth number and said: "Hello, darling, let me talk to Sid? . . . Hello, Sid — Sam. I've got a date with the District Attorney at half-past two this afternoon. Will you give me a ring — here or there — around four, just to see that I'm not in trouble? . . . Hell with your Saturday afternoon golf: your job's to keep me out of jail. . . . Right, Sid. 'Bye."

He pushed the telephone away, yawned, and stretched, felt his bruised temple, looked at his watch, and rolled and lighted a cigarette. He smoked sleepily until Effie Perine came in.

Effie Perine came in smiling, bright-eyed and rosy-faced. "Ted says it could be," she reported, "and he hopes it is. He says he's not a specialist in that field, but the names and dates are all right, and at least none of your authorities or their works are out-and-out fakes. He's all excited over it."

"That's swell, as long as he doesn't get

too enthusiastic to see through it if it's phoney."

"Oh, he wouldn't — not Ted! He's too good at his stuff for that."

"Uh-huh, the whole damned Perine family's wonderful," Spade said, "including you and the smudge of soot on your nose."

"He's not a Perine, he's a Christy." She bent her head to look at her nose in her vanity-case-mirror. "I must've got that from the fire." She scrubbed the smudge with the corner of a handkerchief.

"The Perine-Christy enthusiasm ignite Berkeley?" he asked.

She made a face at him while patting her nose with a powdered pink disc. "There was a boat on fire when I came back. They were towing it out from the pier and the smoke blew all over our ferry-boat."

Spade put his hands on the arms of his chair. "Were you near enough to see the name of the boat?" he asked.

"Yes. *La Paloma*. Why?"

Spade smiled ruefully. "I'm damned if I know why, sister," he said.

15
Every Crackpot

Spade And Detective-Sergeant Polhaus ate pickled pigs' feet at one of big John's tables at the States Hof Brau.

Polhaus, balancing pale bright jelly on a fork half-way between plate and mouth, said: "Hey, listen, Sam! Forget about the other night. He was dead wrong, but you know anybody's liable to lose their head if you ride them thataway."

Spade looked thoughtfully at the police-detective. "Was that what you wanted to see me about?" he asked.

Polhaus nodded, put the forkful of jelly into his mouth, swallowed it, and qualified his nod: "Mostly."

"Dundy send you?"

Polhaus made a disgusted mouth. "You know he didn't. He's as bullheaded as you are."

Spade smiled and shook his head. "No,

he's not, Tom," he said. "He just thinks he is."

Tom scowled and chopped at his pig's foot with a knife. "Ain't you ever going to grow up?" he grumbled. "What've you got to beef about? He didn't hurt you. You came out on top. What's the sense of making a grudge of it? You're just making a lot of grief for yourself."

Spade placed his knife and fork carefully together on his plate, and put his hands on the table beside his plate. His smile was faint and devoid of warmth. "With every bull in town working overtime trying to pile up grief for me a little more won't hurt. I won't even know it's there."

Polhaus's ruddiness deepened. He said: "That's a swell thing to say to me."

Spade picked up his knife and fork and began to eat. Polhaus ate.

Presently Spade asked: "See the boat on fire in the bay?"

"I saw the smoke. Be reasonable, Sam. Dundy was wrong and he knows it. Why don't you let it go at that?"

"Think I ought to go around and tell him I hope my chin didn't hurt his fist?"

Polhaus cut savagely into his pig's foot.

Spade said: "Phil Archer been in with any more hot tips?"

"Aw, hell! Dundy didn't think you shot Miles, but what else could he do except run the lead down? You'd've done the same thing in his place, and you know it."

"Yes?" Malice glittered in Spade's eyes. "What made him think I didn't do it? What makes you think I didn't? Or don't you?"

Polhaus's ruddy face flushed again. He said: "Thursby shot Miles."

"You think he did."

"He did. That Webley was his, and the slug in Miles came out of it."

"Sure?" Spade demanded.

"Dead sure," the police-detective replied. "We got hold of a kid — a bellhop at Thursby's hotel — that had seen it in his room just that morning. He noticed it particular because he'd never saw one just like it before. I never saw one. You say they don't make them any more. It ain't likely there'd be another around and — anyway — if that wasn't Thursby's what happened to his? And that's the gun the slug in Miles come out of." He started to put a piece of bread into his mouth, withdrew it, and asked:

"You say you've seen them before: where was that at?" He put the bread into his mouth.

"In England before the war."

"Sure, there you are."

Spade nodded and said: "Then that leaves Thursby the only one I killed."

Polhaus squirmed in his chair and his face was red and shiny. "Christ's sake, ain't you never going to forget that?" he complained earnestly. "That's out. You know it as well as I do. You'd think you wasn't a dick yourself the way you bellyache over things. I suppose you don't never pull the same stuff on anybody that we pulled on you?"

"You mean that you tried to pull on me, Tom — just tried."

Polhaus swore under his breath and attacked the remainder of his pig's foot.

Spade said: "All right. You know it's out and I know it's out. What does Dundy know?"

"He knows it's out."

"What woke him up?"

"Aw, Sam, he never really thought you'd —" Spade's smile checked Polhaus. He left the sentence incomplete and said: "We dug up a record on Thursby."

"Yes? Who was he?"

Polhaus's shrewd small brown eyes studied Spade's face. Spade exclaimed irritably: "I wish to God I knew half as much about this business as you smart guys think I do!"

"I wish we all did," Polhaus grumbled. "Well, he was a St. Louis gunman the first we hear of him. He was picked up a lot of times back there for this and that, but he belonged to the Egan mob, so nothing much was ever done about any of it. I don't know howcome he left that shelter, but they got him once in New York for knocking over a row of stuss-games — his twist turned him up — and he was in a year before Fallon got him sprung. A couple of years later he did a short hitch in Joliet for pistol-whipping another twist that had given him the needle, but after that he took up with Dixie Monahan and didn't have any trouble getting out whenever he happened to get in. That was when Dixie was almost as big a shot as Nick the Greek in Chicago gambling. This Thursby was Dixie's bodyguard and he took the run-out with him when Dixie got in wrong with the rest of the boys over some debts he couldn't or wouldn't pay off. That was a couple of years back — about the time the Newport Beach Boating Club was shut up. I don't know if Dixie had any part in that. Anyways, this is the first time him or Thursby's been seen since."

"Dixie's been seen?" Spade asked.

Polhaus shook his head. "No." His small eyes became sharp, prying. "Not unless you've seen him or know somebody's seen him."

Spade lounged back in his chair and began to make a cigarette. "I haven't," he said mildly. "This is all new stuff to me."

"I guess it is," Polhaus snorted.

Spade grinned at him and asked: "Where'd you pick up all this news about Thursby?"

"Some of it's on the records. The rest — well — we got it here and there."

"From Cairo, for instance?" Now Spade's eyes held the prying gleam.

Polhaus put down his coffee-cup and shook his head. "Not a word of it. You poisoned that guy for us."

Spade laughed. "You mean a couple of high-class sleuths like you and Dundy worked on that lily-of-the-valley all night and couldn't crack him?"

"What do you mean — all night?" Polhaus protested. "We worked on him for less than a couple of hours. We saw we wasn't getting nowhere, and let him go."

Spade laughed again and looked at his watch. He caught John's eye and asked for the check. "I've got a date with the D.A. this afternoon," he told Polhaus while they waited for his change.

"He send for you?"

"Yes."

Polhaus pushed his chair back and stood

up, a barrel-bellied tall man, solid and phlegmatic. "You won't be doing me any favor," he said, "by telling him I've talked to you like this."

A lathy youth with salient ears ushered Spade into the District Attorney's office. Spade went in smiling easily, saying easily: "Hello, Bryan!"

District Attorney Bryan stood up and held his hand out across his desk. He was a blond man of medium stature, perhaps forty-five years old, with aggressive blue eyes behind black-ribboned nose-glasses, the over-large mouth of an orator, and a wide dimpled chin. When he said, "How do you do, Spade?" his voice was resonant with latent power.

They shook hands and sat down.

The District Attorney put his finger on one of the pearl buttons in a battery of four on his desk, said to the lathy youth who opened the door again, "Ask Mr. Thomas and Healy to come in," and then, rocking back in his chair, addressed Spade pleasantly: "You and the police haven't been hitting it off so well, have you?"

Spade made a negligent gesture with the fingers of his right hand. "Nothing serious," he said lightly. "Dundy gets too enthusiastic."

The door opened to admit two men. The one to whom Spade said, "Hello, Thomas!" was a sunburned stocky man of thirty in clothing and hair of a kindred unruliness. He clapped Spade on the shoulder with a freckled hand, asked, "How's tricks?" and sat down beside him. The second man was younger and colorless. He took a seat a little apart from the others and balanced a stenographer's notebook on his knee, holding a green pencil over it.

Spade glanced his way, chuckled, and asked Bryan: "Anything I say will be used against me?"

The District Attorney smiled. "That always holds good." He took his glasses off, looked at them, and set them on his nose again. He looked through them at Spade and asked: "Who killed Thursby?"

Spade said: "I don't know."

Bryan rubbed his black eyeglass-ribbon between thumb and fingers and said knowingly: "Perhaps you don't, but you certainly could make an excellent guess."

"Maybe, but I wouldn't."

The District Attorney raised his eyebrows.

"I wouldn't," Spade repeated. He was serene. "My guess might be excellent, or it might be crummy, but Mrs. Spade didn't raise any children dippy enough to make guesses in front of a district attorney, an assistant district attorney, and a stenographer."

"Why shouldn't you, if you've nothing to conceal?"

"Everybody," Spade responded mildly, "has something to conceal."

"And you have — ?"

"My guesses, for one thing."

The District Attorney looked down at his desk and then up at Spade. He settled his glasses more firmly on his nose. He said: "If you'd prefer not having the stenographer here we can dismiss him. It was simply as a matter of convenience that I brought him in."

"I don't mind him a damned bit," Spade replied. "I'm willing to have anything I say put down and I'm willing to sign it."

"We don't intend asking you to sign anything," Bryan assured him. "I wish you wouldn't regard this as a formal inquiry at all. And please don't think I've any belief — much less confidence — in those theories the police seem to have formed."

"No?"

"Not a particle."

Spade sighed and crossed his legs. "I'm

glad of that." He felt in his pockets for tobacco and papers. "What's your theory?"

Bryan leaned forward in his chair and his eyes were hard and shiny as the lenses over them. "Tell me who Archer was shadowing Thursby for and I'll tell you who killed Thursby."

Spade's laugh was brief and scornful. "You're as wrong as Dundy," he said.

"Don't misunderstand me, Spade," Bryan said, knocking on the desk with his knuckles. "I don't say your client killed Thursby or had him killed, but I do say that, knowing who your client is, or was, I'll mighty soon know who killed Thursby."

Spade lighted his cigarette, removed it from his lips, emptied his lungs of smoke, and spoke as if puzzled: "I don't exactly get that."

"You don't? Then suppose I put it this way: where is Dixie Monahan?"

Spade's face retained its puzzled look. "Putting it that way doesn't help much," he said. "I still don't get it."

The District Attorney took his glasses off and shook them for emphasis. He said: "We know Thursby was Monahan's bodyguard and went with him when Monahan found it wise to vanish from Chicago. We know Monahan welshed on something like two-hundred-thousand-dollars' worth of bets when he vanished. We don't know — not yet — who his creditors were." He put the glasses on again and smiled grimly. "But we all know what's likely to happen to a gambler who welshes, and to his bodyguard, when his creditors find him. It's happened before."

Spade ran his tongue over his lips and pulled his lips back over his teeth in an ugly grin. His eyes glittered under pulled-down brows. His reddening neck bulged over the rim of his collar. His voice was low and hoarse and passionate. "Well, what do you think? Did I kill him for his creditors? Or just find him and let them do their own killing?"

"No, no!" the District Attorney protested. "You misunderstand me."

"I hope to Christ I do," Spade said.

"He didn't mean that," Thomas said.

"Then what did he mean?"

Bryan waved a hand. "I only mean that you might have been involved in it without knowing what it was. That could —"

"I see," Spade sneered. "You don't think I'm naughty. You just think I'm dumb."

"Nonsense," Bryan insisted: "Suppose someone came to you and engaged you to find Monahan, telling you they had reasons for thinking he was in the city. The someone might give you a completely false story — any one of a dozen or more would do — or might say he was a debtor who had run away, without giving you any of the details. How could you tell what was behind it? How would you know it wasn't an ordinary piece of detective work? And under those circumstances you certainly couldn't be held responsible for your part in it unless" — his voice sank to a more impressive key and his words came out spaced and distinct — "you made yourself an accomplice by concealing your knowledge of the murderer's identity or information that would lead to his apprehension."

Anger was leaving Spade's face. No anger remained in his voice when he asked: "That's what you meant?"

"Precisely."

"All right. Then there's no hard feelings. But you're wrong."

"Prove it."

Spade shook his head. "I can't prove it to you now. I can tell you."

"Then tell me."

"Nobody ever hired me to do anything about Dixie Monahan."

Bryan and Thomas exchanged glances. Bryan's eyes came back to Spade and he said: "But, by your own admission, somebody did hire you to do something about his bodyguard Thursby."

"Yes, about his ex-bodyguard Thursby."

"Ex?"

"Yes, ex."

"You know that Thursby was no longer associated with Monahan? You know that positively?"

Spade stretched out his hand and dropped the stub of his cigarette into an ashtray on the desk. He spoke carelessly: "I don't know anything positively except that my client wasn't interested in Monahan, had never been interested in Monahan. I heard that Thursby took Monahan out to the Orient and lost him."

Again the District Attorney and his assistant exchanged glances.

Thomas, in a tone whose matter-of-factness did not quite hide excitement, said: "That opens another angle. Monahan's friends could have knocked Thursby off for ditching Monahan."

"Dead gamblers don't have any friends," Spade said.

"It opens up two new lines," Bryan said. He leaned back and stared at the ceiling for several seconds, then sat upright quickly. His orator's face was alight. "It narrows down to three things. Number one: Thursby was killed by the gamblers Monahan had welshed on in Chicago. Not knowing Thursby had sloughed Monahan — or not believing it — they killed him because he had been Monahan's associate, or to get him out of the way so they could get to Monahan, or because he had refused to lead them to Monahan. Number two: he was killed by friends of Monahan. Or number three: he sold Monahan out to his enemies and then fell out with them and they killed him."

"Or number four," Spade suggested with a cheerful smile: "he died of old age. You folks aren't serious, are you?"

The two men stared at Spade, but neither of them spoke. Spade turned his smile from one to the other of them and shook his head in mock pity. "You've got Arnold Rothstein on the brain," he said.

Bryan smacked the back of his left hand down into the palm of his right. "In one of those three catagories lies the solution." The power in his voice was no longer latent. His right hand, a fist except for protruding forefinger, went up and then down to stop with a jerk when the finger was leveled at Spade's chest. "And you can give us the information that will enable us to determine the category."

Spade said, "Yes?" very lazily. His face was somber. He touched his lower lip with a finger, looked at the finger, and then scratched the back of his neck with it. Little irritable lines had appeared in his forehead. He blew his breath out heavily through his nose and his voice was an ill-humored growl. "You wouldn't want the kind of information I could give you, Bryan. You couldn't use it. It'd poop this gambler's-revenge-scenario for you."

Bryan sat up straight and squared his shoulders. His voice was stern without blustering. "You are not the judge of that. Right or wrong, I am nonetheless the District Attorney."

Spade's lifted lip showed his eyetooth. "I thought this was an informal talk."

"I am a sworn officer of the law twenty-four hours a day," Bryan said, "and neither formality nor informality justifies your withholding from me evidence of crime, except of course" — he nodded meaningly — "on certain constitutional grounds."

"You mean if it might incriminate me?" Spade asked. His voice was placid, almost amused, but his face was not. "Well, I've got better grounds than that, or grounds that suit me better. My clients are entitled to a decent amount of secrecy. Maybe I can be made to talk to a Grand Jury or even a Coroner's Jury, but I haven't been called before either yet, and it's a cinch I'm not going to advertise my clients' business until I have to. Then again, you and the police have both accused me of being mixed up in the other night's murders. I've had trouble with both of you before. As far as I can see, my best chance of clearing myself of the trouble you're trying to make for me is by bringing in the murderers — all tied up. And my only chance of ever catching them and tying them up and bringing them in is by keeping away from you and the police, because neither of you show any signs of knowing what in hell it's all about." He rose and turned his head over his shoulder to address the stenographer: "Getting this all right, son? Or am I going too fast for you?"

The stenographer looked at him with startled eyes and replied: "No, sir, I'm getting it all right."

"Good work," Spade said and turned to Bryan again. "Now if you want to go to the Board and tell them I'm obstructing justice and ask them to revoke my license, hop to it. You've tried it before and it didn't get you anything but a good laugh all around." He picked up his hat.

Bryan began: "But look here —"

Spade said: "And I don't want any more of these informal talks. I've got nothing to tell you or the police and I'm Goddamned tired of being called things by every crackpot on the city payroll. If you want to see me, pinch me or subpoena me or something and I'll come down with my lawyer." He put his hat on his head, said, "See you at the inquest, maybe," and stalked out.

16
The Third Murder

Spade went into the Hotel Sutter and telephoned the Alexandria. Gutman was not in. No member of Gutman's party was in. Spade telephoned the Belvedere. Cairo was not in, had not been in that day.

Spade went to his office.

A swart greasy man in notable clothes was waiting in the outer room. Effie Perine, indicating the swart man, said: "This gentleman wishes to see you, Mr. Spade."

Spade smiled and bowed and opened the inner door. "Come in." Before following the man in Spade asked Effie Perine: "Any news on that other matter?"

"No, sir."

The swart man was the proprietor of a moving-picture-theater in Market Street. He suspected one of his cashiers and a doorman of colluding to defraud him. Spade hurried him through the story, promised to "take care of it," asked for and received fifty dollars, and got rid of him in less than half an hour.

When the corridor-door had closed behind the showman Effie Perine came into the inner office. Her sunburned face was worried and questioning. "You haven't found her yet?" she asked.

He shook his head and went on stroking his bruised temple lightly in circles with his fingertips.

"How is it?" she asked.

"All right, but I've got plenty of headache."

She went around behind him, put his hand down, and stroked his temple with her slender fingers. He leaned back until the back of his head over the chair-top rested against her breast. He said: "You're an angel."

She bent her head forward over his and looked down into his face. "You've got to find her, Sam. It's more than a day and she —"

He stirred and impatiently interrupted her: "I haven't got to do anything, but if you'll let me rest this damned head a minute or two I'll go out and find her."

She murmured, "Poor head," and stroked it in silence awhile. Then she asked: "You know where she is? Have you any idea?"

The telephone-bell rang. Spade picked up the telephone and said: “Hello. . . . Yes, Sid, it came out all right, thanks. . . . No. . . . Sure. He got snotty, but so did I. . . . He’s nursing a gambler’s-war pipe-dream. . . . Well, we didn’t kiss when we parted. I declared my weight and walked out on him. . . . That’s something for you to worry about. . . . Right. ’Bye.” He put the telephone down and leaned back in his chair again.

Effie Perine came from behind him and stood at his side. She demanded: “Do you think you know where she is, Sam?”

“I know where she went,” he replied in a grudging tone.

“Where?” She was excited.

“Down to the boat you saw burning.”

Her eyes opened until their brown was surrounded by white. “You went down there.” It was not a question.

“I did not,” Spade said.

“Sam,” she cried angrily, “she may be —”

“She went down there,” he said in a surly voice. “She wasn’t taken. She went down there instead of to your house when she learned the boat was in. Well, what the hell? Am I supposed to run around after my clients begging them to let me help them?”

“But, Sam, when I told you the boat was

on fire!"

"That was at noon and I had a date with Polhaus and another with Bryan."

She glared at him between tightened lids. "Sam Spade," she said, "you're the most contemptible man God ever made when you want to be. Because she did something without confiding in you you'd sit here and do nothing when you know she's in danger, when you know she might be —"

Spade's face flushed. He said stubbornly: "She's pretty capable of taking care of herself and she knows where to come for help when she thinks she needs it, and when it suits her."

"That's spite," the girl cried, "and that's all it is! You're sore because she did something on her own hook, without telling you. Why shouldn't she? You're not so damned honest, and you haven't been so much on the level with her, that she should trust you completely."

Spade said: "That's enough of that."

His tone brought a brief uneasy glint into her hot eyes, but she tossed her head and the glint vanished. Her mouth was drawn taut and small. She said: "If you don't go down there this very minute, Sam, I will and I'll take the police down there." Her voice trembled, broke, and was thin and wailing. "Oh, Sam, go!"

He stood up cursing her. Then he said: "Christ! It'll be easier on my head than sitting here listening to you squawk." He looked at his watch. "You might as well lock up and go home."

She said: "I won't. I'm going to wait right here till you come back."

He said, "Do as you damned please," put his hat on, flinched, took it off, and went out carrying it in his hand.

An hour and a half later, at twenty minutes past five, Spade returned. He was cheerful. He came in asking: "What makes you so hard to get along with, sweetheart?"

"Me?"

"Yes, you." He put a finger on the tip of Effie Perine's nose and flattened it. He put his hands under her elbows, lifted her straight up, and kissed her chin. He set her down on the floor again and asked: "Anything doing while I was gone?"

"Luke — what's his name? — at the Belvedere called up to tell you Cairo has returned. That was about half an hour ago."

Spade snapped his mouth shut, turned with a long step, and started for the door.

"Did you find her?" the girl called.

"Tell you about it when I'm back," he

replied without pausing and hurried out.

A taxicab brought Spade to the Belvedere within ten minutes of his departure from his office. He found Luke in the lobby. The hotel-detective came grinning and shaking his head to meet Spade. "Fifteen minutes late," he said. "Your bird has fluttered."

Spade cursed his luck.

"Checked out — gone bag and baggage," Luke said. He took a battered memorandum-book from a vest-pocket, licked his thumb, thumbed pages, and held the book out open to Spade. "There's the number of the taxi that hauled him. I got that much for you."

"Thanks." Spade copied the number on the back of an envelope. "Any forwarding address?"

"No. He just come in carrying a big suitcase and went upstairs and packed and come down with his stuff and paid his bill and got a taxi and went without anybody being able to hear what he told the driver."

"How about his trunk?"

Luke's lower lip sagged. "By God," he said, "I forgot that! Come on."

They went up to Cairo's room. The trunk was there. It was closed, but not locked. They raised the lid. The trunk was empty.

Luke said: "What do you know about that!"

Spade did not say anything.

Spade went back to his office. Effie Perine looked up at him, inquisitively.

"Missed him," Spade grumbled and passed into his private room.

She followed him in. He sat in his chair and began to roll a cigarette. She sat on the desk in front of him and put her toes on a corner of his chair-seat.

"What about Miss O'Shaughnessy?" she demanded.

"I missed her too," he replied, "but she had been there."

"On the *La Paloma?*"

"*The La* is a lousy combination," he said.

"Stop it. Be nice, Sam. Tell me."

He set fire to his cigarette, pocketed his lighter, patted her shins, and said: "Yes, *La Paloma.* She got down there at a little after noon yesterday." He pulled his brows down. "That means she went straight there after leaving the cab at the Ferry Building. It's only a few piers away. The Captain wasn't aboard. His name's Jacobi and she asked for him by name. He was uptown on business. That would mean he didn't expect her, or not at that time anyway. She waited there till he came back at four o'clock. They spent the time from then till mealtime in his cabin and she ate with him."

He inhaled and exhaled smoke, turned his head aside to spit a yellow tobacco-flake off his lip, and went on: "After the meal Captain Jacobi had three more visitors. One of them was Gutman and one was Cairo and one was the kid who delivered Gutman's message to you yesterday. Those three came together while Brigid was there and the five of them did a lot of talking in the Captain's cabin. It's hard to get anything out of the crew, but they had a row and somewhere around eleven o'clock that night a gun went off there, in the Captain's cabin. The watchman beat it down there, but the Captain met him outside and told him everything was all right. There's a fresh bullet-hole in one corner of the cabin, up high enough to make it likely that the bullet didn't go through anybody to get there. As far as I could learn there was only the one shot. But as far as I could learn wasn't very far."

He scowled and inhaled smoke again. "Well, they left around midnight — the Captain and his four visitors all together — and all of them seem to have been walking all right. I got that from the watchman. I haven't been able to get hold of the Custom-

Housemen who were on duty there then. That's all of it. The Captain hasn't been back since. He didn't keep a date he had this noon with some shipping-agents, and they haven't found him to tell him about the fire."

"And the fire?" she asked.

Spade shrugged. "I don't know. It was discovered in the hold, aft — in the rear basement — late this morning. The chances are it got started some time yesterday. They got it out all right, though it did damage enough. Nobody liked to talk about it much while the Captain's away. It's the —"

The corridor-door opened. Spade shut his mouth. Effie Perine jumped down from the desk, but a man opened the connecting door before she could reach it.

"Where's Spade?" the man asked.

His voice brought Spade up erect and alert in his chair. It was a voice harsh and rasping with agony and with the strain of keeping two words from being smothered by the liquid bubbling that ran under and behind them.

Effie Perine, frightened, stepped out of the man's way.

He stood in the doorway with his soft hat crushed between his head and the top of the door-frame: he was nearly seven feet tall. A black overcoat cut long and straight and like a sheath, buttoned from throat to knees, exaggerated his leanness. His shoulders stuck out, high, thin, angular. His bony face — weather-coarsened, age-lined — was the color of wet sand and was wet with sweat on cheeks and chin. His eyes were dark and bloodshot and mad above lower lids that hung down to show pink inner membrane. Held tight against the left side of his chest by a black-sleeved arm that ended in a yellowish claw was a brown-paper-wrapped parcel bound with thin rope — an ellipsoid somewhat larger than an American football.

The tall man stood in the doorway and there was nothing to show that he saw Spade. He said, "You know —" and then the liquid bubbling came up in his throat and submerged whatever else he said. He put his other hand over the hand that held the ellipsoid. Holding himself stiffly straight, not putting his hands out to break his fall, he fell forward as a tree falls.

Spade, wooden-faced and nimble, sprang from his chair and caught the falling man. When Spade caught him the man's mouth opened and a little blood spurted out, and the brown-wrapped parcel dropped from the man's hands and rolled across the floor until a foot of the desk stopped it. Then the man's knees bent and he bent at the waist and his thin body became limber inside the sheath-like overcoat, sagging in Spade's arms so that Spade could not hold it up from the floor.

Spade lowered the man carefully until he lay on the floor on his left side. The man's eyes — dark and bloodshot, but not now mad — were wide open and still. His mouth was open as when blood has spurted from it, but no more blood came from it, and all his long body was as still as the floor it lay on.

Spade said: "Lock the door."

While Effie Perine, her teeth chattering, fumbled with the corridor-door's lock Spade knelt beside the thin man, turned him over on his back, and ran a hand down inside his overcoat. When he withdrew the hand presently it came out smeared with blood. The sight of his bloody hand brought not the least nor briefest of changes to Spade's face. Holding that hand up where it would touch nothing, he took his lighter out of his pocket with his other hand. He snapped on the flame and held the flame close to first one and then the other of the thin man's eyes. The eyes — lids, balls, irises, and pupils — remained frozen, immobile.

Spade extinguished the flame and returned the lighter to his pocket. He moved on his knees around to the dead man's side and, using his one clean hand, unbuttoned and opened the tubular overcoat. The inside of the overcoat was wet with blood and the double-breasted blue jacket beneath it was sodden. The jacket's lapels, where they crossed over the man's chest, and both sides of his coat immediately below that point, were pierced by soggy ragged holes.

Spade rose and went to the wash-bowl in the outer office.

Effie Perine, wan and trembling and holding herself upright by means of a hand on the corridor-door's knob and her back against its glass, whispered: "Is — is he — ?"

"Yes. Shot through the chest, maybe half a dozen times." Spade began to wash his hands.

"Oughtn't we — ?" she began, but he cut her short: "It's too late for a doctor now and I've got to think before we do anything." He finished washing his hands and began to rinse the bowl. "He couldn't have come far with those in him. If he — Why in hell couldn't he had stood up long enough to say something?" He frowned at the girl, rinsed his hands again, and picked up a towel. "Pull yourself together. For Christ's sake don't get sick on me now!" He threw the towel down and ran fingers through his hair. "We'll have a look at that bundle."

He went into the inner office again, stepped over the dead man's legs, and picked up the brown-paper-wrapped parcel. When he felt its weight his eyes glowed. He put it on his desk, turning it over so that the knotted part of the rope was uppermost. The knot was hard and tight. He took out his pocket-knife and cut the rope.

The girl had left the door and, edging around the dead man with her face turned away, had come to Spade's side. As she stood there — hands on a corner of the desk — watching him pull the rope loose and push aside brown paper, excitement began to supplant nausea in her face. "Do you think it is?" she whispered.

"We'll soon know," Spade said, his big fingers busy with the inner husk of coarse gray paper, three sheets thick, that the brown paper's removal had revealed. His face was hard and dull. His eyes were shining. When he had put the gray paper out of the way he had an egg-shaped mass of pale excelsior, wadded tight. His fingers tore the wad apart and then he had the foot-high figure of a bird, black as coal and shiny where its polish was not dulled by wood-dust and fragments of excelsior.

Spade laughed. He put a hand down on the bird. His widespread fingers had ownership in their curving. He put his other arm around Effie Perine and crushed her body against his. "We've got the damned thing, angel," he said.

"Ouch!" she said, "you're hurting me."

He took his arm away from her, picked the black bird up in both hands, and shook it to dislodge clinging excelsior. Then he stepped back holding it up in front of him and blew dust off it, regarding it triumphantly.

Effie Perine made a horrified face and screamed, pointing at his feet.

He looked down at his feet. His last backward step had brought his left heel into contact with the dead man's hand, pinching a quarter-inch of flesh at a side of the palm between heel and floor. Spade jerked his foot away from the hand.

The telephone-bell rang.

He nodded at the girl. She turned to the desk and put the receiver to her ear. She said: "Hello. . . . Yes. . . . Who? . . . Oh, yes!" Her eyes became large. "Yes. . . . Yes. . . .

Hold the line. . . .” Her mouth suddenly stretched wide and fearful. She cried: “Hello! Hello! Hello!” She rattled the prong up and down and cried, “Hello!” twice. Then she sobbed and spun around to face Spade, who was close beside her by now. “It was Miss O’Shaughnessy,” she said wildly. “She wants you. She’s at the Alexandria — in danger. Her voice was — oh, it was awful, Sam! — and something happened to her before she could finish. Go help her, Sam!”

Spade put the falcon down on the desk and scowled gloomily. “I’ve got to take care of this fellow first,” he said, pointing his thumb at the thin corpse on the floor.

She beat his chest with her fists, crying: “No, no — you’ve got to go to her. Don’t you see, Sam? He had the thing that was hers and he came to you with it. Don’t you see? He was helping her and they killed him and now she’s — Oh, you’ve got to go!”

“All right.” Spade pushed her away and bent over his desk, putting the black bird back into its nest of excelsior, bending the paper around it, working rapidly, making a larger and clumsy package. “As soon as I’ve gone phone the police. Tell them how it happened, but don’t drag any names in. You don’t know. I got the phone-call and I told you I had to go out, but I didn't say where." He cursed the rope for being tangled, yanked it into straightness, and began to bind the package. "Forget this thing. Tell it as it happened, but forget he had a bundle." He chewed his lower lip. "Unless they pin you down. If they seem to know about it you'll have to admit it. But that's not likely. If they do then I took the bundle away with me, unopened." He finished tying the knot and straightened up with the parcel under his left arm. "Get it straight, now. Everything happened the way it did happen, but without this dingus unless they already know about it. Don't deny it — just don't mention it. And I got the phone-call — not you. And you don't know anything about anybody else having any connection with this fellow. You don't know anything about him and you can't talk about my business until you see me. Got it?"

"Yes, Sam. Who — do you know who he is?"

He grinned wolfishly. "Uh-uh," he said, "but I'd guess he was Captain Jacobi, master of *La Paloma*." He picked up his hat and put it on. He looked thoughtfully at the dead man and then around the room.

"Hurry, Sam," the girl begged.

"Sure," he said absent-mindedly, "I'll

hurry. Might not hurt to get those few scraps of excelsior off the floor before the police come. And maybe you ought to try to get hold of Sid. No." He rubbed his chin. "We'll leave him out of it awhile. It'll look better. I'd keep the door locked till they come." He took his hand from his chin and rubbed her cheek. "You're a damned good man, sister," he said and went out.

17
Saturday Night

Carrying the parcel lightly under his arm, walking briskly, with only the ceaseless shifting of his eyes to denote wariness, Spade went, partly by way of an alley and a narrow court, from his office-building to Kearny and Post Streets, where he hailed a passing taxicab.

The taxicab carried him to the Pickwick Stage terminal in Fifth Street. He checked the bird at the Parcel Room there, put the check into a stamped envelope, wrote *M. F. Holland* and a San Francisco Post Office box-number on the envelope, sealed it, and dropped it into a mail-box. From the stage-terminal another taxicab carried him to the Alexandria Hotel.

Spade went up to suite 12-C and knocked on the door. The door was opened, when he had knocked a second time, by a small fair-haired girl in a shimmering yellow dressing-gown — a small girl whose face was white and dim and who clung desperately to the inner doorknob with both hands and gasped: "Mr. Spade?"

Spade said, "Yes," and caught her as she swayed.

Her body arched back over his arm and her head dropped straight back so that her short fair hair hung down her scalp and her slender throat was a firm curve from chin to chest.

Spade slid his supporting arm higher up her back and bent to get his other arm under her knees, but she stirred then, resisting, and between parted lips that barely moved blurred words came: "No! Ma' me wa'!"

Spade made her walk. He kicked the door shut and he walked her up and down the green-carpeted room from wall to wall. One of his arms around her small body, that hand under her armpit, his other hand gripping her other arm, held her erect when she stumbled, checked her swaying, kept urging her forward, but made her tottering legs bear all her weight they could bear. They walked across and across the floor, the girl falteringly, with incoordinate steps, Spade surely on the balls of his feet with balance unaffected by her staggering. Her face was chalk-white and eyeless, his sullen, with eyes hardened to watch everywhere at once.

He talked to her monotonously: "That's the stuff. Left, right, left, right. That's the stuff. One, two, three, four, one, two, three, now we turn." He shook her as they turned from the wall. "Now back again. One, two, three, four. Hold your head up. That's the stuff. Good girl. Left, right, left, right. Now we turn again." He shook her again. "That's the girl. Walk, walk, walk, walk. One, two, three, four. Now we go around." He shook her, more roughly, and increased their pace. "That's the trick. Left, right, left, right. We're in a hurry. One, two, three. . . ."

She shuddered and swallowed audibly. Spade began to chafe her arm and side and he put his mouth nearer her ear. "That's fine. You're doing fine. One, two, three, four. Faster, faster, faster, faster. That's it. Step, step, step, step. Pick them up and lay them down. That's the stuff. Now we turn. Left, right, left, right. What'd they do — dope you? The same stuff they gave me?"

Her eyelids twitched up then for an instant over dulled golden-brown eyes and she managed to say all of "Yes" except the final consonant.

They walked the floor, the girl almost trotting now to keep up with Spade, Spade slapping and kneading her flesh through yellow silk with both hands, talking and talking while his eyes remained hard and aloof and watchful. "Left, right, left, right, left, right, turn. That's the girl. One, two, three, four, one, two, three, four. Keep the chin up. That's the stuff. One, two. . . ."

Her lids lifted again a bare fraction of an inch and under them her eyes moved weakly from side to side.

"That's fine," he said in a crisp voice, dropping his monotone. "Keep them open. Open them wide — wide!" He shook her.

She moaned in protest, but her lids went farther up, though her eyes were without inner light. He raised his hand and slapped her cheek half a dozen times in quick succession. She moaned again and tried to break away from him. His arm held her and swept her along beside him from wall to wall.

"Keep walking," he ordered in a harsh voice, and then: "Who are you?"

Her "Rhea Gutman" was thick but intelligible.

"The daughter?"

"Yes." Now she was no farther from the final consonant than *sh.*

"Where's Brigid?"

She twisted convulsively around in his arms and caught at one of his hands with both of hers. He pulled his hand away quickly and looked at it. Across its back was a thin red scratch an inch and a half or more in length.

"What the hell?" he growled and examined her hands. Her left hand was empty. In her right hand, when he forced it open, lay a three-inch jade-headed steel bouquet-pin. "What the hell?" he growled again and held the pin up in front of her eyes.

When she saw the pin she whimpered and opened her dressing-gown. She pushed aside the cream-colored pajama-coat under it and showed him her body below her left breast — white flesh criss-crossed with thin red lines, dotted with tiny red dots, where the pin had scratched and punctured it. "To stay awake . . . walk . . . till you came. . . . She said you'd come . . . were so long." She swayed.

Spade tightened his arm around her and said: "Walk."

She fought against his arm, squirming around to face him again. "No . . . tell you . . . sleep . . . save her . . ."

"Brigid?" he demanded.

"Yes . . . took her . . . Bur-Burlingame . . . twenty-six Ancho . . . hurry . . . too late . . ." Her head fell over on her shoulder.

Spade pushed her head up roughly. "Who

took her there? Your father?"

"Yes . . . Wilmer . . . Cairo." She writhed and her eyelids twitched but did not open. ". . . kill her." Her head fell over again, and again he pushed it up.

"Who shot Jacobi?"

She did not seem to hear the question. She tried pitifully to hold her head up, to open her eyes. She mumbled: "Go . . . she . . ."

He shook her brutally. "Stay awake till the doctor comes."

Fear opened her eyes and pushed for a moment the cloudiness from her face. "No, no," she cried thickly, "father . . . kill me . . . swear you won't . . . he'd know . . . I did . . . for her . . . promise . . . won't . . . sleep . . . all right . . . morning . . ."

He shook her again. "You're sure you can sleep the stuff off all right?"

"Ye'." Her head fell down again.

"Where's your bed?"

She tried to raise a hand, but the effort had become too much for her before the hand pointed at anything except the carpet. With the sigh of a tired child she let her whole body relax and crumple.

Spade caught her up in his arms — scooped her up as she sank — and, holding her easily against his chest, went to the nearest of the three doors. He turned the knob far enough to release the catch, pushed the door open with his foot, and went into a passageway that ran past an open bathroom-door to a bedroom. He looked into the bathroom, saw it was empty, and carried the girl into the bedroom. Nobody was there. The clothing that was in sight and things on the chiffonier said it was a man's room.

Spade carried the girl back to the green-carpeted room and tried the opposite door. Through it he passed into another passageway, past another empty bathroom, and into a bedroom that was feminine in its accessories. He turned back the bedclothes and laid the girl on the bed, removed her slippers, raised her a little to slide the yellow dressing-gown off, fixed a pillow under her head, and put the covers up over her.

Then he opened the room's two windows and stood with his back to them staring at the sleeping girl. Her breathing was heavy but not troubled. He frowned and looked around, working his lips together. Twilight was dimming the room. He stood there in the weakening light for perhaps five minutes. Finally he shook his thick sloping shoulders impatiently and went out, leaving the suite's outer door unlocked.

■ ■ ■ ■

Spade went to the Pacific Telephone and Telegraph Company's station in Powell Street and called Davenport 2020. "Emergency Hospital, please. . . . Hello, there's a girl in suite twelve C at the Alexandria Hotel who has been drugged. . . . Yes, you'd better send somebody to take a look at her. . . . This is Mr. Hooper of the Alexandria."

He put the receiver on its prong and laughed. He called another number and said: "Hello, Frank. This is Sam Spade. . . . Can you let me have a car with a driver who'll keep his mouth shut? . . . To go down the peninsula right away. . . . Just a couple of hours. . . . Right. Have him pick me up at John's, Ellis Street, as soon as he can make it."

He called another number — his office's — held the receiver to his ear for a little while without saying anything, and replaced it on its hook.

He went to John's Grill, asked the waiter to hurry his order of chops, baked potato, and sliced tomatoes, ate hurriedly, and was smoking a cigarette with his coffee when a thick-set youngish man with a plaid cap set askew above pale eyes and a tough cheery face came into the Grill and to his table.

"All set, Mr. Spade. She's full of gas and rearing to go."

"Swell." Spade emptied his cup and went out with the thick-set man. "Know where Ancho Avenue, or Road, or Boulevard, is in Burlingame?"

"Nope, but if she's there we can find her."

"Let's do that," Spade said as he sat beside the chauffeur in the dark Cadillac sedan. "Twenty-six is the number we want, and the sooner the better, but we don't want to pull up at the front door."

"Correct."

They rode half a dozen blocks in silence. The chauffeur said: "Your partner got knocked off, didn't he, Mr. Spade?"

"Uh-huh."

The chauffeur clucked. "She's a tough racket. You can have it for mine."

"Well, hack-drivers don't live forever."

"Maybe that's right," the thick-set man conceded, "but, just the same, it'll always be a surprise to me if I don't."

Spade stared ahead at nothing and thereafter, until the chauffeur tired of making conversation, replied with uninterested yeses and noes.

■ ■ ■ ■

At a drug-store in Burlingame the chauffeur learned how to reach Ancho Avenue. Ten minutes later he stopped the sedan near a dark corner, turned off the lights, and waved his hand at the block ahead. "There she is," he said. "She ought to be on the other side, maybe the third or fourth house."

Spade said, "Right," and got out of the car. "Keep the engine going. We may have to leave in a hurry."

He crossed the street and went up the other side. Far ahead a lone street-light burned. Warmer lights dotted the night on either side where houses were spaced half a dozen to a block. A high thin moon was cold and feeble as the distant street-light. A radio droned through the open windows of a house on the other side of the street.

In front of the second house from the corner Spade halted. On one of the gate-posts that were massive out of all proportion to the fence flanking them a 2 and a 6 of pale metal caught what light there was. A square white card was nailed over them. Putting his face close to the card, Spade could see that it was a *For Sale or Rent* sign. There was no gate between the posts. Spade went up the cement walk to the house. He stood still on the walk at the foot of the porch-steps for a long moment. No sound came from the house. The house was dark except for another pale square card nailed on its door.

Spade went up to the door and listened. He could hear nothing. He tried to look through the glass of the door. There was no curtain to keep his gaze out, but inner darkness. He tiptoed to a window and then to another. They, like the door, were uncurtained except by inner darkness. He tried both windows. They were locked. He tried the door. It was locked.

He left the porch and, stepping carefully over dark unfamiliar ground, walked through weeds around the house. The side-windows were too high to be reached from the ground. The back door and the one back window he could reach were locked.

Spade went back to the gatepost and, cupping the frame between his hands, held his lighter up to the *For Sale or Rent* sign. It bore the printed name and address of a San Mateo real-estate-dealer and a line penciled in blue: *Key at 31.*

Spade returned to the sedan and asked the chauffeur: "Got a flashlight?"

"Sure." He gave it to Spade. "Can I give

you a hand at anything?"

"Maybe." Spade got into the sedan. "We'll ride up to number thirty-one. You can use your lights."

Number 31 was a square grey house across the street from, but a little farther up than, 26. Lights glowed in its downstairs-windows. Spade went up on the porch and rang the bell. A dark-haired girl of fourteen or fifteen opened the door. Spade, bowing and smiling, said: "I'd like to get the key to number twenty-six."

"I'll call Papa," she said and went back into the house calling: "Papa!"

A plump red-faced man, bald-headed and heavily mustached, appeared, carrying a newspaper.

Spade said: "I'd like to get the key to twenty-six."

The plump man looked more doubtful. He said: "The juice is not on. You couldn't see anything."

Spade patted his pocket. "I've a flashlight."

The plump man looked more doubtful. He cleared his throat uneasily and crumpled the newspaper in his hand.

Spade showed him one of his business-cards, put it back in his pocket, and said in a low voice: "We got a tip that there might be something hidden there."

The plump man's face and voice were eager. "Wait a minute," he said. "I'll go over with you."

A moment later he came back carrying a brass key attached to a black and red tag. Spade beckoned to the chauffeur as they passed the car and the chauffeur joined them.

"Anybody been looking at the house lately?" Spade asked.

"Not that I know of," the plump man replied. "Nobody's been to me for the key in a couple of months."

The plump man marched ahead with the key until they had gone up on the porch. Then he thrust the key into Spade's hand, mumbled, "Here you are," and stepped aside.

Spade unlocked the door and pushed it open. There was silence and darkness. Holding the flashlight — dark — in his left hand, Spade entered. The chauffeur came close behind him and then, at a little distance, the plump man followed them. They searched the house from bottom to top, cautiously at first, then, finding nothing, boldly. The house was empty — unmistakably — and there was nothing to indicate that it had been visited in weeks.

■ ■ ■ ■

Saying, "Thanks, that's all," Spade left the sedan in front of the Alexandria. He went into the hotel, to the desk, where a tall young man with a dark grave face said: "Good evening, Mr. Spade."

"Good evening." Spade drew the young man to one end of the desk. "These Gutmans — up in twelve C — are they in?"

The young man replied, "No," darting a quick glance at Spade. Then he looked away, hesitated, looked at Spade again, and murmured: "A funny thing happened in connection with them this evening, Mr. Spade. Somebody called the Emergency Hospital and told them there was a sick girl up there."

"And there wasn't?"

"Oh, no, there was nobody up there. They went out earlier in the evening."

Spade said: "Well, these practical-jokers have to have their fun. Thanks."

He went to a telephone-booth, called a number, and said: "Hello. . . . Mrs. Perine? . . . Is Effie there? . . . Yes, please. . . . Thanks.

"Hello, angel! What's the good word? . . . Fine, fine! Hold it. I'll be out in twenty minutes. . . . Right."

Half an hour later Spade rang the door-bell of a two-storybrick building in Ninth Avenue. Effie Perine opened the door. Her boyish face was tired and smiling. "Hello, boss," she said. "Enter." She said in a low voice: "If Ma says anything to you, Sam, be nice to her. She's all up in the air."

Spade grinned reassuringly and patted her shoulder.

She put her hands on his arm. "Miss O'Shaughnessy?"

"No," he growled. "I ran into a plant. Are you sure it was her voice?"

"Yes."

He made an unpleasant face. "Well, it was hooey."

She took him into a bright living-room, sighed, and slumped down on one end of a Chesterfield, smiling cheerfully up at him through her weariness.

He sat beside her and asked: "Everything went OK? Nothing said about the bundle?"

"Nothing. I told them what you told me to tell them, and they seemed to take it for granted that the phone-call had something to do with it, and that you were out running it down."

"Dundy there?"

"No. Hoff and O'Gar and some others I didn't know. I talked to the Captain too."

"They took you down to the Hall?"

"Oh, yes, and they asked me loads of questions, but it was all — you know — routine."

Spade rubbed his palms together. "Swell," he said and then frowned, "though I guess they'll think up plenty to put to me when we meet. That damned Dundy will, anyway, and Bryan." He moved his shoulders. "Anybody you know, outside of the police, come around?"

"Yes." She sat up straight. "That boy — the one who brought the message from Gutman — was there. He didn't come in, but the police left the corridor-door open while they were there and I saw him standing there."

"You didn't say anything?"

"Oh, no. You had said not to. So I didn't pay any attention to him and the next time I looked he was gone."

Spade grinned at her. "Damned lucky for you, sister, that the coppers got there first."

"Why?"

"He's a bad egg, that lad — poison. Was the dead man Jacobi?"

"Yes."

He pressed her hands and stood up. "I'm

going to run along. You'd better hit the hay. You're all in."

She rose. "Sam, what is — ?"

He stopped her words with his hand on her mouth. "Save it till Monday," he said. "I want to sneak out before your mother catches me and gives me hell for dragging her lamb through gutters."

Midnight was a few minutes away when Spade reached his home. He put his key into the street-door's lock. Heels clicked rapidly on the sidewalk behind him. He let go the key and wheeled. Brigid O'Shaughnessy ran up the steps to him. She put her arms around him and hung on him, panting: "Oh, I thought you'd never come!" Her face was haggard, distraught, shaken by the tremors that shook her from head to foot.

With the hand not supporting her he felt for the key again, opened the door, and half lifted her inside. "You've been waiting?" he asked.

"Yes." Panting spaced her words. "In a — doorway — up the — street."

"Can you make it all right?" he asked. "Or shall I carry you?"

She shook her head against his shoulder. "I'll be — all right — when I — get where

— I can — sit down."

They rode up to Spade's floor in the elevator and went around to his apartment. She left his arm and stood beside him — panting, both hands to her breast — while he unlocked his door. He switched on the passageway light. They went in. He shut the door and, with his arm around her again, took her back towards the living-room. When they were within a step of the living-room-door the light in the living-room went on.

The girl cried out and clung to Spade.

Just inside the living-room-door fat Gutman stood smiling benevolently at them. The boy Wilmer came out of the kitchen behind them. Black pistols were gigantic in his small hands. Cairo came from the bathroom. He too had a pistol.

Gutman said: "Well, sir, we're all here, as you can see for yourself. Now let's come in and sit down and be comfortable and talk."

18
The Fall-Guy

Spade, with his arms around Brigid O'Shaughnessy, smiled meagerly over her head and said: "Sure, we'll talk."

Gutman's bulbs jounced as he took three waddling backward steps away from the door.

Spade and the girl went in together. The boy and Cairo followed them in. Cairo stopped in the doorway. The boy put away one of his pistols and came up close behind Spade.

Spade turned his head far around to look down over his shoulder at the boy and said: "Get away. You're not going to frisk me."

The boy said: "Stand still. Shut up."

Spade's nostrils went in and out with his breathing. His voice was level. "Get away. Put your paw on me and I'm going to make you use the gun. Ask your boss if he wants me shot up before we talk."

"Never mind, Wilmer," the fat man said.

He frowned indulgently at Spade. "You are certainly a most headstrong individual. Well, let's be seated."

Spade said, "I told you I didn't like that punk," and took Brigid O'Shaughnessy to the sofa by the windows. They sat close together, her head against his left shoulder, his left arm around her shoulders. She had stopped trembling, had stopped panting. The appearance of Gutman and his companions seemed to have robbed her of that freedom of personal movement and emotion that is animal, leaving her alive, conscious, but quiescent as a plant.

Gutman lowered himself into the padded rocking chair. Cairo chose the armchair by the table. The boy Wilmer did not sit down. He stood in the doorway where Cairo had stood, letting his one visible pistol hang down at his side, looking under curling lashes at Spade's body. Cairo put his pistol on the table beside him.

Spade took off his hat and tossed it to the other end of the sofa. He grinned at Gutman. The looseness of his lower lip and the droop of his upper eyelids combined with the v's in his face to make his grin lewd as a satyr's. "That daughter of yours has a nice belly," he said, "too nice to be scratched up with pins."

Gutman's smile was affable if a bit oily.

The boy in the doorway took a short step forward, raising his pistol as far as his hip. Everybody in the room looked at him. In the dissimilar eyes with which Brigid O'Shaughnessy and Joel Cairo looked at him there was, oddly, something identically reproving. The boy blushed, drew back his advanced foot, straightened his legs, lowered the pistol and stood as he had stood before, looking under lashes that hid his eyes at Spade's chest. The blush was pale enough and lasted for only an instant, but it was startling on his face that habitually was so cold and composed.

Gutman turned his sleek-eyed fat smile on Spade again. His voice was a suave purring. "Yes, sir, that was a shame, but you must admit that it served its purpose."

Spade's brows twitched together. "Anything would've," he said. "Naturally I wanted to see you as soon as I had the falcon. Cash customers — why not? I went to Burlingame expecting to run into this sort of a meeting. I didn't know you were blundering around, half an hour late, trying to get me out of the way so you could find Jacobi again before he found me."

Gutman chuckled. His chuckle seemed to hold nothing but satisfaction. "Well, sir," he said, "in any case, here we are having our little meeting, if that's what you wanted."

"That's what I wanted. How soon are you ready to make the first payment and take the falcon off my hands?"

Brigid O'Shaughnessy sat up straight and looked at Spade with surprised blue eyes. He patted her shoulder inattentively. His eyes were steady on Gutman's. Gutman's twinkled merrily between sheltering fat-puffs. He said: "Well, sir, as to that," and put a hand inside the breast of his coat.

Cairo, hands on thighs, leaned forward in his chair, breathing between parted soft lips. His dark eyes had the surface-shine of lacquer. They shifted their focus warily from Spade's face to Gutman's, from Gutman's to Spade's.

Gutman repeated, "Well, sir, as to that," and took a white envelope from his pocket. Ten eyes — the boy's now only half obscured by his lashes — looked at the envelope. Turning the envelope over in his swollen hands, Gutman studied for a moment its blank white front and then its back, unsealed, with the flap tucked in. He raised his head, smiled amiably, and scaled the envelope at Spade's lap.

The envelope, though not bulky, was heavy enough to fly true. It struck the lower part of Spade's chest and dropped down on his thighs. He picked it up deliberately and opened it deliberately, using both hands, having taken his left arm from around the girl. The contents of the envelope were thousand-dollar bills, smooth and stiff and new. Spade took them out and counted them. There were ten of them. Spade looked up smiling. He said mildly: "We were talking about more money than this."

"Yes, sir, we were," Gutman agreed, "but we were talking then. This is actual money, genuine coin of the realm, sir. With a dollar of this you can buy more than with ten dollars of talk." Silent laughter shook his bulbs. When their commotion stopped he said more seriously, yet not altogether seriously: "There are more of us to be taken care of now." He moved his twinkling eyes and his fat head to indicate Cairo. "And — well, sir, in short — the situation has changed."

While Gutman talked Spade had tapped the edges of the ten bills into alignment and returned them to their envelope, tucking the flap in over them. Now, with forearms on knees, he sat hunched forward, dangling the envelope from a corner held lightly by finger and thumb down between his legs. His reply to the fat man was careless: "Sure.

You're together now, but I've got the falcon."

Joel Cairo spoke. Ugly hands grasping the arms of his chair, he leaned forward and said primly in his high-pitched thin voice: "I shouldn't think it would be necessary to remind you, Mr. Spade, that though you may have the falcon yet we certainly have you."

Spade grinned. "I'm trying to not let that worry me," he said. He sat up straight, put the envelope aside — on the sofa — and addressed Gutman: "We'll come back to the money later. There's another thing that's got to be taken care of first. We've got to have a fall-guy."

The fat man frowned without comprehension, but before he could speak Spade was explaining: "The police have got to have a victim — somebody they can stick for those three murders. We —"

Cairo, speaking in a brittle excited voice, interrupted Spade. "Two — only two — murders, Mr. Spade. Thursby undoubtedly killed your partner."

"All right, two," Spade growled. "What difference does that make? The point is we've got to feed the police some —"

Now Gutman broke in, smiling confidently, talking with good-natured assurance:

"Well, sir, from what we've seen and heard of you I don't think we'll have to bother ourselves about that. We can leave the handling of the police to you, all right. You won't need any of our inexpert help."

"If that's what you think," Spade said, "you haven't seen or heard enough."

"Now come, Mr. Spade. You can't expect us to believe at this late date that you are the least bit afraid of the police, or that you are not quite able to handle —"

Spade snorted with throat and nose. He bent forward, resting forearms on knees again, and interrupted Gutman irritably: "I'm not a damned bit afraid of them and I know how to handle them. That's what I'm trying to tell you. The way to handle them is to toss them a victim, somebody they can hang the works on."

"Well, sir, I grant you that's one way of doing it, but —"

" 'But' hell!" Spade said. "It's the only way." His eyes were hot and earnest under a reddening forehead. The bruise on his temple was liver-colored. "I know what I'm talking about. I've been through it all before and expect to go through it again. At one time or another I've had to tell everybody from the Supreme Court down to go to hell, and I've got away with it. I got away with it because I never let myself forget that a day of reckoning was coming. I never forget that when the day of reckoning comes I want to be all set to march into headquarters pushing a victim in front of me, saying: 'Here, you chumps, is your criminal!' As long as I can do that I can put my thumb to my nose and wriggle my fingers at all the laws in the book. The first time I can't do it my name's Mud. There hasn't been a first time yet. This isn't going to be it. That's flat."

Gutman's eyes flickered and their sleekness became dubious, but he held his other features in their bulbous pink smiling complacent cast and there was nothing of uneasiness in his voice. He said: "That's a system that's got a lot to recommend it, sir — by Gad, it has! And if it was anyway practical this time I'd be the first to say: 'Stick to it by all means, sir.' But this just happens to be a case where it's not possible. That's the way it is with the best of systems. There comes a time when you've got to make exceptions, and a wise man just goes ahead and makes them. Well, sir, that's just the way it is in this case and I don't mind telling you that I think you're being very well paid for making an exception. Now maybe it will be a little more trouble to you than if you had your victim to hand over to the police, but" — he laughed and spread his hands — "you're not the man that's afraid of a little bit of trouble. You know how to do things and you know you'll land on your feet in the end, no matter what happens." He pursed his lips and partly closed one eye. "You'll manage that, sir."

Spade's eyes had lost their warmth. His face was dull and lumpy. "I know what I'm talking about," he said in a low, consciously patient, tone. "This is my city and my game. I could manage to land on my feet — sure — this time, but the next time I tried to put over a fast one they'd stop me so fast I'd swallow my teeth. Hell with that. You birds'll be in New York or Constantinople or some place else. I'm in business here."

"But surely," Gutman began, "you can —"

"I can't," Spade said earnestly. "I won't. I mean it." He sat up straight. A pleasant smile illuminated his face, erasing its dull lumpishness. He spoke rapidly in an agreeable, persuasive tone: "Listen to me, Gutman. I'm telling you what's best for all of us. If we don't give the police a fall-guy it's ten to one they'll sooner or later stumble on information about the falcon. Then you'll have to duck for cover with it — no matter where you are — and that's not going to help you make a fortune off it. Give them a fall-guy and they'll stop right there."

"Well, sir, that's just the point," Gutman replied, and still only in his eyes was uneasiness faintly apparent. "Will they stop right there? Or won't the fall-guy be a fresh clue that as likely as not will lead them to information about the falcon? And, on the other hand, wouldn't you say they were stopped right now, and that the best thing for us to do is leave well enough alone?"

A forked vein began to swell in Spade's forehead. "Jesus! you don't know what it's all about either," he said in a restrained tone. "They're not asleep, Gutman. They're lying low, waiting. Try to get that. I'm in it up to my neck and they know it. That's all right as long as I do something when the time comes. But it won't be all right if I don't." His voice became persuasive again. "Listen, Gutman, we've absolutely got to give them a victim. There's no way out of it. Let's give them the punk." He nodded pleasantly at the boy in the doorway. "He actually did shoot both of them — Thursby and Jacobi — didn't he? Anyway, he's made to order for the part. Let's pin the necessary evidence on him and turn him over to them."

The boy in the doorway tightened the corners of his mouth in what may have been a minute smile. Spade's proposal seemed to have no other effect on him. Joel Cairo's dark face was open-mouthed, open-eyed, yellowish, and amazed. He breathed through his mouth, his round effeminate chest rising and falling, while he gaped at Spade. Brigid O'Shaughnessy had moved away from Spade and had twisted herself around on the sofa to stare at him. There was a suggestion of hysterical laughter behind the startled confusion in her face.

Gutman remained still and expressionless for a long moment. Then he decided to laugh. He laughed heartily and lengthily, not stopping until his sleek eyes had borrowed merriment from his laughter. When he stopped laughing he said: "By Gad, sir, you're a character, that you are!" He took a white handkerchief from his pocket and wiped his eyes. "Yes, sir, there's never any telling what you'll do or say next, except that it's bound to be something astonishing."

"There's nothing funny about it." Spade did not seem offended by the fat man's laughter, nor in any way impressed. He spoke in the manner of one reasoning with a recalcitrant, but not altogether unreasonable, friend. "It's our best bet. With him in their hands, the police will —"

"But, my dear man," Gutman objected, "can't you see? If I even for a moment thought of doing it — But that's ridiculous too. I feel towards Wilmer just exactly as if he were my own son. I really do. But if I even for a moment thought of doing what you propose, what in the world do you think would keep Wilmer from telling the police every last detail about the falcon and all of us?"

Spade grinned with stiff lips. "If we had to," he said softly, "we could have him killed resisting arrest. But we won't have to go that far. Let him talk his head off. I promise you nobody'll do anything about it. That's easy enough to fix."

The pink flesh on Gutman's forehead crawled in a frown. He lowered his head, mashing his chins together over his collar, and asked: "How?" Then, with an abruptness that set all his fat bulbs to quivering and tumbling against one another, he raised his head, squirmed around to look at the boy, and laughed uproariously. "What do you think of this, Wilmer? It's funny, eh?"

The boy's eyes were cold hazel gleams under his lashes. He said in a low distinct voice: "Yes, it's funny — the son of a bitch."

Spade was talking to Brigid O'Shaughnessy: "How do you feel now, angel? Any better?"

"Yes, much better, only" — she reduced her voice until the last words would have been unintelligible two feet away — "I'm frightened."

"Don't be," he said carelessly and put a hand on her gray-stockinged knee. "Nothing very bad's going to happen. Want a drink?"

"Not now, thanks." Her voice sank again. "Be careful, Sam."

Spade grinned and looked at Gutman, who was looking at him. The fat man smiled genially, saying nothing for a moment, and then asked: "How?"

Spade was stupid. "How what?"

The fat man considered more laughter necessary then, and an explanation: "Well, sir, if you're really serious about this — this suggestion of yours, the least we can do in common politeness is to hear you out. Now how are you going about fixing it so that Wilmer" — he paused here to laugh again — "won't be able to do us any harm?"

Spade shook his head. "No," he said, "I wouldn't want to take advantage of anybody's politeness, no matter how common, like that. Forget it."

The fat man puckered up his facial bulbs. "Now come, come," he protested, "you make me decidedly uncomfortable. I shouldn't have laughed, and I apologize most humbly and sincerely. I wouldn't want to seem to ridicule anything you'd suggest, Mr. Spade, regardless of how much I disagreed with you, for you must know that I have the greatest respect and admiration for your astuteness. Now mind you, I don't see how this suggestion of yours can be in any way practical — even leaving out the fact that I couldn't feel any different towards Wilmer if he was my own flesh and blood — but I'll consider it a personal favor as well as a sign that you've accepted my apologies, sir, if you'll go ahead and outline the rest of it."

"Fair enough," Spade said. "Bryan is like most district attorneys. He's more interested in how his record will look on paper than anything else. He'd rather drop a doubtful case than try it and have it go against him. I don't know that he ever deliberately framed anybody he believed innocent, but I can't imagine him letting himself believe them innocent if he could scrape up, or twist into shape, proof of their guilt. To be sure of convicting one man he'll let half a dozen equally guilty accomplices go free — if trying to convict them all might confuse his case.

"That's the choice we'll give him and he'll gobble it up. He wouldn't want to know about the falcon. He'll be tickled pink to persuade himself that anything the punk tells him about it is a lot of chewing-gum, an attempt to muddle things up. Leave that end to me. I can show him that if he starts fooling around trying to gather up everybody he's going to have a tangled case that no jury will be able to make heads or tails of, while if he sticks to the punk he can get a conviction standing on his head."

Gutman wagged his head sidewise in a slow smiling gesture of benign disapproval. "No, sir," he said, "I'm afraid that won't do, won't do at all. I don't see how even this District Attorney of yours can link Thursby and Jacobi and Wilmer together without having to —"

"You don't know district attorneys," Spade told him. "The Thursby angle is easy. He was a gunman and so's your punk. Bryan's already got a theory about that. There'll be no catch there. Well, Christ! they can only hang the punk once. Why try him for Jacobi's murder after he's been convicted of Thursby's? They simply close the record by writing it up against him and let it go at that. If, as is likely enough, he used the same gun on both, the bullets will match up.

Everybody will be satisfied."

"Yes, but —" Gutman began, and stopped to look at the boy.

The boy advanced from the doorway, walking stiff-legged, with his legs apart, until he was between Gutman and Cairo, almost in the center of the floor. He halted there, leaning forward slightly from the waist, his shoulders raised towards the front. The pistol in his hand still hung at his side, but his knuckles were white over its grip. His other hand was a small hard fist down at his other side. The indelible youngness of his face gave an indescribably vicious — and inhuman — turn to the white-hot hatred and the cold white malevolence in his face. He said to Spade in a voice cramped by passion: "You bastard, get up on your feet and go for your heater!"

Spade smiled at the boy. His smile was not broad, but the amusement in it seemed genuine and unalloyed.

The boy said: "You bastard, get up and shoot it out if you've got the guts. I've taken all the riding from you I'm going to take."

The amusement in Spade's smile deepened. He looked at Gutman and said: "Young Wild West." His voice matched his smile. "Maybe you ought to tell him that shooting me before you get your hands on the falcon would be bad for business."

Gutman's attempt at a smile was not successful, but he kept the resultant grimace on his mottled face. He licked dry lips with a dry tongue. His voice was too hoarse and gritty for the paternally admonishing tone it tried to achieve. "Now, now, Wilmer," he said, "we can't have any of that. You shouldn't let yourself attach so much importance to these things. You —"

The boy, not taking his eyes from Spade, spoke in a choked voice out the side of his mouth: "Make him lay off me then. I'm going to fog him if he keeps it up and there won't be anything that'll stop me from doing it."

"Now, Wilmer," Gutman said and turned to Spade. His face and voice were under control now. "Your plan is, sir, as I said in the first place, not at all practical. Let's not say anything more about it."

Spade looked from one of them to the other. He had stopped smiling. His face held no expression at all. "I say what I please," he told them.

"You certainly do," Gutman said quickly, "and that's one of the things I've always admired in you. But this matter is, as I say, not at all practical, so there's not the least bit of use of discussing it any further, as you can see for yourself."

"I can't see it for myself," Spade said, "and you haven't made me see it, and I don't think you can." He frowned at Gutman. "Let's get this straight. Am I wasting time talking to you? I thought this was your show. Should I do my talking to the punk? I know how to do that."

"No, sir," Gutman replied, "you're quite right in dealing with me."

Spade said: "All right. Now I've got another suggestion. It's not as good as the first, but it's better than nothing. Want to hear it?"

"Most assuredly."

"Give them Cairo."

Cairo hastily picked up his pistol from the table beside him. He held it tight in his lap with both hands. Its muzzle pointed at the floor a little to one side of the sofa. His face had become yellowish again. His black eyes darted their gaze from face to face. The opaqueness of his eyes made them seem flat, two-dimensional.

Gutman, looking as if he could not believe he had heard what he had heard, asked: "Do what?"

"Give the police Cairo."

Gutman seemed about to laugh, but he did not laugh. Finally, he exclaimed: "Well, by Gad, sir!" in an uncertain tone.

"It's not as good as giving them the punk," Spade said. "Cairo's not a gunman and he carries a smaller gun than Thursby and Jacobi were shot with. We'll have to go to more trouble framing him, but that's better than not giving the police anybody."

Cairo cried in a voice shrill with indignation: "Suppose we give them you, Mr. Spade, or Miss O'Shaughnessy? How about that if you're so set on giving them somebody?"

Spade smiled at the Levantine and answered him evenly: "You people want the falcon. I've got it. A fall-guy is part of the price I'm asking. As for Miss O'Shaughnessy" — his dispassionate glance moved to her white perplexed face and then back to Cairo and his shoulders rose and fell a fraction of an inch — "if you think she can be rigged for the part I'm perfectly willing to discuss it with you."

The girl put her hands to her throat, uttered a short strangled cry, and moved farther away from him.

Cairo, his face and body twitching with excitement, exclaimed: "You seem to forget that you are not in a position to insist on anything."

Spade laughed, a harsh derisive snort.

Gutman said, in a voice that tried to make firmness ingratiating: "Come now, gentlemen, let's keep our discussion on a friendly basis; but there certainly is" — he was addressing Spade — "something in what Mr. Cairo says. You must take into consideration the —"

"Like hell I must." Spade flung his words out with a brutal sort of carelessness that gave them more weight than they could have got from dramatic emphasis or from loudness. "If you kill me, how are you going to get the bird? If I know you can't afford to kill me till you have it, how are you going to scare me into giving it to you?"

Gutman cocked his head to the left and considered these questions. His eyes twinkled between puckered lids. Presently he gave his genial answer: "Well, sir, there are other means of persuasion besides killing and threatening to kill."

"Sure," Spade agreed, "but they're not much good unless the threat of death is behind them to hold the victim down. See what I mean? If you try anything I don't like I won't stand for it. I'll make it a matter of your having to call it off or kill me, knowing you can't afford to kill me."

"I see what you mean." Gutman chuckled. "That is an attitude, sir, that calls for the most delicate judgment on both sides, because, as you know, sir, men are likely to forget in the heat of action where their best interest lies and let their emotions carry them away."

Spade too was all smiling blandness. "That's the trick, from my side," he said, "to make my play strong enough that it ties you up, but yet not make you mad enough to bump me off against your better judgment."

Gutman said fondly: "By Gad, sir, you are a character!"

Joel Cairo jumped up from his chair and went around behind the boy and behind Gutman's chair. He bent over the back of Gutman's chair and, screening his mouth and the fat man's ear with his empty hand, whispered. Gutman listened attentively, shutting his eyes.

Spade grinned at Brigid O'Shaughnessy. Her lips smiled feebly in response, but there was no change in her eyes; they did not lose their numb stare. Spade turned to the boy: "Two to one they're selling you out, son."

The boy did not say anything. A trembling in his knees began to shake the knees of his trousers.

Spade addressed Gutman: "I hope you're not letting yourself be influenced by the guns these pocket-edition desperadoes are waving."

Gutman opened his eyes. Cairo stopped whispering and stood erect behind the fat man's chair.

Spade said: "I've practiced taking them away from both of them, so there'll be no trouble there. The punk is —"

In a voice choked horribly by emotion the boy cried, "All right!" and jerked his pistol up in front of his chest.

Gutman flung a fat hand out at the boy's wrist, caught the wrist, and bore it and the gun down while Gutman's fat body was rising in haste from the rocking chair. Joel Cairo scurried around to the boy's other side and grasped his other arm. They wrestled with the boy, forcing his arms down, holding them down, while he struggled futilely against them. Words came out of the struggling group: fragments of the boy's incoherent speech — "right . . . go . . . bastard . . . smoke" — Gutman's "Now, now, Wilmer!" repeated many times; Cairo's "No, please, don't" and "Don't do that, Wilmer."

Wooden-faced, dreamy-eyed, Spade got up from the sofa and went over to the group. The boy, unable to cope with the weight against him, had stopped struggling.

Cairo, still holding the boy's arm, stood partly in front of him, talking to him soothingly. Spade pushed Cairo aside gently and drove his left fist against the boy's chin. The boy's head snapped back as far as it could while his arms were held, and then came forward. Gutman began a desperate "Here, what — ?" Spade drove his right fist against the boy's chin.

Cairo dropped the boy's arm, letting him collapse against Gutman's great round belly. Cairo sprang at Spade, clawing at his face with the curved stiff fingers of both hands. Spade blew his breath out and pushed the Levantine away. Cairo sprang at him again. Tears were in Cairo's eyes and his red lips worked angrily, forming words, but no sound came from between them.

Spade laughed, grunted, "Jesus, you're a pip!" and cuffed the side of Cairo's face with an open hand, knocking him over against the table. Cairo regained his balance and sprang at Spade the third time. Spade stopped him with both palms held out on long rigid arms against his face. Cairo, failing to reach Spade's face with his shorter arms, thumped Spade's arms.

"Stop it," Spade growled. "I'll hurt you."

Cairo cried, "Oh, you big coward!" and backed away from him.

Spade stooped to pick up Cairo's pistol from the floor, and then the boy's. He straightened up holding them in his left hand, dangling them upside-down by their trigger-guards from his forefinger.

Gutman had put the boy in the rocking chair and stood looking at him with troubled eyes in an uncertainly puckered face. Cairo went down on his knees beside the chair and began to chafe one of the boy's limp hands.

Spade felt the boy's chin with his fingers. "Nothing cracked," he said. "We'll spread him on the sofa." He put his right arm under the boy's arm and around his back, put his left forearm under the boy's knees, lifted him without apparent effort, and carried him to the sofa.

Brigid O'Shaughnessy got up quickly and Spade laid the boy there. With his right hand Spade patted the boy's clothes, found his second pistol, added it to the others in his left hand, and turned his back on the sofa. Cairo was already sitting beside the boy's head.

Spade clinked the pistols together in his hand and smiled cheerfully at Gutman. "Well," he said, "there's our fall-guy."

Gutman's face was gray and his eyes were clouded. He did not look at Spade. He looked at the floor and did not say anything.

Spade said: "Don't be a damned fool again. You let Cairo whisper to you and you held the kid while I pasted him. You can't laugh that off and you're likely to get yourself shot trying to."

Gutman moved his feet on the rug and said nothing.

Spade said: "And the other side of it is that you'll either say yes right now or I'll turn the falcon and the whole Goddamned lot of you in."

Gutman raised his head and muttered through his teeth: "I don't like that, sir."

"You won't like it," Spade said. "Well?"

The fat man sighed and made a wry face and replied sadly: "You can have him."

Spade said: "That's swell."

19
The Russian's Hand

The boy lay on his back on the sofa, a small figure that was — except for its breathing — altogether corpse-like to the eye. Joel Cairo sat beside the boy, bending over him, rubbing his cheeks and wrists, smoothing his hair back from his forehead, whispering to him, and peering anxiously down at his white still face.

Brigid O'Shaughnessy stood in an angle made by table and wall. One of her hands was flat on the table, the other to her breast. She pinched her lower lip between her teeth and glanced furtively at Spade whenever he was not looking at her. When he looked at her she looked at Cairo and the boy.

Gutman's face had lost its troubled cast and was becoming rosy again. He had put his hands in his trousers-pockets. He stood facing Spade, watching him without curiosity.

Spade, idly jingling his handful of pistols,

nodded at Cairo's rounded back and asked Gutman: "It'll be all right with him?"

"I don't know," the fat man replied placidly. "That part will have to be strictly up to you, sir."

Spade's smile made his v-shaped chin more salient. He said: "Cairo."

The Levantine screwed his dark anxious face around over his shoulder.

Spade said: "Let him rest awhile. We're going to give him to the police. We ought to get the details fixed before he comes to."

Cairo asked bitterly: "Don't you think you've done enough to him without that?"

Spade said: "No."

Cairo left the sofa and went close to the fat man. "Please don't do this thing, Mr. Gutman," he begged. "You must realize that —"

Spade interrupted him: "That's settled. The question is, what are you going to do about it? Coming in? Or getting out?"

Though Gutman's smile was a bit sad, even wistful in its way, he nodded his head. "I don't like it either," he told the Levantine, "but we can't help ourselves now. We really can't."

Spade asked: "What are you doing, Cairo? In or out?"

Cairo wet his lips and turned slowly to

face Spade. "Suppose," he said, and swallowed. "Have I — ? Can I choose?"

"You can," Spade assured him seriously, "but you ought to know that if the answer is *out* we'll give you to the police with your boy-friend."

"Oh, come, Mr. Spade," Gutman protested, "that is not —"

"Like hell we'll let him walk out on us," Spade said. "He'll either come in or he'll go in. We can't have a lot of loose ends hanging around." He scowled at Gutman and burst out irritably: "Jesus God! is this the first thing you guys ever stole? You're a fine lot of lollipops! What are you going to do next — get down and pray?" He directed his scowl at Cairo. "Well? Which?"

"You give me no choice." Cairo's narrow shoulders moved in a hopeless shrug. "I come in."

"Good," Spade said and looked at Gutman and at Brigid O'Shaughnessy. "Sit down."

The girl sat down gingerly on the end of the sofa by the unconscious boy's feet. Gutman returned to the padded rocking chair, and Cairo to the armchair. Spade put his handful of pistols on the table and sat on the table-corner beside them. He looked at the watch on his wrist and said: "Two o'clock. I can't get the falcon till daylight, or maybe eight o'clock. We've got plenty of time to arrange everything."

Gutman cleared his throat. "Where is it?" he asked and then added in haste: "I don't really care, sir. What I had in mind was that it would be best for all concerned if we did not get out of each other's sight until our business has been transacted." He looked at the sofa and at Spade again, sharply. "You have the envelope?"

Spade shook his head, looking at the sofa and then at the girl. He smiled with his eyes and said: "Miss O'Shaughnessy has it."

"Yes, I have it," she murmured, putting a hand inside her coat. "I picked it up. . . ."

"That's all right," Spade told her. "Hang on to it." He addressed Gutman: "We won't have to lose sight of each other. I can have the falcon brought here."

"That will be excellent," Gutman purred. "Then, sir, in exchange for the ten thousand dollars and Wilmer you will give us the falcon and an hour or two of grace — so we won't be in the city when you surrender him to the authorities."

"You don't have to duck," Spade said. "It'll be air-tight."

"That may be, sir, but nevertheless we'll feel safer well out of the city when Wilmer is being questioned by your District Attorney."

"Suit yourself," Spade replied. "I can hold him here all day if you want." He began to roll a cigarette. "Let's get the details fixed. Why did he shoot Thursby? And why and where and how did he shoot Jacobi?"

Gutman smiled indulgently, shaking his head and purring: "Now come, sir, you can't expect that. We've given you the money and Wilmer. That is our part of the agreement."

"I do expect it," Spade said. He held his lighter to his cigarette. "A fall-guy is what I asked for, and he's not a fall-guy unless he's a cinch to take the fall. Well, to cinch that I've got to know what's what." He pulled his brows together. "What are you belly-aching about? You're not going to be sitting so damned pretty if you leave him with an out."

Gutman leaned forward and wagged a fat finger at the pistols on the table beside Spade's legs. "There's ample evidence of his guilt, sir. Both men were shot with those weapons. It's a very simple matter for the police-department-experts to determine that the bullets that killed the men were fired from those weapons. You know that; you've mentioned it yourself. And that, it seems to me, is ample proof of his guilt."

"Maybe," Spade agreed, "but the thing's more complicated than that and I've got to know what happened so I can be sure the parts that won't fit in are covered up."

Cairo's eyes were round and hot. "Apparently you've forgotten that you assured us it would be a very simple affair," Cairo said. He turned his excited dark face to Gutman. "You see! I advised you not to do this. I don't think —"

"It doesn't make a damned bit of difference what either of you think," Spade said bluntly. "It's too late for that now and you're in too deep. Why did he kill Thursby?"

Gutman interlaced his fingers over his belly and rocked his chair. His voice, like his smile, was frankly rueful. "You are an uncommonly difficult person to get the best of," he said. "I begin to think that we made a mistake in not letting you alone from the very first. By Gad, I do, sir!"

Spade moved his hand carelessly. "You haven't done so bad. You're staying out of jail and you're getting the falcon. What do you want?" He put his cigarette in a corner of his mouth and said around it: "Anyhow you know where you stand now. Why did he kill Thursby?"

Gutman stopped rocking. "Thursby was a notorious killer and Miss O'Shaughnessy's ally. We knew that removing him in just that manner would make her stop and think that perhaps it would be best to patch up her differences with us after all, besides leaving her without so violent a protector. You see, sir, I am being candid with you?"

"Yes. Keep it up. You didn't think he might have the falcon?"

Gutman shook his head so that his round cheeks wobbled. "We didn't think that for a minute," he replied. He smiled benevolently. "We had the advantage of knowing Miss O'Shaughnessy far too well for that and, while we didn't know then that she had given the falcon to Captain Jacobi in Hongkong to be brought over on the *Paloma* while they took a faster boat, still we didn't for a minute think that, if only one of them knew where it was, Thursby was the one."

Spade nodded thoughtfully and asked: "You didn't try to make a deal with him before you gave him the works?"

"Yes, sir, we certainly did. I talked to him myself that night. Wilmer had located him two days before and had been trying to follow him to wherever he was meeting Miss O'Shaughnessy, but Thursby was too crafty for that even if he didn't know he was being watched. So that night Wilmer went to his hotel, learned he wasn't in, and waited outside for him. I suppose Thursby returned immediately after killing your partner. Be that as it may, Wilmer brought him to see me. We could do nothing with him. He was quite determinedly loyal to Miss O'Shaughnessy. Well, sir, Wilmer followed him back to his hotel and did what he did."

Spade thought for a moment. "That sounds all right. Now Jacobi."

Gutman looked at Spade with grave eyes and said: "Captain Jacobi's death was entirely Miss O'Shaughnessy's fault."

The girl gasped, "Oh!" and put a hand to her mouth.

Spade's voice was heavy and even. "Never mind that now. Tell me what happened."

After a shrewd look at Spade, Gutman smiled. "Just as you say, sir," he said. "Well, Cairo, as you know, got in touch with me — I sent for him — after he left police headquarters the night — or morning — he was up here. We recognized the mutual advantage of pooling forces." He directed his smile at the Levantine. "Mr. Cairo is a man of nice judgment. The *Paloma* was his thought. He saw the notice of its arrival in the papers that morning and remembered that he had heard in Hongkong that Jacobi and Miss O'Shaughnessy had been seen together. That was when he had been trying to find her there, and he thought at first that she had left on the *Paloma,* though later he learned that she hadn't. Well, sir, when he saw the notice of arrival in the paper he guessed just what had happened: she had given the bird to Jacobi to bring here for her. Jacobi did not know what it was, of course. Miss O'Shaughnessy is too discreet for that."

He beamed at the girl, rocked his chair twice, and went on: "Mr. Cairo and Wilmer and I went to call on Captain Jacobi and were fortunate enough to arrive while Miss O'Shaughnessy was there. In many ways it was a difficult conference, but finally, by midnight we had persuaded Miss O'Shaughnessy to come to terms, or so we thought. We then left the boat and set out for my hotel, where I was to pay Miss O'Shaughnessy and receive the bird. Well, sir, we mere men should have known better than to suppose ourselves capable of coping with her. *En route,* she and Captain Jacobi and the falcon slipped completely through our fingers." He laughed merrily. "By Gad, sir, it was neatly done."

Spade looked at the girl. Her eyes, large and dark with pleading, met his. He asked

Gutman: "You touched off the boat before you left?"

"Not intentionally, no, sir," the fat man replied, "though I dare say we — or Wilmer at least — were responsible for the fire. He had been out trying to find the falcon while the rest of us were talking in the cabin and no doubt was careless with matches."

"That's fine," Spade said. "If any slip-up makes it necessary for us to try him for Jacobi's murder we can also hang an arson-rap on him. All right. Now about the shooting."

"Well, sir, we dashed around town all day trying to find them and we found them late this afternoon. We weren't sure at first that we'd found them. All we were sure of was that we'd found Miss O'Shaughnessy's apartment. But when we listened at the door we heard them moving around inside, so we were pretty confident we had them and rang the bell. When she asked us who we were and we told her — through the door — we heard a window going up.

"We knew what that meant, of course; so Wilmer hurried downstairs as fast as he could and around to the rear of the building to cover the fire-escape. And when he turned into the alley he ran right plumb smack into Captain Jacobi running away with the falcon under his arm. That was a difficult situation to handle, but Wilmer did every bit as well as he could. He shot Jacobi — more than once — but Jacobi was too tough to either fall or drop the falcon, and he was too close for Wilmer to keep out of his way. He knocked Wilmer down and ran on. And this was in broad daylight, you understand, in the afternoon. When Wilmer got up he could see a policeman coming up from the block below. So he had to give it up. He dodged into the open back door of the building next the Coronet, through into the street, and then up to join us — and very fortunate he was, sir, to make it without being seen.

"Well, sir, there we were — stumped again. Miss O'Shaughnessy had opened the door for Mr. Cairo and me after she had shut the window behind Jacobi, and she —" He broke off to smile at a memory. "We persuaded — that is the word, sir — her to tell us that she had told Jacobi to take the falcon to you. It seemed very unlikely that he'd live to go that far, even if the police didn't pick him up, but that was the only chance we had, sir. And so, once more, we persuaded Miss O'Shaughnessy to give us a little assistance. We — well — persuaded her to phone your office in an attempt to draw you away before Jacobi got there, and we sent Wilmer after him. Unfortunately it had taken us too long to decide and to persuade Miss O'Shaughnessy to —"

The boy on the sofa groaned and rolled over on his side. His eyes opened and closed several times. The girl stood up and moved into the angle of table and wall again.

"— cooperate with us," Gutman concluded hurriedly, "and so you had the falcon before we could reach you."

The boy put one foot on the floor, raised himself on an elbow, opened his eyes wide, put the other foot down, sat up, and looked around. When his eyes focused on Spade bewilderment went out of them.

Cairo left his armchair and went over to the boy. He put his arm on the boy's shoulders and started to say something. The boy rose quickly to his feet, shaking Cairo's arm off. He glanced around the room once and then fixed his eyes on Spade again. His face was set hard and he held his body so tense that it seemed drawn in and shrunken.

Spade, sitting on the corner of the table, swinging his legs carelessly, said: "Now listen, kid. If you come over here and start cutting up I'm going to kick you in the face. Sit down and shut up and behave and you'll last longer."

The boy looked at Gutman.

Gutman smiled benignly at him and said: "Well, Wilmer, I'm sorry indeed to lose you, and I want you to know that I couldn't be any fonder of you if you were my own son; but — well, by Gad! — if you lose a son it's possible to get another — and there's only one Maltese falcon."

Spade laughed.

Cairo moved over and whispered in the boy's ear. The boy, keeping his cold hazel eyes on Gutman's face, sat down on the sofa again. The Levantine sat beside him.

Gutman's sigh did not affect the benignity of his smile. He said to Spade: "When you're young you simply don't understand things."

Cairo had an arm around the boy's shoulders again and was whispering to him. Spade grinned at Gutman and addressed Brigid O'Shaughnessy: "I think it'd be swell if you'd see what you can find us to eat in the kitchen, with plenty of coffee. Will you? I don't like to leave my guests."

"Surely," she said and started towards the door.

Gutman stopped rocking. "Just a moment, my dear." He held up a thick hand. "Hadn't you better leave the envelope in here? You don't want to get grease-spots on it."

The girl's eyes questioned Spade. He said in an indifferent tone: "It's still his."

She put her hand inside her coat, took out the envelope, and gave it to Spade. Spade tossed it into Gutman's lap, saying: "Sit on it if you're afraid of losing it."

"You misunderstand me," Gutman replied suavely. "It's not that at all, but business should be transacted in a business-like manner." He opened the flap of the envelope, took out the thousand-dollar bills, counted them, and chuckled so that his belly bounced. "For instance there are only nine bills here now." He spread them out on his fat knees and thighs. "There were ten when I handed it to you, as you very well know." His smile was broad and jovial and triumphant.

Spade looked at Brigid O'Shaughnessy and asked: "Well?"

She shook her head sidewise with emphasis. She did not say anything, though her lips moved slightly, as if she had tried to. Her face was frightened.

Spade held his hand out to Gutman and the fat man put the money into it. Spade counted the money — nine thousand-dollar bills — and returned it to Gutman. Then Spade stood up and his face was dull and placid. He picked up the three pistols on the table. He spoke in a matter-of-fact voice. "I want to know about this. We" — he nodded at the girl, but without looking at her — "are going in the bathroom. The door will be open and I'll be facing it. Unless you want a three-story drop there's no way out of here except past the bathroom door. Don't try to make it."

"Really, sir," Gutman protested, "it's not necessary, and certainly not very courteous of you, to threaten us in this manner. You must know that we've not the least desire to leave."

"I'll know a lot when I'm through." Spade was patient but resolute. "This trick upsets things. I've got to find the answer. It won't take long." He touched the girl's elbow. "Come on."

In the bathroom Brigid O'Shaughnessy found words. She put her hands up flat on Spade's chest and her face up close to his and whispered: "I did not take that bill, Sam."

"I don't think you did," he said, "but I've got to know. Take your clothes off."

"You won't take my word for it?"

"No. Take your clothes off."

"I won't."

"All right. We'll go back to the other room

and I'll have them taken off."

She stepped back with a hand to her mouth. Her eyes were round and horrified. "You would?" she asked through her fingers.

"I will," he said. "I've got to know what happened to that bill and I'm not going to be held up by anybody's maidenly modesty."

"Oh, it isn't that." She came close to him and put her hands on his chest again. "I'm not ashamed to be naked before you, but — can't you see? — not like this. Can't you see that if you make me you'll — you'll be killing something?"

He did not raise his voice. "I don't know anything about that. I've got to know what happened to the bill. Take them off."

She looked at his unblinking yellow-gray eyes and her face became pink and then white again. She drew herself up tall and began to undress. He sat on the side of the bathtub watching her and the open door. No sound came from the living-room. She removed her clothes swiftly, without fumbling, letting them fall down on the floor around her feet. When she was naked she stepped back from her clothing and stood looking at him. In her mien was pride without defiance or embarrassment.

He put his pistols on the toilet-seat and, facing the door, went down on one knee in front of her garments. He picked up each piece and examined it with fingers as well as eyes. He did not find the thousand-dollar bill. When he had finished he stood up holding her clothes out in his hands to her. "Thanks," he said. "Now I know."

She took the clothing from him. She did not say anything. He picked up his pistols. He shut the bathroom-door behind him and went into the living-room.

Gutman smiled amiably at him from the rocking chair. "Find it?" he asked.

Cairo, sitting beside the boy on the sofa, looked at Spade with questioning opaque eyes. The boy did not look up. He was leaning forward, head between hands, elbows on knees, staring at the floor between his feet.

Spade told Gutman: "No, I didn't find it. You palmed it."

The fat man chuckled. "I palmed it?"

"Yes," Spade said, jingling the pistols in his hand. "Do you want to say so or do you want to stand for a frisk?"

"Stand for — ?"

"You're going to admit it," Spade said, "or I'm going to search you. There's no third way."

Gutman looked up at Spade's hard face and laughed outright. "By Gad, sir, I believe you would. I really do. You're a character, sir, if you don't mind my saying so."

"You palmed it," Spade said.

"Yes, sir, that I did." The fat man took a crumpled bill from his vest-pocket, smoothed it on a wide thigh, took the envelope holding the nine bills from his coat-pocket, and put the smoothed bill in with the others. "I must have my little joke every now and then and I was curious to know what you'd do in a situation of that sort. I must say that you passed the test with flying colors, sir. It never occurred to me that you'd hit on such a simple and direct way of getting at the truth."

Spade sneered at him without bitterness. "That's the kind of thing I'd expect from somebody the punk's age."

Gutman chuckled.

Brigid O'Shaughnessy, dressed again except for coat and hat, came out of the bathroom, took a step towards the living-room, turned around, went to the kitchen, and turned on the light.

Cairo edged closer to the boy on the sofa and began whispering in his ear again. The boy shrugged irritably.

Spade, looking at the pistols in his hand and then at Gutman, went out into the passageway, to the closet there. He opened the door, put the pistols inside on the top of a trunk, shut the door, locked it, put the key in his trousers-pocket, and went to the kitchen-door.

Brigid O'Shaughnessy was filling an aluminum percolator.

"Find everything?" Spade asked.

"Yes," she replied in a cool voice, not raising her head. Then she set the percolator aside and came to the door. She blushed and her eyes were large and moist and chiding. "You shouldn't have done that to me, Sam," she said softly.

"I had to find out, angel." He bent down, kissed her mouth lightly, and returned to the living-room.

Gutman smiled at Spade and offered him the white envelope, saying: "This will soon be yours; you might as well take it now."

Spade did not take it. He sat in the armchair and said: "There's plenty of time for that. We haven't done enough talking about the money-end. I ought to have more than ten thousand."

Gutman said: "Ten thousand dollars is a lot of money."

Spade said: "You're quoting me, but it's not all the money in the world."

"No, sir, it's not. I grant you that. But it's

a lot of money to be picked up in as few days and as easily as you're getting it."

"You think it's been so damned easy?" Spade asked, and shrugged. "Well, maybe, but that's my business."

"It certainly is," the fat man agreed. He screwed up his eyes, moved his head to indicate the kitchen, and lowered his voice. "Are you sharing with her?"

Spade said: "That's my business too."

"It certainly is," the fat man agreed once more, "but" — he hesitated — "I'd like to give you a word of advice."

"Go ahead."

"If you don't — I dare say you'll give her some money in any event, but — if you don't give her as much as she thinks she ought to have, my word of advice is — be careful."

Spade's eyes held a mocking light. He asked: "Bad?"

"Bad," the fat man replied.

Spade grinned and began to roll a cigarette.

Cairo, still muttering in the boy's ear, had put his arm around the boy's shoulders again. Suddenly the boy pushed his arm away and turned on the sofa to face the Levantine. The boy's face held disgust and anger. He made a fist of one small hand and struck Cairo's mouth with it. Cairo cried out as a woman might have cried and drew back to the very end of the sofa. He took a silk handkerchief from his pocket and put it to his mouth. It came away daubed with blood. He put it to his mouth once more and looked reproachfully at the boy. The boy snarled, "Keep away from me," and put his face between his hands again. Cairo's handkerchief released the fragrance of *chypre* in the room.

Cairo's cry had brought Brigid O'Shaughnessy to the door. Spade, grinning, jerked a thumb at the sofa and told her: "The course of true love. How's the food coming along?"

"It's coming," she said and went back to the kitchen.

Spade lighted his cigarette and addressed Gutman: "Let's talk about money."

"Willingly, sir, with all my heart," the fat man replied, "but I might as well tell you frankly right now that ten thousand is every cent I can raise."

Spade exhaled smoke. "I ought to have twenty."

"I wish you could. I'd give it to you gladly if I had it, but ten thousand dollars is every cent I can manage, on my word of honor. Of course, sir, you understand that is simply the first payment. Later —"

Spade laughed. "I know you'll give me millions later," he said, "but let's stick to this first payment now. Fifteen thousand?"

Gutman smiled and frowned and shook his head. "Mr. Spade, I've told you frankly and candidly and on my word of honor as a gentleman that ten thousand dollars is all the money I've got — every penny — and all I can raise."

"But you don't say positively."

Gutman laughed and said: "Positively."

Spade said gloomily: "That's not any too good, but if it's the best you can do — give it to me."

Gutman handed him the envelope. Spade counted the bills and was putting them in his pocket when Brigid O'Shaughnessy came in carrying a tray.

The boy would not eat. Cairo took a cup of coffee. The girl, Gutman, and Spade ate the scrambled eggs, bacon, toast, and marmalade she had prepared, and drank two cups of coffee apiece. Then they settled down to wait the rest of the night through.

Gutman smoked a cigar and read *Celebrated Criminal Cases of America,* now and then chuckling over or commenting on the parts of its contents that amused him. Cairo nursed his mouth and sulked on his end of the sofa. The boy sat with his head in his hands until a little after four o'clock. Then he lay down with his feet towards Cairo, turned his face to the window, and went to sleep. Brigid O'Shaughnessy, in the armchair, dozed, listened to the fat man's comments, and carried on wide-spaced desultory conversations with Spade.

Spade rolled and smoked cigarettes and moved, without fidgeting or nervousness, around the room. He sat sometimes on an arm of the girl's chair, on the table-corner, on the floor at her feet, on a straight-backed chair. He was wide-awake, cheerful, and full of vigor.

At half-past five he went into the kitchen and made more coffee. Half an hour later the boy stirred, awakened, and sat up yawning. Gutman looked at his watch and questioned Spade: "Can you get it now?"

"Give me another hour."

Gutman nodded and went back to his book.

At seven o'clock Spade went to the telephone and called Effie Perine's number. "Hello, Mrs. Perine? . . . This is Mr. Spade. Will you let me talk to Effie, please? . . . Yes, it is. . . . Thanks." He whistled two lines of *En Cuba,* softly. "Hello, angel. Sorry to get you up. . . . Yes, very. Here's the plot: in our Holland box at the Post Office you'll find an envelope addressed in my scribble. There's a Pickwick Stage parcel-room-check in it — for the bundle we got yesterday. Will you get the bundle and bring it to me — p. d. q.? . . . Yes, I'm home. . . . That's the girl — hustle. . . . 'Bye."

The street-door-bell rang at ten minutes of eight. Spade went to the telephone-box and pressed the button that released the lock. Gutman put down his book and rose smiling. "You don't mind if I go to the door with you?" he asked.

"OK," Spade told him.

Gutman followed him to the corridor-door. Spade opened it. Presently Effie Perine, carrying the brown-wrapped parcel, came from the elevator. Her boyish face was gay and bright and she came forward quickly, almost trotting. After one glance she did not look at Gutman. She smiled at Spade and gave him the parcel.

He took it saying: "Thanks a lot, lady. I'm sorry to spoil your day of rest, but this —"

"It's not the first one you've spoiled," she replied, laughing, and then, when it was apparent that he was not going to invite her in, asked: "Anything else?"

He shook his head. "No, thanks."

She said, "Bye-bye," and went back to the elevator.

Spade shut the door and carried the parcel into the living-room. Gutman's face was red and his cheeks quivered. Cairo and Brigid O'Shaughnessy came to the table as Spade put the parcel there. They were excited. The boy rose, pale and tense, but he remained by the sofa, staring under curling lashes at the others.

Spade stepped back from the table saying: "There you are."

Gutman's fat fingers made short work of cord and paper and excelsior, and he had the black bird in his hands. "Ah," he said huskily, "now, after seventeen years!" His eyes were moist.

Cairo licked his red lips and worked his hands together. The girl's lower lip was between her teeth. She and Cairo, like Gutman, and like Spade and the boy, were breathing heavily. The air in the room was chilly and stale, and thick with tobacco smoke.

Gutman set the bird down on the table again and fumbled at a pocket. "It's it," he said, "but we'll make sure." Sweat glistened on his round cheeks. His fingers twitched as he took out a gold pocket-knife and opened it.

Cairo and the girl stood close to him, one on either side. Spade stood back a little where he could watch the boy as well as the group at the table.

Gutman turned the bird upside-down and scraped an edge of its base with his knife. Black enamel came off in a tiny curl, exposing blackened metal beneath. Gutman's knife-blade bit into the metal, turning back a thin curved shaving. The inside of the shaving, and the narrow plane its removal had left, had the soft gray sheen of lead.

Gutman's breath hissed between his teeth. His face became turgid with hot blood. He twisted the bird around and hacked at its head. There too the edge of his knife bared lead. He let knife and bird bang down on the table where he wheeled to confront Spade. "It's a fake," he said hoarsely.

Spade's face had become somber. His nod was slow, but there was no slowness in his hand's going out to catch Brigid O'Shaughnessy's wrist. He pulled her to him and grasped her chin with his other hand, raising her face roughly. "All right," he growled into her face. "You've had *your* little joke. Now tell us about it."

She cried: "No, Sam, no! That is the one I got from Kemidov. I swear —"

Joel Cairo thrust himself between Spade

and Gutman and began to emit words in a shrill spluttering stream: "That's it! That's it! It was the Russian! I should have known! What a fool we thought him, and what fools he made of us!" Tears ran down the Levantine's cheeks and he danced up and down. "You bungled it!" he screamed at Gutman. "You and your stupid attempt to buy it from him! You fat fool! You let him know it was valuable and he found out how valuable and made a duplicate for us! No wonder we had so little trouble stealing it! No wonder he was so willing to send me off around the world looking for it! You imbecile! You bloated idiot!" He put his hands to his face and blubbered.

Gutman's jaw sagged. He blinked vacant eyes. Then he shook himself and was — by the time his bulbs had stopped jouncing — again a jovial fat man. "Come, sir," he said good-naturedly, "there's no need of going on like that. Everybody errs at times and you may be sure this is every bit as severe a blow to me as to anyone else. Yes, that is the Russian's hand, there's no doubt of it. Well, sir, what do you suggest? Shall we stand here and shed tears and call each other names? Or shall we" — he paused and his smile was a cherub's — "go to Constantinople?"

Cairo took his hands from his face and his eyes bulged. He stammered: "You are — ?" Amazement coming with full comprehension made him speechless.

Gutman patted his fat hands together. His eyes twinkled. His voice was a complacent throaty purring: "For seventeen years I have wanted that little item and have been trying to get it. If I must spend another year on the quest — well, sir — that will be an additional expenditure in time of only" — his lips moved silently as he calculated — "five and fifteen-seventeenths per cent."

The Levantine giggled and cried: "I go with you!"

Spade suddenly released the girl's wrist and looked around the room. The boy was not there. Spade went into the passageway. The corridor-door stood open. Spade made a dissatisfied mouth, shut the door, and returned to the living-room. He leaned against the door-frame and looked at Gutman and Cairo. He looked at Gutman for a long time, sourly. Then he spoke, mimicking the fat man's throaty purr: "Well, sir, I must say you're a swell lot of thieves!"

Gutman chuckled. "We've little enough to boast about, and that's a fact, sir," he said. "But, well, we're none of us dead yet and there's not a bit of use thinking the world's come to an end just because we've run into a little setback." He brought his left hand from behind him and held it out towards Spade, pink smooth hilly palm up. "I'll have to ask you for that envelope, sir."

Spade did not move. His face was wooden. He said: "I held up my end. You got your dingus. It's your hard luck, not mine, that it wasn't what you wanted."

"Now come, sir," Gutman said persuasively, "we've all failed and there's no reason for expecting any one of us to bear the brunt of it, and —" He brought his right hand from behind him. In the hand was a small pistol, an ornately engraved and inlaid affair of silver and gold and mother-of-pearl. "In short, sir, I must ask you to return my ten thousand dollars."

Spade's face did not change. He shrugged and took the envelope from his pocket. He started to hold it out to Gutman, hesitated, opened the envelope, and took out one thousand-dollar bill. He put that bill into his trousers-pocket. He tucked the envelope's flap in over the other bills and held them out to Gutman. "That'll take care of my time and expenses," he said.

Gutman, after a little pause, imitated Spade's shrug and accepted the envelope. He said: "Now, sir, we will say good-bye to you, unless" — the fat puffs around his eyes crinkled — "you care to undertake the Constantinople expedition with us. You don't? Well, sir, frankly I'd like to have you along. You're a man to my liking, a man of many resources and nice judgment. Because we know you're a man of nice judgment we know we can say good-bye with every assurance that you'll hold the details of our little enterprise in confidence. We know we can count on you to appreciate the fact that, as the situation now stands, any legal difficulties that come to us in connection with these last few days would likewise and equally come to you and the charming Miss O'Shaughnessy. You're too shrewd not to recognize that, sir, I'm sure."

"I understand that," Spade replied.

"I was sure you would. I'm also sure that, now there's no alternative, you'll somehow manage the police without a fall-guy."

"I'll make out all right," Spade replied.

"I was sure you would. Well, sir, the shortest farewells are the best. Adieu." He made a portly bow. "And to you, Miss O'Shaughnessy, adieu. I leave you the *rara avis* on the table as a little memento."

20
If They Hang You

For all of five minutes after the outer door had closed behind Casper Gutman and Joel Cairo, Spade, motionless, stood staring at the knob of the open living-room-door. His eyes were gloomy under a forehead drawn down. The clefts at the root of his nose were deep and red. His lips protruded loosely, pouting. He drew them in to make a hard v and went to the telephone. He had not looked at Brigid O'Shaughnessy, who stood by the table looking with uneasy eyes at him.

He picked up the telephone, set it on its shelf again, and bent to look into the telephone-directory hanging from a corner of the shelf. He turned the pages rapidly until he found the one he wanted, ran his finger down a column, straightened up, and lifted the telephone from the shelf again. He called a number and said:

"Hello, is Sergeant Polhaus there? . . . Will you call him, please? This is Samuel

Spade. . . ." He stared into space, waiting. "Hello, Tom, I've got something for you. . . . Yes, plenty. Here it is: Thursby and Jacobi were shot by a kid named Wilmer Cook." He described the boy minutely. "He's working for a man named Casper Gutman." He described Gutman. "That fellow Cairo you met here is in with them too. . . . Yes, that's it. . . . Gutman's staying at the Alexandria, suite twelve C, or was. They've just left here and they're blowing town, so you'll have to move fast, but I don't think they're expecting a pinch. . . . There's a girl in it too — Gutman's daughter." He described Rhea Gutman. "Watch yourself when you go up against the kid. He's supposed to be pretty good with the gun. . . . That's right, Tom, and I've got some stuff here for you. I've got the guns he used. . . . That's right. Step on it — and luck to you!"

Spade slowly replaced receiver on prong, telephone on shelf. He wet his lips and looked down at his hands. Their palms were wet. He filled his deep chest with air. His eyes were glittering between straightened lids. He turned and took three long swift steps into the living-room.

Brigid O'Shaughnessy, startled by the suddenness of his approach, let her breath out in a little laughing gasp.

Spade, face to face with her, very close to her, tall, big-boned and thick-muscled, coldly smiling, hard of jaw and eye, said: "They'll talk when they're nailed — about us. We're sitting on dynamite, and we've only got minutes to get set for the police. Give me all of it — fast. Gutman sent you and Cairo to Constantinople?"

She started to speak, hesitated, and bit her lip.

He put a hand on her shoulder. "God damn you, talk!" he said. "I'm in this with you and you're not going to gum it. Talk. He sent you to Constantinople?"

"Y-yes, he sent me. I met Joe there and — and asked him to help me. Then we —"

"Wait. You asked Cairo to help you get it from Kemidov?"

"Yes."

"For Gutman?"

She hesitated again, squirmed under the hard angry glare of his eyes, swallowed, and said: "No, not then. We thought we would get it for ourselves."

"All right. Then?"

"Oh, then I began to be afraid that Joe wouldn't play fair with me, so — so I asked Floyd Thursby to help me."

"And he did. Well?"

"Well, we got it and went to Hongkong."

"With Cairo? Or had you ditched him before that?"

"Yes. We left him in Constantinople, in jail — something about a check."

"Something you fixed up to hold him there?"

She looked shamefacedly at Spade and whispered: "Yes."

"Right. Now you and Thursby are in Hongkong with the bird."

"Yes, and then — I didn't know him very well — I didn't know whether I could trust him. I thought it would be safer — anyway, I met Captain Jacobi and I knew his boat was coming here, so I asked him to bring a package for me — and that was the bird. I wasn't sure I could trust Thursby, or that Joe or — or somebody working for Gutman might not be on the boat we came on — and that seemed the safest plan."

"All right. Then you and Thursby caught one of the fast boats over. Then what?"

"Then — then I was afraid of Gutman. I knew he had people — connections — everywhere, and he'd soon know what we had done. And I was afraid he'd have learned that we had left Hongkong for San Francisco. He was in New York and I knew if he heard that by cable he would have plenty of time to get here by the time we did, or before. He did. I didn't know that then, but I was afraid of it, and I had to wait here until Captain Jacobi's boat arrived. And I was afraid Gutman would find me — or find Floyd and buy him over. That's why I came to you and asked you to watch him for —"

"That's a lie," Spade said. "You had Thursby hooked and you knew it. He was a sucker for women. His record shows that — the only falls he took were over women. And once a chump, always a chump. Maybe you didn't know his record, but you'd know you had him safe."

She blushed and looked timidly at him.

He said: "You wanted to get him out of the way before Jacobi came with the loot. What was your scheme?"

"I — I knew he'd left the States with a gambler after some trouble. I didn't know what it was, but I thought that if it was anything serious and he saw a detective watching him he'd think it was on account of the old trouble, and would be frightened into going away. I didn't think —"

"You told him he was being shadowed," Spade said confidently. "Miles hadn't many brains, but he wasn't clumsy enough to be spotted the first night."

"I told him, yes. When we went out for a

walk that night I pretended to discover Mr. Archer following us and pointed him out to Floyd." She sobbed. "But please believe, Sam, that I wouldn't have done it if I had thought Floyd would kill him. I thought he'd be frightened into leaving the city. I didn't for a minute think he'd shoot him like that."

Spade smiled wolfishly with his lips, but not at all with his eyes. He said: "If you thought he wouldn't you were right, angel."

The girl's upraised face held utter astonishment.

Spade said: "Thursby didn't shoot him."

Incredulity joined astonishment in the girl's face.

Spade said: "Miles hadn't many brains, but, Christ! he had too many years' experience as a detective to be caught like that by the man he was shadowing. Up a blind alley with his gun tucked away on his hip and his overcoat buttoned? Not a chance. He was as dumb as any man ought to be, but he wasn't quite that dumb. The only two ways out of the alley could be watched from the edge of Bush Street over the tunnel. You'd told us Thursby was a bad actor. He couldn't have tricked Miles into the alley like that, and he couldn't have driven him in. He was dumb, but not dumb enough for that."

He ran his tongue over the inside of his lips and smiled affectionately at the girl. He said: "But he'd've gone up there with you, angel, if he was sure nobody else was up there. You were his client, so he would have had no reason for not dropping the shadow on your say-so, and if you caught up with him and asked him to go up there he'd've gone. He was just dumb enough for that. He'd've looked you up and down and licked his lips and gone grinning from ear to ear — and then you could've stood as close to him as you liked in the dark and put a hole through him with the gun you had got from Thursby that evening."

Brigid O'Shaughnessy shrank back from him until the edge of the table stopped her. She looked at him with terrified eyes and cried: "Don't — don't talk to me like that, Sam! You know I didn't! You know —"

"Stop it." He looked at the watch on his wrist. "The police will be blowing in any minute now and we're sitting on dynamite. Talk!"

She put the back of a hand on her forehead. "Oh, why do you accuse me of such a terrible — ?"

"Will you stop it?" he demanded in a low

impatient voice. "This isn't the spot for the schoolgirl-act. Listen to me. The pair of us are sitting under the gallows." He took hold of her wrists and made her stand up straight in front of him. "Talk!"

"I — I — How did you know he — he licked his lips and looked — ?"

Spade laughed harshly. "I knew Miles. But never mind that. Why did you shoot him?"

She twisted her wrists out of Spade's fingers and put her hands up around the back of his neck, pulling his head down until his mouth all but touched hers. Her body was flat against his from knees to chest. He put his arms around her, holding her tight to him. Her dark-lashed lids were half down over velvet eyes. Her voice was hushed, throbbing: "I didn't mean to, at first. I didn't, really. I meant what I told you, but when I saw Floyd couldn't be frightened I —"

Spade slapped her shoulder. He said: "That's a lie. You asked Miles and me to handle it ourselves. You wanted to be sure the shadower was somebody you knew and who knew you, so they'd go with you. You got the gun from Thursby that day — that night. You had already rented the apartment at the Coronet. You had trunks there and none at the hotel and when I looked the apartment over I found a rent-receipt dated five or six days before the time you told me you rented it."

She swallowed with difficulty and her voice was humble. "Yes, that's a lie, Sam. I did intend to if Floyd — I — I can't look at you and tell you this, Sam." She pulled his head farther down until her cheek was against his cheek, her mouth by his ear, and whispered: "I knew Floyd wouldn't be easily frightened, but I thought that if he knew somebody was shadowing him either he'd — Oh, I can't say it, Sam!" She clung to him, sobbing.

Spade said: "You thought Floyd would tackle him and one or the other of them would go down. If Thursby was the one then you were rid of him. If Miles was, then you could see that Floyd was caught and you'd be rid of him. That it?"

"S-something like that."

"And when you found that Thursby didn't mean to tackle him you borrowed the gun and did it yourself. Right?"

"Yes — though not exactly."

"But exact enough. And you had that plan up your sleeve from the first. You thought Floyd would be nailed for the killing."

"I — I thought they'd hold him at least until after Captain Jacobi had arrived with the falcon and —"

"And you didn't know then that Gutman was here hunting for you. You didn't suspect that or you wouldn't have shaken your gunman. You knew Gutman was here as soon as you heard Thursby had been shot. Then you knew you needed another protector, so you came back to me. Right?"

"Yes, but — oh, sweetheart! — it wasn't only that. I would have come back to you sooner or later. From the first instant I saw you I knew —"

Spade said tenderly: "You angel! Well, if you get a good break you'll be out of San Quentin in twenty years and you can come back to me then."

She took her cheek away from his, drawing her head far back to stare up without comprehension at him.

He was pale. He said tenderly: "I hope to Christ they don't hang you, precious, by that sweet neck." He slid his hands up to caress her throat.

In an instant she was out of his arms, back against the table, crouching, both hands spread over her throat. Her face was wild-eyed, haggard. Her dry mouth opened and closed. She said in a small parched voice: "You're not —" She could get no other words out.

Spade's face was yellow-white now. His mouth smiled and there were smile-wrinkles around his glittering eyes. His voice was soft, gentle. He said: "I'm going to send you over. The chances are you'll get off with life. That means you'll be out again in twenty years. You're an angel. I'll wait for you." He cleared his throat. "If they hang you I'll always remember you."

She dropped her hands and stood erect. Her face became smooth and untroubled except for the faintest of dubious glints in her eyes. She smiled back at him, gently. "Don't, Sam, don't say that even in fun. Oh, you frightened me for a moment! I really thought you — You know you do such wild and unpredictable things that —" She broke off. She thrust her face forward and stared deep into his eyes. Her cheeks and the flesh around her mouth shivered and fear came back into her eyes. "What — ? Sam!" She put her hand to her throat again and lost her erectness.

Spade laughed. His yellow-white face was damp with sweat and though he held his smile he could not hold softness in his voice. He croaked: "Don't be silly. You're taking the fall. One of us has got to take it, after the talking those birds will do. They'd hang me sure. You're likely to get a better break. Well?"

"But — but, Sam, you can't! Not after what we've been to each other. You can't —"

"Like hell I can't."

She took a long trembling breath. "You've been playing with me? Only pretending you cared — to trap me like this? You didn't — care at all? You didn't — don't — l-love me?"

"I think I do," Spade said. "What of it?" The muscles holding his smile in place stood out like wales. "I'm not Thursby. I'm not Jacobi. I won't play the sap for you."

"That is not just," she cried. Tears came to her eyes. "It's unfair. It's contemptible of you. You know it was not that. You can't say that."

"Like hell I can't," Spade said. "You came into my bed to stop me asking questions. You led me out yesterday for Gutman with that phoney call for help. Last night you came here with them and waited outside for me and came in with me. You were in my arms when the trap was sprung — I couldn't have gone for a gun if I'd had one on me and couldn't have made a fight of it if I had wanted to. And if they didn't take you away with them it was only because Gutman's got too much sense to trust you except for short stretches when he has to and because he thought I'd play the sap for you and — not wanting to hurt you — wouldn't be able to hurt him."

Brigid O'Shaughnessy blinked her tears away. She took a step towards him and stood looking him in the eyes, straight and proud. "You called me a liar," she said. "Now you are lying. You're lying if you say you don't know down in your heart that, in spite of anything I've done, I love you."

Spade made a short abrupt bow. His eyes were becoming bloodshot, but there was no other change in his damp and yellowish fixedly smiling face. "Maybe I do," he said. "What of it? I should trust you? You who arranged that nice little trick for — for my predecessor, Thursby? You who knocked off Miles, a man you had nothing against, in cold blood, just like swatting a fly, for the sake of double-crossing Thursby? You who double-crossed Gutman, Cairo, Thursby — one, two, three? You who've never played square with me for half an hour at a stretch since I've known you? I should trust you? No, no, darling. I wouldn't do it even if I could. Why should I?"

Her eyes were steady under his and her hushed voice was steady when she replied:

"Why should you? If you've been playing with me, if you do not love me, there is no answer to that. If you did, no answer would be needed."

Blood streaked Spade's eyeballs now and his long-held smile had become a frightful grimace. He cleared his throat huskily and said: "Making speeches is no damned good now." He put a hand on her shoulder. The hand shook and jerked. "I don't care who loves who, I'm not going to play the sap for you. I won't walk in Thursby's and Christ knows who else's footsteps. You killed Miles and you're going over for it. I could have helped you by letting the others go and standing off the police the best way I could. It's too late for that now. I can't help you now. And I wouldn't if I could."

She put a hand on his hand on her shoulder. "Don't help me then," she whispered, "but don't hurt me. Let me go away now."

"No," he said. "I'm sunk if I haven't got you to hand over to the police when they come. That's the only thing that can keep me from going down with the others."

"You won't do that for me?"

"I won't play the sap for you."

"Don't say that, please." She took his hand from her shoulder and held it to her face. "Why must you do this to me, Sam?

Surely Mr. Archer wasn't as much to you as —"

"Miles," Spade said hoarsely, "was a son of a bitch. I found that out the first week we were in business together and I meant to kick him out as soon as the year was up. You didn't do me a damned bit of harm by killing him."

"Then what?"

Spade pulled his hand out of hers. He no longer either smiled or grimaced. His wet yellow face was set hard and deeply lined. His eyes burned madly. He said: "Listen. This isn't a damned bit of good. You'll never understand me, but I'll try once more and then we'll give it up. Listen. When a man's partner is killed he's supposed to do something about it. It doesn't make any difference what you thought of him. He was your partner and you're supposed to do something about it. Then it happens we were in the detective business. Well, when one of your organization gets killed it's bad business to let the killer get away with it. It's bad all around — bad for that one organization, bad for every detective everywhere. Third, I'm a detective and expecting me to run criminals down and then let them go free is like asking a dog to catch a rabbit and let it go. It can be done, all right, and sometimes it is done, but it's not the natural thing. The only way I could have let you go was by letting Gutman and Cairo and the kid go. That's —"

"You're not serious," she said. "You don't expect me to think that these things you're saying are sufficient reason for sending me to the —"

"Wait till I'm through and then you can talk. Fourth, no matter what I wanted to do now it would be absolutely impossible for me to let you go without having myself dragged to the gallows with the others. Next, I've no reason in God's world to think I can trust you and if I did this and got away with it you'd have something on me that you could use whenever you happened to want to. That's five of them. The sixth would be that, since I've also got something on you, I couldn't be sure you wouldn't decide to shoot a hole in *me* some day. Seventh, I don't even like the idea of thinking that there might be one chance in a hundred that you'd played me for a sucker. And eighth — but that's enough. All those on one side. Maybe some of them are unimportant. I won't argue about that. But look at the number of them. Now on the other side we've got what? All we've got is the fact that maybe you love me and maybe I love you."

"You know," she whispered, "whether you do or not."

"I don't. It's easy enough to be nuts about you." He looked hungrily from her hair to her feet and up to her eyes again. "But I don't know what that amounts to. Does anybody ever? But suppose I do? What of it? Maybe next month I won't. I've been through it before — when it lasted that long. Then what? Then I'll think I played the sap. And if I did it and got sent over then I'd be sure I was the sap. Well, if I send you over I'll be sorry as hell — I'll have some rotten nights — but that'll pass. Listen." He took her by the shoulders and bent her back, leaning over her. "If that doesn't mean anything to you forget it and we'll make it this: I won't because all of me wants to — wants to say to hell with the consequences and do it — and because — God damn you — you've counted on that with me the same as you counted on that with the others." He took his hands from her shoulders and let them fall to his sides.

She put her hands up to his cheeks and drew his face down again. "Look at me," she said, "and tell me the truth. Would you have done this to me if the falcon had been real and you had been paid your money?"

"What difference does that make now?

Don't be too sure I'm as crooked as I'm supposed to be. That kind of reputation might be good business — bringing in high-priced jobs and making it easier to deal with the enemy."

She looked at him, saying nothing.

He moved his shoulders a little and said: "Well, a lot of money would have been at least one more item on the other side of the scales."

She put her face up to his face. Her mouth was slightly open with lips a little thrust out. She whispered: "If you loved me you'd need nothing more on that side."

Spade set the edges of his teeth together and said through them: "I won't play the sap for you."

She put her mouth to his, slowly, her arms around him, and came into his arms. She was in his arms when the door-bell rang.

Spade, left arm around Brigid O'Shaughnessy, opened the corridor-door. Lieutenant Dundy, Detective-sergeant Tom Polhaus, and two other detectives were there.

Spade said: "Hello, Tom. Get them?"

Polhaus said: "Got them."

"Swell. Come in. Here's another one for you." Spade pressed the girl forward. "She killed Miles. And I've got some exhibits — the boy's guns, one of Cairo's, a black statuette that all the hell was about, and a thousand-dollar bill that I was supposed to be bribed with." He looked at Dundy, drew his brows together, leaned forward to peer into the Lieutenant's face, and burst out laughing. "What in hell's the matter with your little playmate, Tom? He looks heart-broken." He laughed again. "I bet, by God! when he heard Gutman's story he thought he had me at last."

"Cut it out, Sam," Tom grumbled. "We didn't think —"

"Like hell he didn't," Spade said merrily. "He came up here with his mouth watering, though you'd have sense enough to know I'd been stringing Gutman."

"Cut it out," Tom grumbled again, looking uneasily sidewise at his superior. "Anyways we got it from Cairo. Gutman's dead. The kid had just finished shooting him up when we got there."

Spade nodded. "He ought to have expected that," he said.

Effie Perine put down her newspaper and jumped out of Spade's chair when he came into the office at a little after nine o'clock Monday morning.

He said: "Morning, angel."

"Is that — what the papers have — right?" she asked.

"Yes, ma'am." He dropped his hat on the desk and sat down. His face was pasty in color, but its lines were strong and cheerful and his eyes, though still somewhat red-veined, were clear.

The girl's brown eyes were peculiarly enlarged and there was a queer twist to her mouth. She stood beside him, staring down at him.

He raised his head, grinned, and said mockingly: "So much for your woman's intuition."

Her voice was queer as the expression on her face. "You did that, Sam, to her?"

He nodded. "Your Sam's a detective." He looked sharply at her. He put his arm around her waist, his hand on her hip. "She did kill Miles, angel," he said gently, "offhand, like that." He snapped the fingers of his other hand.

She escaped from his arm as if it had hurt her. "Don't, please, don't touch me," she said brokenly. "I know — I know you're right. You're right. But don't touch me now — not now."

Spade's face became pale as his collar.

The corridor-door's knob rattled. Effie

Perine turned quickly and went into the outer office, shutting the door behind her. When she came in again she shut it behind her.

She said in a small flat voice: "Iva is here."

Spade, looking down at his desk, nodded almost imperceptibly. "Yes," he said, and shivered. "Well, send her in."

ABOUT THE AUTHOR

Dashiell Hammett was born in St. Marys County, Maryland, in 1894. He grew up in Philadelphia and Baltimore. He left school at the age of fourteen and held several kinds of jobs thereafter — messenger boy, newsboy, clerk, timekeeper, yardman, machine operator, and stevedore. He finally became an operative for Pinkerton's Detective Agency.

World War I, in which he served as a sergeant, interrupted his sleuthing and injured his health. When he was finally discharged from the last of several hospitals, he resumed detective work. Subsequently, he turned to writing, and in the late 1920s he became the unquestioned master of detective-story fiction in America. During World War II, Mr. Hammett again served as sergeant in the Army, this time for more than two years, most of which he spent in the Aleutians. He died in 1961.

0